Driving Justice, Equity, Diversity, and Inclusion

P9-CDD-715

Driving Justice, Equity, Diversity, and Inclusion

Kristina Kohl

CRC Press
Taylor & Francis Group
Boca Raton London New York

CRC Press is an imprint of the
Taylor & Francis Group, an **informa** business

AN AUERBACH BOOK

First Edition published 2022
by CRC Press
6000 Broken Sound Parkway NW, Suite 300, Boca Raton, FL 33487-2742

and by CRC Press
4 Park Square, Milton Park, Abingdon, Oxon, OX14 4RN

CRC Press is an imprint of Taylor & Francis Group, LLC

© 2022 Kristina Kohl

Reasonable efforts have been made to publish reliable data and information, but the author and publisher cannot assume responsibility for the validity of all materials or the consequences of their use. The authors and publishers have attempted to trace the copyright holders of all material reproduced in this publication and apologize to copyright holders if permission to publish in this form has not been obtained. If any copyright material has not been acknowledged please write and let us know so we may rectify in any future reprint.

Except as permitted under U.S. Copyright Law, no part of this book may be reprinted, reproduced, transmitted, or utilized in any form by any electronic, mechanical, or other means, now known or hereafter invented, including photocopying, microfilming, and recording, or in any information storage or retrieval system, without written permission from the publishers.
For permission to photocopy or use material electronically from this work, access www.copyright.com or contact the Copyright Clearance Center, Inc. (CCC), 222 Rosewood Drive, Danvers, MA 01923, 978-750-8400. For works that are not available on CCC please contact mpkbookspermissions@tandf.co.uk

Trademark notice: Product or corporate names may be trademarks or registered trademarks and are used only for identification and explanation without intent to infringe.

ISBN: 978-1-032-18416-6 (hbk)
ISBN: 978-0-367-76679-5 (pbk)
ISBN: 978-1-003-16807-2 (ebk)

DOI: 10.1201/9781003168072

Typeset in Garamond
by SPi Technologies India Pvt Ltd (Straive)

I am dedicating this book to my children, Joshua and Madeline. They represent the future and the opportunity for us to redesign our systems to promote justice, equity, diversity, and inclusion. Thank you for being who you are and for making the world a better place every day.

Contents

Acknowledgements

Thank you to everyone who has contributed to the writing of this book. Some of you were part of the original concept review and vetting process, others contributed thought leadership or cases, others agreed to be interviewed and to share your J.E.D.I. expertise, others served as editors adding valuable insights and comments, and others gave me inspiration and encouragement. I am especially grateful to the Bard MBA in Sustainability community for their many contributions to this project. Thank you to IBM's P-TECH team for sharing their unique model, offering resources, and arranging interviews. Thank you to all who agreed to be interviewed and worked with me to get your interviews approved for publication. Thank you to my contributing authors for dedicating their time and talents to writing their unique and very valuable pieces. I am very grateful to my family for your support, proof reading, and graphic designing. Thank you to all who have shared their insights and experiences in making our world a more just and equitable place.

I would especially like to thank the following people for their contributions:

Contributing Authors	Contribution
Kathy Hipple, Finance, Bard MBA in Sustainability	Must Organizations Excel in ESG Metrics to be Sustainable?
Daniel Farber Huang, Strategic Consultant, Journalist, and Documentary Photographer	Human Resource and Human Rights
Gilles Mesrobian, Managing Director, Red Queen Group	The View from Within: The Sustainability Leader's Relationship to the System
Erika White, Diversity, Equity and Inclusion Leader	Pennsylvania Convention Center: Driving Impact Through Supplier Diversity

Interviewees	Interview/Case
Shudon Brown, Continuous Improvement & Robotics Process Automation Leader, IBM	IBM Driving Impact Through P-TECH
Fiona Jamison, CEO, Spring International	Gaining DEI Perspective Through Assessment and Stakeholder Engagement
Katherine Pease, Managing Director, Pathstone	The Crucial Role for Impact Investing in Driving Systemic Change
Cara Pelletier, Diversity, Equity, and Belonging Leader	Designing a Playbook to Build a Culture of Belonging for People of All Abilities
Grace Suh, Vice President, Education, CSR, IBM	IBM Driving Impact Through P-TECH
Reviewers/Facilitators	
Laurie Garrett, Human Capital Management Leader	
Twana Harris, DEI Leader	
Cara Kiewel, Sustainability Leader	
Kathleen Leasor, CSR, IBM	
Charlotte Lysohir, CSR, IBM	
Caitlin O'Donnell, Community & Civic Engagement Leader	
Roxanne Sharif, Data-driven Solutions Leader	
Madeline Yankell, Educator	

I would like to thank the many people who have supported my own J.E.D.I. growth and development over the years. This book would not be possible without the support of my husband, Morris. Thank you to my editors for your guidance. If I have overlooked someone, please accept my appreciation and personal thank you. Best wishes on your J.E.D.I. journey.

Author

Kristina Kohl, MBA, PMP is the managing principal of HRComputes, a management consulting firm, providing advisory and technical support for people management digital solution selection and client-side implementation and optimization. HRComputes focuses on delivery on people strategy using technology, change management, and program and project management. HRComputes is a registered NJ WBE and NJ SBE and is in the NJ Sustainable Business Registry.

Kristina leads the Becoming Sustainable practice developing people strategy to build more equitable and inclusive organizations. Services include strategy development, assessment, gap analysis, workforce data analytics, ERG development, talent strategies to promote diversity, building an inclusive culture, and digital solution selection and implementation. She is a diversity, equity, and inclusion thought leader and frequent speaker. Kristina brings executive business management experience from the corporate and not for profit worlds. Her background includes serving as Vice President and Manager at JPMorgan Chase. She is the Building Sustainable Organizations professor and DEI Committee faculty advisor for the Bard MBA in Sustainability, She is the author of *Becoming a Sustainable Organization* published by CRC Press. Her new book, *Driving Transformative and Equitable Change to Build Inclusive Organizations*, which focuses on rebalancing power and breaking down systemic barriers to create organizations that authentically welcome diverse voices, will be released next year. She is a frequent speaker at conferences and events including the PMI Global Congress EMEA, Society for Human Resource Management, the Great IT Pro, Boston University, and other industry groups. She has served on a number of not for profit boards and is currently the EVP for the Wharton Club of New Jersey. She was named a 2020 Beacon ICON Award recipient for her work in women's leadership and to the SJBiz 2020 Women to Watch List. Kristina holds an MBA from the Wharton School, University of Pennsylvania. She is a PMP.

Contributing Author Biographies

Daniel Farber Huang is a strategic consultant and advisor on cyber security and other risk mitigation issues to a broad array of companies and organizations, ranging from entrepreneurial start-ups to multi-national corporations. He has worked closely with numerous federal, state, and local law enforcement agencies across the U.S. on providing solutions to their mobile technology requirements.

Before founding his own independent advisory firm, Daniel worked at major investment banks advising corporations and investors on domestic and international corporate finance transactions. Daniel is an Advisor to Princeton University's Keller Center for Innovation in Engineering Education, where he advises start-up founders on business' best practices.

Outside of his consulting work, Daniel is a journalist and documentary photographer focused on women's and children's issue and the alleviation of poverty around the world. Daniel is a co-founder of The Power of Faces, a major portrait project raising awareness of the global refugee crisis. As an independent humanitarian advocate, Daniel has documented refugee camps around the world, and has actively raised awareness through multiple Talks on TED.com and other platforms. His documentary work has been exhibited at Amnesty International, the Middle East Institute, and numerous universities and colleges. His work is included in the permanent collections of The International Center of Photography, The Museum of the City of New York, New York Historical Society, Museum of Chinese in the Americas, New York City Fire Museum, and other institutions.

Daniel is a National Member of The Explorers Club, a multidisciplinary professional society dedicated to the advancement of field research and the ideal that it is vital to preserve the instinct to explore. He is a Brand Ambassador for OP/TECH USA camera accessories. Daniel is an Ambassador for the Wharton Alumni Social Impact Club.

Daniel earned his Master's degree (A.L.M.) in Journalism and a Certificate in International Security from Harvard University, an M.B.A. from The Wharton School, University of Pennsylvania in Finance and Entrepreneurial Management, and a B.A. from New York University in Economics.

 **Erika L. White**, CDE is a Diversity Equity & Inclusion leader who currently serves as the first head of Diversity Equity and Inclusion for Pennoni Associates, a national Civil Engineering firm headquartered in Philadelphia. Erika joined Pennoni from the Pennsylvania Convention Center, an ASM Global managed facility, where she served as the head of Diversity and Inclusion. She worked to revitalize the DEI strategy especially with regards to the supplier diversity program. Previously, Erika held the position of Senior Diversity & Inclusion Coordinator for the American Lawyer top 100 law firm, Ballard Spahr LLP. Erika also supported the Philadelphia community holding positions such as Director of the West Oak Lane Jazz and Arts Festival and Director of Community and Government Affairs for the Ogontz Avenue Revitalization Corporation.

Erika has expertise in DEI education, multicultural marketing, supplier diversity, community outreach, and workforce development. She continues to lend her talents as a DEI subject matter expert and consultant and serves on several diversity related advisory boards and is the co-founder of the networking group, The Philadelphia Diversity Professionals Consortium. She serves as a Board of Trustee for the Shipley School as well as a Board of Director for the Center City Proprietors Association.

She has a Bachelor of Science in Business and Administration from Drexel University Lebow College of Business and has received her designation as a Certified Diversity Executive from the Institute for Diversity Certification. Erika is a mentor to young women, a regular volunteer in her faith, and a member of Alpha Kappa Alpha Sorority Incorporated.

Gilles Mesrobian is the Managing Director of The Red Queen Group as well as a Senior Associate at the Support Center for Nonprofit Management. His credentials include over 26 years senior management experience in the non-profit arena, with nearly 20 years as an Executive Director. His consulting experience covers a broad range of organizational work in the non-profit and philanthropic sector, including executive leadership transition and executive search.

Gilles is also a Certified Governance trainer through BoardSource as well as a faculty member of Bard's MBA in Sustainability where he teaches leadership development in Sustainability. He is a member of the national training faculty for Neighborworks America and facilitates several leadership training programs including the New York Foundation for the Arts' Emerging Leaders program, a yearlong cohort-learning program for senior non-profit professionals.

Kathy Hipple teaches the finance sequence at Bard's MBA in Sustainability. She is a research fellow at the Ohio River Valley Institute (ORVI) and a senior advisor in financial services at Corporate Citizenship. She has written extensively on sustainable, responsible, and impact investing. Her research on fossil fuel divestment and the financial decline of the fossil fuel industry from her work at the Institute for Energy Economics and Financial Analysis (IEEFA) has been widely cited. As Vice President at Merrill Lynch for 10 years, Hipple placed fixed income securities with international institutions and advised Japanese insurance companies and pension funds. She later served as founder and CEO of Ambassador Media, a New York-based local search company with revenues of more than $35 million. She has an MBA in Sustainability and splits her time between New York City and Vermont.

A Justice, Equity, Diversity, and Inclusion (J.E.D.I.) Primer

I.1 Foundational Terms

Justice Fairness in the way people are treated from environmental, social, and economic perspective.

Equity Ensuring fair treatment, access, opportunity, and advancement for all people, while at the same time striving to identify root causes and eliminate barriers that have prevented the full participation of some groups.

Diversity Variety of characteristics that makes everyone unique including race, ethnicity, gender identity, sexual orientation, veteran status, socioeconomic status, age, disability, thought, experience, talent, religious beliefs, political beliefs, or other ideologies.

Inclusion Practices and policies designed to provide equal access to opportunities and resources for people who might otherwise be excluded or marginalized, such as those who have physical or mental disabilities and members of other underrepresented groups.

I.2 Key Terms

AAPI Asian American and Pacific Islander.

Affirmative Action The practice of providing resources or favorable policy toward members of groups that have been historically disadvantaged, oppressed, or discriminated against. Often a set of procedures created to eliminate unlawful discrimination toward job applicants or students applying for matriculation in educational institutions.

DOI: 10.1201/9781003168072-1

Ally An ally is someone that actively promotes an identity group other than one's own and aspires to advance the culture of belonging through intentional, positive, and conscious efforts that benefit all people.

Anti-racism Actively opposing racism by advocating for changes in political, economic, and social life.

Bias A form of prejudice that results from our neuro process of classifying individuals into categories.

BIPOC Black, Indigenous, People of Color.

Belonging Create a culture where individuals feel welcome and are treated fairly, have equal access to opportunities and resources, and are able to bring their true selves, and to contribute fully to the organization.

Cisgender Identify with the sex that was assigned at birth.

Disability Physical or mental impairment that affects a person's ability to perform routine functions without the need for reasonable accommodation.

Discrimination Unequal treatment of members of certain groups.

Dominant Culture One in which its values, language, behaviors, and attitudes are imposed on subordinate cultures through social constructs such as economic or political power and institutions such as educational.

Dominant Group Advantage and superior rights to resources and societal institutions.

Gender Expression Expression of one's gender identity to others, often through behavior, clothing, hairstyles, voice, or body characteristics.

Gender Identity The subjective experience of one's own gender.

Harassment Unwelcome conduct based on race, color, religion, sexual orientation, gender identity, national origin, age, disability and is a form of employment discrimination.

Hostile Work Environment A work environment where a boss' or co-worker's actions, communication, or behaviors are unwelcome or discriminatory in nature and makes doing your job impossible. Harassment creates a hostile work environment.

Identity Group A particular group of people share a sense of belonging or bonding because of their common experiences, heritage, interests, beliefs, cultures, etc.

Implicit Bias Bias that people unknowingly hold, which impact our perceptions, actions, and decisions.

Intersectionality Reflects multiple identities that intersect such as race, gender identity, education, socio-economic status causing us to experience privilege or oppression in certain situations, cultures, or environments.

J.E.D.I. Justice, equity, diversity, inclusion.

LGBTQ+ Lesbian, gay, bisexual, transgender, queer or questioning

Microaggressions Comment or insult which harms another individual based on their gender, social class, race, religion, sexual orientation, or any other aspect of the person's identity often with a negative, or even hostile connotation, whether intended or unintended.

Model Minority Collection of stereotypes about Asian Americans depicting all members of this diverse group as smart, wealthy, hard-working, docile, and spiritually enlightened.

Neurodiversity The range of differences in brain function and behavioral traits considered to be typical in the range for humans.

Non-Binary One of the terms used to describe people whose gender is not male or female.

Power Reflecting control of access to and allocation of resources from private and public institutions through control of policies, laws, and other social constructs.

POC People of color

Privilege Reflecting the dominant group's advantage and superior access to resources and societal rights usually through oppression or exploitation of others.

Quid Pro Quo Tying a job benefit to unwelcome sexual advances or sexual harassment.

Racial Equity Equal distribution of society's benefits and burdens regardless of race.

Racism Unequal access to opportunities, education, healthcare, social support, employment, and other social and economic norms because of race.

Reasonable Accommodation Assistance or modifications for a person with a disability to a job function or workplace environment that will enable an employee to perform their job. Under the ADA, employers are required to provide reasonable accommodations unless they can demonstrate undue hardship.

Sexual Harassment Unwelcome sexual advances, requests for sexual favors, and other verbal or physical harassment of a sexual nature.

Sexual Orientation Romantic, sexual identity, and behavior.

Stereotyping A standardized mental picture of members of an identity group that represents an oversimplified opinion, prejudiced attitude, or uncritical judgment.

Systemic Racism The normalization and legitimization throughout societal systems such as political, economic, social, educational, cultural, institutional, and interpersonal that advantage White people but create chronic adverse outcomes for BIPOC people.

Tokenism Inclusion without meaningful impact.

Transitioning Process of changing one's gender presentation to match one's internal sense of gender.

Transgender People who know themselves to be one gender but who were labeled a different gender at birth.

Unconscious Bias or Implicit Bias Cognitive shortcuts that impact the way we perceive, interpret, and prefer people, which often leads to inequities.

Underrepresented Group Disadvantaged and unequal access to resources and societal institutions owing to the dominant group.

White Privilege Reflecting that member of the White race have dominant social group advantage and superior access to resources and societal rights over other racial groups. Check your privilege.

I.3 Leveling the Playing Field

After reading through the foundational and key terms, I hope that you have an appreciation for the distinctions between Diversity, Equity, and Inclusion. Diversity represents over 40 characteristics that define identity, experience, and thought. The Diversity Wheel gives a perspective on the multitude of components and combinations that represent diversity (https://www.researchgate.net/figure/Diversity-Wheel-as-used-at-Johns-Hopkins-University-12_fig1_320178286). These include identity characteristics, such as age, gender identity, or expression, national origin, and race, and experience characteristics such as work experience, cultural exposure, family, professional training, language, religious beliefs, and education. People are unique with intersectionalities that cross groups and experiences. Through diversity, new ideas and solutions are brought to organizations allowing for innovation. Equity is offering equal opportunity for all persons including fair treatment, equal access, and advancement. In order to achieve equity, we must actively eliminate systemic barriers. Inclusion ensures our society including our workplaces welcome differences and that different perspectives are respectfully heard. Every individual must feel that they belong. Equity and inclusion are crucial for supporting a diverse workforce.

When we talk about leveling the playing field, we are talking about removing barriers and opening pathways to create conditions that support equal access for all. Because of White privilege, we have a dominant social construct that affords greater opportunity and access to members of the White race. This privilege has been in existence for hundreds of years in the U.S.; as a result, White people have had a cumulative unfair advantage in terms of access to resources and social rights such as in the legal, political, healthcare, and financial systems. This construct has contributed to significant education, pay, healthcare, and wealth gaps in our society creating underrepresented and marginalized communities. Because of the historical and cumulative impacts of these inequities, providing *equal* support to all citizens doesn't level the playing field. As depicted in Figure I.1, underrepresented or marginalized populations are much further below the bar than those who have benefitted from White privilege. Providing equal support to all raises everyone equally, but it doesn't reallocate or address the foundational inequities. While the first figure depicted can access the view over the barrier, the second figure can just barely access it, and the third figure cannot access it at all. This model helps us to understand why equal treatment to all doesn't create equity because based on power and privilege, underrepresented and marginalized groups are beginning from a significantly more disadvantaged position. In Figure I.2, we provide *equitable* support to raise everyone equally above the barrier so that all can access the view. To address the challenge of systemic inequity and to achieve equal access, we must give multiple levels of support to underserved and marginalized people. This diagram is foundational to the reason for programs such as Affirmative Action, which are designed to compensate for historical and cumulative lack of access and resources for underserved and marginalized groups. Figure I.3 depicts the removal of systemic barriers that prevent people from accessing a level playing field. *Equity* is achieved when all people have equal access to resources and opportunities because systemic barriers have been removed. Removing power and privilege and providing equal access is the focus of this book – Driving toward justice, equity, diversity, and inclusion – The J.E.D.I. Journey.

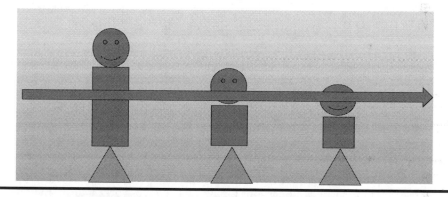

Figure I.1   Equal Support.

Figure I.2   Equitable Support.

Figure I.3 Equity.

I.4 Pronouns

A pronoun is a word used to refer to an individual or group instead of using their name. Some people feel that traditional gender pronouns do not align with their gender identities. Transgender, genderqueer, or other gender-variant people may choose different pronouns for themselves. Some people go by just one set of pronouns, others use more than one set. In Figure I.4, we share some commonly used pronouns.

In order to promote inclusion and belonging, it is important to ask someone their preferred pronouns and to use those pronouns when referring to them. In the age of virtual meetings on platforms such as Zoom, encouraging participants to include their pronouns after their names is a convenient tool for sharing pronouns. Another way to introduce pronouns is to ask that people share their preferred pronouns when introducing themselves in a meeting or to colleagues.

Here are some suggested questions for asking peers, co-workers, team members, employees, and clients their preferred pronouns:

1. What pronouns do you use?
2. How would you like me to refer to you?

they	them	their	theirs	themselves
she/he	her/him	her/his	hers/his	herself/himself
ze	hir (pronounced "here")	hir	hirs	hirself
ze	zim	zir	zirs	zirself

Figure I.4 Pronouns.

3. My name is Kristina, and my pronouns are she/her. What is your name and preferred pronouns?

I.5 Resource List

1. Diversity Wheel: https://www.researchgate.net/figure/Diversity-Wheel-as-used-at-Johns-Hopkins-University-12_fig1_320178286
2. Implicit Bias Tests: https://implicit.harvard.edu/implicit/takeatest.html
3. Talking About Race Toolkit: https://www.centerforsocialinclusion.org/wp-content/uploads/2015/08/CSI-Talking-About-Race-Toolkit.pdf
4. DEI Plan: https://www.shrm.org/resourcesandtools/tools-and-samples/how-to-guides/pages/how-to-develop-a-diversity-and-inclusion-initiative.aspx
5. "Why Diversity Matters." https://www.mckinsey.com/business-functions/organization/our-insights/why-diversity-matters

Chapter 1

Leveraging ESG on the J.E.D.I. Journey

As we build and adapt organizations to address 21st century challenges, we must consider that models that worked in the 20th century are no longer applicable. We operate in a Volatile, Uncertain, Changing, Complex, and Ambiguous (VUCA) world. Organizations need to be agile and adaptive to build resiliency and thrive. Megatrends impacting organizations include population growth and demographic changes, increasing urbanization and growth of megacities, warming temperatures, rising sea levels, loss of habitat, loss of biodiversity, pandemics, social protests, and increased political polarization, to name a few. Advances in technology and connectivity mean that the world is aware of events both good and bad minutes after they happen. Transparency is necessary to effectively meet stakeholder requirements. In addition, the average lifecycle of a business is shrinking. McKinsey reports that the average life span of organizations included in Standard & Poor's 500 was 14 years in 2010, and getting shorter, vs. 90 years in 1935.[1] This increased velocity of change heightens the complexity of managing organizations and requires a new framework that values planet, people, and profit to thrive. A new model for success is found in the U.N. Sustainable Development Goals (SDGs), which provide a roadmap to build more environmentally and socially just and equitable organizations.

1.1 Sustainable Development Goals

In order to move forward, leaders need to think more broadly about creating organizational value using the U.N. SDGs as a guiding principle. These goals serve as a roadmap for organizations seeking to create an integrated bottom line return – planet, people, and profit. These goals and their interconnectivity are pillars of

The content of this publication has not been approved by the United Nations and does not reflect the views of the United Nations or its officials or Member States.
https://www.un.org/sustainabledevelopment/

Figure 1.1 The U.N. Sustainable Development Goals.[2]

environment and social justice. While these goals will apply to organizations differently with some being more material than others, we will not achieve success in creating transformative change unless all organizational leaders think deeply about these issues and their role in driving transformative change.

Figure 1.1 lays out each of the 17 goals for improved environmental, societal, and organizational health. These 17 goals serve as a framework for leaders creating a more just, equitable, diverse, and inclusive (J.E.D.I.) organization. The vision is to achieve these goals by 2030, which will require major transformation by both public and private institutions. Table 1.1 provides more details on each of the goals and further insight and information is available through the U.N. Sustainable Goals websites referenced.

Table 1.1 U.N. Sustainable Development Goals and Descriptions[3]

Sustainable Development Goals	Descriptions
SDG #1-No Poverty	Promote inclusive economic growth to provide sustainable jobs and promote equality.
SDG #2-Zero Hunger	Promote development and innovation in the food and agriculture sector to eradicate hunger and poverty.
SDG #3-Good Health & Well-Being	Ensure access to resources to promote healthy lives and promote well-being across all age groups.

(Continued)

Table 1.1 *(Continued)* U.N. Sustainable Development Goals and Descriptions

Sustainable Development Goals	Descriptions
SDG #4-Quality Education	Provide a quality education equitably to improve global prosperity.
SDG #5-Gender Equity	Promote gender equality globally by removing legal and societal barriers and creating greater access and opportunity.
SDG #6-Clean Water and Sanitation	Focus on providing clean and accessible water to promote healthy communities.
SDG #7-Affordable and Clean Energy	Develop and expand the use of affordable and clean energy to drive change and create new opportunities for solutions.
SDG #8-Decent Work and Economic Growth	Focus on creating conditions that support quality jobs that promote economic prosperity.
SDG #9-Industry, Innovation, & Infrastructure	Promote innovation and investments in infrastructure to support a more sustainable future.
SDG #10-Reduce Inequalities	Develop policies that are universal in principle and include addressing the needs of disadvantaged and marginalized populations.
SDG #11-Sustainable Cities and Communities	Design cities and communities to provide opportunities for all including access to basic services, energy, housing, transportation, and education.
SDG #12-Responsible Consumption and Production	Revise consumption and production patterns to reduce the destructive impact on natural environment and resources.
SDG #13-Climate Action	Reduce CO_2 levels and other greenhouse gas emissions to combat temperature rise and corresponding severe weather events and sea level rise.
SDG #14-Life Below Water	Reverse water degradation and manage this essential global resource sustainably for future generations.

(Continued)

Table 1.1 *(Continued)* **U.N. Sustainable Development Goals and Descriptions**

Sustainable Development Goals	Descriptions
SDG #15-Life on Land	Reverse land degradation, halt biodiversity loss, manage forests more sustainably, and combat desertification.
SDG #16-Peace, Justice and Strong Institutions	Provide access to justice for all and build effective and accountable institutions across all levels.
SDG #17-Partnerships	Leverage public and private partnerships globally to promote sustainable development.

The SDG roadmap is built on foundation of planetary health-*SDG #6-Clean Water and Sanitation, SDG-#7-Affordable Clean Energy, SDG #12-Responsible Consumption and Production, SDG #13-Climate Action, SDG #14-Life Below Water, and SDG #15-Life on Land.* Building on top of a healthy planet, we look to have a more just and equitable society-*SDG #1-No Poverty, SDG #2-Zero Hunger, SDG #3-Good Health and Well-Being, SDG #4-Quality Education, SDG #5-Gender Equity, SDG #9-Industry, Innovation, & Infrastructure, and SDG #10-Reduced Inequalities.* Building on the environmental and social platforms, we create economic prosperity for all – *SDG #8-Decent Work and Economic Growth, SDG #11-Sustainable Cities and Communities, SDG #16-Peace, Justice and Strong Institutions, and SDG #17-Partnerships.* Each of these 17 SDGs are interconnected with each affecting the other. For example, access to quality education impacts the ability to find decent work, which in turn eliminates poverty and hunger and promotes health and well-being. This framework functions as a system delivering an integrated bottom line strategy that allows leaders to build regenerative organizations contributing to their business value (Profits) through improved management of natural resources (Planet) and stakeholders (People).

Societal outcomes such as health and well-being are often a function of underlying environmental factors. As we have seen from the COVID-19 pandemic, there is intersectionality between climate change, increased human and animal interactions owing to habitat loss, and the health and well-being of global populations. While COVID-19 is not the first climate-related virus, it has been one of the deadliest viruses. There have been a number of viruses stemming from human and animal interaction such as SARS, Ebola, and Zika. As the human footprint expands, wildlife loses habitat, and human and wildlife interactions increase resulting in viruses morphing and spreading. In addition, as the climate changes, hosts and viruses move into areas that were not previously habituated. As a result, all types of bacterial and viral infections are moving into new populations.[4] The health of people and the health of the planet are intertwined.

For our most vulnerable populations, we see significantly higher infection rates, hospitalization rates, and mortality rates related to COVID-19. The virus has impacted racial and ethnically diverse groups differently owing to social inequities such as access to and utilization of healthcare, income, wealth, education, housing, occupation, and discrimination. These outcomes are a result of government and private programs that have systematically disadvantaged Black, Indigenous, and people of color (BIPOC) communities. In the U.S., high density, urban locations where many BIPOC people live were highly impacted at the beginning of the pandemic. In addition, many people in this group take public transportation because they don't have the means for or access to private transportation further exposing them to the virus. Black Americans are 2.6 times more likely to contract COVID-19, 4.7 times more likely to be hospitalized with the virus, and 2.1 times more likely to die from virus related health causes.[5] Other inequities come from BIPOC communities' higher exposure to air pollution and toxic chemicals because of housing stock availability, income inequality, and lack of educational opportunities. All of these factors have contributed to the disproportional rates of infection and mortality for the BIPOC population. While we are seeing it very clearly as it relates to the coronavirus, we have consistently seen BIPOC communities disproportionally impacted by extreme weather events and flooding owing to climate change and sea level rise. While the pandemic has starkly highlighted these inequalities, there have been systemic barriers to the BIPOC community for generations.

Project Drawdown research further demonstrates the intersectionality of environmental and social SDGS. As part of their climate action response, Project Drawdown advocates for education of girls, globally, as one of the most impactful ways to improve planetary health by reducing emissions through controlling population growth. Women with more education have better economic outcomes, living standards, and reproductive health. Both maternal and infant mortality rates improve with education and economic stability. Women's stewardship of agricultural land improves soil health and crop yield providing a better quality of life for their families while preserving natural resources.[6] As this research highlights, environmental, social, and economic SDGs are intertwined and the intersectionality of planetary health and people well-being is crucial to delivering on economic viability.

THE INTERSECTION OF ENVIRONMENTAL AND SOCIAL JUSTICE

In June 2020, Chevron joined many other major corporations in espousing their support of Black communities and calling for systemic change to eliminate racism. Chevron tweeted "Racism has no place in America" with links to quotations from several Chevron leaders on their thoughts on systemic racism.[7] While the intent of these communiques was clearly in support of

SDG #10-Reduce Inequalities, the reaction from stakeholders including community members and environmental justice supporters has been to call into question Chevron's commitment to communities of color given their history of environmental injustice.

In the U.S., the poor and people of color are disproportionally impacted by air and water pollution. (These outcomes reinforce the need for *SDG #7-Clean Water* and Sanitation and *SDG #13-Climate Action to* promote equity.) These communities have higher rates of cancer, asthma, and mortality and overall poorer health rates than affluent and White communities. Clearly, these outcomes are a detriment to *SDG #3-Good Health and Well-Being*. Furthering the cycle of environmental injustice, property located in areas with high level of pollution has a lower value impacting wealth accumulation for residents. Pollution related disease impacts the ability to work and to perform well in school. These factors negatively impact SDG #1-No Poverty and SDG #8-Decent Work and Economic Growth further degrading social justice. Vulnerable populations bear the largest burden of our society's environmental degradation and the corresponding impacts on health, wealth, and education. Environmental injustice is most often found in communities that lack the resources for adequate representation to protect themselves.

While Chevron is a major employer, it is also a major polluter in the communities in which it operates. In Richmond, CA, where they operate a refinery, people live within a ring of five major oil refineries, three chemical companies, eight Superfund sites, dozens of other toxic waste sites, highways, two rail yards, ports, and marine terminals where tankers dock.[8] The median household income for residents is below the California state average, with more than 15% of residents living in poverty. In addition, over 80% of Richmond residents are people of color. The population in closest proximity to the refinery has disproportionately high rates of cancer. California EPA information indicates communities bordering the Chevron facility fall in the 99th centile for asthma.[9] In addition, the Chevron facility has had several major fires with the last one in 2012 impacting over 15,000 residents sending them to the hospital with respiratory distress.[10] A subsequent investigation in 2013 by the California Division of Occupational Safety and Health resulted in 25 citations against the company. Yet, Chevron's settlement with the City of Richmond was only $5 million.[11] Given the negative environmental and social impact of the Chevron facility on the Richmond community, which is primarily a community of color, their social media post in support of Black lives and their comments around systemic racism, their institutional commitment has been questioned by many stakeholders. Several impact investors are submitting shareholder proposals requesting that Chevron address this disparity between public relations and organizational actions.

In addition to environmental degradation, environmental justice supporters have questioned Chevron's financial commitment to the communities in which they operate as they paid no federal taxes in 2018. Among the biggest winners from the Trump Administration's Tax Cuts and Jobs Act (TCJA) was the oil and gas industry, in which companies' average tax rates dropped to 3.6%. In the case of Chevron, they reported a U.S. pre-tax income of $4.5 billion on which they paid a negative $181 million in taxes. Even if they had paid the 2018 greatly reduced oil industry average, it would have generated $162 million in taxes for the federal government. While Chevron is not the only corporation to have avoided taxes under this legislation, it does raise the question of how a company that is espousing support for communities of color is demonstrating that commitment when they aren't paying their fair share of societal costs. In the case of Chevron, the largest portion of the $1.1 billion in tax avoidance was in the form of a tax deferral, which enables businesses to postpone paying taxes until a later fiscal year perhaps indefinitely. In addition, there were new accelerated depreciation rules established under the TCJA for capital equipment allowing for more rapid depreciation, which also reduced taxes. According to Chevron's 10-K form, various deferments moved $738 million into the future for Chevron to pay taxes on later.[12] While taking advantage of these tax savings is perfectly legal, it does raise the question as to how the government is to fund programs to promote environmental justice and social equity in support of SDG# 16-Peace, Justice & Strong Institutions.

While Chevron is far from the only example, taking a deeper dive into their statements and their actions around systemic racism and supporting communities of color reveals the intersectionality of environmental and social impact highlighting the importance of environmental justice on the journey to building a more just and equitable organization. As business leaders, we need to take a deep look at our institutional practices and begin the process of meaningful transformation. While many corporate statements have been made in support of Black Lives Matter (BLM), the true impact will be known in future years as we unravel our past environmental and social injustices.

As leaders, we can leverage these lessons to develop a sustainable approach to deliver agility and resiliency for our organizations to meet the challenges of the 21st century. "Sustainable strategy provides a framework for a management philosophy that transforms people, process, and practice, creating business value while addressing financial, environmental, and social challenges."[13] Using the SDGs as a framework is a pathway forward to delivering on an integrated bottom line strategy, which incorporates environmental and social outcomes, required to address today's VUCA world. Driving systemic change requires hard work and a significant commitment at all levels of the organization. The process involves peeling back the layers and making significant changes to organizational culture, values, policies, and processes.

1.2 J.E.D.I. Value Creation

Stakeholders, such as investors, employees, customers, suppliers, public institutions, regulators, press, unions, and communities are requiring organizations and their leaders to be more authentic and transparent around their environmental and social responsibility. A singular focus on shareholder value creation is no longer sufficient, even for the shareholders, because they are much more aware of the risks not identified and the opportunities lost from viewing value creation through this singular lens.

As a result, we have seen a rise in money flowing into funds that target environmental, social, and governance (ESG) investing. "The value of global assets applying environmental, social and governance data to drive investment decisions has almost doubled over four years, and more than tripled over eight years, to $40.5 trillion in 2020."[14] "The number of ESG strategies launched in the Morningstar investment universe in 2019 rose to 400, compared with around 160 launches in 2016."[15] Clearly, ESG investing strategy has become a mainstream investment strategy. As a result, there are advantages to organizations that report on their ESG performance in terms of lower cost of capital and debt issuance rates.

In response to funding COVID-19 recovery, the European Commission, the executive branch of the European Union, committed to funding 30% with green debt, approximately €225 billion ($269 billion) of issuance. This commitment is the world's largest issuance of green debt and effectively doubles the current size of the market.[16] The impact of this action is that 30% of the coronavirus recovery spend for the EU will be dedicated for building resilience in society and health of the environment. In addition to renewable energy, cleaner transportation, and improved infrastructure, the plan funds a number of social initiatives such as:

1. European Unemployment Reinsurance Scheme providing €100 billion in support for workers and businesses.
2. Skills Agenda for Europe and a Digital Education Action Plan designed to provide digital skills for EU citizens.
3. Improved connectivity.
4. Fair minimum wage and binding pay transparency to support vulnerable workers.[17]

The EU is committed to reducing its carbon footprint, jumpstarting its economy, and investing for future generations to build a more just and equitable society for all citizens.

Expanding on the social perspective, organizational performance demonstrates that companies with diverse workforces outperform their peers. According to McKinsey & Co research in 2019, organizations with top quartile representation for gender diversity on executive teams were 25% more likely to earn above-average profitability than companies with gender representation in the fourth quartile. Over the past 5 years, we have seen this profitability differential grow from 15% in 2014 to 25% in 2019.[18] In terms of ethnic and cultural diversity, the outcomes for more diverse workforces are even stronger. Top quartile performance companies were 36% more likely to outperform bottom quartile performers.[19] These impressive results reflect benefits such as higher employee engagement, quality talent attraction, and improved collaboration. Additional benefits include gaining access to new market opportunities, new partnerships, greater sources of financing, and more innovative solutions. The results are clear that diversity of identity, thought, and experience drives organizational value.

Over the many years McKinsey and others have performed this research, we find that organizations with diversity of identity, experience, and thought outperform their peers. Yet, we continue to see very little movement in gender, racial, ethnic, and cultural diversity at the most senior levels of organizations. Over the past 20 years, we have seen a very small rise in the diversity of CEOs.

> Among CEOs of S&P 500 companies, 11% are ethnic minorities. Of the total, 3% are Latino, 3% are Indian, 2% are Asian, 1% are Middle Eastern and 1% are multiracial. Just 1% are Black, according to an analysis by MyLog IQ, a data tracker.[20]

In the U.S., approximately 13% of the population identifies as Black. Clearly, these leadership numbers are not representative of the U.S. population, and this lack of leadership diversity creates a risk for organizations from both a license to operate and stakeholder engagement perspective.

As organizations seek to address 21st century challenges by building organizations with agility and resiliency, investor, employee, supplier, and customer diversity offers a new pathway for innovation and risk mitigation. From an innovation perspective, research done by Boston Consulting Group found that "companies that reported above-average diversity on their management teams also reported innovation revenue that was 19 percentage points higher than that of companies with below-average leadership diversity—45% of total revenue versus just 26%."[21] Correspondingly, these same organizations reported higher financial performance.

As indicated in Figure 1.2, there are many avenues for creating organizational value through a holistic strategy that develops diversity in their key stakeholders such as employees, clients, suppliers, and advisors by building an inclusive organization with equitable policies, practices, and processes. The first rung on the ladder is compliance with various federal and state laws and regulations that are enforced by agencies

Figure 1.2   J.E.D.I. Value Creation.

Table 1.2 Equal Employment Opportunity Laws and Regulations[22]

13th Amendment/ Abolished Slavery	Equal Pay Act-1963	Pregnancy Discrimination-1978
14th Amendment/Equal Protection and Due Process for Citizens	Title VII-CRA-1964- Prohibits Discrimination Based on Race, Color, National Origin, Sex, or Religion	Americans with Disabilities Act-1990- Prohibits Discrimination Against Those with Disabilities
Civil Rights Act-1866, 1871	Age Discrimination Act-1967	Genetic Information Nondiscrimination Act-2008

such as the Equal Employment Opportunity Commission (EEOC). While Table 1.2 does not include an exhaustive list, it highlights protected classes of employees and the magnitude of federal compliance requirements. It also demonstrates that the U.S. has been attempting to address equity issues for hundreds of years.

State requirements will vary, with California having some of the most stringent requirements. In the Fall of 2020, Governor Gavin Newsome signed into law a requirement that all publicly traded companies, within the state's borders, have at least one Board of Director from a racially, ethnically, or some other underserved group.[23] This legislation is in addition to a law passed in California several years ago requiring female representation on publicly traded company Board of Directors (Board) operating within its state borders.

Moving beyond compliance, organizational value is created by productivity gains generated by higher employee engagement arising from allowing people to bring their full and best selves to work. Attracting top talent is another key value creator. If your organization is looking for all of their talent from a few sources, they are missing opportunities to recruit and engage top talent. By promoting a culture of belonging, you become an employer of choice where the most talented individuals can contribute their talents and feel as if their contributions are valued by management, co-workers, and clients. Promoting belonging drives engagement and offers an opportunity to recoup a portion of the hundreds of billions of dollars employee disengagement costs U.S. companies each year.

In addition, innovation and creativity suffer as employees from similar backgrounds and experiences often share similar perspectives, thus, limiting ideation and creative problem solving. A more diverse workforce provides new opportunities including opening new markets, developing new products, services, and solutions. These benefits of diversity provide leaders with a more agile workforce allowing for improved customer response as well as organizational resiliency.

While most of this discussion has focused on organizations internally, focusing externally on a broader group of stakeholders, such as suppliers, can create a whole new offering of improved products and services at more competitive prices. Gaining a new outside perspective into a challenge or opportunity may result in additional services, new markets, and even additional value-added offerings. Diversity of identity, thought, and experience drive organizational value.

Conversely, those organizations that do not embrace diversity, equity, and inclusion (DEI) authentically are exposing themselves to brand, reputational, and image risk potentially resulting in loss of their social license to operate. Over the summer of 2020, we have seen many organizations issue statements in support of BLM. These statements have been in response to social justice protests highlighting police brutality against BIPOC communities as well as other systemic inequities. Many stakeholders have questioned the authenticity of these statements and the commitment of leadership to change their business practices both internally and externally to address the root cause of these inequities. Some believe these statements are made in response to perceived enterprise risk to their brands and organizations rather than a true commitment of support and alliance with the BIPOC community. It is really a question of authenticity, and a lack of authenticity can impact an organization's social license to operate.

As a result, a new term, "woke-washing," has entered the conversation suggesting that leaders are issuing statements to preserve image, brand, and profitability rather than doing the hard work to drive deep systemic change to promote organizational transparency, belonging, and opportunity for all.

WHAT IS WOKE WASHING?

While issuing a statement supporting BLM might be considered a positive by some, many are questioning the authenticity of corporate statements because of their long history of racist and sexist actions and behaviors. Many employees, customers, investors, and communities are pushing back and sharing their stories.

Complaints are being made by employees and former employees against employers as they find a lack of internal policy and procedure alignment with corporate issued statements around social justice and BLM. "Woke washing" is the most recent iteration of "green washing" in which companies adopt the trappings of the social justice movement in their media and promotional coverage but their internal policies and practices remain unchanged and are often biased, racist, and sexist.

Employees of organizations such as Whole Foods and Chick-fil-A have reported being fired or sent home for wearing BLM face masks. At the Whole Foods in Cambridge, MA, protestors gathered, calling for a boycott of the store. Many customers sought other alternatives rather than entering the store.[24] While this example is for one location, protestors leveraging social media platforms can have a tremendous impact on organizations, their brands, and their license to operate.

Employees of sporting apparel giants, Adidas, Nike Inc., and Under Armour Inc. have complained that while these organizations have benefitted from marketing black sports stars to generate sales and selling sneakers and apparel to Black communities, their leadership ranks remain under-representational for women and people of color.[25]

The previous case on Chevron is another example of being called out for "woke washing." Investors are pushing back with shareholder proposals demanding greater insight into meaningful organizational change around its history of environmental injustice.

Whistleblowers and protestors focus on the authenticity of corporate leaders to really address systemic racism, sexism, and biases within their organizations. Employees and other stakeholders are looking for meaningful change not just a one-off program. Making this type of change takes time and requires significant engagement and effort.

Some best practices to avoid "woke washing" include:

1. Ensuring your brand and organization have real purpose and that it is baked into your culture, values, business model, and exemplified in your actions and behaviors.

2. Authentically storytelling about your organization, its history, actions, and impacts to build credibility and trust.

3. Owning your mistakes and seeking to engage a broad base of stakeholders to gather input to drive change.

4. Investing time and resources to drive authentic change both internally and externally.

As with reporting of any results, it is best practice to share the good, the bad, and the ugly because anything short of authenticity will be deemed "woke washing." Stakeholders are demanding meaningful change and demonstrated action rather than Public Relation (PR) statements that lack organizational strategic alignment.

1.3 Driving Strategic Alignment

To drive systemic change, it is crucial to ensure strategic alignment so that vision, action, and resources align with organizational mission. Systemic change to deliver a J.E.D.I. strategy must be baked into an organization's culture rather than be bolted on to it. Many organizations have DEI training programs, some have DEI leaders, others require DEI concepts to be included in leadership training; but most of these initiatives are siloed rather than embedded into core operations. They are more check the box approaches that allow leadership to respond in the affirmative about the existence of such programs rather than to truly inculcate J.E.D.I. principles into culture, strategy, and core business functionality.

When we speak about J.E.D.I. systemic change to drive belonging and engagement, we are focusing on:

1. **Board of Directors and C-suite Alignment and Support** – In order to drive systemic change, we need Board and C-suite sponsorship and engagement. Creating a culture of belonging is part of an organization's core values and it is practiced by both the Board and the C-suite. Justice, equity, diversity and inclusion (J.E.D.I.) strategy alignment, performance results, and goal tracking are on the agenda for both groups. Board and C-suite composition is reflective of the broader community in which it operates. Leadership serves as a role model for both employees and peer organizations. Resource support includes training and development as well as accountability and compensation alignment for desired outcomes.

2. **Strategy Alignment** – Building a culture for inclusion must be part of an organization's core values. As a result, it is baked into its strategy for engaging clients, investors, employees, suppliers, and community members. Often J.E.D.I. projects are undertaken because a competitor is offering a similar program. Or a member of the senior leadership team met someone at a conference, and they think a DEI training session is a competitive requirement. One-off DEI trainings or programs are not effective in driving systemic change. Building a culture of belonging requires alignment with organizational strategy so that it is part of everyone's responsibility cascading from the C-suite all the way to the lowest level employee. Siloed efforts do not result in systemic change.

3. **Portfolio Alignment** – Projects need to be selected and resourced based on their impact toward strategic goals including J.E.D.I. goals. While specific projects are more easily aligned to J.E.D.I. goals, all projects should have a set of criteria related to these issues. Portfolio managers need to assess all program and project selection based on organizational J.E.D.I. criteria such as strategic alignment, product or service target outcome, people assignments, supplier selection, and community impacts.

4. **Resource Allocation** – One of the most common barriers to an organization's J.E.D.I. strategic transformation is unfunded or underfunded mandates. Driving systemic change requires resources in terms of budget, time, and people. If leadership supports a more just, equitable, and inclusive organization, then resources need to be appropriately allocated so that impact viewed from both an internal and external lens can be delivered across the organization.

5. **Reward Alignment** – I'm sure you have heard that what gets measured gets managed. The same is true with performance-based Key Performance Indicators (KPIs) and performance scorecards. If leadership, managers, and employees are not held accountable for creating a more inclusive culture, which is necessary for a diverse workforce to thrive, then there is insufficient incentive to drive change. It is the classic problem of "Asking for A but rewarding B." It is crucial to have alignment between compensation and strategic initiatives to hold everyone accountable for building an inclusive and equitable organization.

1.4 Capital Markets

As we have seen in the prior cases, investors are requiring disclosure on environmental, social. and governance (ESG) issues. The growing trend is known by several names: Socially Responsible, Social Impact, Sustainable, Impact, and ESG investing. Global assets applying ESG criteria reached $40.5 trillion in 2020 representing a tripling of this market over the past 8 years.[26] While much of the early focus was on carbon footprint and environmental concerns, increasingly investors are focusing on equity and social justice issues. For the 2020 proxy season, there were over 400 shareholder proposals focused on ESG issues such as climate change, gender diversity, and political contributions.[27] Another significant topic has been Board and C-suite diversity. The E.U. is reinvigorating a proposal, originally drafted in 2012 that requires European-listed companies to ensure that at least 40% of their non-executive board member seats are held by women. The representation of women on Boards rose initially but stagnated in 2015 at 26% without the passing of this legislation.[28]

Tesla, which is lauded for its development of electric vehicles (EVs) and battery technology, scores well on environmental impact, but it has come under fire because of its social impact, specifically its requirement that employees need to sign arbitration agreements as a condition for employment. According to an Institutional Shareholder Services, Inc report, "Although the company's code of conduct bans harassment and discrimination in the workplace, Tesla has faced multiple allegations of racial discrimination and harassment at its factory in Fremont, California."[29] The impact of these arbitration clauses as a condition for employment stifles employees right to shine a light on discrimination and harassment publicly. GM, by contrast, has, until recently been an environmental laggard. Its transformation to becoming a leader in EV production has followed a company-wide culture transformation, a cornerstone of which has been expanding its DEI strategy and leadership. As we look deeply at organizations and follow the pathway of their systems, we see how policies and procedures impact achieving one's J.E.D.I. vision, and how system redesign drives organizational benefit realization and creates value (Case Study: Tesla vs. GM in Appendix 1A).

As You Sow issues an annual report looking at CEO pay relative to organizational performance. Using a regression analysis, their research highlights a series of variables to determine organizational performance and CEO impact. In the last several years, U.S. public companies have been required to report on the ratio of CEO pay to average worker pay. The pay multiple ratios are staggering; the ratio of CEO to average worker compensation was 320-to-1 in 2019 in comparison to 21-to-1 in 1965. This significant wealth gain for CEOs has come at the expense of workers and has exacerbated the wealth gap and income inequality.

Investors are requiring greater disclosure on non-financial related risk and opportunity factors as these variables significantly impact organizational performance and investor returns. In order to better understand the risks associated with human capital policies, the U.S. Securities and Exchange Committee (SEC) passed new non-financial reporting guidelines requesting companies disclose details of their workforce management. The new ruling, which passed in August of 2020, is expected to generate additional human capital data such as information on workforce composition and practices around recruitment, development, and engagement.[30] Human capital and management systems are being much more closely scrutinized by both regulators and investors because of the risks and opportunities for competitive advantage that they represent.

1.5 Technology and Digital Systems

Algorithms have become ubiquitous and drive much of the decision-making happening in organizations. While data-driven decisions are impactful in reducing bias and improving organizational decision-making, it is important to understand that algorithms can exacerbate bias when the data driving the algorithmic formula is biased. Amazon famously developed an Artificial Intelligence (AI) recruiting tool that was biased against women. Based on Amazon's past hiring data for developer and technical roles, the machine learning tool taught itself that male candidates were preferred. The tool penalized resumes that included the word "women" and lowered scores for graduates of two all-women's colleges.[31] Because the AI tool was learning from past hiring data that historically had resulted in men being much more successful as candidates, it used this learning to recommend candidates that were male. As we embrace digital transformation to become more agile organizations, it is crucial that management understand the benefits and risks of AI and machine learning as it relates to bias and decision-making.

As a country, the U.S. has had many examples of algorithmic bias in terms of incorporating data on education, zip codes, job titles, etc. into all kinds of offerings including insurance coverage and rates, mortgage rates, terms and availability, and credit scores and credit availability. It is important to understand the impacts of algorithmic formulas on potential outcomes and on the people they impact. While AI can be a tool to improve data-driven decision-making and to reduce bias, it must be thoughtfully and knowledgeably utilized. There are no silver bullets, and instituting new tools without full vetting, change management plans, and adoption support is a recipe for disaster. The good news is that there are best practices and checklists to facilitate effective usage of AI, and other technologies to improve data driven decision making.

1.6 ESG Reporting Frameworks

Increasingly, diverse stakeholders are requiring companies to disclose their non-financial data, including human capital strategy and workforce data, in order to better assess both risks and opportunities. The frameworks highlighted in Table 1.3 include ESG reporting for both public and private organizations. These frameworks serve as useful tools for management leading their organizations toward an integrated bottom-line strategy as they require reporting on material, ESG issues.

Each reporting framework highlights social, environmental, and governance differently, which results in different reporting outcomes based upon the framework utilized. SASB standards address diversity and inclusion topics through its human capital lens focusing on the following categories – Employee Health and Safety, Labor Practices, and Employee Engagement, Diversity & Inclusion. Of the current 77 industry standards, 13 focus on DEI.[32] Because of SASB's focus on financial materiality, not all industries have the same DEI materiality requirements. (Note materiality is discussed in detail in my first book, *Becoming a Sustainable Organization*.) Under the Human Capital Research Project, SASB is reviewing the materiality of human capital issues and has found support for broadening their materiality standards across their 77 industry standards. Work continues on this Human Capital project, but this approach does highlight the discussion of materiality. One might argue that all organizations should consider their people as material.

GRI 405 Diversity and Equal Opportunity guidelines recommend topic-specific disclosures such as gender and age group stratification for governing bodies such as board of directors and for employees and pay equity by gender. This approach is more quantitative rather than a deep dive into organizational systems, policies, and processes. The B Impact Assessment delves more deeply into organizational system questions around equity and inclusion and is designed to be used by small and mid-size organizations.

Table 1.3 Reporting Frameworks for ESG Risk Management

Reporting Organization	Website	Human Rights and Equity Impact
Sustainability Accounting Standards Board (SASB)	https://www.sasb.org/	Human Capital Project-Human capital management, employee health and wellness, diversity, equity, & inclusion, and labor practices
Global Reporting Initiative (GRI)	https://www.globalreporting.org/	Mapping of GRI reporting standards to SDGs
Task Force on Climate-related Financial Disclosure (TCFD)	https://www.fsb-tcfd.org/	Systemic risk framework.
ISO 26000-Social Responsibility	https://www.iso.org/iso-26000-social-responsibility.html	Framework to respect human rights, ethical behavior, employee health and well-being, accountability, and transparency.
Certified B Corp B Impact Assessment	https://bimpactassessment.net/	Measuring business impact on employees, community, environment, and customers.
Taskforce on Inequality-related Financial Disclosure (TIFD)	https://thetifd.org/	Systemic risk framework-accounting for company and investor impacts on inequality.

Taskforce on Inequality-related Financial Disclosure (TIFD) is a new framework proposal designed to address the fragility of the economy and especially the most underserved populations revealed during the COVID-19 pandemic. Workers are facing increasing job insecurity, below living standard wages, no minimum hour contracts, and contract only positions that lack benefits. These trends are creating a less stable environment for families and communities. TIFD is calling for a collaboration between investors, the business community, and public entities to create a framework to better address these issues.

B Corp offers private, public, and global organizations certification using the B Impact Assessment to rate your organization on its ESG impacts including its policies around diversity representation, living wage, benefits, working conditions, employee ownership, and several other human capital related factors. Each of these reporting frameworks seeks to highlight the importance of non-financial factors on the performance of organizations and many take a deeper look at the role of business in society.

The discussion around ESG reporting frameworks highlights their variation in approaches with differing criteria and areas of focus especially as it relates to human capital. These differences in ESG ratings and risk assessment are further highlighted in the GM vs. Tesla case in which the major ESG investment rating agencies assign widely different ratings to these companies.

1.7 Summary

As we navigate the VUCA world of the 21st century, leaders need a new strategic approach and toolkit to build equitable, just, and resilient organizations that promotes worker and community stability allowing for a more prosperous future for all. Investors, communities, employees, and customers are all demanding a holistic, ESG model for business value creation. Using the U. N. SDGs as a roadmap helps leadership create a blueprint for creating a J.E.D.I. strategy and delivering on its goals. Leveraging frameworks such as SASB, GRI, and the B Impact Assessment as tools facilitates tying a sustainable strategy to actions and metrics. Each of these tools incorporates human capital factors that, while not part of traditional financial reporting, need to be considered and analyzed as part of building an equitable and inclusive organization. While candidates and employees are important stakeholders for these initiatives so are investors, customers, and regulators.

Understanding the economic impact of J.E.D.I. focused organizations from both a risk mitigation and opportunity creation perspective lays the foundation for driving significant change and cascading transformation throughout the organization. Moving forward requires Board and senior level commitment from a strategic, modeling, and resource perspective. Peeling back the layers of an organization to really understand its internal systems must be part of the process. This approach identifies barriers and impediments to progress as well as organizational excellence that can be modeled across the organization. Digital tools may be part of the solution, but understanding the tool itself and its benefits and limitations is crucial for successful adoption and integration. Let's move forward to discuss broadening the stakeholder conversation so that we can be authentic in our organizational transformation rather than be accused of "woke washing."

Questions

1. What megatrends are impacting global society? What megatrends are impacting your organization?
2. Why do you believe environmental and social justice are intertwined?

3. What #SDGs are strong fits for impact for your organization?
4. How might your organization begin to address environmental and social justice issues?
5. If you were asked to explain the benefits of adopting a J.E.D.I. strategy to your senior leadership team, what would you say?
6. Are there examples of "woke washing" that you have experienced? If so, what could have been done to improve alignment?
7. Do you agree that a J.E.D.I. strategy must be integrated into organizational strategy to drive impact? Why?
8. How do you think COVID-19 impacted organizations? Did leadership require the systemic shock of COVID-19 to reassess their ESG strategies?
9. How might a J.E.D.I. strategic approach improve your organizational performance and outcome?
10. What recommendation might you make relative to ESG reporting to facilitate comparable reporting for stakeholders?

Appendix 1A

Case Study: Tesla vs. General Motors

Must Organizations Excel in Environmental, Social, and Governance (ESG) Metrics to Be Sustainable?

By Kathy Hipple

Kathy Hipple teaches the finance sequence at Bard's MBA in Sustainability. She is a research fellow at the Ohio River Valley Institute (ORVI) and a senior advisor in financial services at Corporate Citizenship. She has written extensively on sustainable, responsible, and impact investing. Her research on fossil fuel divestment and the financial decline of the fossil fuel industry from her work at the Institute for Energy Economics and Financial Analysis (IEEFA) has been widely cited. As Vice President at Merrill Lynch for 10 years, Hipple placed fixed income securities with international institutions and advised Japanese insurance companies and pension funds. She later served as founder and CEO of Ambassador Media, a New York-based local search company with revenues of more than $35 million. She has an MBA in Sustainability and splits her time between New York City and Vermont.

While both Tesla and General Motors (GM) make vehicles, they are radically different companies, with radically different leaders, corporate cultures, and missions. Their industry is rapidly being disrupted by the global transition to a low-carbon economy resulting in slowing demand for their primary products with some speculating that demand for vehicles may have peaked. Each company has chosen a different approach to the industry disruption, illustrated by their disparate approaches toward ESG issues, which couldn't be more different, at least on the surface. Tesla is a leader in Environment (E), but its scores on Social (S) and Governance (G) metrics are mixed. A teacher who grades generously might give that company a "Needs Improvement" in governance.[33] Despite its poor environmental history as the nation's largest manufacturer of gas-guzzling trucks and SUVs, GM is transforming, aspiring to become a leader in E by selling only EVs by 2035. GM's score on S and G metrics, already respectable, continues to improve.

Comparing these two iconic companies and their CEOs sheds light on questions:

- Can an organization have a poor record on either E, S, or G, yet still be considered a sustainable organization?
- Can ESG accelerate a company's journey – be it an innovation or a transformation journey?
- How can ESG be a value driver?

Tesla: With Climate as Proxy, Environmental Leadership is in the Company's DNA; Social Metrics and Governance, Not So Much

Tesla is rightly considered an environmental leader. No wonder. Its mission, until mid-2016, was "to accelerate the world's transition to sustainable transport," by eliminating transportation emissions, the largest contributor to greenhouse gas emissions in the U.S., accounting for nearly 30% of total emissions[34] and 24% of global CO_2 emissions.[35] Light vehicles account for almost 60% of transport emissions. The company now produces EVs on a scale – half a million in 2020, nearly a quarter of the global EV market – that will result in billions of tons of avoided carbon emissions, changing the trajectory of climate change from a doomsday scenario to a more hopeful one.

Its current mission, seeking to "accelerate the world's transition to sustainable energy," is even more ambitious. Tesla now sells solar panels and solar roof tiles, battery storage from home to grid scale. It is building massive battery factories around the world. Growth plans include ride-hailing or ride-sharing services.[36] Tesla has a 50/50 shot of creating fully autonomous vehicles (AVs)[37] by 2025, enabled by data from its vehicle fleet, which log 30–40 million miles of data per day, according to some analysts who believe Tesla could be worth nearly $3 trillion by 2025.[38] Those analysts expect Tesla to enter and dominate the robotaxi business, increasing the company's role in creating sustainable transport at a global scale.

Viewed through an environmental lens, Tesla is on an innovation journey, one that is only accelerating.

Viewed through a social lens, however, Tesla has work to do, as its diversity report acknowledged. Its human capital management, according to Sustainalytics, reveal "significant shortcomings."[39] A recent shareholder proposal, for example, has targeted the company's stance on mandatory arbitration. The company's reliance on lithium-ion batteries to power its electric fleet has thrown into question its supply chain especially around extraction of rare earth minerals and human rights. And the company's record on governance, under Musk's leadership, has arguably been abysmal. Musk was fined by the Securities and Exchange Commission (SEC) in 2019 and required to relinquish his Chairmanship of the company, retaining his role as CEO. Despite changes to its board to include more independent directors and fewer Musk family members or those with close ties to Musk, critics still suggest Tesla's board should be more independent.

General Motors (GM): Its Transformation Journey Underway, GM Seeks a Leadership Role in Environmental Metrics to Match its Impressive Record on Social and Governance

GM, the nation's largest manufacturer of Internal Combustion Engines (ICE) vehicles, is on a transformation journey. In many ways, this journey is as radical as Tesla's disruption and innovation journey. GM's vehicle sales have steadily declined each year since 2016, from 10 million to 6.83 million in 2020, a decline of more than 30%, according to its annual filings. It has restructured its business, closing plants in the U.S., eliminating brands, and exiting the European market – to boost profitability and to spur innovation. GM entered the AV space in 2016, with its timely acquisition of Cruise Automation. And Mary Barra, the company's CEO, shocked the world in early 2021 when she announced GM would aspire to produce only EVs by 2035.

Based on the company's long history of building gas-guzzling trucks, cozying up to the oil and gas industry, allegedly killing the firm's early attempts to build EVs,[40] and arguing against stringent fuel efficiency standards,[41] it would be hard to call GM an environmental or climate leader. But this is changing rapidly.

Under Barra's leadership, GM has also transformed its corporate culture, improving its social impact. A product of diversity initiatives, Barra was named CEO in 2014, becoming the world's first female CEO of a major automobile company. She has disclosed and publicly addressed safety problems, led the company's diversity initiatives, and announced GM's aspiration "to be the most inclusive company in the world" following the murder of George Floyd.[42] GM closed the gender pay gap in 2018.[43]

GM is also considered a leader in Governance. Highlights include the company's majority-female board since 2019. A comparison is highlighted in Table 1.4.

Table 1.4 Scorecard: Tesla vs. General Motors (GM) an ESG Perspective

	Tesla	*General Motors (GM)*
Environmental	Industry-Leading	Aspirational
Social	Improving	Leading, with Important Caveats
Governance	Historically Poor, But Improving	Very Good

ESG METRICS: RATINGS REMAIN LESS PRECISE THAN FINANCIAL METRICS

Stakeholders, including board members, impact investors, and ESG rating firms such as MSCI and Sustainalytics, struggle to assess companies' current ESG-performance and ESG-specific risks. The field is relatively young. It's important to remember that it took years, even decades, after the Securities Acts of 1933 and 1934 before financial metrics were sufficiently standardized and refined to be useful to investors.

Ratings firms struggle to determine *which* ESG metrics are most vital and how these metrics should be weighted and ranked.[44] Refinitiv, a database that tracks ESG and financial data, includes approximately 125 separate components within each broad E, S, and G category. As a further illustration of the complexity, three recent Sustainalytics reports, "Sustainalytics ESG Risk Rating Report," "Tesla Controversy Report," and "GM Controversy Report," are 71, 59, and 70 pages, respectively.

Adding to the confusion, the major ESG rating companies often produce wildly different, often conflicting, ESG scores for the same company.[45] MSCI, for example, gives Tesla an overall A rating for ESG on a scale ranging from AAA (highest) to CCC (lowest).[46] It describes Tesla as an ESG leader for its corporate governance. However, Institutional Shareholder Services (ISS), scores Tesla's Governance as high risk.

GM received a CCC ESG rating (the lowest) from July 2017 through April 2020, when it was upgraded to a B (below average for the automotive industry). MSCI noted GM was an ESG laggard in product safety and quality, product carbon footprint, and labor relations.[47]

Sustainalytics, which uses a framework to assess "a company's exposure to industry-specific material ESG issues … and how well the company is managing those issues," currently gives Tesla and GM widely varied scores on separate ESG Risk categories, but ultimately assigns each the same overall ESG Risk score of 31, which is considered high risk, just below severe risk. GM's greatest risk exposure is in S, with G as the lowest. Tesla's greatest risk exposure is also in S, with E as its lowest risk.

CSRHub, another ESG rating system that assesses Corporate Social Responsibility (CSR) performance, rated Tesla as 31[48] and GM 91 on a 100-point scale, with 100 being the highest.[49]

S&P DJI ESG Score rated Tesla a dismal 22 out of 100 in 2021, up from an even more dismal score in 2020. Notably, its G score, at 49, was up 21 points over the prior year. GM, by contrast, scored a near-perfect 95, the highest in the Eligible S&P 500 Automobiles & Components sector.[50]

TruCost, which S&P Global acquired, gives Tesla a poor ESG rating of 15, out of 100, compared to the auto industry's 51.[51] Tesla's S score was a dismal

2, and its E and G scores, at 21, were also poor. GM, by contrast, was awarded a 79, scoring equally well on E, S, and G metrics.[52]

ISS now includes ESG rankings. Currently, only its Governance scores were publicly available on Yahoo! Finance, as part of each corporate Profile. Tesla's Governance Quality Score was 10, ISS's highest governance risk rating. GM's Governance score is 4, reflecting much lower governance risk, according to ISS.

As Table 1.5 ESG Risk Rating: Tesla vs. GM highlights, each rating agency focuses on ESG issues and metrics issuing a range of ratings. As a result, both Tesla and GM have mixed performance – depending upon the rating agency and its lens.

It's little wonder that ESG and impact investors are confused – comparing Tesla and GM through an ESG lens *is* complicated. And the current state of ESG ratings only intensify this complexity. Stakeholders, in effect, must choose which ESG factors they consider most relevant, and make their own determinations about ESG-specific risks and opportunities. Despite the complexity, the following analysis of Tesla and GM will attempt an ESG-based comparison.

Table 1.5 ESG Risk Ratings: Tesla vs. GM

	Tesla	*GM*
MSCI ESG From AAA (best) to CCC (worst)	• A (average) • Has been rated A since 2019	• B (below average) • From 2017-4/2020, rating was CCC
Sustainalytics: ESG Risk (1-50, with higher scores representing greater risk)	• 31 overall ESG • Product Governance, or "responsibilities to clients," represents the most severe risk stemming from its lead-in deploying autopilot • Corporate governance risk is perceived as a medium	• 31 • Its greatest risk is S • GM's highest controversy risk is in Customer Incidences
CSRHub CSR/ESG Ranking (1-100 scoring, with 100 the highest)	• 31	• 91

(*Continued*)

Table 1.5 *(Continued)* **ESG Risk Ratings: Tesla vs. GM**

	Tesla	GM
S&P DJI ESG (1-100 scoring, with 100 the highest, or best, score)	• 22[53] • Score improved by eight points in 2021 • Governance was the highest component of the ESG score, at 49	• 95
TruCost ESG score (1-100, with 100 as the highest, or best, score)	• 15, compared to the auto industry average of 51 • Social Score of 2 is seen as the area with the highest risk • E and G are each ranked 21	• 79 compared to the auto industry average of 51 • GM scores well above the industry average on E, S, and G

Environmental (E) Perspective

Tesla, from its inception, has sought to be an environmental leader. Its mission is ambitious: to "accelerate the world's transition to sustainable energy." Perhaps its biggest environmental impact has been to prove it can profitably sell EVs, achieving five consecutive profitable quarters through Q1 2021. It sold 500,000 EVs in 2020, capturing more than 20% of the global market, and is on track to nearly double sales in 2021. Its rocketing share price ballooned its market capitalization to nearly $850 billion in early 2021. Tesla's financial success has encouraged the growth of the EV market with legacy automakers joining the rush into the EV market. Many, such as Volkswagen and GM, seek to displace Tesla as the world's largest manufacturer of EVs. Ford's introduction of an all-electric version of its F-150 truck, currently the best-selling vehicle in the U.S., helped push its stock price to a five-year high. Investors have also enthusiastically backed EV start-ups, sending the valuations of start-ups that have yet to manufacture a single auto into the billions.

Forecasts for growth in EVs vary, with most analysts forecasting modest penetration by EVs throughout the decade. Bloomberg New Energy Finance (BNEF) projects sales of 8.5 million EVs by 2025, 26 million by 2030, and 54 million by 2040.[54] ARK Invest, a famous Tesla bull, believes global EV sales will increase 20 times by 2025, from 2.2 to 40 million – nearly five times BNEF's forecast.[55] Tesla has a commanding competitive position in China, the world's largest auto market.

Beyond transforming the auto industry, Tesla appears to have a massive competitive advantage with AVs based on its head start in the EV market, which provides an enormous trove of data from its fleet. Both AVs and ride-sharing platforms depend on vast quantities of high-quality data. Tesla had already amassed more than

3 billion driving miles from its vehicles by March 2020.[56] Its closest competitor in driving mile collection data, Google-owned Waymo, has collected roughly 20 million real-world driving miles, by contrast.[57]

If Tesla launches the first autonomous ride-sharing platform, or Mobility as a Service (MaaS), sales could dwarf those of current ride-share leaders, Uber and Lyft, at currently more than $150 billion a year. Both Uber and Lyft have recently exited the AV space, likely because of the complexity and costs of developing AV technology. Eliminating the cost of human drivers, which accounts for more than 75% of the cost of a ride service, could make an autonomous ride-hailing platform wildly profitable.

GM, by contrast, has been, until recently, an environmental laggard. No longer. For example, GM has moved from being sued by the Environmental Protection Agency (EPA) in 1995 to receiving its Green Power Leadership Award for efforts to expand the company's renewable energy supply.[58]

The transformation to environmental leader remains bumpy, however. As recently as 2018, GM's chief executive lobbied the then-president Trump to ease up on Corporate Average Fuel Economy (CAFE) standards, which, under President Obama, had called for increasingly stringent fuel efficiency levels.[59] After California challenged Trump's proposed changes in 2019, GM and other automakers joined the Trump administration lawsuit against California. Only after the Biden victory did Barra change course, dropping the lawsuit. By early 2021, GM was planning for an all-electric vehicle future. The company plans to invest $27 billion between now and 2025 on electrification, R&D, and capex to support this move.

This aspiration will be challenging, as GM's most profitable vehicles have long been pick-up trucks and SUVs, which contribute $5,000 – $15,000, per vehicle, in earnings before interest and tax. It is unclear if electric pick-up trucks will have the same profit margins as their ICE counterparts. Making the transition to a slightly smaller, less profitable fleet will be financially challenging.

Supply chain issues, particularly semiconductor chip shortages, have caused GM to idle eight plants throughout the U.S. But GM opted to keep open a few plants that manufactures its most profitable SUVs, luxury cars and heavy-duty trucks, all of which are gas-guzzling ICE vehicles. While this decision makes sense from a strictly financial standpoint, it does belie GM's aspiration to lead on climate issues.

Legacy companies rarely pivot successfully, especially when new technologies disrupt their primary business. Often, the revenues, profits, and cash flows generated from their legacy business keep management's focus on the past, rather than on new opportunities with disruptive technology. GM's aspiration is to be the outlier – a legacy company that successfully transforms. If it succeeds, this may be GM's most lasting legacy.

GM's aspirations to be an environmental leader have faced recent challenges. The massive recall of batteries in its all-electric Bolts, produced between 2017 and 2022 at two different factories, led GM to suspend sales and production of Bolts.

Measuring environmental aspirations for GM, however, remains complicated. Even as it struggles with batteries for its EVs, GM plans a big future for the robotaxi business. While GM was late coming to the EV revolution at scale, it had forged ahead in AVs, turbo-charged in 2016 through its acquisition of Cruise Automation for $580 million. GM formed a separate company for autonomy, allowing it to collaborate with other car companies while remaining majority owner.

Cruise, formerly called Cruise Automation, received authorization to test its self-driving cars in California,[60] bringing it a step closer to producing a fleet, or even launching a platform, of robotaxis (or driverless cars) – the holy grail for car companies seeking to dominate what many believe will be the transportation of the future. Cruise could add $50 billion in revenues as it ramps, according to company officials. It hopes to begin charging for rides as early as 2022. These ambitious plans may have hit a snag as Cruise expected to use modified Bolts for its ride-hailing business.

Advanced technology, requiring massive amounts of data, AI, and Deep Learning, is not generally associated with a 100-year-old car company. GM, however, has access to an unlikely data source from its OnStar, an in-vehicle safety system. All new, and many older, GM cars are equipped with OnStar, enabling the company to create a central database connecting individual cars to GM's telematics platform. This database may prove useful to GM as it builds out its AV capabilities.

Forecasting the impact of this shift to autonomous is furiously debated by futurists. But clearly, the potential environmental impact of autonomous taxi networks will be profound. Currently, cars spend roughly 80–90% of the time parked, highly inefficient use of space in urban areas, and a massive waste of resources to build cars that operate so infrequently. Fleets of robotaxis may blend what is currently considered public transport with privately owned cars, resulting in fewer cars on the road. Car ownership may continue to decline as passengers could tap into MaaS easily and affordably. The next generation may feel no need ever to own a car. It's a brave new world. Table 1.6 Environmental Scorecard: Tesla vs. GM highlights key comparisons between the two companies on several key points.

Table 1.6 Environmental Scorecard: Tesla vs. GM

	Tesla	*GM*
Mission/Vision	• Accelerate the world's transition to sustainable energy.	• Create a future of zero crashes, zero emissions, and zero congestion.

(Continued)

Table 1.6 *(Continued)* **Environmental Scorecard: Tesla vs. GM**

	Tesla	*GM*
Company History	• Focused on sustainable transport since its inception. • World's largest manufacturer of EVs launched Gigafactories globally. • Acquired SolarCity.	• Slow to move toward EVs. • Despite introduction of 2015 Chevy Bolt, company's EV strategy has stumbled. • In 2019, GM allocated a portion of the $6 billion savings from reducing its workforce by 15% and discontinuing several models, and idling factories in a broad restructuring effort designed, in part, to spur innovation.
Aspiration	• Company builds only all-EV cars but "also infinitely scalable" clean energy generation and storage products. • Creating an ambitious energy ecosystem. • "Tesla believes the faster the world stops relying on fossil fuels and moves toward a zero-emission future, the better."[61]	• Company set a goal to sell only EVs by 2035. • Seeks leadership role in autonomous vehicle ride-sharing market.[62] • Purchased Cruise Automation in 2016 to accelerate move into AVs.
Sustainability Goals	• Published First Impact Report in 2019. • Goal to operate global manufacturing, vehicle charging, and other operations using 100 renewable energy.[63]	• Published First Sustainability Report in 2010. • Global operations and vehicles will be carbon neutral by 2040.

(Continued)

Table 1.6 *(Continued)* **Environmental Scorecard: Tesla vs. GM**

	Tesla	GM
Current Mitigating Factors	• Supply chain concerns include products that rely on batteries, which currently use both lithium and cobalt. • Company Investment of $1.5 billion in Bitcoin criticized for leading to increase in carbon emissions.[64] • Company then suspended use of Bitcoin for payment due to concerns about "rapidly increasing use fossil fuels for Bitcoin mining and transactions." • Gigafactory in Texas may be fueled by fossil gas.[65]	• GM's most profitable vehicles have been SUVs and pick-up trucks, which have poor safety implications for pedestrians and cyclists. • EVgo partnership, to "democratize" EV charging.[66]
Additional Notes	• Musk resigned from Trump advisory councils, following the then-president's withdrawal from the Paris Climate Agreement.	• In 2016–2017, Barra urged Trump to relax Obama-era emission standards, which had called for greater fuel efficiency. • Climate Action 100+, the largest global coalition on climate change, supports a proxy resolution at GM calling for Paris-aligned lobbying disclosure.

Social (S) Perspective

Evaluating a company through a Social lens is arguably even more complex than through an Environmental lens. Stakeholders are forced to select which metrics, among dozens, they deem most relevant.

Overall, Tesla produces EVs that promise to improve society on a grand scale. Its models consistently receive the highest safety rankings.[67] Its customers, early on, were exclusively affluent since its first models were too expensive for the average consumer. With the introduction of the Model 3 in 2017, its customer base broadened considerably, though its customers' median income in the U.S. remains far higher than the national average. It plans to offer a $25,000 car, noting "Affordability is key to how we scale."[68] Its customers are insanely loyal. Its board composition includes two females, but its overall diversity needs improvement.

In other areas, however, Tesla's social scores are suboptimal. Its U.S. workforce is heavily male, with women holding just 17% of leadership roles (director and vice president), and Black (and African American) each represent just 4% of leadership positions, which, the company notes, does "not represent the deep talent pools ... that exist in the U.S. at every level."[69] Latinx (and Hispanic) also represent only 4% of leadership positions, though they make up 22% of the U.S. workforce.[70] Tesla has been criticized for requiring its employees to agree to mandatory arbitration, and a shareholder resolution was filed in 2020 asking the company to end this practice.[71] Two recent cases alleging Black workers faced racism in Tesla's workplace have resulted in hefty fines. In October, Owen Diaz was awarded a jaw-dropping $137 million in damages, which may be the largest such award in history. (The $130 million punitive damages are likely to be reduced.) As a contract worker, he had not signed a mandatory arbitration agreement.

The social impact of its production has come under fire, especially the company's supply chain, which currently includes cobalt used for its batteries, though it plans to make cobalt-free batteries in the future.[72] Tesla and several tech companies were sued in 2019[73] by a human rights group, claiming they used cobalt that was mined by children in the Democratic Republic of Congo (DRC).

The broader social impact of EVs in general, however, is widely perceived as beneficial. BIPOC communities suffer disproportionately from living near highways, and as EV adoption rates increase, fewer emissions will pollute these communities. If Tesla launches an autonomous ride-hailing platform at scale, many of the roughly 1.35 million annual traffic fatalities globally could be eliminated.[74]

Another positive social impact of AVs includes adding hours a day to commuters' lives, particularly those in megacities such as Los Angeles, who cannot afford to live near their workplaces.

While the future of EVs and AVs is uncertain, mass adoption of EVs and AVs will be extremely disruptive. There will be winners and losers. More than 100,000 gas stations in the U.S. alone will close. The supply chain that creates parts for ICE cars will cease to exist. Robotaxis could potentially displace thousands of taxi and ride-share drivers.[75] Since Lyft and Uber have already abandoned plans to create their own AVs, Tesla will have a competitive advantage launching a ride-hailing platform without needing to conduct a managed decline of its own workforce of drivers.

GM rightly claims to be a leader in Social. Its female CEO acknowledges she was a "product of diversity." It aspires to be the "most inclusive company in the world." The company closed the gender pay gap in 2018, and its board has been majority female since 2019. Diversity initiatives focused on Black Americans are long-standing. During the Great Migration, Black Americans moved to Detroit factories and ultimately moved into high-paying, union jobs that gave them a pathway to join the middle class. In 1960, Detroit was the richest city per capita in the U.S., according to the U.S. Census bureau. And Detroit's African-American community was the wealthiest in America at one point. As the largest auto company in the U.S. during this era, GM touts this history. With the decline of the auto industry and the collapse of Detroit, however, the auto industry no longer offers workers the predictable pathway toward a secure job, let alone a permanent place in the middle class, is no longer a given.

GM has been named one of the most ethical companies in the world.[76] But its Social *bona fides* are not unblemished. After suspending contributions to Republican politicians who voted not to certify the presidential elections votes on January 6, GM resumed these donations in September 2021.[77] [Toyota, which also resumed such contributions, discontinued them after a firestorm of opposition.] To date, GM has not addressed the criticism around these donations to the Republican politicians who opposed certification of the votes. Table 1.7 takes a deeper dive into several key social comparisons.

Table 1.7 Social Scorecard: Tesla vs. GM

	Tesla	*GM*
Gender Diversity on the Board	• Two of the nine board members are women.	• Seven of 13 board members are women. Board has been majority female since 2019.
Racial/Ethnic Diversity on the Board	• Board members are not identified on the Tesla site, based on their racial or ethnic identity.	• Two board members identify as African-American. • Among the seven women on GM's board, one identifies as Hispanic, one as Asian-American, one as African-American.[78]
Workforce Culture and Composition	• 70,757 Full-time employees as of December 31, 2020.	• 155,000 employees, of which 87,000 are hourly, and 68,000 salaried, as of December 31, 2020.

(Continued)

Table 1.7 *(Continued)* **Social Scorecard: Tesla vs. GM**

	Tesla	GM
Gender Composition	• Gender breakdown in U.S. Workforce: 79% Male; 21% Female. • Gender breakdown in Leadership roles in U.S. Workforce: 83% Male; 17% Female.[79]	• Gender breakdown in U.S. Workforce: 88% Male; 12% Female. • Gender breakdown globally: 72% Male, 28% Female.[80] • Females represent 34% of GM's management.[81]
Average Worker Pay/Median Worker Pay and Pay Inequity	• $96,000/year average.[82] • $58,500/year median in FY 2019.[83] • CEO to median pay is largely irrelevant as Musk's compensation is tied to a series of metrics[84] that, for a period in 2021, made him the richest man in the world. • In 2018, Musk earned $2.3 billion, making his pay 40,668 times the median salary of $56,163.[85]	• $85,000/year average.[86] • $107,000/year median in FY 2019.[87] • In 2018, Barra made $21.9 million, 281 times the median worker pay that year $78,000.[88]
Gender Pay Gap	• Median pay was 9% higher for women in Tesla U.K., taken from a snapshot in April 2018.[89] • It appears they have not done a pay gap analysis	• GM closed the gender pay gap in 2018, one of only two global companies with no gender pay gap.[90]
Supplier Diversity Programs and Human Rights	• Efforts to promote supplier diversity include formalizing collaboration within the company and partnerships with suppliers.	• Launched the first supplier diversity program in the auto industry in 1968. • Recognized as an industry leader in supplier diversity initiatives.[91]

(Continued)

Table 1.7 *(Continued)* **Social Scorecard: Tesla vs. GM**

	Tesla	GM
DEI Metrics DEI Programming	• Overall, the majority of employees are from minority groups. • U.S. Workforce: 34% White; 22% Hispanic; 21% Asian; and 10% Black. • Leadership in U.S. Workforce: 59% are White; 25% are Asian; 10% are Black; and 4% are Hispanic.[92] • Named Forbes "Best Employer for Diversity" in 2019. • First DEI Report issued for 2019.	• U.S. Workforce: 69% White; 17% Black; 7% Asian; and 5% Latino.[93] • 40% of corporate officers are women and minorities.[94] • GM appears to have a much more mature DEI initiative.
Safety Ratings on Products	• All Tesla models had received the highest safety awards, until May 2021, when Consumer Reports pulled its top ratings for some Tesla vehicles that would use only cameras, rather than radar and cameras.[95]	• GM's most profitable vehicles have been SUVs and pick-up trucks, which have grown larger, causing safety issues for pedestrians and cyclists. Women, despite being safer drivers, have been disproportionately impacted by the explosion of larger pick-up trucks.[96] • In the U.S., 51% of GM cars received the highest safety award in 2019.[97] • No GM cars received the highest safety rankings in 2021, based on IIHS's top safety picks.[98] Only GM's small SUV, the Equinox, received the highest award. • NHTSA publishes safety records for 1174 GM vehicle models from 2011 to 2021.[99]

(Continued)

Table 1.7 *(Continued)* **Social Scorecard: Tesla vs. GM**

	Tesla	GM
Safety Ratings of Work Environments	• Improving the safety record of the work environment,[100] higher than the auto industry average. The company's global Dart Away, Restricted, or Transferred due to injury (DART) improved by 12% in 2019, compared to 2018. DART. • Tesla is 5% safer than the industry average of large auto manufacturers in terms of injuries, according to BLS data.[101]	• GM measures its workplace safety based on several metrics, including lost work-day injuries and illness, work-related fatalities, and workplace injuries.[102] • Its Sentinel program addresses potential problems proactively to prevent injuries/fatalities. • No fatalities were recorded in 2018 and 2019.
Types of Customers Served, Markets, Customer Demographics, Diversity, Experience, Loyalty	• Of the 500,000 Tesla vehicles sold in 2020, over 450,000 were Models 3/Y, which have sticker prices ranging from $39,000 to $67,500.[103] • When Tesla launched its first model in 2008, the price point was too high for most customers. • Tesla Model 3 owners, in 2018, were mostly male (84%), wealthier than average ($128K household income), older (46 median age, compared to median household 38)[104]	• GM produces dozens of models of vehicles in its four core brands, Chevrolet, Buick, GMC, and Cadillac, and its joint ventures in other countries. It sells vehicles to virtually every demographic.
Social Impact of Production	• Lithium is mined for batteries. Cobalt is expected to be eliminated from its batteries in the future.[105] Most cobalt is mined in the DRC, which has been associated with child labor.	• Transition to EV production offers company opportunity to focus on environmental impact of materials used in production.[106]

(Continued)

Table 1.7 *(Continued)* **Social Scorecard: Tesla vs. GM**

	Tesla	GM
Additional Notes:	• Free medical and dental benefits are offered.[107] • Most employees can buy Tesla stock at a discount. • 100 score (perfect) on LGBTQ equality score in 2021, for the sixth consecutive year.[108]	• Announced intention to be "most inclusive company in the world" following the murder of George Floyd and formed an inclusive advisory board.[109] • GM named among best five gender-equal companies.[110]
Final Thoughts	• If Tesla successfully launched an autonomous ride-hailing service at scale, thousands of taxi and Uber/Lyft drivers' livelihoods would be eliminated.	• GM's EV vision will require transformative change impacting communities and employees, requiring upskilling, and disrupting the ICE supply chain and those workers and communities.

Governance (G) Perspective

A movement to tie corporate governance more closely to sustainability, and away from a sole focus on shareholder primacy, is underway.[111] This shift toward stakeholder capitalism has broad implications for how stakeholders will assess Tesla and GM through a Governance lens.

Corporate governance, the system of rules and principles by which a company is managed and operated, includes financial strategy and risk management, organizational structure, and board structure policies. Governance is where Tesla and GM, differ most. For most of its early history, Tesla's board of directors was comprised of its CEO, Elon Musk, his relatives, and close business partners. Musk has taken a seemingly cavalier attitude toward various stakeholders, including regulators in the U.S., large investor groups, and, more recently, disgruntled consumers in China. Musk's run-in with the SEC, from a tweet in 2018 that implied having received funding to take the company private, resulted in a settlement. Other questionable tweets have followed. When investor groups requested Musk add more independent board members, he suggested they buy Ford stock, which has a dual class of shares, noting "their governance is amazing." As recently as early 2021, Musk was again in questionable Governance territory when he announced Tesla's large investment

Table 1.8 Governance Scorecard: Tesla vs. GM

	Tesla	GM
Board Independence	• In 2016, Tesla was sued after it announced its intention to acquire SolarCity, a company in which Musk was the largest shareholder and served as Chairman. The suit claimed, "six of Tesla's seven board members are either beholden to Musk or directly own SolarCity shares themselves, about $560 million worth."[112] • In 2017, CALSTRS criticized Tesla for its lack of independence on its board. • After a shareholder lawsuit in April 2019, Tesla shed four members who were considered too friendly to Musk. • Currently, five of nine members are independent.[113]	• 12 of GM's 13-member board are independent, with CEO Mary Barra the only corporate executive on the board.[114]
Noteworthy Governance-Related Issues	• In 2018, Musk settled a securities fraud lawsuit with the SEC, which stemmed from his tweet about taking the company private, with "funding secured." The claim appeared to have been false. As part of the settlement, Musk stepped down as Chairman but remained CEO. • When Tesla was criticized in 2017 by two large investors, and asked to add independent board members, Musk tweeted, "This investor group should buy Ford stock. Their governance is amazing. …"	• In 2018, GM announced restructuring plans, which involved cutting jobs and closing five plants, to focus on innovation and autonomous vehicles. The move was approved by GM's Board, and considered effective corporate governance.
Gender Diversity on the Board	Two of the nine board members are women.	• Seven of 13 board members are women. Board has been majority-female since 2019.

in Bitcoin, a cryptocurrency he had often touted. When the company announced quarterly profits that were boosted by the sale of some Bitcoin, critics were quick to suggest Musk had "pumped and dumped," Bitcoin. Shortly after backing away from accepting Bitcoin as payment, Musk has tweeted about Dogecoin, a meme cryptocurrency, and announced he had Asperger's syndrome. The company's Governance woes seem to have no end.

GM, by contrast, has assembled a large 13-person board, with 12 independent members. Its only corporate insider is CEO Barra. When the company has shifted course, internally transforming its culture or externally shifting its strategy, Barra appears to have the support of its board. Barra has been transparent in her efforts to transform the culture – an effort that eluded her predecessors. And she has been equally transparent about shifting the company toward innovation, even when it required closing plants, discontinuing models, and massive layoffs.

Both Musk and Barra have been active in the political realm in the U.S. and China, their largest markets. Both worked on various Trump-era task forces. Barra serves on the Business Roundtable. Barra and Musk each see huge opportunities in the EV market in China, and each has forged political ties to the Chinese government to support these strategies. In short, navigating the geopolitics of a global brand is an extraordinary Governance challenge. Table 1.8 highlights some key governance considerations such as board independence and diversity.

Table 1.9 Shareholder Proposals: Tesla vs GM[115]

	2018	*2019*	*2020*	*2021*
Tesla	• Integrate Sustainability into Financial Reporting • Sustainability Reporting • Climate-related Water Risk Withdrawn after agreement reached	• Sustainability Reporting	• Human Rights Disclosure • Paid Advertising • Mandatory Arbitration	
GM	• Report on GHG Emissions and CAFE Fuel Economy Standards	• Lobbying Expenditures Disclosure	• Human Rights Policy Implementation • Lobbying Expenditures Disclosure – Climate Change	• Paris-Aligned Climate Lobbying • Executive Compensation Linked to Climate Actions (Executive Remuneration Indicator)

Shareholder advocacy and activism, often show-cased through the shareholder resolution process, is one way to interpret a company's Governance. Non-binding resolutions can reveal what shareholders want from management. Often, key shareholders can convince management to make the desired changes through advocacy efforts, and resolutions are withdrawn before coming to a vote. Table 1.9 Shareholder Proposals, Including Withdrawn Proposals: Tesla vs. GM, offers a snapshot of several key comparisons.

Conclusion

Though the history of Tesla and GM are strikingly different, each is navigating the rapid transition to a low-carbon economy and seeking a leadership role in EVs, AVs, and MaaS. They seek to revolutionize transportation as we know it. Tesla is the poster child for radical innovation; GM is the poster child for radical transformation. Similarly, each company's exposure to material ESG factors is also largely different. Management acknowledges their company's journeys are incomplete from an ESG perspective – and recognizes improvement is crucial. Elevating ESG performance may unlock even greater value – for both the companies themselves and society as a whole.

Despite its mission to transform energy, Tesla only issued its first sustainability report in 2018 and maintained in its 2019 report that "Making a significant and lasting impact on environmental sustainability is difficult to achieve without securing financial sustainability for the long term."[116] Yet, given its massive head starts in EVs and AVs and its apparent head start in MaaS, Tesla may ultimately have the most significant impact on sustainability. Arguably, its impact could accelerate further as it improves its Social and Governance performance.

Despite its later start in EVs and AVs, GM appears to have made a radical shift toward an all-electric future, with significant steps toward dominance in AVs. From an ESG perspective, if GM leverages its aspirations for the Environment, its impressive Social ambitions and its excellent Governance record, it may yet have the greatest impact on sustainability. And, if GM proves that legacy companies can pivot to thrive in a low-carbon future, its impact on sustainability may be even greater.

Questions

1. Can an organization be sustainable if it has only environmental or social justice, or are both necessary?
2. Which organization do you believe will thrive and grow in the next five (5) years? Why?
3. What advice would you give each of these CEOs to make their organization more equitable and just?

4. If GM becomes an environmental leader to rival Tesla, what will be the world-wide impact?
5. How important is Governance when you assess the two companies from a sustainability perspective?

Notes

1 "Activate Agility: The Five Avenues to Success | McKinsey & Company," accessed September 28, 2020, https://www.mckinsey.com/business-functions/organization/our-insights/the-organization-blog/activate-agility-get-these-five-things-right.
2 Martin, "Communications Materials," *United Nations Sustainable Development* (blog), accessed October 21, 2020, https://www.un.org/sustainabledevelopment/news/communications-material/.
3 dpicampaigns, "Take Action for the Sustainable Development Goals," *United Nations Sustainable Development* (blog), accessed January 2, 2021, https://www.un.org/sustainabledevelopment/sustainable-development-goals/.
4 Will Peischel, "Chevron Made $4.5 Billion in 2018. So Why Did the IRS Give Them a Refund?," *Mother Jones* (blog), accessed December 31, 2020, https://www.motherjones.com/politics/2020/01/chevron-made-4-5-billion-in-2018-so-why-did-the-irs-give-them-a-refund/.
5 Lauren Bauer O'Donnell Kristen E. Broady, Wendy Edelberg, and Jimmy, "Ten Facts about COVID-19 and the U.S. Economy," *Brookings* (blog), September 17, 2020, https://www.brookings.edu/research/ten-facts-about-Covid-19-and-the-u-s-economy/.
6 "Health and Education @ProjectDrawdown," Project Drawdown, February 5, 2020, https://drawdown.org/sectors/health-and-education.
7 Chevron, "Black Lives Matter. Words from Our Leaders: Https://T.Co/Dl1WEKdCJe Https://T.Co/PjyZEWx498," Tweet, *@Chevron* (blog), June 5, 2020, https://twitter.com/Chevron/status/1268984687927705600.
8 Jane Kay Katz Cheryl, "Pollution, Poverty and People of Color: Living with Industry," Scientific American, accessed December 31, 2020, https://www.scientificamerican.com/article/pollution-poverty-people-color-living-industry/.
9 Ibid.
10 Cagle.
11 "Chevron, Richmond Settle Lawsuit Over 2012 Refinery Fire," KQED, accessed December 31, 2020, https://www.kqed.org/news/11665999/chevron-richmond-move-to-settle-lawsuit-over-2012-refinery-fire-that-sickened-thousands.
12 Will Peischel, "Chevron Made $4.5 Billion in 2018. So Why Did the IRS Give Them a Refund?," *Mother Jones* (blog), accessed December 31, 2020, https://www.motherjones.com/politics/2020/01/chevron-made-4-5-billion-in-2018-so-why-did-the-irs-give-them-a-refund/.
13 Kristina Kohl, *Becoming a Sustainable Organization: A Project and Portfolio Management Approach* (Boca Raton, FL: CRC Press, 2016).
14 "Global ESG-Data Driven Assets Hit $40.5 Trillion," Pensions & Investments, July 2, 2020, https://www.pionline.com/esg/global-esg-data-driven-assets-hit-405-trillion.
15 "Global ESG-Data Driven Assets Hit $40.5 Trillion."

16 Anna Hirtenstein, "Sustainable-Bond Market Boosted by Europe's Top Institutions," *Wall Street Journal*, September 25, 2020, sec. Markets, https://www.wsj.com/articles/sustainable-bond-market-boosted-by-europes-top-institutions-11601048068.

17 "Europe's Moment: Repair and Prepare for the next Generation," Text, European Commission 0150 – European Commission, accessed October 13, 2020, https://ec.europa.eu/commission/presscorner/detail/en/ip_20_940.

18 "Diversity Wins: How Inclusion Matters | McKinsey," accessed September 30, 2020, https://www.mckinsey.com/featured-insights/diversity-and-inclusion/diversity-wins-how-inclusion-matters.

19 "Diversity Wins: How Inclusion Matters | McKinsey."

20 Te-Ping Chen, "Why Are There Still So Few Black CEOs?," *Wall Street Journal*, September 28, 2020, sec. Business, https://www.wsj.com/articles/why-are-there-still-so-few-black-ceos-11601302601.

21 "How Diverse Leadership Teams Boost Innovation," U.S. – EN, July 17, 2020, https://www.bcg.com/en-us/publications/2018/how-diverse-leadership-teams-boost-innovation.

22 "Solutions Manual for Fundamentals of Human Resource Management 8th Edition Noe," *Test Bank Hut* (blog), accessed October 2, 2020, https://testbankhut.com/shop/fundamentals-human-resource-management-8th-noe-solutions-manual/.

23 Anne Steele, "California Rolls Out Diversity Quotas for Corporate Boards," *Wall Street Journal*, October 1, 2020, sec. Business, https://www.wsj.com/articles/california-rolls-out-diversity-quotas-for-corporate-boards-11601507471.

24 Abigail Feldman Globe Correspondent et al., "Boycott Continues against Cambridge Whole Foods That Sent Employees Home for Black Lives Matter Masks - The Boston Globe," BostonGlobe.com, accessed October 5, 2020, https://www.bostonglobe.com/2020/07/05/metro/boycott-continues-against-cambridge-whole-foods-that-sent-employees-home-black-lives-matter-masks/.

25 Jacob Gallagher, Khadeeja Safdar, and Sharon Terlep, "Adidas Tweeted Against Racism. Its Black Workers Say That Isn't Enough.," *Wall Street Journal*, June 9, 2020, sec. Business, https://www.wsj.com/articles/workers-press-adidas-estee-lauder-others-to-act-on-racism-diversity-11591660452.

26 "Global ESG-Data Driven Assets Hit $40.5 Trillion."

27 Davis Polk, "Top 10 Key Trends at 2020 Proxy Mid-Season," n.d., 3.

28 Jennifer Rankin, "EU Revives Plans for Mandatory Quotas of Women on Company Boards," *The Guardian*, March 5, 2020, sec. World news, https://www.theguardian.com/world/2020/mar/05/eu-revives-plans-for-mandatory-quotas-of-women-on-company-boards.

29 "Tesla Is Under Pressure to End Arbitration for Racism Claims - Bloomberg," accessed October 4, 2020, https://www.bloomberg.com/news/articles/2020-09-09/tesla-is-under-pressure-to-end-arbitration-for-racism-claims?srnd=premium&sref=AgsaEEIU.

30 "SEC Wants More Human Capital Disclosures But Won't Say How Much (1)," accessed October 5, 2020, https://news.bloomberglaw.com/securities-law/sec-wants-more-human-capital-disclosures-but-wont-say-how-much.

31 Jeffrey Dastin, "Amazon Scraps Secret AI Recruiting Tool That Showed Bias against Women," *Reuters*, October 10, 2018, https://www.reuters.com/article/us-amazon-com-jobs-automation-insight-idUSKCN1MK08G.

32 "SASB - ESG Reporting - Diversity and Inclusion - SASB Standards," *SASB* (blog), September 28, 2020, https://www.sasb.org/blog/exploring-diversity-inclusion-in-the-sasb-standards/.

33 Its current CSR/ESG ranking, 47% among 18,000 companies. GM is 62%. "Advanced Search." *CSRHub Ratings* https://www.csrhub.com/search/industry/Motor-Vehicle-Manufacturing?page=1

34 "Sources of Greenhouse Gas Emissions." *EPA*, Environmental Protection Agency, April 14, 2021, https://www.epa.gov/ghgemissions/sources-greenhouse-gas-emissions#:~:text=Transportation%20(28.2%20percent%20of%202018,share%20of%20greenhouse%20gas%20emissions.

35 IEA. "Transport – Topics." *IEA*, https://www.iea.org/topics/transport

36 Alonzo, Isaiah. "Tesla Network' to Create Driver Profile for Ride Hailing App and Initiative—Tesla Uber for EVs?" *Tech Times*, February 24, 2021, https://www.tech-times.com/articles/257407/20210224/tesla-network-create-driver-profile-ride-hailing-app-initiative%E2%80%94tesla-uber.htm

37 The term AV is often used interchangeably with Full Self Drive (FSD) or Autopilot though industry experts make distinctions.

38 Keeney, Tasha. "ARK's Price Target for Tesla in 2025." *ARK Invest*, March 19, 2021, https://ark-invest.com/articles/analyst-research/tesla-price-target-2/

39 "Company ESG Risk Ratings." *Sustainalytics*, April 15, 2021, www.sustainalytics.com/esg-rating/tesla-inc/1035322998/.

40 "Who Killed the Electric Car?" *Papercut Films*, 2006, www.whokilledtheelectriccar.com/ and Staley, Oliver. "The General Motors CEO Who Killed the Original Electric Car Is Now in the Electric Car Business." *Quartz*, Quartz, April 7, 2017, https://qz.com/952951/the-general-motors-gm-ceo-who-killed-the-ev1-electric-car-rick-wagoner-is-now-in-the-electric-car-business/

41 Barra speaks with Trump about relaxing CAFÉ standards.

42 "Our Aspiration: Be The Most Inclusive Company In The World." *General Motors*, https://www.gmsustainability.com/highlights-and-features/most-inclusive.html

43 "Mary Barra." *Forbes*, Forbes Magazine, https://www.forbes.com/profile/mary-barra/?sh=332165210ad5

44 MacMahon, Simon. "The Challenge of Rating ESG Performance." *Harvard Business Review*, 2020, https://hbr.org/2020/09/the-challenge-of-rating-esg-performance

45 Staff, Verdict, et al. "Confusing ESG Data Threatens to Hinder Sustainable Investing." *Private Banker International*, January 23, 2020, https://www.privatebankerinterna-tional.com/comments/confusing-esg-data-sustainable-investing/

46 "ESG Ratings Corporate Search Tool." *MSCI*, https://www.msci.com/our-solutions/esg-investing/esg-ratings/esg-ratings-corporate-search-tool/issuer/tesla-inc/IID000000002594878

47 "ESG Ratings Corporate Search Tool." *MSCI*, https://www.msci.com/our-solutions/esg-investing/esg-ratings/esg-ratings-corporate-search-tool/issuer/general-motors-company/IID000000002433496

48 "CSR Information for Tesla Motors, Inc." *CSRHub*, https://www.csrhub.com/CSR_and_sustainability_information/Tesla-Motors-Inc

49 "CSR Information for General Motors Corporation (GM)." *CSRHub*, https://www.csrhub.com/CSR_and_sustainability_information/General-Motors-Corporation-(GM)

50 "Update: Tesla's Standing in the S&P 500 ESG Index." *S&P Global.* May 26, 2021. https://www.spglobal.com/en/research-insights/articles/update-tesla-s-standing-in-the-sp-500-esg-index

51 "Tesla, Incorporated." *S&P Global*, https://www.spglobal.com/esg/scores/results?cid=4574287

52 "General Motors Company." *S&P Global*, https://www.spglobal.com/esg/scores/results?cid=4272273

53 "Update: Tesla's Standing in the S&P 500 ESG Index." *S&P Global*. May 26, 2021. https://www.spglobal.com/en/research-insights/articles/update-tesla-s-standing-in-the-sp-500-esg-index

54 "BNEF EVO Report 2020: BloombergNEF: Bloomberg Finance LP." *BloombergNEF*, https://about.bnef.com/electric-vehicle-outlook/

55 "Big Ideas 2021." *ARK Investment Management LLC*, January 26, 2021, 57, https://research.ark-invest.com/hubfs/1_Download_Files_ARK-Invest/White_Papers/ARK%E2%80%93Invest_BigIdeas_2021.pdf?hsCtaTracking=4e1a031b-7ed7-4fb2-929c-072267eda5fc%7Cee55057a-bc7b-441e-8b96-452ec1efe34c

56 Lambert, Fred. "Tesla Drops a Bunch of New Autopilot Data, 3 Billion Miles and More." *Electrek*, April 22, 2020, https://electrek.co/2020/04/22/tesla-autopilot-data-3-billion-miles/

57 "Big Ideas 2021." *ARK Investment Management LLC*, January 26, 2021, 7, https://research.ark-invest.com/hubfs/1_Download_Files_ARK-Invest/White_Papers/ARK%E2%80%93Invest_BigIdeas_2021.pdf?hsCtaTracking=4e1a031b-7ed7-4fb2-929c-072267eda5fc%7Cee55057a-bc7b-441e-8b96-452ec1efe34c

58 "General Motors' New In-Vehicle Technology Strengthens Connectivity Leadership and Enhances Customer Experience." *Media.gm.com*, September 5, 2019, https://media.gm.com/media/us/en/gm/news.detail.html/content/Pages/news/us/en/2019/sep/0905-epa.html

59 Kulisch, Eric. "Barra: GM Supports Modernizing CAFE Standards." *Automotive News*, May 8, 2018, https://www.autonews.com/article/20180508/RETAIL01/180509816/barra-gm-supports-modernizing-cafe-standards

60 Szymkowski, Sean. "Cruise Automation's Self-Driving Cars Can Now Carry Passengers." *Roadshow*, CNET, February 27, 2020, https://www.cnet.com/roadshow/news/cruise-automation-self-driving-cars-california/

61 "Tesla." *Global Green*, October 12, 2020, https://www.globalgreen.org/directory/listing/tesla/

62 "General Motors, University of Michigan Show Automated Safety Features Preventing Crashes." *Safety Study|General Motors*, https://www.gm.com/safetystudy.html

63 Tesla. *"Impact Report."* 2019. https://www.tesla.com/ns_videos/2019-tesla-impact-report.pdf

64 Staff, Reuters. "Tesla Announces $1.5 Billion Bitcoin Bet, Makes Payments Pledge." *Reuters*, Thomson Reuters, February 8, 2021, https://www.reuters.com/article/us-crypto-currency-tesla-quotes/tesla-announces-1-5-billion-bitcoin-bet-makes-payments-pledge-idUSKBN2A81PD

65 Chapa, Sergio. "Musk's Warming Up to Gas Evident Once More at Texas Gigafactory." *Bloomberg.com*, Bloomberg, March 30, 2021, https://www.bloomberg.com/news/articles/2021-03-30/musk-s-warming-up-to-gas-evident-once-more-at-texas-gigafactory?sref=BY1LwCui

66 "Adding EV Charging Stations on Our Journey Toward an All-Electric Future." *Gm*, https://www.gm.com/masthead-story/electric-charging-stations-infrastructure.html

67 O'Kane, Sean. "Tesla Model 3 Awarded Five-Star Safety Rating." *The Verge*, The Verge, September 20, 2018, https://www.theverge.com/2018/9/20/17882634/tesla-model-3-nhtsa-five-star-safety-rating

68 Calma, Justine. "Tesla to Make EV Battery Cathodes without Cobalt." *The Verge*, The Verge, September 22, 2020, https://www.theverge.com/2020/9/22/21451670/tesla-cobalt-free-cathodes-mining-battery-nickel-ev-cost

69 Impact Report 2020 (U.S.). "Diversity, Equity and Inclusion." *Tesla*, 8, https://www.tesla.com/sites/default/files/downloads/2020-DEI-impact-report.pdf,

70 "Diversity, Equity and Inclusion." *Impact Report 2020*.

71 "An Activist Investor Crusades against Forced Arbitration at Tesla." *Bloomberg*. September 9, 2020, https://www.bloomberg.com/news/articles/2020-09-09/tesla-is-under-pressure-to-end-arbitration-for-racism-claims?sref=BY1LwCui

72 "2020 Annual Meeting of Stockholders and Battery Day." *Tesla*, September 22, 2020, https://www.tesla.com/2020shareholdermeeting

73 Collingsworth, Terrence. "Case 1:19-cv-03737." *United States District Court For The District Of Columbia*, December 15, 2019, http://iradvocates.org/sites/iradvocates.org/files/stamped%20-Complaint.pdf

74 "Global Status Report on Road Safety 2018." *World Health Organization*, World Health Organization, June 17, 2018, https://www.who.int/violence_injury_prevention/road_safety_status/2018/en/

75 Former presidential candidate Andrew Yang and advocate for a Universal Basic Income (UBI), described the devastating impact of truck drivers who will similarly be displaced as AVs become the norm.

76 Ethisphere.com. The 2021 World's Most Ethical Companies Honoree List.

77 Detroit News. PAC Targets GM for Giving to Republicans Who Voted to Overturn the 2020 Election. 17 September, 2021.

78 LaReau, Jamie L. "GM Just Became Only Automaker with Board of Directors That's Majority Women." *Detroit Free Press*, Detroit Free Press, 25 March 2021, https://www.freep.com/story/money/cars/general-motors/2021/03/25/gm-board-women-diversity-meg-whitman-mark-tatum/6969922002/

79 Impact Report 2020 (U.S.). "Diversity, Equity and Inclusion." https://www.tesla.com/sites/default/files/downloads/2020-DEI-impact-report.pdf

80 "Diversity & Inclusion Report." *General Motors*. https://www.gm.com/content/dam/company/us/docs/GM_Diversity_Inclusion_Report.pdf

81 "Building the Female Leaders of Tomorrow at General Motors." *General Motors*. https://www.gm.com/masthead-story/building-female-leaders-of-tomorrow-at-general-motors.html

82 "Average Salary for Tesla Motors Employees." *PayScale*, March 31, 2021, https://www.payscale.com/research/US/Employer=Tesla_Motors/Salary

83 Melin, Anders. "Warren, Sanders Target Firms That Pay CEOs Way More Than Workers." *Bloomberg*, April 28, 2021, https://www.bloomberg.com/graphics/ceo-pay-ratio/?sref=BY1LwCui

84 Tully, Shawn. "The Daring Architecture of Elon Musk's Compensation Plan Has the Tesla CEO on Track to Make History." *Fortune*, March 17, 2021, https://fortune.com/2021/03/16/elon-musk-net-worth-tesla-stock-tsla-options-compensation-plan/

85 26th Annual Report. "Executive Excess 2019: Making Corporations Pay for Big Gaps." *Institute for Policy Studies*, September 2019, 20, https://ips-dc.org/wp-content/uploads/2019/09/EE19-Sept-2019.pdf

86 "Average Salary for General Motors Corporation Employees." *PayScale*, April 22, 2021, https://www.payscale.com/research/US/Employer=General_Motors_Corporation/Salary

87 Melin, Anders. "Warren, Sanders Target Firms That Pay CEOs Way More Than Workers." *Bloomberg*, April 28, 2021, https://www.bloomberg.com/graphics/ceo-pay-ratio/?sref=BY1LwCui

88 LaReau, Jamie L. "GM CEO Mary Barra's Compensation Was $21.87 Million in 2018, 281 Times Median GM Worker." *Detroit Free Press*, April 18, 2019, https://www.freep.com/story/money/cars/general-motors/2019/04/18/gm-ceo-barra-compensation-22-million/3415415002/

89 Dormaar, Julia. "UK Gender Pay Report Summary 2017/18." *Tesla*, March 22, 2019. https://www.tesla.com/sites/default/files/pdfs/UK%20Gender%20Pay%20Report%20Summary%20April%202019.pdf?2017071020170710

90 "Mary Barra." *Forbes*, Forbes Magazine, https://www.forbes.com/profile/mary-barra/?sh=332165210ad5

91 "Diversity & Inclusion Report." *General Motors*. https://www.gm.com/content/dam/company/us/docs/GM_Diversity_Inclusion_Report.pdf

92 Impact Report 2020 (U.S.). "Diversity, Equity and Inclusion." https://www.tesla.com/sites/default/files/downloads/2020-DEI-impact-report.pdf

93 "Diversity & Inclusion Report." *General Motors*. https://www.gm.com/content/dam/company/us/docs/GM_Diversity_Inclusion_Report.pdf

94 "Diversity & Inclusion Report." *General Motors*. https://www.gm.com/content/dam/company/us/docs/GM_Diversity_Inclusion_Report.pdf

95 "Consumer Reports Yanks Safety Ratings from Some Tesla Models." *Fortune*, May 27, 2021, https://fortune.com/2021/05/27/consumer-reports-safety-ratings-tesla-models/

96 Schmitt, Angie. "What Happened to Pickup Trucks?" *Bloomberg CityLab*, March 11, 2021, https://www.bloomberg.com/news/articles/2021-03-11/the-dangerous-rise-of-the-supersized-pickup-truck?sref=BY1LwCui

97 "Keeping People Safe." *General Motors Sustainability Report*, 2019, https://www.gmsustainability.com/material-topics/keeping-people-safe.html

98 "2021 IIHS Top Safety Picks." *IIHS*, https://www.iihs.org/ratings/top-safety-picks

99 "Ratings: Vehicle Safety, Car Seat, Tire." *NHTSA*, October 14, 2020, https://www.nhtsa.gov/ratings

100 "Impact Report 2019." *Tesla*, 41, https://www.tesla.com/ns_videos/2019-tesla-impact-report.pdf

101 Belauste, Alex. "Tesla: The World's Safest Company." *Torque News*. February 10, 2020, https://www.torquenews.com/9895/tesla-worlds-safest-company

102 "Keeping People Safe." *General Motors Sustainability Report*, 2019, https://www.gmsustainability.com/material-topics/keeping-people-safe.html

103 Gorzelany, Jim. "How Much Does A Tesla Cost?" *Motor1.Com*, Motor1.Com, February 27, 2021, https://www.motor1.com/features/313677/how-much-is-a-tesla/

104 "Tesla Model 3 Demographics: Income, Age, Gender And More." *Hedges & Company*, January28, 2021, https://hedgescompany.com/blog/2019/03/tesla-model-3-demographics-income/

105 Calma, Justine. "Tesla to Make EV Battery Cathodes without Cobalt." *The Verge*, September 22, 2020, https://www.theverge.com/2020/9/22/21451670/tesla-cobalt-free-cathodes-mining-battery-nickel-ev-cost

106 "Designing for The Environment." *Designing for The Environment | General Motors 2020 Sustainability Report*, General Motors, https://www.gmsustainability.com/material-topics/designing-for-the-environment/

107 Calma, Justine. "Tesla to Make EV Battery Cathodes without Cobalt." 43.

108 "Tesla Inc." *HRC*, https://www.hrc.org/resources/buyers-guide/tesla-inc.
109 "Our Aspiration: Be The Most Inclusive Company In The World." *General Motors 2019 Sustainability Report*, https://www.gmsustainability.com/highlights-and-features/most-inclusive.html
110 "Gender Equality Global Report & Ranking." *EQUILEAP*, 2021. https://equileap.com/wp-content/uploads/2021/03/Global-Report-2021.pdf
111 Johnston, Andrew. "Corporate Governance for Sustainability Statement." *The Harvard Law School Forum on Corporate Governance*, January 7, 2020, https://corpgov.law.harvard.edu/2020/01/07/corporate-governance-for-sustainability-statement/
112 Caroom, Eliot. "Tesla's Governance Record and ESG Monitoring." *The Harvard Law School Forum on Corporate Governance*, August 4, 2019, https://corpgov.law.harvard.edu/2019/08/04/teslas-governance-record-and-esg-monitoring/
113 "Board of Directors." *Tesla, Inc.*, https://ir.teslamotors.com/corporate-governance/board-of-directors
114 Schnell, Mychael. "General Motors Adds Meg Whitman, NBA COO to Board of Directors." *TheHill*, The Hill, March 25, 2021, https://thehill.com/homenews/news/544892-general-motors-adds-meg-whitman-nbc-coo-to-board-of-directors
115 Lambert, Fred. "Tesla Shareholders Will Vote on Using Paid Advertising, Board Fights to Kill Proposal." *Electrek*, May 28, 2020, https://electrek.co/2020/05/28/tesla-shareholders-vote-paid-advertising/ and also Obtained from ICCR, As You Sow, and BlackRock).
116 "Impact Report 2019." *Tesla*, https://www.tesla.com/ns_videos/2019-tesla-impact-report.pdf

Bibliography

"Activate Agility: The Five Avenues to Success | McKinsey & Company." Accessed September 28, 2020. https://www.mckinsey.com/business-functions/organization/our-insights/the-organization-blog/activate-agility-get-these-five-things-right.

Bauer, Lauren, Kristen E. Broady, Wendy Edelberg, and Jimmy O'Donnell. "Ten Facts about COVID-19 and the U.S. Economy." *Brookings* (blog), September 17, 2020. https://www.brookings.edu/research/ten-facts-about-Covid-19-and-the-u-s-economy/.

Cagle, Susie. "Richmond v Chevron: The California City Taking on Its Most Powerful Polluter." *The Guardian*, October 9, 2019, sec. Environment. https://www.theguardian.com/environment/2019/oct/09/richmond-chevron-california-city-polluter-fossil-fuel.

Chen, Te-Ping. "Why Are There Still So Few Black CEOs?" *Wall Street Journal*, September 28, 2020, sec. Business. https://www.wsj.com/articles/why-are-there-still-so-few-black-ceos-11601302601.

Chevron. "Black Lives Matter. Words from Our Leaders: Https://T.Co/Dl1WEKdCJe Https://T.Co/PjyZEWx498." Tweet. *@Chevron* (blog), June 5, 2020. https://twitter.com/Chevron/status/1268984687927705600.

Correspondent, Abigail Feldman Globe, Updated July 5, 2020, and 8:05 p m Email to a Friend Share on Facebook Share on TwitterPrint this Article View Comments70. "Boycott Continues against Cambridge Whole Foods That Sent Employees Home for Black Lives Matter Masks - The Boston Globe." BostonGlobe.com. Accessed October 5, 2020. https://www.bostonglobe.com/2020/07/05/metro/

boycott-continues-against-cambridge-whole-foods-that-sent-employees-home-black-lives-matter-masks/.

Dastin, Jeffrey. "Amazon Scraps Secret AI Recruiting Tool That Showed Bias against Women." *Reuters*, October 10, 2018. https://www.reuters.com/article/us-amazon-com-jobs-automation-insight-idUSKCN1MK08G.

"Diversity Wins: How Inclusion Matters | McKinsey." Accessed September 30, 2020. https://www.mckinsey.com/featured-insights/diversity-and-inclusion/diversity-wins-how-inclusion-matters.

dpicampaigns. "Take Action for the Sustainable Development Goals." *United Nations Sustainable Development* (blog). Accessed January 2, 2021. https://www.un.org/sustainabledevelopment/sustainable-development-goals/.

European Commission - European Commission. "Europe's Moment: Repair and Prepare for the next Generation." Text. Accessed October 13, 2020. https://ec.europa.eu/commission/presscorner/detail/en/ip_20_940.

Gallagher, Jacob, Khadeeja Safdar and Sharon Terlep. "Adidas Tweeted Against Racism. Its Black Workers Say That Isn't Enough." *Wall Street Journal*, June 9, 2020, sec. Business. https://www.wsj.com/articles/workers-press-adidas-estee-lauder-others-to-act-on-racism-diversity-11591660452.

Hirtenstein, Anna. "Sustainable-Bond Market Boosted by Europe's Top Institutions." *Wall Street Journal*, September 25, 2020, sec. Markets. https://www.wsj.com/articlcs/sustainable-bond-market-boosted-by-europes-top-institutions-11601048068.

Jane Kay, Cheryl Katz. "Pollution, Poverty and People of Color: Living with Industry." *Scientific American*. Accessed December 31, 2020. https://www.scientificamerican.com/article/pollution-poverty-people-color-living-industry/.

Kohl, Kristina. *Becoming a Sustainable Organization: A Project and Portfolio Management Approach*. Boca Raton, FL: CRC Press, 2016.

KQED. "Chevron, Richmond Settle Lawsuit Over 2012 Refinery Fire." Accessed December 31, 2020. https://www.kqed.org/news/11665999/chevron-richmond-move-to-settle-lawsuit-over-2012-refinery-fire-that-sickened-thousands.

Martin. "Communications Materials." *United Nations Sustainable Development* (blog). Accessed October 21, 2020. https://www.un.org/sustainabledevelopment/news/communications-material/.

"Opinion | We Made the Coronavirus Epidemic - The New York Times." Accessed September 28, 2020. https://www.nytimes.com/2020/01/28/opinion/coronavirus-china.html.

Peischel, Will. "Chevron Made $4.5 Billion in 2018. So Why Did the IRS Give Them a Refund?" *Mother Jones* (blog). Accessed December 31, 2020. https://www.mother-jones.com/politics/2020/01/chevron-made-4-5-billion-in-2018-so-why-did-the-irs-give-them-a-refund/.

Pensions & Investments. "Global ESG-Data Driven Assets Hit $40.5 Trillion," July 2, 2020. https://www.pionline.com/esg/global-esg-data-driven-assets-hit-405-trillion.

Polk, Davis. "Top 10 Key Trends at 2020 Proxy Mid-Season," n.d., 3.

Project Drawdown. "Health and Education @ProjectDrawdown," February 5, 2020. https://drawdown.org/sectors/health-and-education.

Rankin, Jennifer. "EU Revives Plans for Mandatory Quotas of Women on Company Boards." *The Guardian*, March 5, 2020, sec. World news. https://www.theguardian.com/world/2020/mar/05/eu-revives-plans-for-mandatory-quotas-of-women-on-company-boards.

SASB. "SASB - ESG Reporting - Diversity and Inclusion - SASB Standards," September 28, 2020. https://www.sasb.org/blog/exploring-diversity-inclusion-in-the-sasb-standards/.

"SEC Wants More Human Capital Disclosures But Won't Say How Much (1)." Accessed October 5, 2020. https://news.bloomberglaw.com/securities-law/sec-wants-more-human-capital-disclosures-but-wont-say-how-much.

Steele, Anne. "California Rolls Out Diversity Quotas for Corporate Boards." *Wall Street Journal*, October 1, 2020, sec. Business. https://www.wsj.com/articles/california-rolls-out-diversity-quotas-for-corporate-boards-11601507471.

"Tesla Is Under Pressure to End Arbitration for Racism Claims - Bloomberg." Accessed October 4, 2020. https://www.bloomberg.com/news/articles/2020-09-09/tesla-is-under-pressure-to-end-arbitration-for-racism-claims?srnd=premium&sref=AgsaE EIU.

Test Bank Hut. "Solutions Manual for Fundamentals of Human Resource Management 8th Edition Noe." Accessed October 2, 2020. https://testbankhut.com/shop/fundamentals-human-resource-management-8th-noe-solutions-manual/.

United States - EN. "How Diverse Leadership Teams Boost Innovation," July 17, 2020. https://www.bcg.com/en-us/publications/2018/how-diverse-leadership-teams-boost-innovation.

Chapter 2

Global Impact

While organizations operate globally, countries have very different perspectives about equity and inclusion. National views on justice, equity, diversity, and inclusion (J.E.D.I.) significantly impact an organization's ability to operate in those countries. It impacts employee safety, wellness, well-being, and their ability to contribute fully. Some of the countries with the fastest growing populations have the least inclusive cultures. As a result, this trend impacts an organization's own ability to create a J.E.D.I. culture.

Gender equity is a U.N. priority and a sustainable development goal. While progress has been made, we see that much work remains in both developed and developing countries to promote gender equity. The trend lines are not really improving with income and wealth inequality growing in our societies. Compounding the challenges are the significant number of global refugees fleeing war, violence, environmental disasters, and genocides. A discussion of global inequities would be incomplete without addressing the rights of Indigenous peoples and the need for these to be honored and upheld. In order to create just and equitable organizations, we must consider our roles in the broader global ecosystem to address these injustices to create social and workplace environments that support equity and inclusion.

2.1 Global Perspective on Equity and Inclusion

Globally, views on equity and inclusion vary greatly and are impacted by governance and legal structures, national population diversity, societal inclusion, workplace inclusion, and governmental inclusion. In a recent Society for Human Resource Management (SHRM) survey of global organizations on diversity and inclusion (D&I), over half of respondents from North America (59%), Asia-Pacific (55%), and Western Europe (55%) promote D&I "strongly" or "very strongly" in their

DOI: 10.1201/9781003168072-3

organizations. Those respondents promoting D&I "moderately" were somewhat lower but still significant Asia-Pacific (31%), North America (31%), and Western Europe (28%).[1] These global firms' DEI initiatives are led by the board of directors, CEO, and top management making them a top strategic priority. While legal compliance remains the most cited reason for DEI initiatives, 58% of respondents say that Corporate Social Responsibility (CSR) considerations drive D&I efforts.[2]

In order to better understand a country's J.E.D.I. maturity, SHRM commissioned the Economist Intelligence Unit to create the Global Diversity Readiness Index. This benchmarking model assesses five areas of Diversity, Equity, and Inclusion using multiple indicators outlined in Table 2.1. The data pointing to both quantitative and qualitative indicators are included in the table to provide a perspective on the scope of the project. These indicators such as workplace inclusion, national diversity representation, social inclusion, government inclusion, and legal structures specifically address systemic facilitators and barriers that both promote and inhibit creating equitable and just organizations. The issues are both societal and organizational and in order to address them we need to understand the governmental, social, legal, and workplace constructs.

The national diversity component is looking at the heterogeneity of a country's population primarily based on identity and cultural factors. The workplace identity component focuses on inclusion metrics especially minority representation in managerial positions and the presence of systemic barriers faced in achieving these positions. (This definition of minority encompasses ethnicity, race, religion, age, disability, and sexual orientation.) The analysis is heavily focused on women's representation in the workplace as data for women in the workplace was available in the 47 countries evaluated. (Data for other underrepresented groups was not so consistently tracked and therefore not available.) Social inclusion dives more deeply into the attitudes exhibited toward minorities in their everyday life. It also considers issues such as the wealth gap and relations between wealthy and poor citizens. Access to and funding of education is also considered as education plays a major role in changing the trajectory of someone's life in terms of opportunities for advancement and living standards. Governmental inclusion considers overall respect of human rights and the recognition that all people have the right to basic human necessities and equality of access and opportunity. It also looks at the representation of minorities in governmental positions of leadership in order to assess the level of power and authority that minority groups have achieved within a country. The attitude toward foreign ownership rights reflects a society's attitude toward wealth and or foreign investment. The following case highlights how these views on foreign ownership impact capital investment and foreigners' rights within a country. Legal structures really speak to a country's governance approach to empowering minorities through laws and regulations and then the enforcement of them through a qualified court system. While there are other metrics that may be considered in evaluating a country's J.E.D.I. contructs, this research provides an excellent framework for the justice, equity, and inclusion conversation on a global level.

Table 2.1 Global Diversity Readiness Index Indicators

Diversity, Equity, and Inclusion Components	Diversity, Equity, and Inclusion Indicators
National Diversity	Male/female population ratio Immigrants as a percentage of population Ethnic and racial diversity Religious diversity Percentage of the population over 65 Income inequality Number of official or major languages
Workplace inclusion	Corporate ethics Female workforce participation Prevalence of glass ceilings Social elitism Ease of hiring foreign national Female access to leadership Female wage equality Meritocracy
Social Inclusion	Cultural openness toward immigrants Tension between religious groups Impact of religion in country politics Tensions toward ethnic or racial diversity Openness to LGBTQ+ communities Social ills, kidnapping, and extortion Female/male ratio in university enrollment Educational attainment of minorities Public education funding relative to GDP
Government Inclusion	Respect for human rights Minorities participation in politics Hostility toward foreigners' or their private property Female head of state Female representation in legislature Minority president or prime minister Government corruption
Legal Structures	Protection of civil liberties. Presence of anti-discrimination laws Laws ensuring paid maternity leave Laws protecting immigrants Immigration policies Independence and quality of judiciary Enforceability of contracts

Source: "Global Diversity and Inclusion; Perceptions, Practices and Attitudes." https://www.shrm.org/hr-today/trends-and-forecasting/research-and-surveys/Documents/09-Diversity_and_Inclusion_Report.pdf, Accessed 1/12/2021

CHINA'S EXPANSION IN THE SOUTH CHINA SEA IMPACTS ACCEPTANCE OF ITS FOREIGN INVESTMENT

Over the last decade, China has expanded its presence and control of the South China Seas. China's motives are partially driven by the abundance of natural resources in the sea estimated at 11 billion barrels of untapped oil and 190 trillion cubic feet of natural gas. Their aggression in the region has antagonized other countries including Brunei, Indonesia, Malaysia, the Philippines, Taiwan, and Vietnam.[3]

This strategy of aggression in the South China Seas backfired when Vietnamese citizens attacked Chinese controlled businesses in Vietnam in retaliation for an oil rig being placed in disputed waters off the coast of Vietnam. The oil rig platform was protected by Chinese military presence. The Vietnamese accused China of attacking its ships in the area by ramming them and firing water cannons at them. In an effort to proactively address these issues, the 10-member Association of Southeast Asian Nations, or ASEAN, had been requesting a code of conduct agreement.[4] While China's approach did not reach the level of full military aggression, both Vietnam and the Philippines were angered by China's moves to claim natural resource rights and fishing rights.

In response, the Philippines launched an international challenge to China's rights at a U.N. tribunal. In Vietnam, the actions were much more aggressive with rioting by citizens in Ho Chi Minh city against Chinese owned businesses. While the initial riots were in response to the Chinese oil rig, rioters expanded their destruction to include other foreign owned facilities. Yen Chen-shen, a research fellow at Taiwan's National Chengchi University's Institute of International Relations, described China's oil rig as a catalyst for the Vietnamese to express their deep-seated anger at foreign investors.

> The influx of foreign companies in Vietnam in recent years has widened the wealth gap there, Mr. Yen said. For the locals, prices have gone up, but wages haven't caught up. Although the protest is about China's oil rig, the core anger and fear is against foreign exploitation of their country.[5]

These riots and property destruction were a clear reflection of anger by locals at foreign investors especially the Chinese and their perceived exploitation of the local labor markets, the widening wealth gap, and their geopolitical influence. Beijing paid the price for their assertiveness in this region both in terms of local investments and in the broader global geopolitical arena. This is an example of the Government Inclusion component of the Global Diversity Readiness Index as it relates to acceptance of foreign investment. It is also reminder that openness of foreign investment is not a static factor and that both governments and investors need to work proactively to ensure equity and inclusion for workers.

Table 2.2 Global Diversity Readiness Index Country Rankings

Top 10		Bottom 10	
Country	**Rank**	**Country**	**Rank**
Sweden	1	Saudi Arabia	47
Norway	2	Indonesia	46
New Zealand	3	Nigeria	45
Canada	4	China	44
Finland	5	Russia	43
Denmark	6	The Philippines	42
The United Kingdom	7	India	41
Australia	7	Thailand	40
Switzerland	9	Turkey	39
Ireland	10	Malaysia	38

Source: "Global Diversity and Inclusion; Perceptions, Practices and Attitudes."

The data analysis and ranking were done for 47 countries with the top and bottom 10 countries listed in Table 2.2.

The top ranking 10 countries, primarily from Scandinavia and Western Europe, reflect their open and developed economies, more inclusive workplaces, and governments and laws that respect and empower minorities. The bottom ranking 10 countries are from Asia, the Middle East, Africa, and Eastern Europe with economies that are restricted and less developed, less inclusive work environments, and governments and laws which lack support for human rights and minorities.

As might be expected, Scandinavia, North America, and Western Europe recorded the higher scores on the Global Diversity Readiness Index. While their scores outrank the world average, they still leave room for improvement with the highest score achieving around 70%. The survey results suggest that governmental inclusion and national inclusion are areas for improvement across the board reinforcing that societal systemic barriers exist to achieving equity and inclusion in countries around the globe.

From a demographic trend perspective, it is important to note that countries in Asia and Africa are growing in population and economic power. China is the second largest economy and it has the largest world's population. India has the second largest population and a rapidly growing economy. Together, these countries represent almost one third of the world's population. In order to drive global equity and inclusion, it is imperative to address J.E.D.I. constructs in these countries as well as in other emerging regions and countries. From an organizational leadership perspective, it is crucial for leaders to understand the risks that they may be taking in setting up operations and relocating employees to locations that are less mature in their national J.E.D.I. journey.

As global business evolves, understanding regional and country perspectives on human rights, racial equity, ethnic and religious freedoms, gender equality, LGBTQ rights, etc. provides guidance for organizational leaders in choosing areas for operation and expansion that reflect their organizational values and protect the rights of their employees, customers, and other stakeholders. Often it is a best practice to engage with a partner organization to better evaluate the global landscape and to develop best practices to promote J.E.D.I.. Out & Equal (https:// outandequal.org) is an organization working for LGBTQ+ workplace equality on a global scale. They partner with Fortune 1000 companies, government agencies, and organizations globally to provide LGBTQ+ executive leadership development, D&I training and consultation, and networking opportunities in order to build inclusive and welcoming work environments where all belong. They have hosted symposiums in China and India to help organizations in these regions share stories, experiences, and best practices to address issues of equity and inclusion for the LGBTQ+ community.

A recent report cosponsored by Out & Equal reporting on the intersectionality of mental health and the LGBTQ+ community in India found that 75% of people identifying as LGBTQ+ felt that they needed to keep their true identities hidden.[6] While India decriminalized homosexuality in 2018, identifying as LGBTQ+ in India is still stigmatized by society. As indicated in the Global Diversity Readiness Index, India is ranked number 44 suggesting that they still have much work to do to realign their social, workplace, and governmental systems to promote equity and inclusion. There have been calls for better protections including anti-discriminatory laws, gender neutral legislation, and extending the right to marriage to same sex couples.

Another resource is Human Dignity Trust (https://www.humandignitytrust. org/), an organization working globally to support strategic litigation to challenge laws that persecute people on the basis of their sexual orientation and/or gender identity. They provide legal, communications, and security assistance to lawyers and activists who are defending human rights in countries where private, same-sex, consensual sexual activity is criminalized. Globally, 72 jurisdictions still criminalize private, consensual same-sex sexual activity. Equality and inclusion remain challenges around the globe but organizations like Out & Equal and Human Dignity Trust offer platforms, research, and resources for those seeking to drive change. Collaborating with partners like these will help protect your organization's global employees while transforming your operations to be a J.E.D.I. focused culture with a workplace where everyone is safe and is able to bring their full selves to work.

2.2 Global Gender Equity

Globally gender equity remains a challenge. While progress has been made, the COVID-19 pandemic has highlighted and exacerbated gender inequities. Women and girls carry a disproportionate amount of unpaid work especially caregiving. During the global pandemic, women and girls have been burdened with much of the caregiving impacting their ability to hold jobs and attend school. Globally, women experience violence at a high rate and the stresses of the pandemic have increased the frequency of violence. Despite gender equity progress, work remains to protect the fragility of those gains and to continue the journey forward toward parity.

While women have greater representation in the labor market, globally gender equity remains a significant issue. In fact, there is not a single country in the world where gender equity has been achieved. Around the world, 750 million women and girls were married before their 18th birthdays. Almost one in three women experience some kind of physical or sexual violence. In Africa and the Middle East, one in three girls (aged 15–19) have experienced some form of female genital mutilation/cutting which exposes them to a risk of prolonged bleeding, infection, childbirth complications, infertility, and even death. Despite the environmental and social benefits of women as agricultural landowners, they represent only 13% of agricultural landholdings. In developing countries, two thirds of women have achieved gender parity in primary education.[7]

Although women are better educated than they have ever been, they still face discrimination in the workplace. Women continue to earn less for the same work earning 77 cents for every $1 a man earns.[8] Worldwide, men own 50% more wealth than women and continue to make up 66% of all managerial positions.[9] These figures compare to women's representation in the global population which is 49.6%.[10] Clearly, representational parity in the workplace has not been reached. A recent Oxfam study found that the value of unpaid work performed by women and girls over 15 was $10.8 trillion, which is three times the value of the world's tech industry.[11] Without this work, which is unpaid, our societies would break down. Women and girls bear this cost of contributing these benefits rather than society. As a result, the bottom tier of an economy is often represented by women and girls. These women and girls, especially those living in poverty and from marginalized groups, are working 12.5 billion hours every day without pay.[12] If we include the numbers of hours worked earning only poverty wages, the number of daily hours is even larger. This work is essential to the health and well-being of families and communities, and society and organizations benefit from this unpaid work. Globally, women remain economically vulnerable and at greater risk of economic and social inequality despite providing great benefit to society.

Even though women vote at the same rates as men, their representation in government remains lower than their percentage of the population. There are only 10 female heads of government out of 193 countries. The representation of female elected parliamentarians as of 2018 was 24%, which reflects an increase from 11%

in 1995.[13] Societal norms and bias run deep making global equality for women an ongoing challenge. Research suggests that both men and women hold these views with 91% of men and 86% of women holding at least one gender bias.[14] Countries with the highest levels of gender bias are Pakistan, Jordan, Nigeria, Qatar, and Zimbabwe. Bias and lack of value attributed to "women's work," the unpaid work done by women and girls remains high in both developed and developing countries requiring work from both the public and private sectors. As we saw with the pandemic, caregiving remains a significant issue for women and resulted in a significant loss of women from the workforce as well as the need for both governments and organizations to reevaluate their policies and support systems.

GLOBAL GENDER GAP PROGRESS IN RWANDA

The World Economic Forum Global Gender Gap Report for 2020 ranks Rwanda as ninth out of 153 countries based on the Global Gender Ranking Index 2020.[15] They are in the top 10 and in the company of consistently high-performing Scandinavian countries such as Iceland, Norway, and Sweden. One might wonder how Rwanda achieved this status. In celebration of International Women's Day in 2021, Katherine Klein, Vice Dean, the Wharton School, University of Pennsylvania, Wharton Social Impact Initiative, Edward H. Bowman Professor of Management hosted a Wharton Webinar Series event, The Transformative Power of Women Leadership: Lessons from Rwanda. The panelist included Agnes Binagwaho, Vice Chancellor, University of Global Health Equity; Diane Karusisi, CEO, Bank of Kigali; and Kampeta Sayinzoga, CEO, Development Bank of Rwanda Plc. Each of these women have incredible stories and achievements.

Agnes Binagwaho, MD, M(Ped), and PhD is a Rwandan pediatrician specializing in emergency pediatrics, neonatology, and the treatment of HIV/AIDS. Her work with the University of Global Health Equity focuses on changing healthcare delivery globally through training health professionals in support of providing more equitable, quality health services for all global citizens. Dr. Diana Karusisi, PhD, has been steering the Bank of Kigali since 2016 through a digital transformation journey in order to improve customer satisfaction, profitability, and drive acquisitions. Kampeta Sayinzoga has over 16 years of experience in international development within Rwanda and the East African Region. In addition to her current role as CEO of the Development Bank of Rwanda Plc., she served as the Director of General of the National Industrial Research and Development Agency under the Ministry of Trade and Industry. In addition, she has served on the Board of Directors for a variety of organizations.

This very impressive group of women gathered on International Women's Day to discuss the transformative change that has occurred in Rwanda for women since the genocide that occurred in 1994. During the genocide, members of the Hutu ethnic majority killed as many as 800,000 people, mostly of the Tutsi minority.[16] From this dark period in their history, they have taken the painful lessons learned and forged them into a new agenda emerging a more diverse and equitable country. Agnes Binagwaho reflected that foundational to the transformation is a culture that emerged from the healing process that prioritizes community above self. Key to the change in status for women has been establishing an agenda focused on equity and providing financial resources to support this agenda. Crucial to the transformation has been developing both laws and an action plan to support female empowerment. Her advice to drive systemic change is to create this same agenda and support for all vulnerable and underserved people.[17]

The success of creating political empowerment and gender equity for women in Rwanda is significant. Prior to 1994, around 18% members of parliament were women.[18] Today, the parliament is predominately female with the representation of females exceeding 60%. Significant progress has been made in other political arenas such as within the Cabinet, where there is an equal gender representation, and the Judiciary where female representation has risen to approximately 40%. A significant part of the progress can be attributed to the 2003 Constitution that mandated 30% of elected posts be held by women. To support more women running in the parliamentary elections, Rwanda holds capacity building training to empower women leaders seeking higher positions in the political arena.

Trainings have been offered under a joint program by the U.N. Women, the U.N. Development Program (UNDP), and the U.N. Population Fund (UNFPA) and funded by the Swedish International Development Agency.[19] One of the impacts of this increased representation of women in parliament is the passing of changes to the Civil Code allowing for equal inheritance and succession rights between men and women. The female dominated Parliament has passed laws promoting equal pay and ending gender-based violence, harassment, and discrimination at work, equal rights to access and own land, and preventing and punishing gender-based violence and violence against children.[20]

To further promote gender equity in Rwanda, Dr. Karusisi highlighted the need to transfer the success in political empowerment into economic empowerment. Her recommendations include supporting greater access to higher education for women. While primary education access is fairly equal between the genders, girls are more likely to be pulled from school to do household chores and to fetch water. While Africa leads the world in women owned businesses, these businesses are less likely to receive financing from a financial institution. As a result, these women owned businesses are often less profitable than male owned businesses. As fewer women (34%) than men (40%) have bank accounts, they don't have access to financial tools and resources.

According to Dr. Karusisi, CEO positions continue to be male dominated (80%).[21] Her advice for women in leadership is to trust your instincts, don't try to fit a stereotype, and be yourself.

Kampeta Sayinzoga reminded us that as Rwanda emerged to heal itself after the genocide, many of the freedom fighters were women. As the government reformed, they focused on the triple threat faced by women during the genocide. Rape was used as a weapon against women, many women found themselves left as the head of the household after the loss of their husbands, and women were facing a greater burden of disease. All of these issues became priorities for the new government with gender being a cross-cutting issue. The programs initiated and laws passed focused on these issues including steps against gender-based violence (2011), and change to codes allowing for women to inherit and own land (2013), and female health, mortality, and reproductive health (2015).

Women carry a disproportional burden in society and the steps that Rwanda has taken to empower women giving them a voice in politics and the judiciary has had a profound impact on gender equity in their country. While Rwanda still has areas for improvement, its progress reminds countries such as the U.S. that we have many equity issues that we need to address including gender equity issues.

2.3 Global Income Inequality

Global inequality is on the rise. The world's richest citizens comprising 1% of the global population have more than twice as much wealth as 6.9 billion people. The authors from the Oxfam report give us a visual perspective. If each person in the world was to sit on their wealth piled up in $100 bills, most of the population would remain sitting on the floor. A middle-class person from a developed country would be sitting at chair height. The world's two richest men, Elon Musk and Jeff Bezos, would be sitting in outer space with their estimated net worth of over $100 billion, each, depending on market fluctuations.[22] Income inequality has grown as real wages have barely moved while shareholder returns have skyrocketed. As a result, laborers share of gains have declined while the wealthiest, frequently investors, have garnered a greater share of the economic pie.

Despite growing income inequality, elected global leaders continue to enact governmental and tax legislation that favors the wealthy. Policy changes supporting low personal and corporate tax rates have helped to build wealth for the top percentile. In G7 countries, – the U.S., Canada, France, Germany, the U.K., Japan, and Italy – -average wages from 2011 and 2017 rose by 3%, while dividends to wealthy shareholders grew by 31%.[23] Increasingly, we have seen global citizens protesting racial and economic inequality as our policymakers and representatives continue to move to protect the few rather than the many. Continued population growth combined with environmental depletion and degradation means that increasingly the world's neediest will not have access to clean drinking water, food, and other human necessities.

The International Labour Organization (ILO) estimates that an additional 100 million older people and a 100 million children (aged 6–14 years) will need care by 2030.[24] The elderly will require more acute and long-term care from healthcare systems that are already stretched without this additional burden. As we saw during the pandemic, the burden of care for children and other family members disproportionally falls to women causing many of them to exit the workforce. The requirements of unpaid care impact women on many levels including the opportunity to attend school, to develop skills and valued credentials, and to earn a living wage.

With an aging population, underfunded public services, strained social safety nets, and continued environmental degradation, we will see even a greater toll on human society. The following recommendations made by Oxfam recognize the value of unpaid work and suggest legislative changes to redistribute wealth and extend protections to marginalized citizens.

1. Invest in national care systems to address the unpaid work primarily performed by women and girls.
2. Address systemic drivers of extreme wealth to end extreme poverty.
3. Legislate to protect the rights of caregivers and ensure living wages for care workers.
4. Ensure that caregivers have a voice in the development of programs and policies.
5. Address societal norms and behaviors that promote gender inequality.
6. Acknowledge the economic value to organizations of unpaid care.[25]

As we see from this research and report, as a global society, we are moving in the wrong direction in terms of addressing income and wealth equality. This issue is not just one for developing nations, it remains an issue for those nations with elected democracies and developed economies.

Racism, sexism, heterosexism, ableism, ageism, and classism remain global challenges impacting human rights, economic prosperity, and environmental degradation. The U.N. Development Program created an alternative to Gross Domestic Product (GDP) as a means of measuring economic growth called human development, which ranks countries by whether their people have the freedom and opportunity to live the lives they desire and value. Table 2.3 lists the following countries as the top 10 globally based on factors such as life expectancy, expected years of schooling, mean years of schooling, and Gross National Income Per Capita. Based on these factors, only one G7 country is listed in the top 10, and the U.S. comes in at 17th place.

Table 2.3 Human Development Index Ranking-2020

Rank	Country
1	Norway
2	Ireland
2	Switzerland
4	Hong Kong (China)
4	Iceland
6	Germany
7	Sweden
8	Australia
9	The Netherlands
10	Denmark

Source: "Human Development Reports | United Nations Development Programme," accessed January 5, 2021, http://hdr.undp.org/.

Globally, gender equity remains an elusive goal as unequal educational opportunities results in fewer skills limiting employment opportunities. Women's and girls' empowerment is a missing key for many countries seeking to expand economic growth and promote social development. As previously discussed, the COVID-19 pandemic has been extremely hard on women and has resulted in increased domestic violence.[26] Inequality based on income, sex, age, disability, sexual orientation, race, class, ethnicity, religion, and opportunity continues to grow globally with inequality growing for more than 70% of the population.[27]

We continue to talk about justice, equity, and inclusion because driving this type of systemic change is hard and long-term work. It requires all of us to engage and to do the work. We need to take the time to understand systemic barriers in both in our national and global societies and how these barriers impact our organizational cultures and workplaces. Senior leadership needs to commit time, money, and resources to drive systemic change in order to create J.E.D.I. aligned organizations and societal ecosystems.

2.4 Global Migration and Refugees

The U.N. has called the global refugee crisis the greatest humanitarian crisis of our time with over 79 million people displaced.[28] As indicated in Figure 2.1, we have experienced an increase in forcibly displaced people from 40 million in 1990 to

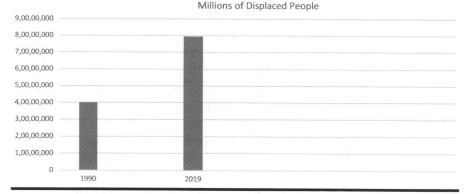

Figure 2.1   100% Growth in Displaced Persons Globally.[29]

80 million at the end of 2019.[29] Currently, 1% of the world's population has been displaced. These figures include refugees, internally displaced people, and asylum seekers, and those that are stateless. People have been forced from their homes by devastation, conflict and persecution. Many of these refugees, including children, are stateless and they have no access to healthcare, education, or a means of employment. Even their freedom of movement has been curtailed. According to the U.N., over half of the refugees come from five countries – Syria, Venezuela, Afghanistan, South Sudan, and Myanmar. The vast majority of these displaced people are relocating to countries or territories that are impacted by food insecurity and malnutrition. The majority of displaced people are hosted in developing countries.

Climate change related events have joined the list of the top drivers of displacement. Natural disasters such as earthquakes, floods, mud slides, and hurricanes have been occurring with increasing frequency. This climate related devastation drives people from their homes. Most of the population relocation owing to climate related events has been within country moves, but some of these events related to environmental degradation and natural disasters have caused cross border migration. Natural resource limitations such as access to drinking water, crop failures, and livestock survival, owing to climate change such as rising temperatures or changing rainfall, contribute to human migration and creation of refugees. These climate related events threaten livelihoods and food stability. While people are trying to adapt to their changing environments, new patterns of migration are developing resulting in conflicts within communities and even further stresses on limited resources.

The COVID-19 pandemic continues to have an adverse impact on immigrants and refugees. While the source of the COVID-19 virus remains unclear, the loss of wildlife habitat and the increased interactions between humans and wildlife is thought to be a contributing factor. The environmental and social intersectionality of the pandemic has again reinforced the vulnerability of our least resourced people. The difference in how developed vs. developing countries have been able to support pandemic fiscal relief is marked, with developed countries spending 24% of GDP and emerging countries spending 2–6% of GDP.[30] Emerging economy governmental leaders have less resources to deploy monetary and fiscal stimulus packages. In addition, they are more impacted by tourism and immigration and have greater exposure to global protectionism and trade barriers. Often, governance standards in emerging countries are lower resulting in high levels of corruption and crime. In 2020, the World Bank estimated that the global figure for people in poverty rose for the first time in 20 years increasing by $90 million.[31] This increase in poverty levels eliminates 4 years of progress. As a result, the number of the world's most vulnerable citizens is growing giving rise to more refugees.

While initially many emerging countries populations have experienced lower mortality rates from the virus because of younger population demographics and lower prevalence of comorbidities, they have been dramatically impacted from an economic perspective. As a result, we anticipate a rise in immigration to more developed countries. In Honduras, the impact of the virus was recently compounded by two tropical cyclones that struct within 2 weeks. These devastating events left roads and bridges destroyed, over 100,000 homeless, hundreds of thousands without electricity for months, neighborhoods buried in mud, and a population exposed to mosquito borne illnesses. These levels of devastation are on top of an already inadequate infrastructure and corrupt government. Non-governmental organizations (NGOs) report that humanitarian relief has been diverted, corruption reigns, and that gangs are extorting businesses and threatening citizens.[32] As a result, the stream of Hondurans heading for the U.S. border is expected to rise impacting immigration and leading to more refugees.

As we consider equity and inclusion, refugees and immigrants must be part of the conversation. They face tremendous barriers in rebuilding their lives and supporting their families. What role might there be for leveraging technology such as blockchain to provide the world's citizens with credentialing allowing them to verify their identities, health records, professional status, education, and even financial records. As environmental degradation continues, we can expect more destructive storms and diseases resulting in increased refugees and immigrants seeking an opportunity to build a new life.

HUMAN RESOURCES AND HUMAN RIGHTS

Daniel Farber Huang

As a strategic consultant, documentary photographer, and journalist, Daniel Farber Huang has traveled to 40 countries, regularly documenting humanitarian crises or politically sensitive situations. His projects include a collaboration with his wife and photo partner, Theresa Menders, entitled The Power of Faces in which they provide refugees across the world with physical family photos and seek to raise awareness of the global refugee crisis. He holds a Master's degree from Harvard University in Journalism with a Certificate in International Security as well as an MBA from The Wharton School, University of Pennsylvania.

Over 70 years ago, back in 1948, 48 out of 58 member countries of the United Nations voted to adopt the Universal Declaration of Human Rights ("UDHR"), which sought to promote mutual respect and equity "without distinction of any kind, such as race, colour, sex, language, religion, political or other opinion, national or social origin, property, birth or other status."[33]

While there have been some minor successes over the past seven decades in the name of human rights, let's face it, the small wins are too often outnumbered by humanity's failures. The concept behind the UDHR is noble, some might even call it beautiful. All people – whoever, wherever – are entitled to certain fundamental rights such as freedom from slavery, freedom from torture, equality under the law, freedom of movement (including leaving and returning to their home country), the right to asylum, freedom of thought, choice of religion, and many other privileges that lay out the architecture for the peaceful world most people would want to live in.

Of particular interest is the UDHR Article 23 regarding every individual's human right to earn a living for oneself. Article 23 includes four key points:

1. Everyone has the right to work, to free choice of employment, to just and favorable conditions of work, and to protection against unemployment.

2. Everyone, without any discrimination, has the right to equal pay for equal work.

3. Everyone who works has the right to just and favorable remuneration ensuring for himself and his family an existence worthy of human dignity, and supplemented, if necessary, by other means of social protection.

4. Everyone has the right to form and to join trade unions for the protection of his interests.[34]

The U.N. today boasts all its member States have ratified at least one of the nine core international human rights treaties, and 80% have ratified four or more, giving concrete expression to the universality of the UDHR and international human rights. But what does it mean in practice, when push literally comes to shove?

In direct contrast to the grandiose intentions of the UDHR, our collective performance has been abysmal. The U.N. calls the current global refugee crisis "the greatest humanitarian crisis of our time." As of mid-2020, 80 million men, women, and children have been forced to flee their homes due to conflict and persecution.[35] That obscene level of violence equates to one person becoming a refugee every 2 seconds.

Every 2 Seconds.

That's over 60 people since you started reading this article and more than 150 new refugees created by the time you finish.

As a Trustee of an international non-profit organization, I was recently required to sign an affidavit confirming that I personally have not been involved in activities that would be considered "Mandatory grounds for exclusion" according to a generally-accepted European procurement standards, specifically Article 67 of the Belgium Act of June 17, 2016 (the "Act"). The purpose of the Act, in part, is to establish a uniform set of standards and requirements for public bidding situations.

The mandatory grounds for disqualifying a prospective contract bidder included several of the typical "bad behavior" standards that would be expected, including any person who has been convicted of

1. participation in a criminal organization,
2. corruption,
3. fraud,
4. terrorist offences or offences linked to terrorist activities, or the instigation of, the aiding and abetting in or the attempt to commit such crime or offence,
5. money laundering and terrorist financing,
6. child labor and other forms of trafficking in human beings.

Disqualification Point #7 stood out to me, which stated:

7. the employment of illegal residents from third countries who reside here illegally.[36]

I fully recognize that Points 1 through 6 are criminal activities that rightfully warrant the full weight of local and international laws and penalties. Point 7, however, one might argue should fall into a more of a gray area, which can take into account a more nuanced delineation of who (or "what") an "illegal resident" is or is not. There also is the debate that no human being should be considered "illegal." A more accurate descriptor would be labeling someone "undocumented" to represent better their current citizenship status.

I understand the legal minds writing the Act had to contend with the inevitable politics that would attach itself to these issues, but I believe it is a grave mistake to group undocumented individuals (whether they are displaced individuals, refugees, asylum seekers, or other men and women from third countries residing in a new country) in the same category as criminal, terrorists, and human traffickers.

Undocumented individuals may be vulnerable to exploitation by unscrupulous employers, but I do not believe the spirit of Point #7 is intended to protect undocumented people in that manner. Rather, I believe it is intended to restrict further that vulnerable population's ability to earn a living and to develop greater self-sufficiency.

The U.S. has comparable standards against the hiring or employment of undocumented individuals. The net effect is that people who displaced, often fleeing war or persecution in their countries of origin, are further marginalized and forced into poverty by arbitrarily penalizing them for seeking safety in a new country.

Ultimately, denying capable individuals the ability to obtain self-sufficiency through employment, by applying their existing skills and talents (as well as preventing people from obtaining advanced or new skills) does not protect any host country's best interests. Host countries should consider integrating, welcoming, and leveraging the significant pools of talent, manpower, and knowledge that is ready to willingly contribute to their new communities.

The Universal Declaration on Human Rights thought that was a sound, humane philosophy over seven decades ago. It still is today.

2.5 Supporting Indigenous Peoples' Rights

Indigenous peoples are distinct social and cultural groups that share ancestral rights or ties to lands where they live, or from which they have been displaced.[37] According to the World Bank, Indigenous peoples own, occupy, or use only 25% of the world's land but they are actively protecting 80% of the planet's remaining biodiversity.[38] Their ecosystem is highly vulnerable to the impacts of climate change and other environmental degradation. In addition, Indigenous peoples have suffered from being displaced by colonization of other cultures. They remain a vulnerable and underserved and are often the very last to receive public investment in basic services and infrastructure. While they make up 6% of the global population, they represent over double that percentage of the impoverished. Given these systemic barriers, their life expectancy can be 20 years lower than the general population average.

Because of these impediments, Indigenous peoples are often displaced separating them from their land, traditional practices, community, and natural resources creating additional pressure on their survival. Recommendations to facilitate integration of Indigenous peoples into communities of other cultures include:

1. Honor and value their traditional skills and knowledge.
2. Buy products and services from Indigenous peoples to provide economic stability and to support traditional methodologies.

3. Respect Indigenous peoples' collective and ancestral rights to land, water, and natural resources.
4. Establish community protocols to offer empathy and support for Indigenous peoples who may lack identification documents such as identity cards, birth certificates, or marriage licenses making access to a procedure or service challenging.
5. Include Indigenous languages or alternative forms of communication through community based social and other services to facilitate interactions and understanding.[39]

Many Indigenous peoples are displaced because of environmental, social, political, and economic factors. As organizations pursue their agendas for growth often including access to land and resources, it is incumbent on all of us to reflect on the impact that our requests are having on Indigenous peoples around the world. On June 9, 2021, TransCanada Energy announced that it was terminating its Keystone XL pipeline project. The Rosebud Sioux Tribe (Sicangu Lakota Oyate), the Fort Belknap Indian Community (Assiniboine (Nakoda)), and the Gros Ventre (Aaniih) Tribes, along with their counsel the Native American Rights Fund, sued the Trump Administration for numerous legal violations in the Keystone XL pipeline permitting process. In January 2021, President Biden signed an Executive Order revoking the Keystone XL pipeline permit. The Tribes have been fighting to protect their people and lands and to ensure that the treaties and laws are honored and upheld.[40] Even though the pipeline's projected construction would cross Tribal homelands, the Tribes were not consulted as required by law and U.S. Department of the Interior policy. In granting the right-of-way, the Bureau of Land Management failed to uphold U.S. treaty obligations. In addition, the environmental and social impacts on land, water, health, and safety have not been fully vetted.[41] This case is a clear example of business failing to recognize Indigenous peoples' rights, and in the end, it was a costly mistake for TransCanada Energy.

Most organizations have not developed the skill sets to properly address the rights of Indigenous peoples either externally or internally. In the U.S., a foundational issue is understanding the differences between federal, state, and tribal laws and that tribal law often takes precedence as tribes are sovereign nations. As such, they have the right to govern themselves with the same level of authority as federal and state governments including enacting legislation and establishing courts.

As a starting point, recognize that in most countries we share the territory previously inhabited and occupied by Indigenous peoples. Acknowledging Indigenous land and territorial rights is a first step. It begins with developing a Land or Territorial Acknowledgment statement that recognizes the Indigenous peoples who have been dispossessed of their homelands and territories on which we have built our own societies and institutions. These acknowledgments are important because our collective history, which is taught in schools, depicted in media, and memorialized in museums often omits the voices of Indigenous peoples. Best practice is to reach out to your local Indigenous communities to solicit their voices in this acknowledgment creation. The entire process should be conducted with the utmost respect for Indigenous peoples and communities.

LAND OR TERRITORIAL ACKNOWLEDGMENT

"We are gathered on the unceded land of the ( ) peoples. I ask you to join me in acknowledging the ( ) community, their elders both past and present, as well as future generations. (Name of institution) also acknowledges that it was founded upon exclusions and erasures of many Indigenous peoples, including those on whose land this institution is located. This acknowledgment demonstrates a commitment to beginning the process of working to dismantle the ongoing legacies of settler colonialism."[42]

If you are unfamiliar with the Indigenous peoples' land and territory rights associated with your institution, https://native-land.ca/ is a useful tool for identifying Indigenous peoples with ties to the lands that your organization may be occupying.

The U.S. has signed over 350 treaties with Indigenous peoples, but honoring those treaties, as highlighted in the Keystone Pipeline example, have often been unfulfilled. These treaties have some common characteristics: a guarantee of peace, a definition of land boundaries, preservation of hunting and fishing rights, and arrangements for protection against domestic and foreign enemies.[43] There are 573 federally recognized Tribes in the U.S. and most Tribes are empowered to establish their own employment laws or rights. "Tribes, for example, are not required to follow the Fair Labor Standards Act or the Americans with Disabilities Act, although most do as a business practice, according to Vivian Santistevan."[44] Vivian is the owner of Taos HR ganics in New Mexico. As an organization, you could be called to a tribal court for your practices that intersect with Indigenous communities. Understanding your organization's points of intersectionality with Indigenous communities is imperative for building a collaborate and equitable relationship.

In order to build a workplace that is inclusive for Indigenous community members, spend some time and resources on understanding the Indigenous communities who are your stakeholders. The following is a list of suggestions for broadening your perspective on Indigenous rights and issues:

1. Engage with Indigenous communities taking the time to understand their needs as community members, customers, and suppliers of workforce labor.
2. Educate your people on Indigenous communities and their culture in your areas of operation. Remember that each Indigenous community is unique.
3. Investigate best practices on creating an Indigenous-friendly workplace program.

4. Ensure C-suite and Board commitment to adopting an inclusive culture for Indigenous peoples.
5. Communicate with Indigenous communities' elders and be prepared for different customs such as time off for hunting, fishing, and other Indigenous traditions and cultural events.[45]

Changing your internal systems to become more inclusive begins with listening and communication, and grows to appreciation and better understanding. As with all inclusion efforts, it is about making Indigenous peoples feel as if they can bring their true selves to work, and that they have an opportunity to contribute and thrive while remaining true to their own heritage and values.

In order to broaden our cultural competency and gain a broader perspective on Indigenous peoples' heritage and issues, Table 2.4 provides resources for learning more about Indigenous peoples and issues of erasure, political correctness, and historical inclusion and accuracy. November is Native American Heritage month. As Americans know, Thanksgiving is a major holiday also celebrated in November. During Thanksgiving, most U.S. citizens focus on gratitude and the celebration of European colonization. There are alternative ways to acknowledge gratitude as practiced by Indigenous peoples. The "All My Relations" November 20, 2020 podcast entitled "ThanksTaking or ThanksGiving?" hosted by Matika Wilbur (Swinomish and Tulalip) and Adrienne Keene (Cherokee Nation) discusses the traditions of Indigenous peoples to regularly give thanks and to practice gratitude on a daily basis. In order to create a more inclusive culture, consider how your organization can honor Native American Heritage month especially given the prominence of the Thanksgiving holiday in our culture and its focus on celebrating European colonization of the Americas.

The "History of Indigenous America" investigates Indigenous population in all of the Americas expanding the views beyond U.S. and Canadian Indigenous peoples. We have much to learn from Indigenous peoples about their history, culture, and beliefs and the ways in which we can address the inequities created by our past and current actions. Bringing their issues to the foreground begins the process of leveling the playing field in terms of public and private policies and practices.

Diving deeper into Indigenous peoples' culture, history, perspectives, and requirements is an example of the work that needs to be done by organizations to

Table 2.4 Indigenous Peoples' Podcasts

All My Relations	Coffee with My Ma	The Secret Life of Canada
The Red Nation Podcast	This Land	The Cuts
Let's Talk Negative, with John Kane	History of Indigenous America	

educate their leaders and employees. In order to drive transformative change, we need to develop awareness and then continue along on the journey to dig deeply into our organization's systems, beliefs, values, attitudes, and behaviors to develop practices, policies, and programs that create a culture of belonging and inclusion. As we have learned from this brief discussion of Indigenous peoples, there is much to be done to improve their rights, opportunities, health, and wellness.

2.6 Summary

Globally, we continue to face challenges to achieving environmental and social equality and justice. As a global business community, we prioritize and approach issue of justice, equity, and inclusion differently based on our own countries' values and beliefs. Top ranking countries on DEI criteria reflect their open and developed economies, more inclusive workplaces, governments, and laws that respect and empower minorities. However, national economic prosperity doesn't translate into environmental and social equity in developed countries. Even in the most developed nations with the largest economies, inequities continue in terms of access, opportunity, and earning a living wage. Bias and prejudice continue against women, LGBTQ+ communities, the elderly, BIPOC community members, minorities, and people with disabilities. The trend lines on promoting equity especially around income equality and wealth accumulation indicate that we continue to be heading in the wrong direction. The wealthy increasingly are receiving a disproportionate number of resources, and the most underserved and most vulnerable populations are receiving less. Environmental degradation results in increasing devastation, disease, and even wars over resources increasing the number of refugees and widen the equity gap. In order to become more equitable and inclusive, we need to seek public–private partnership solutions to address the ever-growing refugee crisis. Progress includes providing support for refugees in regaining their lives and a means to support themselves and their families.

Indigenous peoples' rights have been under threat for hundreds of years. In order to become a J.E.D.I. organization, leadership must acknowledge their past and their present impacts on Indigenous peoples. Creating a culture of inclusion involves acknowledging their rights and considering their cultures and norms as you create workforce policies and processes.

In order to drive global transformative change, governments around the world must assess their current situation and prioritize governance, environmental, and social changes to bridge the equity gap. There is a role for organizational leaders to partner with governments and NGOs to help drive change in social, governmental, legal, and workplace systems redesigned to build a more equitable and just global society. Transforming an organization requires understanding your broader ecosystem and the relationship between that ecosystem and your own organization's systems.

Questions

1. How would you feel if your employer asked you to relocate to one of the 10 best countries for Global Diversity Readiness? What if it were one of the 10 worst countries?
2. What recommendation would you make to promote greater national inclusion in your country?
3. What recommendations would you make to promote greater social inclusion?
4. What recommendations would you make to promote greater government or legal inclusion?
5. What ideas do you have for promoting workplace inclusion?
6. Why do think gender equity has been hard to achieve? How would you recommend addressing this challenge?
7. How are immigrants perceived in your country? What programs or support systems might make them feel more welcome and included?
8. Indigenous people's rights including legal rights such as treaties have often been ignored. How might you recommend your organization promote awareness and education of Indigenous people's rights?
9. How has environmental degradation impacted the number of and plight of refugees in your country?
10. What do you anticipate will happen as the world's population continues to grow and the demand for resources rises?

Notes

1 "Global Diversity and Inclusion; Perceptions, Practices and Attitudes," n.d., 68, accessed January 12, 2021,. https://www.shrm.org/hr-today/trends-and-forecasting/research-and-surveys/Documents/09-Diversity_and_Inclusion_Report.pdf
2 "Global Diversity and Inclusion; Perceptions, Practices and Attitudes."
3 "Territorial Disputes in the South China Sea," Global Conflict Tracker, accessed January 16, 2021, https://cfr.org/global-conflict-tracker/conflict/territorial-disputes-south-china-sea.
4 Andrew Browne, "Beijing Pays a Price for Assertiveness in South China Sea," *Wall Street Journal*, May 14, 2014, sec. Asia, http://online.wsj.com/news/articles/SB10001424052702303627504579558913140862896.
5 Vu Trong Khanh in Hanoi, Jenny W, and Hsu in Taipei, "Anti-China Rioting Turns Deadly in Vietnam," *Wall Street Journal*, May 16, 2014, sec. Asia, http://online.wsj.com/news/articles/SB10001424052702304908304579562962349248496.
6 "The Intersections of Mental Health and LGBTIQ People in the Indian Workplace," Out & Equal, accessed June 14, 2021, https://outandequal.org/mental-health-lgbtqi-india/.
7 "Goal 5: Gender Equality," UNDP, accessed January 18, 2021, https://www.undp.org/content/undp/en/home/sustainable-development-goals/goal-5-gender-equality.html.
8 "Goal 5."

9 Clare Coffey et al., "Time to Care: Unpaid and Underpaid Care Work and the Global Inequality Crisis" (Oxfam, January 20, 2020), https://doi.org/10.21201/2020.5419.

10 "Population, Female (% of Total Population) | Data," accessed June 14, 2021, https://data.worldbank.org/indicator/SP.POP.TOTL.FE.ZS.

11 Coffey et al., "Time to Care."

12 Coffey et al.

13 "Goal 5."

14 "Bias and Backlash," accessed January 18, 2021, https://feature.undp.org/bias-and-backlash/.

15 Klaus Schwab et al., *Global Gender Gap Report 2020 Insight Report.* (Geneva: World Economic Forum, 2019).

16 History com Editors, "Rwandan Genocide," HISTORY, accessed March 10, 2021, https://www.history.com/topics/africa/rwandan-genocide.

17 Diana Karusis et al., "The Transformative Power of Women Leadership Lessons from Rwanda." (Wharton Webinar Series, March 8, 2021).

18 "These Countries Have the Most Women in Parliament," World Economic Forum, accessed March 10, 2021, https://www.weforum.org/agenda/2019/02/chart-of-the-day-these-countries-have-the-most-women-in-parliament/.

19 "Revisiting Rwanda Five Years after Record-Breaking Parliamentary Elections," UN Women, accessed March 10, 2021, https://www.unwomen.org/en/news/stories/2018/8/feature-rwanda-women-in-parliament.

20 Diana Karusis et al., "The Transformative Power of Women Leadership Lessons from Rwanda."

21 Ibid.

22 Coffey et al., "Time to Care."

23 Ibid.

24 Ibid.

25 Ibid.

26 "5_Why-It-Matters-2020.Pdf," accessed January 5, 2021, https://www.un.org/sustainabledevelopment/wp-content/uploads/2016/08/5_Why-It-Matters-2020.pdf.

27 "10_Why-It-Matters-2020.Pdf," accessed January 5, 2021, https://www.un.org/sustainabledevelopment/wp-content/uploads/2018/01/10_Why-It-Matters-2020.pdf.

28 United Nations High Commissioner for Refugees, "Figures at a Glance," UNHCR, accessed January 16, 2021, https://www.unhcr.org/figures-at-a-glance.html.

29 Refugees.

30 Greg Ip, "Post-Covid Recovery Divides Rich Nations From Poor," *Wall Street Journal*, January 17, 2021, sec. U.S., https://www.wsj.com/articles/post-covid-recovery-divides-rich-nations-from-poor-11610879400.

31 Ip.

32 Ip.

33 United Nations, "Universal Declaration of Human Rights," United Nations (United Nations), accessed May 10, 2021, https://www.un.org/en/about-us/universal-declaration-of-human-rights.

34 Nations.

35 United Nations High Commissioner for Refugees, "UNHCR – Refugee Statistics," UNHCR, accessed May 10, 2021, https://www.unhcr.org/refugee-statistics/.

36 "Loi Du 17 Juin 2016," Public Procurement, July 27, 2018, https://www.publicprocurement.be/fr/documents/loi-du-17-juin-2016.

37 "Indigenous Peoples," Text/HTML, World Bank, accessed November 25, 2020, https://www.worldbank.org/en/topic/indigenouspeoples.
38 Ibid.
39 agalarcon, "5 Actions to Facilitate the Social Inclusion of Indigenous Displaced People," Text, Regional Office for Central America, North America and the Caribbean, March 4, 2019, https://rosanjose.iom.int/SITE/en/blog/5-actions-facilitate-social-inclusion-indigenous-displaced-people.
40 "Keystone XL Pipeline Project Terminated," Native American Rights Fund, June 9, 2021, https://www.narf.org/keystone-xl/.
41 "Rosebud Sioux and Fort Belknap File Suit against Keystone XL," Native American Rights Fund, accessed June 13, 2021, https://www.narf.org/cases/keystone/.
42 "GUIDE TO INDIGENOUS LAND AND TERRITORIAL ACKNOWLEDGEMENTS FOR CULTURAL INSTITUTIONS," accessed November 25, 2020, https://as.nyu.edu/content/nyu-as/as/research-centers/npf/Land0.html.
43 Rory Taylor, "6 Native Leaders on What It Would Look like If the US Kept Its Promises," Vox, September 23, 2019, https://www.vox.com/first-person/2019/9/23/20872713/native-american-indian-treaties.
44 Kathy Gurchiek and Kathy Gurchiek, "SHRM State Council at Work on Native American Initiative," SHRM, January 30, 2020, https://www.shrm.org/about-shrm/news-about-shrm/pages/shrm-state-council-at-work-on-native-american-initiative-.aspx.
45 Bob Joseph, "6 Steps to Create an Inclusive Environment for Indigenous Workers," accessed November 25, 2020, https://www.ictinc.ca/blog/inclusive-worksite-for-indigenous-worker.

Bibliography

"5_Why-It-Matters-2020.Pdf." Accessed January 5, 2021. https://www.un.org/sustainabledevelopment/wp-content/uploads/2016/08/5_Why-It-Matters-2020.pdf.
"10_Why-It-Matters-2020.Pdf." Accessed January 5, 2021. https://www.un.org/sustainabledevelopment/wp-content/uploads/2018/01/10_Why-It-Matters-2020.pdf.
agalarcon. "5 Actions to Facilitate the Social Inclusion of Indigenous Displaced People." Text. Regional Office for Central America, North America and the Caribbean, March 4, 2019. https://rosanjose.iom.int/SITE/en/blog/5-actions-facilitate-social-inclusion-indigenous-displaced-people.
"Bias and Backlash." Accessed January 18, 2021. https://feature.undp.org/bias-and-backlash/.
Browne, Andrew. "Beijing Pays a Price for Assertiveness in South China Sea." *Wall Street Journal*, May 14, 2014, sec. Asia. http://online.wsj.com/news/articles/SB10001424052702303627504579558913140862896.
Coffey, Clare, Patricia Espinoza Revollo, Rowan Harvey, Max Lawson, Anam Parvez Butt, Kim Piaget, Diana Sarosi, and Julie Thekkudan. "Time to Care: Unpaid and Underpaid Care Work and the Global Inequality Crisis." *Oxfam*, January 20, 2020. https://doi.org/10.21201/2020.5419.
Editors, History com. "Rwandan Genocide." *HISTORY*. Accessed March 10, 2021. https://www.history.com/topics/africa/rwandan-genocide.
Global Conflict Tracker. "Territorial Disputes in the South China Sea." Accessed January 16, 2021. https://cfr.org/global-conflict-tracker/conflict/territorial-disputes-south-china-sea.
"Global Diversity and Inclusion; Perceptions, Practices and Attitudes," n.d., 68.

"Guide to Indigenous Land and Territorial Acknowledgements for Cultural Institutions." Accessed November 25, 2020. https://as.nyu.edu/content/nyu-as/as/research-centers/npf/Land0.html.

Gurchiek, Kathy, and Kathy Gurchiek. "SHRM State Council at Work on Native American Initiative." *SHRM*, January 30, 2020. https://www.shrm.org/about-shrm/news-about-shrm/pages/shrm-state-council-at-work-on-native-american-initiative-.aspx.

Hanoi, Vu Trong Khanh in, Jenny W, and Hsu in Taipei. "Anti-China Rioting Turns Deadly in Vietnam." *Wall Street Journal*, May 16, 2014, sec. *Asia*. http://online.wsj.com/news/articles/SB10001424052702304908304579562962349248496.

"Human Development Reports | United Nations Development Programme." Accessed January 5, 2021. http://hdr.undp.org/.

Ip, Greg. "Post-Covid Recovery Divides Rich Nations From Poor." *Wall Street Journal*, January 17, 2021, sec. US. https://www.wsj.com/articles/post-covid-recovery-divides-rich-nations-from-poor-11610879400.

Joseph, Bob. "6 Steps to Create an Inclusive Environment for Indigenous Workers." Accessed November 25, 2020. https://www.ictinc.ca/blog/inclusive-worksite-for-indigenous-worker.

Karusis, Diana, Katherine Klein, Agnes Binagwaho, and Kampeta Pitchette Sayinzoga. "The Transformative Power of Women Leadership Lessons from Rwanda." *Wharton Webinar Series*, March 8, 2021.

Nations, United. "Universal Declaration of Human Rights." *United Nations*. United Nations. Accessed May 10, 2021. https://www.un.org/en/about-us/universal-declaration-of-human-rights.

Native American Rights Fund. "Keystone XL Pipeline Project Terminated," June 9, 2021a. https://www.narf.org/keystone-xl/.

Native American Rights Fund. "Rosebud Sioux and Fort Belknap File Suit against Keystone XL." Accessed June 13, 2021b. https://www.narf.org/cases/keystone/.

Out&Equal. "The Intersections of Mental Health and LGBTIQ People in the Indian Workplace." Accessed June 14, 2021. https://outandequal.org/mental-health-lgbtqi-india/.

"Population, Female (% of Total Population) | Data." Accessed June 14, 2021. https://data.worldbank.org/indicator/SP.POP.TOTL.FE.ZS.

Public Procurement. "Loi Du 17 Juin 2016," July 27, 2018. https://www.publicprocurement.be/fr/documents/loi-du-17-juin-2016.

Refugees, United Nations High Commissioner for. "Figures at a Glance." *UNHCR*. Accessed January 16, 2021a. https://www.unhcr.org/figures-at-a-glance.html.

Refugees, United Nations High Commissioner for. "UNHCR - Refugee Statistics." *UNHCR*. Accessed May 10, 2021b. https://www.unhcr.org/refugee-statistics/.

Schwab, Klaus, Robert Crotti, Thierry Geiger, Vesselina Ratcheva, and World Economic Forum. *Global Gender Gap Report 2020 Insight Report*. Geneva: World Economic Forum, 2019.

Taylor, Rory. "6 Native Leaders on What It Would Look like If the US Kept Its Promises." *Vox*, September 23, 2019. https://www.vox.com/first-person/2019/9/23/20872713/native-american-indian-treaties.

UN Women. "Revisiting Rwanda Five Years after Record-Breaking Parliamentary Elections." Accessed March 10, 2021. https://www.unwomen.org/en/news/stories/2018/8/feature-rwanda-women-in-parliament.

UNDP. "Goal 5: Gender Equality." Accessed January 18, 2021. https://www.undp.org/content/undp/en/home/sustainable-development-goals/goal-5-gender-equality.html.

World Bank. "Indigenous Peoples." *Text/HTML*. Accessed November 25, 2020. https://www.worldbank.org/en/topic/indigenouspeoples.

World Economic Forum. "These Countries Have the Most Women in Parliament." Accessed March 10, 2021. https://www.weforum.org/agenda/2019/02/chart-of-the-day-these-countries-have-the-most-women-in-parliament/.

Chapter 3

Why Are We Still Talking about Delivering Equity?

Organizations have been investing in diversity, equity, and inclusion trainings and programs for over 20 years, but the needle has barely moved on creating equal access, pay, and opportunity. Systemic racism, sexism, heterosexism, ableism, ageism, and classism continue to reflect the power imbalance in our society and workplaces. Issues such as power, privilege, and access to opportunity remain unequal. Looking at the history of racism provides a framework to better understand White privilege in our culture. Taking a deeper dive into current issues around equity and inclusion including the Me Too and Black Lives Matter (BLM) movements, and LGBTQ+ rights provide insights into how both societal and organizational systems lead to patriarchal and heteronormative privilege. This privilege creates inequities in access to basic services resulting in health and education divides as well as lack of opportunities generating pay and wealth gaps. Gaining insights into our nation's long history of inequity offers greater understanding into how embedded these beliefs and values are in our cultural norms. We are still discussing justice, equity, diversity and inclusion (J.E.D.I.) despite it being a priority for many organizational leaders, because outcomes continue to fall far short of leveling the playing field. The imbalance of power remains, and in many ways, it has been growing rather than receding.

3.1 History of Racial Inequity

In the U.S., we have a history of colonialization, which is reflected in the taking of land and natural resources and the imposition of culture and control over Indigenous peoples. We set up colonies based on the culture, values, and norms of our origin

DOI: 10.1201/9781003168072-4

countries and applied them to the U.S. and its Indigenous peoples. Justification for colonization and the treatment of non-Christian people as "lesser" beings was supported by the Church. "Towards the middle of the 15th century, the Catholic Church, in particular the Papacy, took an active role in offering justifications for enslavement of Saracens, pagans, infidels, and 'other enemies of Christ.'"[1] Any country not ruled by Christian leaders could be taken in the name of God and its peoples controlled through enslavement. The history of humankind tells the tale of cultures, peoples, and religions dehumanizing of "others" through this justification process. This dehumanization of Indigenous and later Black peoples served as the justification for genocide, enslavement, and bondage.[2] Table 3.1 highlights several systemic

Table 3.1 U.S. History of Systemic Barriers

Legal Barriers	Dates	Description
Slavery	1619–1865	Over 300 years of bondage
Segregation	1865–1877	Post-Civil War reconstruction Black Codes limit civil and economic rights
Jim Crow Laws	1896–1964	Laws that systemized social and economic inequities
Civil Rights Movement	1955–1968	The Civil Rights Act of 1964 ended segregation in public places and banned employment discrimination based on race, color, religion, sex, or national origin
Housing Restrictions	1920–1968	White flight New Deal Homeowners' Loan Corporation Federal Housing Administration Redlining
Voting Rights	1867-present	Voter suppression Gerrymandering
Criminal Justice		
Police Brutality	1865-Present	Lynching, burning, and beating of POC Higher arrest rates Stop and frisk George Floyd's murder
War on Drugs	1971–2008	Mandatory minimum sentencing Three strikes law

(Continued)

Table 3.1 *(Continued)*   **U.S. History of Systemic Barriers**

Legal Barriers	Dates	Description
Mass Incarceration	1971-Present	The War on Drugs and minimum mandatory sentencing escalated the rate of incarceration. U.S. – highest prison population in the world and the highest percentage of its population in prisons Disproportional representation of people of color School to prison pipeline Employment discrimination for returning citizens
Private Prisons	1984-Present	Relieve strain on public sector institutions from mass incarceration Quality and security concerns Generating a profit from incarceration
Education		
Historically Black Colleges and Universities (HBCUs)	1837[5]	Formed to serve Black students as they were denied admission to traditional educational institutions. Provide education for the majority of Black doctors, military officers, and judges
School Integration	1954–1970	Brown vs. Board of Education ruling
School Funding Formulas	Present	Schools are predominately funded by local, property, and state taxes
Healthcare		
Healthcare Systems and Services	Present	Unequal access to care The Tuskegee Study Less preventative care Prejudice/suboptimal care from providers

Source: Janice Hammond, A. Kamau Massey, and Mayra A. Gaza, "African American Inequality in the United States" (Harvard Business School, June 15, 2020); Reshmann Hussam and Holly Fetter, "Race and Mass Incarceration in the United States" (Harvard Business School, June 19, 2020).

impediments such as legal, voting rights, criminal justice, economic, education, and healthcare systems that have supported and enabled inequities. The data offers a modified historical timeline to give magnitude to the sustained depth and breadth of events that have impacted Black people's civil, economic, and legal rights in the U.S.

In the U.S., we have a history of slavery and unfortunately it is a foundational pillar on which we build our country. As a justification of slavery, many cited the Bible and its mention of slavery. "Some argued that, far from being an evil or a human institution merely permitted by God, slavery was in fact a 'positive good' because it exposed 'heathens' to Christianity."[3] Slavery was a system that dehumanized Black people and cast them as the "other" creating inherent indenture, children born into slavery, and a lifetime of terror and torture. Slavery was an integral component of the capitalist system providing free labor to drive economic gain. It was also part of politics. The 1787 Constitutional Convention provided for counting enslaved peoples as 3/5s of one White person for determining population and representation in the House of Representatives.[4] The questions of "Who is White?" and "What does it mean to be White?" are rooted in our history of slavery. If you aren't White, you are considered "other," and you need to be controlled to protect those who are White.

Even when slavery was abolished, we had a series of laws and regulation during Segregation that limited Black people's civil and economic rights. While they were no longer enslaved people in the U.S., the White establishment was still seeking to control and dehumanize people of color (POC). Then came Jim Crow Laws, which further systemized social and economic inequality and laid the foundation for segregation. Even the New Deal had racist provisions around home ownership, mortgage lending, and availability and rates on homeowners' insurance. The 1970s ushered in the "War on Drugs" and the resulting mass incarcerations of people of color. The barriers don't stop there, they spill over into access and availability of healthcare, voting rights, and education. These barriers lead to health and pay gaps and contribute to the significant wealth gap between BIPOC and White Americans. While this list not exhaustive, it provides perspective on the scope and extend of the embedded systemic barriers faced by people of color in the U.S. over the past several hundred years. The playing field is clearly not even. Driving systemic change and really beginning the process of promoting J.E.D.I. values require listening to the stories of our employees, customers, community members, and other key stakeholders to better understand the barriers both within our own organizations and our broader society.

Police brutality and mass incarceration grew out of these Black Codes and Jim Crow laws to keep the "other" under the control of Whites. In the U.S., we are a world leader for incarceration rates. For Black Americans, the rate is significantly higher. Black citizens make up 40% of the incarcerated population even though they only make up 13% of U.S. population.[6] Poverty is a key driver of incarceration rates, and POC represent a disproportionate percentage of those living at poverty levels. Policies that increase the rate of police and BIPOC citizens interactions such as "Stop and Frisk," the intersection of school zones an urban density for mandatory sentencing, and biased use of discretion from prosecutors contribute to the higher arrests and incarceration rates.[7] In order to break the trend line in incarceration rates, we need to invest in counseling, education, training, and support systems to halt the school-to-prison pipeline, where children are funneled out of school and into the criminal justice system. Zero-tolerance policies, which criminalize minor school rules infractions, and the presence of law enforcement in schools leads to a disproportionate percentage of student of color being pushed into the school-prison pipeline.[8] The long-term impacts of the prison industrial system on education, pay, health, and wealth gaps is significant. As we follow the timeline of history, we see the threads that link our current social justice climate back to our country's foundational pillar of slavery and our history of White privilege.

Historically, Black Colleges and Universities (HBCUs) were formed to serve the needs of Black Americans as they were generally denied admission to White institutions. While the history of HBCUs predates the Civil War, the primary mission of these higher education institutions was to provide elementary and secondary education to their students who had no previous access to education. In the early 1900s, HBCUs began offering post-secondary education. Over 80% of all Black Americans who received degrees in medicine and dentistry attended two traditionally Black institutions of medicine and dentistry – Howard University and Meharry Medical College. HBCUs offers a strong foundation for Black students seeking and obtaining doctorate degrees conferring 75% of their undergraduate degrees. They also educated 75% of all Black officers in the armed forces and 80% of all Black federal judges.[9]

Until the Brown vs. the Board of Education Supreme Court ruling, public schools were operated on the principal of separate but equal. However, segregated schools were anything but equal in terms of funding, facilities, resources, and student outcomes and opportunities. In Arkansas, school integration was met with great resistance including riots, violence, and death threats known as the "Little Rock Crisis.". Governor Faubus ordered the Arkansas National Guard to surround Central High School to keep nine Black students from entering the school. In response, President Eisenhower ordered the 101st Airborne Division into Little Rock to ensure the safety of these Black students.[10] Integration was not just a southern issue. In the 1970s, Boston public schools were desegregated by court order. In Boston, school segregation was primarily a result of geographic separation of communities of color. Despite this landmark case, today, many schools remain segregated because school districts are based on geographically defined areas such as townships and municipalities, whose population tend to be representationally homogenous.

School funding at a national level remains unequal as most school funding (over 90%) comes from state, local, and property taxes rather than federal taxes. Some states, such as New Jersey, have funding formulas that allocate school funding more equitably. In 1990, the NJ Supreme Court ruled in *Abbott v. Burke II* that

> inadequate and unequal funding denies students in urban districts a thorough and efficient education and requires the state to equalize funding between suburban and urban districts for regular education and to provide extra or "supplemental" programs to wipe out disadvantages as much as a school district can.[11]

Access to high-quality education remains a challenge for many disadvantaged socio-economic communities of which most residents are POC.

Lack of access to quality healthcare and lack of clear information on healthcare options compounded by poor diet due to food deserts and socioeconomic status often leads to poor healthcare outcomes for members of communities of color. We are in the middle of the COVID-19 pandemic and POC have been disproportionally impacted by the disease in terms of infection rates, hospitalization rates, and mortality rates. Some of the issues around health and well-being run even deeper and arise from lack of trust in the government and healthcare system. Despite their higher COVID-19 contraction rate, communities of color are reluctant to sign up for vaccine trials. Only about 3% of the people who have signed up for the vaccine trials nationally are Black.[12] Some blame their reluctance on the Black community's history with the governmental healthcare systems namely the Tuskegee Study now known as "USPHS Syphilis Study at Tuskegee".

The Tuskegee Study was undertaken by the Public Health Service in 1932 to record the natural history of syphilis with a goal of justifying treatment programs for Black men. The study was conducted without obtaining informed consent of the patients. The study subjects were told that they were being treated for "bad blood," which was a term used to cover aliments such as syphilis, anemia, and fatigue. The study was conducted over 40 years, and participants never received adequate treatment to cure their illness, even when penicillin was discovered and recommended as a highly effective treatment.[13] While studying the impact of the COVID-19 vaccine on POC is crucial for getting the vaccine to be effective to help communities of color, one can certainly understand POC's reluctance to participate in trials given this history.

Slavery was a foundational element of capitalism. In the later part of the 19th century, the British Atlantic slave trade was one of the largest and most valuable businesses. In 1860, a value of over $13 billion was assigned to the bodies of enslaved Black Americans used for labor.[14] In comparison, this figure exceeded the combined investment in factories and railroads at that time. Slavery enriched White slave owners and by extension those who did business with those slave owners at the expense of the enslaved. Capitalism is rooted in this history of systemic racism. Power and privilege stem from this relationship. The history of racism is layered with economic barriers related to wealth accumulation, access to capital, and access to education to provide a pathway to better careers, access to fair mortgages, and devaluation of assets like homes and business franchises. Black former franchisees sued McDonald's citing a systematic process to steer Black owners to purchase franchises located in undesirable locations in inner cities. Because of the location, owners often experienced higher operating costs and even lower sales. As a result, many of these locations were destined to fail and many Black franchise owners have in fact lost their businesses.[15]

The history of POC in the U.S. is one of continuous systemic barriers. When we speak about leveling the playing field, we are really looking at the over 400 years of slavery, oppression, and dehumanization for which we need to account and reparate.

As a nation, we have a great deal of work to do to make reparations for our past and create solutions to eliminate current and future barriers. As business leaders, we need to consider the broader societal systems in which our organizations operate. Only with this perspective can we develop meaningful pathways to level the playing field within our organizations and their broader ecosystem. (See The J.E.D.I. Primer, Leveling the Playing Field for further information.)

3.2 Social Justice Movement

The Civil Rights movement began in the 1960s during the Kennedy and Johnson Administrations. This movement was led by Black leaders, the most prominent being Dr. Martin Luther King, Jr., who led peaceful protests supporting justice, equality, and human rights for POC and other disadvantaged people. His leadership in the Montgomery Bus Boycott and the 1963 March on Washington served as a catalyst ushering in The Civil Rights Act of 1964, which ended segregation in public places and banned employment discrimination based on race, color, religion, sex, or national origin. Yet, over 55 years later, we continue to fight the battle of injustice, racism, and inequity.

The BLM movement emerged when its three women founders' – Patrisse Cullors, Alicia Garza, and Opal Tometi – joined together in response to their outrage over the killing of Trayvon Martin and the subsequent acquittal of George Zimmerman, the person who killed him. The BLM movement has evolved into an influential organization with significant funding to support its message around defunding the police as a pathway to address systemic racism. During the summer of 2020, the call for social justice accelerated with the murder of George Floyd at the hands of police officers causing many around the world to rally around preventing Black deaths at the hands of the police. This social activism has been more grassroots and universal in nature. Rather than working within the system, organizers are pushing back against the system that has created this system of injustice. In an interview given by Rashad Robinson, CEO of the Color of Change, he suggests that their movement is about changing the system to make it more just. He highlights the difference of Black people being present vs. having power pointing to examples of the rise in Black leaders and celebrities, but the lack of a commensurate rise in Black communities in general. While many believe that U. S. society reached a post-racial stage with the presidency of Barack Obama, we see clearly that we have not yet turned that corner. As the protests in response to police brutality in the deaths of George Floyd, Breonna Taylor, and others demonstrate, systemic barriers are interwoven into our culture and society. They are embedded into our systems for criminal justice, voting rights and access, media portrayals, access to and availability of healthcare, education, and career opportunities. Protests reignited the conversation around race in the U.S. but, leaders and activists are focusing on moving beyond awareness toward driving lasting systemic change.

Philadelphia is one of the poorest cities in the U.S. with 25% of the population living in poverty and most of the population identifying as Black (42%).[16] While BLM activists have taken to the streets in Philadelphia with numerous protests throughout the city, they are focused on moving beyond protests and outlining solutions to drive systemic change. They are identifying their vision for the future of the city, creating community group models to work in neighborhoods that they have identified for city investment, and engaging with residents through a series of events and outreach programs. Their goal is to improve the lives of Black community members in Philadelphia in terms of housing, education, employment, and access to healthcare. They are also seeking to find solutions to challenges that create high levels of interactions for this community with the criminal justice system.[17] The hope is that from the chaos and devastation comes lasting systemic change to promote justice, equity, and inclusion for all.

Some outcomes of the protest in Philadelphia have been the cancelling of a $19,000,000 budget increase for Philadelphia police, and the removal of a controversial statue of former police commissioner and mayor, Frank Rizzo, who was known for his law-and-order policies. His tactics and policies were seen by many in the Black community as being racist and fostering a culture of police brutality. There has also been a procedural change to embed a behavioral health specialist alongside 911 dispatchers to redirect issues related to mental health crisis to social services rather than the criminal justice system. Conversations continue around reallocating money from policing budgets to social services.[18]

Across the river in Camden, NJ, we have a model of a city that has transformed its police department. Camden was once considered one of the most dangerous cities in America. Rather than double down on policing, they abolished their police force. Instead, they used a newly formed county program to create a new police force based on a culture of community policing that reframed the role of police officers as facilitators and conveyors rather than arbitrators of justice. Training and reframing the role for officers were key to the process. Performance metrics were changed from tickets written and number of arrests to measures of integration into the community. Police now host block parties and interact regularly with community residents. The department implemented a use-of-force guidebook developed with New York University's Policing Project, which outlines when deadly force can be used. Officers are empowered to intervene if a fellow officer violates these rules, and violation is cause for termination. The transformation was met with a resistance from the police union, some residents, and others but they forged a head, and the data indicates that Camden is a much safer city for residents with significantly fewer complaints of excessive use of force by residents. This transformation was most publicly visible with the photo of Joseph D. Wysocki, Chief of Camden Police, marching in solidarity with the BLM protestors. This photo of solidarity stands as a stark contrast to the looting and riots in other cities along with the outcries against police brutality.[19] This story serves as an example of the deep changes that are needed to address systemic social justice challenges. To design a new law enforcement paradigm, the New Blue

Project offers fellowship training to develop forward-thinking police leaders in pursuit of a more equitable law enforcement system (https://www.newblueproject.org/).

3.3 Sexism and the Me Too Movement

The term sexual harassment began being used more widely in the 1970s.

> That year the feminist legal scholar Catharine MacKinnon put forward the argument that workplace harassment constitutes sex discrimination, which is illegal under the Civil Rights Act of 1964. Federal judges had previously rebuffed this idea, but by 1978 three courts had agreed with MacKinnon, and in 1986 the Supreme Court concurred.[20]

By the late 1990s, many companies in the U.S. developed mandatory harassment training programs explaining to employees the behaviors that are prohibited by law and detailing grievance procedures. Sexual harassment trainings are compliance based often highlight unacceptable behaviors and illegal practices such as quid pro quo or tying job benefits to unwanted sexual advances or sexual harassment. Despite significant training initiatives, we still have sexual harassment and hostile work environments today. Research conducted by Frank Dobbins and Alexandra Kalev found that in organizations that instituted sexual harassment training programs, women actually lost ground in terms of representation in management by 5%.[21] Their research suggests that mandatory sexual harassment training frames the issue as a problem, and that men, in particular, need to be fixed to address this problem. Reframing the issue and presenting training as a tool for effective management is a much more successful approach. By-stander intervention training, which refocuses the training on treating participants as allies who are trying to solve problems of sexual harassment and assault rather than those who are likely to engage in inappropriate behavior has been more successful. Rather than focusing on what not to do, the training focuses on what to do if you hear inappropriate jokes, see an interaction that constitutes harassment, or other behaviors that constitute sexual harassment. This approach gives employees and volunteers an actionable plan to impact change.

Most organizations also instituted sexual harassment grievance protocols, but these have had limited success. With grievance procedures, the reason for failure often lies with the intent of the grievance process. While most large organizations have sexual harassment grievance protocols, many have been designed to protect the organization and its leaders rather than the individual being harassed. While confidentiality is to be maintained around the investigation, in reality, it rarely remains confidential. Rather than supporting the whistleblower, many organizations launch an investigation that leaves the accuser exposed with their story and credibility being attacked. Resolutions are often not equitable requiring the victim rather than the accused to change their role or work environment to avoid a hostile work environment. Examples include being offered a transfer to position that is a demotion or one requiring physical relocation. Often, women have no other recourse than to leave the organization in fear of retaliation. In companies with an underrepresentation of women in management, organizations with grievance policies saw the most significant declines of women in management level positions. This hostility was felt even more significantly by women of color with declines of − 14% among African American, 10% among Latina, and 10% among Asian American managers.[22] Another excellent case for more diversity in senior management. Instead of allowing women to report sexual harassment and expect a reasonable resolution that addresses their issue while leaving them wholly intact within their organization, the research suggests that the solution is most harmful to the accuser.

When women chose to leave an employer after leveling a sexual harassment complaint, they may be subject to a mandatory arbitration clause that was part of their terms of employment. So, they have already given up their right to sue their employer and agree to abide by the ruling of the arbitrator and to keep the outcome confidential. If the arbitration goes in the favor of the employee, which happens less frequently as the arbitrator is retained by the company, they may be asked to sign a non-disclosure agreement (NDA). As part of the NDA, the employee receives a financial payment in exchange for signing an agreement that limits their recourse to the organization and prohibits them from discussing the case publicly. The Me Too movement put a spotlight on how NDAs protect companies and perpetrators by suppressing prior accusations of sexual harassment and assault. In some states, laws have been enacted to limit the use of confidentiality provisions in matters involving sexual harassment. In addition, the 2017 federal tax overhaul prohibits organizations from deducting expenses related to sexual harassment and misconduct settlements.

Sometimes the sexual harassment perpetrator is a crucial member of an organization such as a superstar performer, popular entertainment personality, politician, and even an owner or family member of the owner. When the Me Too movement broke, one of the distinguishing factors is that many of these high-profile employees were brought down to earth and required to resign, face criminal charges, or both. While this very public reckoning had an immediate impact, the longer-term impacts for women in the workplace are less clear. Research indicates that 80% of women do not feel that progress has been made toward equity since the movement began in 2006.[23] In 2019, McDonalds terminated their then CEO, Steve Easterbrook, for an inappropriate relationship with an employee involving sexting.[24] Within a year of the termination, another employee made a new allegation of sexual harassment against Mr. Easterbrook. Further investigation into data stored on company servers indicated a pattern of this type of behavior by the then CEO. The company has undertaken a lawsuit against Mr. Easterbrook seeking to recoup stock options and other compensation totaling $40 million. McDonald's lawsuit accuses Mr. Easterbrook of having a sexual relationship with three employees in the year before his termination. While having a relationship with one of those employees, he awarded her stock options worth several hundreds of thousand dollars.[25] Although

McDonald's is publicly going after Easterbrook to claw back his compensation, one wonders if the action is driven more by the compensation package, he walked away with than by the sexual harassment accusations. While the new CEO, Mr. Kempczinski, has emphasized transparency, inclusion, and integrity, it seems that the Board of Directors was initially willing to allow Easterbrook to depart with his compensation and reputation mainly intact despite the initial sexual harassment allegation. Their lack of action suggests that they didn't want to dig too deeply into their corporate records to unearth any additional information until the disclosure of the inappropriate preferment of stock options.

This case highlights that the imbalance of power and privilege are still intact. When CEOs earn multiples of 300 to 400 times the average workers' pay, do the rules still apply to them? In 2019, McDonalds reported that their CEO's compensation was 1,939 times higher than the median workers compensation.[26] In little more than a decade since the beginning of the Me Too movement and within the 2 years of the publishing of the Harvey Weinstein allegation, we see yet another example of a major corporation's CEO behaving inappropriately with employees. Women have reason to be skeptical about the long-term and lasting impact of changes being adopted to address power and privilege in the workplace.

Research conducted by Leanne Atwater, a management professor at the University of Houston, in the wake of the Me Too movement found that the results might not be as beneficial to women as many had hoped. The 2018 survey indicated,

> Twenty-two percent of men and 44% of women predicted that men would be more apt to exclude women from social interactions, such as after-work drinks; and nearly one in three men thought they would be reluctant to have a one-on-one meeting with a woman.[27]

The follow-up survey in 2019 reported a significant negative impact,

> For instance, 19% of men said they were reluctant to hire attractive women, 21% said they were reluctant to hire women for jobs involving close interpersonal interactions with men (jobs involving travel, say), and 27% said they avoided one-on-one meetings with female colleagues.[28]

This research suggests that rather than leadership modifying behaviors and creating cultures and work environments that support women, the impact has been to limit access, options and opportunities for women. The system has been rewired to increasingly shut the door for women as a means of minimizing sexual harassment making the victim the bearer of the burden rather than the perpetrator. The power imbalance remains as does the risk to the victim's career and livelihood.

Women, especially mothers and other caregivers, have been put under tremendous stress during the COVID-19 pandemic. As a mother, I often joke with my women colleagues, who are also mothers, that we are all like ducks on a pond with our legs going a million miles an hour below the surface to keep our heads above water. With the COVID-19 pandemic, it has not been possible to keep up this pace as working mothers have lost their support systems – childcare, babysitting, school, etc. As a result, women of all ages and levels are leaving the workforce – many permanently. A new term, "she-cession," has been coined to describe this phenomenon. The economic impact for women is significant as leaving the labor force to take care of children or another family member lowers a women's lifetime earnings, retirement savings, and future career opportunities. [29] Often, women chose to leave the workforce because their partner earns a higher income. When faced with which partner must remain at home to provide caregiving during the pandemic, the agreed upon choice is the lower income earner. As a result of the gender pay gap, this person is more likely to be a woman. Childcare and other caregiving demands remain a pressing long-term issue for working women as the bulk of this unpaid work falls predominately to women in our society.

Women have been disproportionally impacted by job loss during the pandemic with the unemployment rate for adult women rising from 3% in February to 15% by April of 2020.[30] The corresponding rate for men was 13%.[31] Women of color have been especially hard hit because they make up a significant portion of the labor force in industries directly impacted by the pandemic – retail, hospitality, leisure. The unemployment rates for Black women and Latina women were even higher at 16.1% and 20.2%, respectively.[32] These levels of unemployment for women are a reversal of the gains that they have made in recent years. Women comprise much of the workforce for the rapidly growing leisure, hospitality, education, and healthcare industries. Their loss of jobs is further compounded by a lack of safety net as many of these jobs were at low wage rates. The gender wealth gap is making these vulnerable women and the families they support even more vulnerable during this pandemic.

While we have had the Me Too movement, we have yet to see the elimination of the power imbalance and other systemic barriers for women especially women of color in our workplaces. The pandemic has shed light on systemic problems that have always existed, but were masked.

3.4 Pay and Wealth Gap

The gender pay gap has been narrowing over the past 40 years as women have increased their education, work experience, and chosen higher paying occupations. Yet, women still make only up to 85% of what men make as defined by median salaries.[33] Other studies put this figure at 81% to 82% depending upon the data included in the analysis. Factors that explain the continuing differential in compensation between genders include gender discrimination such as receiving unequal pay for the same job, being excluded from important assignments and projects, or being treated as if not competent, and being passed over for a promotion. Other factors such as caregiver responsibilities, especially childcare, require women to take breaks in their careers resulting in offtrack career paths and lower earnings. In addition, women tend to make up the largest percentage of lower paying occupations further lowering the average pay for women. Lower pay rates for women translate into higher poverty rates for families. If working women received equal pay to men, poverty rates would be decreased by 50% and the U.S. economy would add $482 billion.[34]

While the overall gender wage gap is a serious issue, the wage gap for women of color is even more startling. Black women earn 62 cents for every dollar a man makes. Indigenous and Hispanic women earn even less at 57 cents and 52 cents, respectively. (These figures are derived from comparing 2018 earnings for full-time year-round workers.) Equal Pay Day is the date that symbolizes how long into the subsequent year women must work to earn what men did in the previous year. It serves as a public awareness event to demonstrate the gap between men's and women's wages. Reflecting on these wage differences over a lifetime gives perspective to the magnitude of the issue. Over a 40-year period, gender wage differentials for an individual can exceed $1 million depending upon the occupational category. While these statistics look at the intersectionality of race and gender, there are additional factors such as being a member of the LGBTQ+ community or being in a subsection of a larger racial category that also impact earnings. The bottom line is that there is much work that remains to be done to address gender and race related pay differentials.

EQUAL PAY LEGISLATION

To combat the pay gap, many states have passed laws requiring pay equality. In 2018, New Jersey passed the Diane B. Allen Equal Pay Act requiring pay equity across all protected categories including race, gender identity or expression, national origin, disability, age, marital status, pregnancy, and sexual orientation, and other protected classes as part of the state's anti-discrimination laws. The law allows employees to recoup up to 6 years of back pay, and the clock restarts each pay period that the employee receives compensation that is deemed to be the result of a discriminatory decision. The law also prohibits retaliation against employees for discussing their compensation with others. Employers that have contracts with the state of New Jersey must report information regarding compensation broken down by gender, race, ethnicity, and job category. Employers can justify pay differentials based on a seniority or merit system or on bona fide factors such as training, education, and experience if the factors are job related, reasonable, and based on a business requirement.

The wealth gap between America's richest and poorest families has more than doubled since 1989. Middle-class incomes have grown at significantly slower rates than upper-tier incomes with the share of adult households living in middle-income households falling from 61% in 1971 to 51% in 2019.[35] Since the Great Recession in 2007, the only group to have gained wealth is families with incomes in top 5% category. Compared to its peers in the Group of 7 (G7) nations – Canada, France, Germany, Italy, Japan, the U.K., and the U.S., income inequality in the U.S. is the highest of the G7 nations. It turns out that many people feel as if we are not doing as well as we were in the late 1990s and the early 2000s, and this data verifies their experiences.

For Black, Hispanic, and Indigenous Americans, the wealth and pay differentials are even greater. Table 3.2 provides data on workforce composition and earnings of racial and ethnic minorities compared to a benchmark of $1.00 for White workers. While Asian Americans exceeded the benchmark at $1.12 in earnings for every $1.00 earned by White workers, all other racial and ethnic minorities earn less. While the wage differential reported for Asian workers tends to reinforce the model minority myth in which a very diverse group is seen as a homogeneous group that is smart, wealthy, hard-working and uniformly successful, we will discuss this bias further in Chapter 8. These earnings differentials impact standards of living, health, wellness, education accessibility, and financial security. Over a lifetime, earnings differentials impact the amount that an individual can save and invest further impacting both income and wealth accumulation for future generations.

While discrimination and earnings differentials account for a portion of the wealth gap between White and Black Americans, there are a variety of other factors contributing to the wealth gap including homeownership, access to higher education, terms of and access to credit, living conditions, poverty rates, and intergenerational wealth transfer. If the wealth gap for Black people had been closed 20 years ago, the U.S. GDP could have benefitted by an estimated $16 trillion. Closing the wealth gap today could add $5 trillion to the U.S. economy over the next 5 years.[36] The gap between White and Black families' household net worth, which is defined as total assets less total liabilities, remains significant. Based on Federal Reserve data,

Table 3.2 Workforce Composition and Earnings

Race/Ethnicity	Percentage of Workforce	Earnings/Dollar
White	63%	1.00
Hispanic/Latino	17%	0.73
Black	11%	0.76
Asian	7%	1.12
Multiracial/Other	2%	0.81

Source: "Earnings Disparities by Race and Ethnicity | U.S. Department of Labor," accessed October 28, 2020, https://www.dol.gov/agencies/ofccp/about/data/earnings/race-and-ethnicity.

Black families' average net worth has been in the $15,000 to $25,000 range over the last 30 years. For the same period, average net worth for White families has been in the range of $115,000 and $200,000. The average wealth gap multiple is eight times. With each passing generation, the impact is magnified as generational transfer of wealth compounds the differential.

Many of these underlying systemic problems have been laid bare by the pandemic. In terms of access to credit, the Cares Act of 2020 and the Paycheck Protection Program (PPP) were enacted to provide protections for the most vulnerable citizens. The PPP was designed to provides loans to small and mid-size organizations experiencing business loss and disruption because of the pandemic. In its first iteration, it had suboptimal performance in distributing loans to minority owned businesses. Many minority business owners did not have relationships with the financial institutions that were empowered to offer these loans. As a result, they were unable to apply for PPP loans. While in the second round of PPP, minority business fared better and the results evened out, the systemic problem of access to lending institutions for minorities was clearly highlighted. There has been a long history of lack of access for BIPOC community members to financial institutions for loans to support businesses and mortgages to support home ownership. Access to credit and capital for women and members of BIPOC communities is an area that requires significant change to level the playing field for pay equity and wealth accumulation.

3.5 Including People with Disabilities

In 2019, less than 20% of people with a disability were employed compared to 66% of people without a disability.[37] The prevalence of disability as a percentage of population continues to be higher for people classifying themselves as Black and White than for those classifying as Hispanics and Asians. In the U.S., the Equal Employment Opportunity Commission (EEOC) requires Reasonable Accommodation, which means that employers are required to provide accommodations such as modifications to the work environment or adjustments in how and when a job is performed. These may include:

- Making existing facilities accessible
- Restructuring of jobs
- Offering part-time or modified work schedules
- Acquiring or adapting equipment
- Modifying tests, training materials, or policies
- Supplying qualified readers or interpreters
- Offering reassignment to a vacant position[38]

Despite organizations offering reasonable accommodations, people with disabilities face many stigmas in the workplace. Best practices suggest that organizations focus on changing their culture and work practices and policies to create a culture of belonging for people with disabilities. Some organizations are focusing on changing the paradigm to provide a more equal playing field for people with disabilities, and they are finding that tapping into a broader talent pool that includes people with disabilities provides a competitive advantage.

AUTISM 2 WORK

CAI is a program and project management and technical contracting staffing agency. As part of their culture, they believe that making the world a more equitable and just place is part of their mission for their customers, employees, and communities. CAI has a disability inclusion program called Autism 2 Work (A2W) that embraces employees with autism and provides meaningful job opportunities through contract work with clients. The program begins with training and mentoring for workers diagnosed with autism spectrum disorder (ASD). Once ready, these employees are assigned to clients for positions in IT, legal, accounting, and business operations. In addition, they are supported through ongoing workplace coaching to help them become a valued team member. The A2W program was developed by DisabilityIN.

DisabilityIN (https://disabilityin.org) is a non-profit resource for business disability inclusion worldwide with a network of over 220 corporations offering opportunities for people with disabilities. They host an Disability:IN Global Roundtables whose members include IBM, Deloitte, E&Y, HP, Microsoft, CAI, and many other leading organizations. The A2W program leverages key skills and strengths that individuals diagnosed with ASD demonstrate including attention to detail, concentration, problem-solving skills, and pattern recognition.[39]

Through the A2W program, CAI partners with other business and educational institutions who have identified expanding neurodiversity within their workforce as an organizational goal. Through the structure and support systems built into this program, CAI provides clients with valuable employees who meet their business needs while enhancing organizational diversity. Several of their clients are recognized as a Best Place to Work by the Disability Equity Index. This index considers an organization's culture, leadership, enterprise-wide access, employment practices such as benefits, recruitment, employment, education, retention, advancement and accommodations, community engagement, and supplier diversity in their assessment and rankings.

Creating an inclusive work environment for all is not only the right thing to do, it also creates a competitive advantage by building a workforce with a wide variety of skill sets, knowledge, experiences, and thought processes. It also provides employers with a pool of top talent for technical roles, which are often hard for recruiters to fill.

3.6 Ageism

While the Age Discrimination in Employment Act (ADEA) prohibits discrimination against anyone over 40, age discrimination remains a challenge for older employees, their families, and the economy. Many older workers who lost their jobs during the Great Recession either never reentered the workforce or had to accept positions with lower compensation. Older workers are often more familiar with the corporate ladder vs. the more common corporate lattice of today's work environment. With five generations currently in the workplace, navigating generational requirements can be complex. While many younger employees consider older employees to be less valuable, evidence shows that creating work groups that combine older and younger workers delivers better outcomes and improves intergenerational perceptions. Older workers have different experiences and skills than younger workers.[40] These skills can be of significant organizational value if leveraged effectively.

Unfortunately, organizational workforce development structures aren't always aligned to support ongoing training and development of older workers. Some retraining efforts require significant time and even outlays of personal funds to retrain in digital and or technical fields. Older workers may have competing priorities for family resources like children attending college. Often, it is not possible for workers to leave the workforce to train in a new area such as data science or coding because of their other responsibilities. As organizational leaders, we need to plan workforce requirements including skills and consider the resources and work structures needed to support employee development and growth.

From a macroeconomic perspective, older workers leaving the workforce too early without sufficient investments and income for retirement place a greater burden on society and social programs. As the Baby Boomers retire, we have large numbers of people entering the Social Security and Medicare systems. Keeping older workers actively working reduces stress on those systems. In addition, early retirement often creates significant institutional knowledge loss. There are benefits to organizations and to the economy to keeping older workers employed longer especially with improving mortality rates and less private retirement support.

AT&T: RESKILLING THE WORKFORCE FOR THE FUTURE OF WORK

AT&T made a strategic pivot to wireless technology requiring a workforce with cloud computing and digital skill, but the majority of its 250,000-person workforce had skills that were based on decades of working on infrastructure of cables and hardware. To meet this demand, leadership faced a decision to hire new talent with these skills or to retrain its existing workforce. Their decision was to retain the existing work force and they launched a retraining initiative called Workforce 2020 to build skills to make their employees future ready. Part of their decision was based on the availability of desired skills in the outside labor pool. Their internal labor pool included unions, and the average employee tenure was over 12 years.

Through a workforce planning initiative, jobs were consolidated and redefined to reflect the new skills required to support their digital transformation. Approximately 100,000 jobs would be eliminated in the coming decade.[41] These roles supported old technology that would be sunsetted as new platforms and technologies emerged. Workers that had been with the company for over 25 years had to decide whether to learn new skills such as data science, engineering, math, and technology or to retire when the company retired the hardware on which they had spent their career.

Performance metrics were streamlined and focused on contribution to business goals. Performance expectations were increased and compensation plans were redesigned to deemphasize seniority and prioritize performance. Compensation plans were structured to reward high performers and those with in-demand skills. The frameworks for success and achievement for employees were reformulated.

To facilitate the transformation, AT&T provided employees with a platform of tools for performance management, career development, and talent planning to help them better assess their skills, skills gaps, and to offer potential opportunities to gain these skills. A variety of tools were leveraged to help employees bridge their skills gap including online classes, certifications, and degree programs. The programs required employees to dedicate their personal time for retraining, but AT&T reimbursed a significant portion of the cost of retraining. [42] For many workers this retraining created opportunities that were lateral, diagonal, or even descending within the corporate structure.

While the AT&T massive retraining program to retool its workforce for the future of work was truly transformative, it raised concerns for workers. Some workers were concerned about returning to school, taking classes on their own time, and being responsible for their own training and development. Many of the union jobs that were cable and hardware related required an entirely different aptitude and skill set than those for cloud computing roles.

> According to the company, more than half of its employees have completed 2.7 million online courses in areas such as data science, cybersecurity, Agile project management and computer science. The company has awarded 177,000 virtual "badges" to about 57,000 employees on their internal career profile pages, indicating they've completed the coursework. Further, about 475 AT&T employees have enrolled in Georgia Tech's online Master of Science in computer science program, and nearly 80 have graduated.[43]

Those employees training for in-demand jobs such as data scientist, computer analytics, app developers, and cloud computing roles are twice as likely to be hired into these new roles offering career advancement and job security.

For older employees, reskilling with outside programs may require brushing off their academic skills in a way that many have not used in decades. Existing training and development programs were shorter and more targeted in design for a specific skill and allowed for a quick return to work. Undertaking a new degree program, often requires a reduction in workload that needs to be discussed with managers in order balance their office and school workloads. In addition, older workers often have childcare or elder care responsibilities that fill personal time. The reimbursement structure also serves as a barrier as financing the training for degree programs upfront is cost prohibitive for some employees because of lack of savings, low wages, and wealth gap issues. Other employees are contributing to their children's education and do not have extra savings for retraining.

Many organizations face this need for massive workforce upskilling; yet few have undertaken the holistic approach that AT&T launched suggesting labor shortages and layoffs to come especially for older workers. While AT&T should be applauded for their extensive workforce planning and retraining initiatives, this type of massive employee reskilling is not without pain for both employer and employees, especially older workers.

Ageism occurs in a number of areas such as recruitment, hiring, on the job bias, and termination. When applying for jobs, candidates may be eliminated based on indicators of age which can be identified based on language usage or even resume formatting. When working, older workers are often overlooked for training opportunities, stretch assignments, and promotions. Some older workers share that they have been moved to lesser roles to make way for younger people. During economic downturns, organizations often use the opportunity to layoff older more senior employees or offer early retirement programs. Our bias in the U.S. is toward youth. The fastest growing sector of the economy is technology companies, and they favor a youthful workforce. "According to a 2016 report by Statista, the average median employee age at 17 top tech companies was 32, compared with 42 for the total U.S. workforce."[44] Google paid $11 million in 2019 to settle the claims by over 200 job applicant claiming age discrimination.[45] As part of the settlement, Google agreed to train managers on ageism and to create a committee focused on improving age diversity in its workplace. Like other systemic biases, ageism is so pervasive in our workplace culture that it is often invisible to those not directly experiencing it. Organizations must reconsider their policies and programs to offer support to the many generations in the workplace including those in the over 40 category who may need different resources than younger workers.

3.7 LGBTQ+ Rights and the Ongoing Journey for Equity

In the past several decades, we have seen tremendous progress in rights for the lesbian, gay, bisexual, transgender, queer or questioning (LGBTQ+)community in the U.S. such as eliminating Don't Ask Don't Tell from the military, allowing gay marriage, and new protective legislation for LGBTQ+ rights. In 2020, the Supreme Court of the U.S. (SCOTUS) ruled that the 1964 Civil Rights Act protects gay, lesbian, and transgender employees from workplace discrimination based on gender identity or sexual orientation. While this ruling is historic for the LGBTQ+ community, systemic challenges remain.

Equity for the LGBTQ+ community is very uneven depending upon the state that one is a resident. A study conducted by 24/7 Wall St. ranks each of the states based on an index of three measures – hate crimes motivated by gender identity or sexual orientation, laws protecting the LGBTQ+ community, and the percentage of the state's population identifying as belonging to the LGBTQ+ community. The top three states for members of the LGBTQ+ community are Nevada, Vermont, and New York. Each of these states had higher percentages of LGBTQ+ identifying residents and a higher number of Pride centers to support the LGBTQ+ community. They also have extensive non-discrimination laws. Nevada has a lower percentage of hate crimes motivated by gender identity or sexual orientation. It also has a high percentage of laws suggested by the Human Rights Campaign for LGBTQ+ rights, such as non-discrimination laws, parenting laws, statutes against hate crimes, and those ensuring protections for healthcare system access. From 2009 to 2019, Nevada passed 34 laws protecting the rights and safety of its LGBTQ+ citizens. Vermont offers some of the most comprehensive health and safety laws for LGBTQ+ residents ensuring that transgender people cannot be excluded from healthcare. It collects data on the health and well-being of LGBTQ+ youth and adults as well.[46]

At the other end of the spectrum are Alabama, Wyoming, and Montana. Alabama has few laws that positively impact the LGTBQ+ community. It is hard to track hate crimes motivated by gender identity or sexual orientation as police do not participate in reporting on them. Inclusion of LGBTQ+ topics is restricted in schools. In addition, Alabama joins with 26 other states in criminalizing behaviors that carry low or negligible risk of HIV transmission. In Montana, LGBTQ+ residents face challenges as the state legislature has not passed non-discrimination protections based on gender identity for employment, housing, public accommodations, education, adoption, foster care, insurance, credit, or jury selection.[47]

Equity in terms of access to services, employment, quality of life, pay equity vary greatly based on the state in which an individual that identifies as LGBTQ+ resides. Even if employees are safe in their work environments based on the SCOTUS ruling, LGBTQ+ community members may not be able to live and thrive in their local communities. Many in the LGBTQ+ community have fewer employment opportunities that pay a living wage. Before COVID-19, the national unemployment rate was very low at 3.6%, but the unemployment rate for LGBTQ+ workers remained high at 9%.[48] The unemployment numbers are even worse in a state like Wyoming, which has a low LGBTQ+ equity index, with unemployment numbers reported at 17% for members of the LGBTQ+ population.[49] This high level of unemployment is reflected in disproportionally high rates of food insecurity and uninsured for the LGBTQ+ community. While the LGBTQ+ community has made many strides over the past several decades, many issues remain for members of this community in terms of access and equity across the U.S. Fundamentally, these barriers impact where and how members of the LGBTQ+ community live in the U.S.

For disabled LGBTQ+ people, the challenges are compounded by this intersectionality. Accessing affordable, accessible, and inclusive healthcare, community services, and other services is challenging for LGBTQ+ people with disabilities. Employment discrimination is a significant barrier as we already know the high unemployment figures for people with disabilities without the added impact of discrimination from identifying as a LGBTQ+ person. Research suggests that LGBTQ+ and gender non-conforming youth and LGBTQ+ people are greatly overrepresented in the criminal and juvenile justice systems, as are people with disabilities and POC.[50] Bullying and exclusion for LGBTQ+ youth with disabilities occurs at significantly higher rates impacting their ability to remain and thrive in school. Research finds that experiences of discrimination based on sexual orientation, gender identity, race, ethnicity, disability status, prejudice, barriers to competent healthcare, lower rates of health insurance, poverty, and experiences of violence contribute more to mental health conditions in this group. Mental health issues for LGBTQ+ youth include higher rates of depression, anxiety, and substance use disorders.[51] As we think about improving access and removing barriers to allow all people to bring their full selves to work, it is imperative that we consider individuals' intersectionalities, which reflect their multiple identities including factors such as race, gender identity, education, and socio-economic status. An individual's intersectionality can either enhance their privilege or conversely compound their disadvantage.

3.8 Non-Binary and Transgender Rights

Non-binary and transgender people face discrimination in society and in the workplace. Often, their very lives are in danger. From legal rights to social services to workplaces, we need to make members of the non-binary and transgender communities' lives safer, healthier, and better. Even accessing medical services can be fraught with trauma if the healthcare institution has not developed protocols that respect gender identities, gender expression, and sexual orientation.

According to National Center for Transgender Equality, the term non-binary is used to describe people who do not fall into our society's traditional male or female gender binary categories. "Some people have a gender that blends elements of being a man or a woman, or a gender that is different than either male or female. Some people don't identify with any gender. Some people's gender changes over time."[52] Other terms used by people who identify in the manner include genderqueer, agender, and bigender. Here are some basic facts about non-binary people:

1. Non-binary people are not a new fad. Non-binary identities have existed for millennia, and they have been recognized globally by cultures and societies.
2. Some non-binary people undergo medical procedures to more align their body with their gender identity.
3. Transgender people are not necessarily non-binary. Most transgender people have a gender identity that is either male or female.
4. Non-binary people differ from intersex people, who have anatomy or genes that don't align with typical definitions of male and female.[53]

Transgender people are those who know themselves to be one gender, but who were labeled a different gender at birth. Gender identity is the gender that a person recognizes themselves to be. Gender expression is how a person represents their gender through behavior, clothing, hairstyles, and body characteristics. By recognizing a transgender person's gender identity, you are treating them with respect. Regardless of a transgender person's stage of transition, it is important to respect their identities including using their preferred name and pronouns. (Pronouns are outlined in the J.E.D.I. Primer.) While many transgender people identify their gender as either male or female, some do not and identify their gender as non-binary or genderqueer.[54]

Becoming an ally for supporting transgender and non-binary people means being open to the needs of that individual. Both the transgender and non-binary communities include a diverse representation and everyone has a unique intersectionality of identifying factors and therefore individuals have different needs and requirements in the workplace. For example, a Black, transgender woman, living in poverty has very different needs than a White, transgender man, who is a technology executive. Best practices include using the same terms and language that the individual uses for themselves. In conversation, listen to the pronouns that they use to describe themselves. In meetings, you can ask that pronouns be shared as part of introductions to level the playing field for all participants. Sharing your own pronouns as part of your regular introduction is another good way to socialize pronoun normalization. In many cases, you will not know that someone is transgender so making gender identity a routine part of the introductory process helps to alleviate awkwardness and promotes belonging. A best practice to build a culture of inclusion is to speak respectfully to everyone and to be open to listening and learning more about who colleagues and employees are as individuals.

While you may be curious about a transgender colleague or a friend's experiences, please be considerate about the types of questions that you ask. It is not appropriate to ask about:

- Birth names or photos pretransition
- Types of hormones being taken
- Types of surgeries
- Sexual relationships

Please recognize that someone's gender identity is their private information to share or not to share. If a friend or colleague has shared their identity as transgender with you, respect their privacy and do not share this information with others. Act as an ally to the transgender community by supporting transgender people and their rights, speaking out when you see discrimination, and modeling behavior that aligns with these recommendations. Encourage representation of transgender people as guest speakers or in other capacities as appropriate in your work environment, community, and industry. In short, act as an ally to ensure that transgender people are included and valued not just tolerated.

From an organizational and societal level, we need to go further. Organizations must reevaluate their protocols including forms and documents requesting gender data. When collecting demographic data that relates to gender identity, make sure that options are provided for gender identification by members of the transgender and non-binary communities. From an organizational access perspective, ensure that everyone has a safe bathroom and other gender specific facilities such as locker rooms to use. If you have an Employee Resource Group (ERG) that supports the transgender community, empower them to invite transgender speakers for the organization and to promote not for profits supporting the transgender community for organizational support. The National Center for Transgender Equality has many resources to support building a more inclusive work and societal environment for transgender and non-binary people (https://transequality.org/). The best advice is to look at your policies, processes, and requirements to determine if they are inclusive to all people. In addition to being the right thing to do, a growing segment of the workforce identifies as a gender other than male or female. Organizations that want to recruit and retain top talent especially with the millennial and Gen Z generations must build gender inclusive workplaces to remain competitive.[55]

3.9 Understanding the Impacts of Intersectionality

Intersectionality is defined as "the complex, cumulative way in which the effects of multiple forms of discrimination (such as racism, sexism, and classism) combine, overlap, or intersect especially in the experiences of marginalized individuals or groups."[56] Figure 3.1 depicts how these identifiers overlap to impact individual experience, access, privilege, or disadvantage. The concept of intersectionality was developed by Kimberlé Crenshaw and based on the concepts found in Black feminism and Critical Race Theory, which addresses the marginalization of Black women in

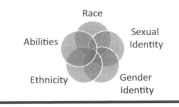

Figure 3.1   Intersectionality.

anti-discrimination law as well as in feminist and anti-racist theory and politics.[57] Since the introduction of the concept, activist, DEI practitioners, and researchers have expanded the concept to encompass a broader range of issues, identities, social identities, and power dynamics. In thinking about intersectionality, it helps to consider the interconnectivity in social categorizations such as race, class, and gender identity within an individual or a larger group and the impact these intersections have in creating overlapping and interdependent systems of discrimination or disadvantage.

Many different groups have been discussed in this chapter, intersectionality comes into play in considering the multiple layers of discrimination an individual or group of individuals face within society. For example, a Black, female, lesbian, who is on the autism spectrum faces discrimination and disadvantages on compounded levels and fronts because of their intersectionality. Unfortunately, the likelihood is that they will experience greater disadvantage and oppression than an individual that falls into a singular identification group. The lived experience of someone based on their intersectionality can vary significantly from other members of an identity group. As we develop policies and programs to address diversity, equity, and inclusion, it is important to consider the impact of intersectionality. Building inclusive and equitable organizations requires creating a culture of belonging for all. This focus reframes the concept of a dominate culture to which all must conform to an equitable culture in which all have access, opportunity, and belonging.

3.10 Summary

We continue to talk about diversity, equity, and inclusion because driving systemic change is hard and long-term work. It requires all of us to engage and to do the work. We need to take the time to understand origins and long history of systemic barriers in our society and how these barriers are reflected in the workplace. Until we spend the time, money, and resources to drive systemic change, we will continue to talk about J.E.D.I. related issues rather than create an action plan to drive meaningful change toward a more equitable and just society.

We have highlighted historical events, legal challenges, social barriers, and other discriminatory patterns that have created power and privilege for predominately White people and left many BIPOC people with very little opportunity, access, or hope. The events, data, and trends highlighted detail the long history of inequity against minorities and privilege for primarily White, heteronormative people. While there is much more that can be written about racism, sexism, ageism, ableism, heterosexism, and classism, these inequities have created systemic barriers that must be proactively addressed to create equitable cultures within our workplaces. White privilege creates inequities in access to basic services resulting in health and education divides as well as lack of opportunities generating pay and wealth gaps. Gaining insights into our nation's long history of inequity provides insight into how embedded these beliefs and values are in our cultural norms and allows us to focus on driving meaningful change to reshape our values and norms driving impactful systemic change. We will begin the process of taking a deeper dive into driving organizational change and the interconnectivity of organizations and social systems.

Questions

1. Before reading the chapter, how familiar are you with history of racism and slavery in the U.S.?
2. What was the most surprising fact to learn?
3. How do you believe racism and White privilege contributed to a POC wealth gap?
4. Given the history covered in this chapter, do you feel that affirmative action programs are justified?
5. How would you explain the use of affirmative action programs to someone who feels that everyone should be given equitable resources? (Hint: the J.E.D.I. Primer)
6. Given the "MeToo" movement and the "She-cession" from the COVID-19 pandemic, what do you expect the representation of women in the U.S. workforce to look like in the next 3–5 years? Why?
7. How do you think we can make workplaces more accessible and inclusive to people with disabilities?
8. If you were a member of an ERG with a mission of being allies to members of the LGBTQ+ community, what would be your top three asks of leadership?
9. How do you think organizations can make people who identify themselves as transgender and non-binary feel as if they belong in their workplace?
10. How do you think intersectionality increases discrimination and disadvantage? What are some ideas to address these challenges?

Notes

1 Stephen B. Young, "Slavery: A Widespread Affliction Form Middle Ages to 19th Century Abolition" XI, no. VII (July 2020).
2 "This Far by Faith. 1526–1775: From AFRICA to AMERICA | PBS," accessed October 23, 2020, https://www.pbs.org/thisfarbyfaith/journey_1/p_6.html.

3 "This Far by Faith. 1526–1775: From AFRICA to AMERICA | PBS."

4 "15.5: The Constitutional Convention and Federal Constitution," Social Sci LibreTexts, July 1, 2020, https://socialsci.libretexts.org/Courses/Lumen_Learning/Book%3A_United_States_History_I%3A_OpenStax_(Lumen)/15%3A_Module_7%3A_Creating_a_Government_(1776%E2%80%931783)/15.5%3A_The_Constitutional_Convention_and_Federal_Constitution.

5 "Historically Black Colleges and Universities and Higher Education Desegregation," Policy Guidance; Guides (US Department of Education (ED), January 10, 2020), https://www2.ed.gov/about/offices/list/ocr/docs/hq9511.html.

6 Prison Policy Initiative and Wendy Sawyer and Peter Wagner, "Mass Incarceration: The Whole Pie 2020," accessed October 23, 2020, https://www.prisonpolicy.org/reports/pie2020.html.

7 "Report to the United Nations on Racial Disparities in the U.S. Criminal Justice System," The Sentencing Project, accessed October 23, 2020, https://www.sentencingproject.org/publications/un-report-on-racial-disparities/.

8 "School-to-Prison Pipeline," American Civil Liberties Union, accessed June 25, 2021, https://www.aclu.org/issues/juvenile-justice/school-prison-pipeline.

9 "Historically Black Colleges and Universities and Higher Education Desegregation," Policy Guidance; Guides (U.S. Department of Education (ED), January 10, 2020), https://www2.ed.gov/about/offices/list/ocr/docs/hq9511.html.

10 "Historically Black Colleges and Universities and Higher Education Desegregation."

11 "Abbotts – History of Funding Equity," accessed October 22, 2020, https://www.state.nj.us/education/archive/abbotts/chrono/.

12 Jan Hoffman and Chang W. Lee, "I Won't Be Used as a Guinea Pig for White People," *The New York Times*, October 7, 2020, sec. Health, https://www.nytimes.com/2020/10/07/health/coronavirus-vaccine-trials-african-americans.html.

13 "Tuskegee Study – Timeline – CDC – NCHHSTP," July 16, 2020, https://www.cdc.gov/tuskegee/timeline.htm.

14 Rashawn Ray and Andre M. Perry, "Why We Need Reparations for Black Americans," *Brookings* (blog), April 15, 2020, https://www.brookings.edu/policy2020/bigideas/why-we-need-reparations-for-black-americans/.

15 Heather Haddon, "McDonald's Seeks Dismissal of Discrimination Lawsuit Filed by Black Former Franchisees," *Wall Street Journal*, October 23, 2020, sec. Business, https://www.wsj.com/articles/mcdonalds-seeks-dismissal-of-discrimination-lawsuit-filed-by-black-former-franchisees-11603476224.

16 "U.S. Census Bureau QuickFacts: Philadelphia City, Pennsylvania," accessed October 26, 2020, https://www.census.gov/quickfacts/philadelphiacitypennsylvania.

17 Oona Goodin-Smith Hardnett Anna Orso, Raishad, "Philadelphia Black Lives Matter Activists Say the Historic Summer of Protests Was Only the Beginning," https://www.inquirer.com, accessed October 26, 2020, https://www.inquirer.com/news/philadelphia/a/philadelphia-defund-police-black-lives-matter-20201021.html.

18 Hardnett.

19 "The City That Really Did Abolish the Police – POLITICO," accessed October 23, 2020, https://www.politico.com/news/magazine/2020/06/12/camden-policing-reforms-313750.

20 Frank Dobbin and Alexandra Kalev, "Why Sexual Harassment Programs Backfire," *Harvard Business Review*, May 1, 2020, https://hbr.org/2020/05/confronting-sexual-harassment.

21 Dobbin and Kalev.

22 Dobbin and Kalev.

23 "Are Women Really No Better off in the Workplace after #MeToo?," DiversityJobs.com, December 16, 2019, https://www.diversityjobs.com/2019/12/women-in-the-workplace-metoo/.

24 David Yaffe-Bellany, "McDonald's Fires C.E.O. Steve Easterbrook After Relationship With Employee (Published 2019)," *The New York Times*, November 3, 2019, sec. Business, https://www.nytimes.com/2019/11/03/business/mcdonalds-ceo-fired-steve-easterbrook.html.

25 David Enrich and Rachel Abrams, "McDonald's Sues Former C.E.O., Accusing Him of Lying and Fraud," *The New York Times*, August 10, 2020, sec. Business, https://www.nytimes.com/2020/08/10/business/mcdonalds-ceo-steve-easterbrook.html.

26 "McDonald's CEO Made 1,939 Times as Much as Average Worker in 2019 – Business Insider," accessed November 9, 2020, https://www.businessinsider.com/mcdonalds-ceo-made-1939-times-as-much-average-worker-2019-2020-4.

27 "The #MeToo Backlash," *Harvard Business Review*, September 1, 2019, https://hbr.org/2019/09/the-metoo-backlash.

28 "The #MeToo Backlash."

29 Podcasts, Wharton Business Daily, and North America, "How the Pandemic Is Affecting Working Mothers," Knowledge@Wharton, accessed October 22, 2020, https://knowledge.wharton.upenn.edu/article/how-the-pandemic-is-affecting-working-mothers/

30 Alisha Haridasani Gupta, "Why Some Women Call This Recession a 'Shecession,'" *The New York Times*, May 13, 2020, sec. U.S., https://www.nytimes.com/2020/05/09/us/unemployment-coronavirus-women.html.

31 Gupta.

32 Gupta.

33 1615 L. St NW, Suite 800Washington, and DC 20036USA202-419-4300 | Main202-857-8562 | Fax202-419-4372 | Media Inquiries, "The Narrowing, but Persistent, Gender Gap in Pay," *Pew Research Center* (blog), accessed October 26, 2020, https://www.pewresearch.org/fact-tank/2019/03/22/gender-pay-gap-facts/.

34 "The Economic Impact of Equal Pay by State," Women in the States, February 24, 2016, https://statusofwomendata.org/featured/the-economic-impact-of-equal-pay-by-state/.

35 1615 L. St NW, Suite 800Washington, and DC 20036USA202-419-4300 | Main202-857-8562 | Fax202-419-4372 | Media Inquiries, "6 Facts about Economic Inequality in the U.S.," *Pew Research Center* (blog), accessed October 27, 2020, https://www.pewresearch.org/fact-tank/2020/02/07/6-facts-about-economic-inequality-in-the-u-s/.

36 "Boyle – 2020 – CLOSING THE RACIAL INEQUALITY GAPS The Economic C.Pdf," accessed September 23, 2020, https://ir.citi.com/NvIUklHPilz14Hwd3oxq ZBLMn1_XPqo5FrxsZD0x6hhil84ZxaxEuJUWmak51UHvYk75VKeHCMI%3D.

37 "Persons with a Disability: Labor Force Characteristics Summary," accessed October 26, 2020, https://www.bls.gov/news.release/disabl.nr0.htm.

38 "Enforcement Guidance on Reasonable Accommodation and Undue Hardship under the ADA | U.S. Equal Employment Opportunity Commission," accessed October 27, 2020, https://www.eeoc.gov/laws/guidance/enforcement-guidance-reasonable-accommodation-and-undue-hardship-under-ada.

39 "Autism2Work," CAI, accessed October 27, 2020, https://www.cai.io/capabilities/autism2work/.

40 "WHO | Ageism in the Workplace," WHO (World Health Organization), accessed October 27, 2020, http://www.who.int/ageing/features/workplace-ageism/en/.

41 Susan Caminiti CNBC.com special to, "AT&T's $1 Billion Gambit: Retraining Nearly Half Its Workforce for Jobs of the Future," CNBC, March 13, 2018, https://www.cnbc.com/2018/03/13/atts-1-billion-gambit-retraining-nearly-half-its-workforce.html.

42 John Donovan and Cathy Benko, "AT&T's Talent Overhaul," *Harvard Business Review*, October 1, 2016, https://hbr.org/2016/10/atts-talent-overhaul.

43 CNBC.com, "AT&T's $1 Billion Gambit."

44 Joe Kita, "Age Discrimination Still Thrives in America," AARP, accessed October 28, 2020, http://www.aarp.org/work/working-at-50-plus/info-2019/age-discrimination-in-america.html.

45 Kent Allen, "Google Settles Age Discrimination Lawsuit," AARP, accessed October 28, 2020, http://www.aarp.org/work/working-at-50-plus/info-2019/age-discrimination-google-lawsuit.html.

46 Hristina Byrnes Suneson John Harrington and Grant, "Supreme Court Decision aside, Some States Are Better – and Some Are Worse – for LGBTQ Community," *USA TODAY*, accessed November 5, 2020, https://www.usatoday.com/story/money/2020/06/19/the-best-and-worst-states-for-lgbtq-people/111968524/.

47 Suneson.

48 Suneson.

49 "LGBT Data & Demographics – The Williams Institute," accessed November 5, 2020, https://williamsinstitute.law.ucla.edu/visualization/lgbt-stats/?topic=LGBT#density.

50 "LGBT People with Disabilities," n.d., 4.

51 "LGBT People with Disabilities."

52 "Understanding Non-Binary People: How to Be Respectful and Supportive," National Center for Transgender Equality, July 9, 2016, https://transequality.org/issues/resources/understanding-non-binary-people-how-to-be-respectful-and-supportive.

53 "Understanding Non-Binary People."

54 "Understanding Non-Binary People."

55 "Higher: Building Gender Inclusive Organizations," accessed February 10, 2021, http://hellohigher.com/.

56 "Definition of INTERSECTIONALITY," accessed March 26, 2021, https://www.merriam-webster.com/dictionary/intersectionality.

57 Devon W. Carbado et al., "INTERSECTIONALITY: Mapping the Movements of a Theory1," *Du Bois Review: Social Science Research on Race* 10, no. 2 (ed 2013): 303–12, https://doi.org/10.1017/S1742058X13000349.

Bibliography

"Abbotts – History of Funding Equity." Accessed October 22, 2020. https://www.state.nj.us/education/archive/abbotts/chrono/.

Allen, Kent. "Google Settles Age Discrimination Lawsuit." *AARP*. Accessed October 28, 2020. http://www.aarp.org/work/working-at-50-plus/info-2019/age-discrimination-google-lawsuit.html.

American Civil Liberties Union. "School-to-Prison Pipeline." Accessed June 25, 2021. https://www.aclu.org/issues/juvenile-justice/school-prison-pipeline.

"As Supreme Court Affirms Workplace Rights, LGBTQ Americans Have a Long Way to Go for Economic Equality – MarketWatch." Accessed November 5, 2020. https://www.marketwatch.com/story/50-years-after-the-stonewall-riots-lgbt-americans-still-grapple-with-these-financial-struggles-2019-06-28.

"Boyle - 2020 - CLOSING THE RACIAL INEQUALITY GAPS The Economic C.Pdf." Accessed September 23, 2020. https://ir.citi.com/NvIUklHPilz14Hwd3oxqZBLMn1_XPqo5FrxsZD0x6hhil84ZxaxEuJUWmak51UHvYk75VKeHCMI%3D.

CAI. "Autism2Work." Accessed October 27, 2020. https://www.cai.io/capabilities/autism2work/.

Carbado, Devon W., Kimberlé Williams Crenshaw, Vickie M. Mays, and Barbara Tomlinson. "INTERSECTIONALITY: Mapping the Movements of a Theory1." *Du Bois Review: Social Science Research on Race* 10, no. 2 (2013): 303–12. https://doi.org/10.1017/S1742058X13000349.

"Civil Rights: The Little Rock School Integration Crisis | Eisenhower Presidential Library." Accessed October 22, 2020. https://www.eisenhowerlibrary.gov/research/online-documents/civil-rights-little-rock-school-integration-crisis.

CNBC.com, Susan Caminiti, special to. "AT&T's $1 Billion Gambit: Retraining Nearly Half Its Workforce for Jobs of the Future." *CNBC*, March 13, 2018. https://www.cnbc.com/2018/03/13/atts-1-billion-gambit-retraining-nearly-half-its-workforce.html.

DiversityJobs.com. "Are Women Really No Better off in the Workplace after #MeToo?," December 16, 2019. https://www.diversityjobs.com/2019/12/women-in-the-workplace-metoo/.

Dobbin, Frank, and Alexandra Kalev. "Why Sexual Harassment Programs Backfire." *Harvard Business Review*, May 1, 2020. https://hbr.org/2020/05/confronting-sexual-harassment.

Donovan, John, and Cathy Benko. "AT&T's Talent Overhaul." *Harvard Business Review*, October 1, 2016. https://hbr.org/2016/10/atts-talent-overhaul.

"Earnings Disparities by Race and Ethnicity | U.S. Department of Labor." Accessed October 28, 2020. https://www.dol.gov/agencies/ofccp/about/data/earnings/race-and-ethnicity.

"Enforcement Guidance on Reasonable Accommodation and Undue Hardship under the ADA | U.S. Equal Employment Opportunity Commission." Accessed October 27, 2020. https://www.eeoc.gov/laws/guidance/enforcement-guidance-reasonable-accommodation-and-undue-hardship-under-ada.

Enrich, David, and Rachel Abrams. "McDonald's Sues Former C.E.O., Accusing Him of Lying and Fraud." *The New York Times*, August 10, 2020, sec. Business. https://www.nytimes.com/2020/08/10/business/mcdonalds-ceo-steve-easterbrook.html.

Gupta, Alisha Haridasani. "Why Some Women Call This Recession a 'Shecession.'" *The New York Times*, May 13, 2020, sec. U.S. https://www.nytimes.com/2020/05/09/us/unemployment-coronavirus-women.html.

Haddon, Heather. "McDonald's Seeks Dismissal of Discrimination Lawsuit Filed by Black Former Franchisees." *Wall Street Journal*, October 23, 2020, sec. Business. https://www.wsj.com/articles/mcdonalds-seeks-dismissal-of-discrimination-lawsuit-filed-by-black-former-franchisees-11603476224.

Hammond, Janice, A. Kamau Massey, and Mayra A. Gaza. "African American Inequality in the United States." *Harvard Business School*, June 15, 2020.

Hardnett, Oona Goodin-Smith, Anna Orso, Raishad. "Philadelphia Black Lives Matter Activists Say the Historic Summer of Protests Was Only the Beginning." https://www.inquirer.com. Accessed October 26, 2020. https://www.inquirer.com/news/philadelphia/a/philadelphia-defund-police-black-lives-matter-20201021.html.

"Higher: Building Gender Inclusive Organizations." Accessed February 10, 2021. http://hellohigher.com/.

"Historically Black Colleges and Universities and Higher Education Desegregation." Policy Guidance; Guides. US Department of Education (ED), January 10, 2020. https://www2.ed.gov/about/offices/list/ocr/docs/hq9511.html.

Hoffman, Jan, and Chang W. Lee. "I Won't Be Used as a Guinea Pig for White People." *The New York Times*, October 7, 2020, sec. Health. https://www.nytimes.com/2020/10/07/health/coronavirus-vaccine-trials-african-americans.html.

Hussam, Reshmann and Holly Fetter. "Race and Mass Incarceration in the United States." *Harvard Business School*, June 19, 2020.

Initiative, Prison Policy, and Wendy Sawyer and Peter Wagner. "Mass Incarceration: The Whole Pie 2020." Accessed October 23, 2020. https://www.prisonpolicy.org/reports/pie2020.html.

Kita, Joe. "Age Discrimination Still Thrives in America." *AARP*. Accessed October 28, 2020. http://www.aarp.org/work/working-at-50-plus/info-2019/age-discrimination-in-america.html.

"LGBT Data & Demographics – The Williams Institute." Accessed November 5, 2020. https://williamsinstitute.law.ucla.edu/visualization/lgbt-stats/?topic=LGBT#density.

"LGBT People with Disabilities," n.d., 4.

"McDonald's CEO Made 1,939 Times as Much as Average Worker in 2019 - Business Insider." Accessed November 9, 2020. https://www.businessinsider.com/mcdonalds-ceo-made-1939-times-as-much-average-worker-2019-2020-4.

National Center for Transgender Equality. "Understanding Non-Binary People: How to Be Respectful and Supportive," July 9, 2016a. https://transequality.org/issues/resources/understanding-non-binary-people-how-to-be-respectful-and-supportive.

National Center for Transgender Equality. "Understanding Transgender People: The Basics," July 9, 2016b. https://transequality.org/issues/resources/understanding-transgender-people-the-basics.

NW, 1615 L. St, Suite 800Washington, and DC 20036USA202-419-4300 | Main202-857-8562 | Fax202-419-4372 | Media Inquiries. "6 Facts about Economic Inequality in the U.S." *Pew Research Center* (blog). Accessed October 27, 2020a. https://www.pewresearch.org/fact-tank/2020/02/07/6-facts-about-economic-inequality-in-the-u-s/.

NW, 1615 L. St, Suite 800Washington, and DC 20036USA202-419-4300 | Main202-857-8562 | Fax202-419-4372 | Media Inquiries. "The Narrowing, but Persistent, Gender Gap in Pay." *Pew Research Center* (blog). Accessed October 26, 2020b. https://www.pewresearch.org/fact-tank/2019/03/22/gender-pay-gap-facts/.

Perry, Rashawn Ray and Andre M. "Why We Need Reparations for Black Americans." *Brookings* (blog), April 15, 2020. https://www.brookings.edu/policy2020/bigideas/why-we-need-reparations-for-black-americans/.

"Persons with a Disability: Labor Force Characteristics Summary." Accessed October 26, 2020. https://www.bls.gov/news.release/disabl.nr0.htm.

Podcasts, Wharton Business Daily, and North America. "How the Pandemic Is Affecting Working Mothers." *Knowledge@Wharton*. Accessed October 22, 2020. https://knowledge.wharton.upenn.edu/article/how-the-pandemic-is-affecting-working-mothers/.

Social Sci LibreTexts. "15.5: The Constitutional Convention and Federal Constitution," July 1, 2020. https://socialsci.libretexts.org/Courses/Lumen_Learning/Book%3A_United_States_History_I%3A_OpenStax_(Lumen)/15%3A_Module_7%3A_Creating_a_Government_(1776%E2%80%931783)/15.5%3A_The_Constitutional_Convention_and_Federal_Constitution.

Suneson, Grant, Hristina Byrnes, John Harrington. "Supreme Court Decision aside, Some States Are Better – and Some Are Worse – for LGBTQ Community." *USA Today*. Accessed November 5, 2020. https://www.usatoday.com/story/money/2020/06/19/the-best-and-worst-states-for-lgbtq-people/111968524/.

"The #MeToo Backlash." *Harvard Business Review*, September 1, 2019. https://hbr.org/2019/09/the-metoo-backlash.

"The City That Really Did Abolish the Police - POLITICO." Accessed October 23, 2020. https://www.politico.com/news/magazine/2020/06/12/camden-policing-reforms-313750.

The Sentencing Project. "Report to the United Nations on Racial Disparities in the U.S. Criminal Justice System." Accessed October 23, 2020. https://www.sentencingproject.org/publications/un-report-on-racial-disparities/.

"This Far by Faith. 1526-1775: From AFRICA to AMERICA | PBS." Accessed October 23, 2020. https://www.pbs.org/thisfarbyfaith/journey_1/p_6.html.

"Tuskegee Study - Timeline - CDC - NCHHSTP," July 16, 2020. https://www.cdc.gov/tuskegee/timeline.htm.

"U.S. Census Bureau QuickFacts: Philadelphia City, Pennsylvania." Accessed October 26, 2020. https://www.census.gov/quickfacts/philadelphiacitypennsylvania.

WHO. "WHO | Ageism in the Workplace." World Health Organization. Accessed October 27, 2020. http://www.who.int/ageing/features/workplace-ageism/en/.

Women in the States. "The Economic Impact of Equal Pay by State," February 24, 2016. https://statusofwomendata.org/featured/the-economic-impact-of-equal-pay-by-state/.

Yaffe-Bellany, David. "McDonald's Fires C.E.O. Steve Easterbrook After Relationship With Employee (Published 2019)." *The New York Times*, November 3, 2019, sec. Business. https://www.nytimes.com/2019/11/03/business/mcdonalds-ceo-fired-steve-easterbrook.html.

Young, Stephen B. "Slavery: A Widespread Affliction Form Middle Ages to 19th Century Abolition" XI, no. VII (July 2020).

Chapter 4

Building a More Inclusive Organization

Building an inclusive and equitable organization begins with developing a J.E.D.I. North Star vision that is supported by the board of directors and the C-suite. This visioning exercise requires reflection on an organization's current state as well as perspective from leadership and stakeholders on what is possible to create a just and equitable organization. From this process organizational values are identified, and strategic goals selected. The roadmap to deliver on an organization's J.E.D.I. North Star vision is the strategy. We term this the J.E.D.I. North Star strategy, and it reflects your organization's mission and strategic roadmap to achieve the organizational vision of justice, equity, and inclusion. Each organization will have a unique J.E.D.I. strategy that is based upon their vision, organizational readiness, resources, industry, competitive position, and regulatory requirements. The process begins with establishing a baseline by measuring the organization's current justice, equity, diversity, and inclusion (J.E.D.I.) state using both internal assessment and stakeholder engagement. This process includes measuring and considering a variety of indicators including assessment results around stakeholder views, program offerings, and workforce diversity representation to "take the pulse " of the organization. Once leadership has an understanding of where the organization resides in its J.E.D.I. maturity journey, then the J.E.D.I. North Star strategy is developed. This strategy includes a roadmap for system redesign with goals and objectives set for the next 3–5 years. The benefits of embracing a J.E.D.I. strategy are numerous and include improved operating performance, greater innovation, higher employee engagement, and improved brand image. While the strategy development begins with an organization's board and C-suite, it is imperative to engage internal and external stakeholders to gather information necessary to target and drive systemic change. External stakeholders such as investors and suppliers are

DOI: 10.1201/9781003168072-5

integral to driving impact. Investors are demanding greater transparency around environmental, social, and governance (ESG) issues and are using their collective voices to drive change within the financial services industry and the organizations in which they invest. Supplier diversity is critical to reallocating purchasing power and driving wealth redistribution. While 2020 has been full of pledges and financial commitments from large organizations, not much has been heard from leaders of mid-size and small businesses. To drive systemic impact, all business leaders for all levels of organizations must be part of the conversation and transformation. Developing a North Star J.E.D.I. vision and strategy to drive impact is a crucial part of leaderships' role in their leading organizations for long-term viability.

4.1 Garnering Board and C-Suite Support

Since 2020, conversations with leadership around the imperative for inclusive and equitable change has become more accepted and welcomed. There are many boards and C-suites that are making J.E.D.I. strategy development and implementation a top priority on their agendas. They are formulating action plans, allocating resources, and hiring Chief Diversity Officers. Since the summer of 2020, corporate America has pledged over $30 billion to address systemic racism, promote educational opportunities, improve supplier diversity, and address pay and wealth gap issues. In the 4th quarter of 2020, 37 CEOs came together to form an organization, OneTen, combining the resources and influence of leading American organizations to upskill, hire, and promote 1 million Black Americans over the next 10 years. The goal is to enable participants to obtain family sustaining jobs with opportunities for advancement. Their plan is to establish an ecosystem of major employers, leading non-profits and skill-credentialing organizations to create a more flexible talent pipeline, develop a skill-based talent model, and promote practices that allow employees and employers to succeed. Founding members are Accenture, ADP, Allstate, American Express, Amgen, Aon, AT&T, Bain & Company, Bank of America, Cargill, Caterpillar, Cisco, Cleveland Clinic, Comcast, Deloitte, Delta Air Lines, Eli Lilly, General Motors, HP Inc., Humana, IBM, Illinois Tool Works, Intermountain Healthcare, Johnson & Johnson, Lowe's, Medtronic, Merck, Nike, Nordstrom, PepsiCo, Roper Technologies, Stryker, Target, Trane Technologies, Verizon, Walmart, and Whirlpool Corporation.[1]

While many commitments are being made by corporate America, it remains to be seen if these are one-off pledges to address social unrest and stakeholder demands or, if we are truly seeing transformative change within our societal and corporate structures. OneTen is offering a more sustained commitment by focusing on foundational systemic barriers around education, access, and bias. While the goals outlined by OneTen are commendable, the member organizations are all large organizations. The issue remains around how to engage the leadership teams of small and mid-size businesses. While presenting at a business meeting for small and mid-size professional services practitioners in the fall of 2020, I asked what was being discussed on the topics of diversity, equity, and inclusion (DEI) at their own organizations or at their clients' organizations. Unfortunately, the predominate answer was that DEI was not being really being discussed or prioritized. With small and mid-size organizations employing 47% of the workforce, engaging boards, C-suite, owners, and entrepreneurs remains a significant issue to drive impactful systemic change.[2] In order for meaningful change to be enacted, we need real buy-in and commitment from the board and leadership teams of organizations of all sizes.

Garnering support from and organization's board and C-suite requires engaging both hearts and minds. From a heart perspective, promoting equity and justice is the right thing to do and appeals to leaders' legacy concerns. From a financial perspective, driving J.E.D.I. values makes good business sense. Research demonstrates that there are numerous business reasons for creating a more inclusive and equitable organization such as improved:

1. Financial performance
2. Decision-making
3. Employee engagement and productivity
4. Innovation
5. Customer focus
6. Access to new markets
7. Access to capital
8. Access to a broader talent pool
9. CEO legacy
10. Compliance

According to a recent study from McKinsey, higher diversity correlates with increased profitability and value creation for organizations. Companies with the most ethnically diverse executive teams are 33% more likely to outperform their peers in terms of profitability. Organizations with greater gender diversity up through the executive level outperform their peers. Organizations in the top-quartile in executive-level gender diversity worldwide are 21% more likely to outperform their fourth-quartile industry peers on earnings before interest and taxes (EBIT). They also were 27% more likely to outperform their fourth-quartile peers in terms of longer-term value creation, as measured using an economic profit margin.[3] (Economic profit is like accounting profit but, it also includes opportunity costs for taking one action vs. another in a given time period.) In the U.S., McKinsey's research demonstrates a linear relationship between racial and ethnic diversity and financial performance. For every 10% increase in senior management diversity, there is a 8% rise in EBIT.[4]

Additional research by Boston Consulting Group (BCG) demonstrates that diversity within the leadership team promotes innovation in both developed and developing countries. Their research includes identity diversity, but it also considers experiential and cognitive diversity. They considered diversity characteristics including gender, age, nation of origin, career path, industry background, and education. Innovation is defined as the percentage of revenues generated by new products or services over the past 3 years. Their research found that companies reporting above-average diversity on their management teams generated innovation revenue that was 19 percentage points higher than that of companies with below-average leadership diversity (45% of total revenue vs. 26%.)[5] The research is clear that higher levels of diversity on leadership teams generates improved organizational performance.

Members of the Gen Z and millennial generations are a growing percentage of the workforce and will comprise 75% of the workforce in 2025.[6] They define diversity much more broadly including diversity of experience, background, and perspectives, and they believe that an organization that creates a culture of belonging is more innovative. If you are seeking to attract top talent especially Gen Z and millennials, it is important to note that these generations of workers are evaluating an organization's J.E.D.I. performance when considering career choices and job offers. To both attract and retain top talent, it is imperative that organizational leaders align their J.E.D.I. strategy with their overall organizational strategy to ensure external and internal consistency.

Over the years, I have coached and advised millennials who were recruited by companies that appeared to be promoting social and environmental justice when viewed from an external lens. After a few months of working with the organization, they realized that there was a disconnect between external messaging and the internal reality of daily life around the execution of company values, mission, and strategy. As a result, these new employees are looking to leave these organizations in order to find an employer that better aligns with their own J.E.D.I. values. Organizations with high employee turnover face a competitive disadvantage as the costs are significant and often represent a multiple of an employee's annual salary to recruit, hire, train, and back fill for unplanned employee turnover. While unwanted employee turnover is costly and disruptive, disengaged employees also negatively impact organizational performance. In the U.S., Gallup estimates the cost of employee disengagement at $350 billion annually. These costs reflect employees performing poorly, undermining coworkers' performance, creating dissatisfaction with customers, and taking more sick days. Ignoring Gen Z and the millennial workforce demands around equitable and inclusive workplaces leaves business owners and leaders vulnerable as they may not be able to attract and retain top talent needed to operate. This talent drain spills over into operational performance, customer satisfaction, innovation, and community image and support. The reasons for leadership to support building a more just, inclusive and equitable organization are many, and leaders that authentically embrace a J.E.D.I. North Star strategy will create organizations that thrive.

4.2 Investor Requirements

Access to capital is another area of impact for an organization's board and the C-suite to consider as part of their J.E.D.I. journey. Investors are demanding greater disclosure on environmental and social justice issues. In the 2020 U.S. SIF survey, ESG investors highlighted the importance of transitioning to a low carbon economy, as well as human capital management (HCM), diversity, and health and wellness as priority issues. At the beginning of 2020, the U.S. SIF reports that there were $16.6 trillion in U.S.-based assets held by 530 institutional investors, 384 money managers, and 1,204 community investment institutions using ESG criteria in their investment analysis and portfolio selection protocols.[7] Support for ESG related shareholder proposals in the 2020 proxy season remained strong and broadened to incorporate more traditional shareholders with six proposals related to DEI and HCM issues receiving majority shareholder approval.

> This year's proxy disclosures demonstrate that many companies are pay-
> ing attention: the percentage of Fortune 100 companies that voluntarily
> highlighted human capital initiatives and commitments more than dou-
> bled over the past three years, rising from 32% in 2017 to 77% in 2020.
> Similarly, the percentage of companies that explicitly assigned board or
> committee oversight of human capital jumped from 28% in 2017 to
> 69% in 2020, with those responsibilities generally assigned to compen-
> sation committees.[8]

The human capital areas of focus are diversity, health, wellness and safety, compensation, culture, and employee development. Board diversity especially around gender and race was also a top priority. Investors are challenging boards and asking what is being done to change the composition of their workforce in terms of gender, race, and ethnic diversity as well as employee skill set diversity. As organizations undergo J.E.D.I. transformation, the skill sets of their board members must reflect the new requirements to support its J.E.D.I. strategic vision. Investors are looking for transparent communication on these efforts as well as seeking demonstrated actions from organizations in support of their J.E.D.I. strategy. The Security and Exchange Commission (SEC) adopted rule amendments to modernize the disclosure requirements in Items 101, 103, and 105 of Regulation S-K to allow investors to make better informed decisions. Reporting organization's human capital disclosures will include:

- "The number of employees and a description of its human capital resources, if material to the business as a whole; and if material to a particular segment, that segment should be identified
- any human capital measures or objectives, if material, that the registrant focuses on in managing its business, such as those related to the development, attraction, safety, engagement, and retention of employees"[9]

If an organization's leadership team is not actively developing a meaningful strategy to respond to investor ESG related demands and questions, especially in the area J.E.D.I. and HCM impact, their ability to raise capital to support growth may be limited. In addition, they may find themselves out of regulatory compliance. For private companies, the financial sector is also increasing disclosure requirements to better address ESG risk and opportunity. So, even if you are not subject to SEC disclosure, anticipate inquiries from investors, bankers, and financers on environmental and social justice issues. A more detailed view of these topics is covered in the following conversation with Katherine Pease, Managing Director, Pathstone.

THE CRUCIAL ROLE FOR IMPACT INVESTING IN DRIVING SYSTEMIC CHANGE

A Conversation with Katherine Pease, Managing Director, Pathstone
Katherine Pease is Managing Director at Pathstone. She works with clients and provides strategic guidance to the integration of impact strategies across the firm. Prior to joining Pathstone, Katherine was Chief Impact Strategist at Cornerstone Capital Group, where she led Cornerstone's thematic research team and co-managed the firm's impact measurement effort (Cornerstone was acquired by Pathstone in March 2021). Katherine previously served as a philanthropic advisor to foundations and high net worth individuals and was a foundation executive. In addition, Katherine is a board member of Global Greengrants Fund and the Colorado Nonprofit Association and serves on numerous corporate and non-profit advisory boards.

As an investment advisory service to individuals, families, foundations, and endowments, what are the major themes that you are seeing in impact investing?

We're seeing significant growth in the level of understanding and adoption of sustainable and impact investment strategies. Investors tend to fall into three categories in terms of their depth of focus. The first is the investor who wants to ensure that their investments are making a generally positive impact while achieving competitive market rate returns. The second is an investor focused on climate and environmental issues. These investors may want to focus on a specific vertical such as land, deforestation, sustainable agriculture, water, renewable energy, or ocean health; or they may simply want to invest their assets in a broad suite of solutions that have an overall positive impact on the environment. Another approach that is gaining attention among this group of investors is innovations in the circular economy, which focuses on natural resource use and reuse, and minimizing waste throughout the life cycle of a product and, ultimately, the supply chain. The third investor group is focused on social issues around racial and economic justice, gender equity, and an emerging category that looks at the intersection of gender, gender identity, and sexual orientation.

Intersectionality between environmental and social impacts is another area of growth. Regenerative agriculture is one example. Unlike with conventional agriculture, regenerative practices seek to ensure that workers are treated fairly – the value of social justice and ecologically balanced practices go hand in hand.

Linking all of these major themes is a focus on governance issues. As Pathstone's Chief Impact Officer, Erika Karp, says, "The G in ESG is first among equals." Well-governed companies practice what's become known as "stakeholder capitalism," fully considering the environmental and social impacts of their activities on all stakeholders. Without strong governance, a company's commitment to environmental and social issues can be inconsistent or insincere – what some have dubbed greenwashing.

We have seen exponential growth in investing with an ESG/impact lens. Since 1995, when the U.S. SIF Foundation first measured the size of the U.S. sustainable investment universe at $639 billion, assets have increased more than 25-fold, a compound annual growth rate of 14%.[10] We anticipate that the industry will continue to grow at a similar pace until at some point, all investing will be done with an ESG lens. This is because it has become abundantly clear that ESG factors are material and that incorporating ESG factors into the investment analysis process can reduce risk while achieving comparable or better returns within an asset class (Figure 4.1).[11]

The largest growth in the last couple of years has been in investing with a focus on social issues. This is likely due to the increased awareness of sexual and gender-based harassment and violence in the workplace that has been exposed through the Me too movement as well as increased awareness of racial justice issues after the murder of George Floyd in 2020. Moreover, the COVID-19 pandemic has exposed alarming structural weaknesses in the fundamental

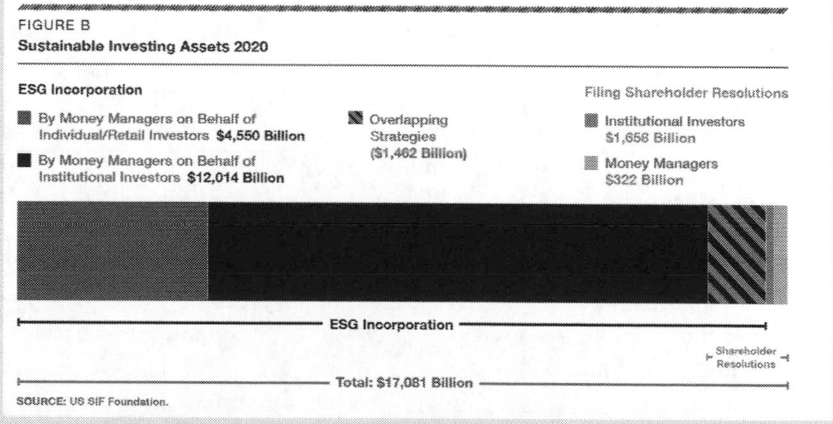

FIGURE B
Sustainable Investing Assets 2020

ESG Incorporation   Filing Shareholder Resolutions

By Money Managers on Behalf of   Overlapping   Institutional Investors
Individual/Retail Investors **$4,550 Billion**   Strategies $1,658 Billion
                                        ($1,462 Billion)
By Money Managers on Behalf of   Money Managers
Institutional Investors **$12,014 Billion** $322 Billion

ESG Incorporation

Shareholder Resolutions

Total: $17,081 Billion

SOURCE: US SIF Foundation.

Figure 4.1   Sustainable Investing Assets 2020.[13]

systems that support our society and economy – including the finance, education, and healthcare systems. As a result, the benefits of ESG analysis are starting to really sink in for investors – it's clear that the global economic risks associated with climate change and social inequities require investment in solutions. It is thus not surprising that through the 2nd quarter of 2020 (as the pandemic was hitting its first peak), inflows into ESG investment strategies were about the same as all of 2019.[12]

In light of the heightened awareness around social injustice in the U.S. and around the world, how has the conversation with investors been reframed on materiality and intersectionality of the components in ESG investing?

Investors use a frame of risk and reward to evaluate investments. They have become aware of the risks associated with not having insight into a company's ESG risk and opportunity factors. Investors are looking for companies with a governance structure that recognizes and addresses material ESG factors. Importantly, ESG factors are interrelated – for example, climate change is affecting all sorts of industries that one might not necessarily think of as relating directly to climate change. For example, one study we conducted (https://www.pathstone.com/app/uploads/2021/10/No-Place-to-Hide_Pathstone.pdf) found that $3–24 trillion or 2–17%, of global financial assets are at risk of loss from climate change. The transportation sector (air, road, rail, and sea) and agriculture face the highest risk, with more than 60% of the financial value of these sectors vulnerable to climate change. Similarly, racial and gender justice issues are cross-cutting – they affect all companies insofar as all companies are at risk of reputational risk, legal costs that result from harassment claims, and an overall failure to effectively manage a diverse workforce.

Our firm does not invest directly in companies; rather, we select funds and fund managers for our clients based on their financial return targets, risk-return profile and impact priorities, within a defined asset allocation. Many clients prefer to steer clear of certain industries such as fossil fuels, private prisons, and weapons and firearms. Our clients may have other industries that they wish to avoid based on their own investment goals.

From a diversity perspective, we look at who is making decisions on behalf of a fund manager. We look at fund managers' views on diversity including the kind of questions they are asking. We are looking for fund managers who move beyond Board and C-suite representation and seek to understand the company's broader view on diversity, equity, and inclusion and how that view is baked into their culture.

From your perspective, what information should leadership teams be including in their investor calls to shed light on their social impact performance especially around social justice issues and systemic impacts?

There are some basic issues that all investors should be asking regarding the companies and industries in their portfolios. Some of key questions we ask fund managers include:

1. Does the company understand risk and opportunities as they relate to their industry, including supply chain risk?
2. Has the company done a risk analysis on ESG factors? Where does the analysis show up in their business plan?
3. Is the company disclosing material ESG risk factors to its shareholders?
4. Has the company done a complete climate risk assessment that includes where they do business? Where are warehouses and other facilities located and what type of climate risk is there related to the operation and physical location of those facilities?
5. Does the company have the right talent at the Board, C-Suite, and operating level to lead the organization, considering the material ESG factors that have been identified? For example, if they are an engineering company, do the engineers have a diversity of thought and experience around ESG risks and opportunities?
6. What is the company actually doing where the rubber hits the road? For example, we had a client focused on addressing deforestation and child labor in food companies' supply chains. So, we spent time asking a global food company about how they ranked their suppliers and then what they were doing about addressing issues identified through this ranking process. The investor wanted to see evidence that the company not only understood the issue but that it was doing something to address the problem.
7. What kinds of ESG-related audits are being done on a regular basis? What is being audited? Does leadership embrace a continuous improvement model? Are they performing cultural audits and are they continually learning and evaluating?
8. What intentional practices are baked into the company's culture and practices?
9. Are the company's ESG-related goals tied to executive compensation?

Are there key ESG metrics that you consider when selecting assets managers to build portfolios for clients?

We do not have a specific litmus test that we use to evaluate asset managers. Instead, we look at an array of factors including: their investment thesis and how it relates to ESG/impact, their financial performance, their knowledge of the specific industries or geographies in which their portfolio companies work, and the experience and diversity of their leadership team. We specifically track the number of women and people of color in ownership, on management teams, and in roles as portfolio managers of asset management companies we work with. While we have tracked this information for a long time, our clients are now more interested in these details than they ever have been. In fact, we are seeing a movement of investors, especially foundations and other institutional investors such as pension funds, requiring that fund managers disclose their diversity and that of the companies in their portfolios.

Is there a paradigm or model that you leverage when guiding clients in selecting impact investment to impact systemic racism, access to education, access and quality of healthcare, community investment, etc.?

We use different frameworks to guide our understanding of how companies and fund managers are performing, relative to specific impact areas. For example, we have developed a framework for racial equity investing that is rooted in our understanding of structural racism. As an illustration, we firmly believe that racism is rooted in the history of this country and was reinforced through a series of laws and norms that gave White people economic and social advantages. For example, through redlining practices, people of color were denied opportunities to live in neighborhoods with good schools, access to quality healthcare, distance from environmentally toxic industrial sites, etc. We therefore believe that investments that provide people of color access to affordable mortgages is an important strategy to disrupt the legacy of racism and economic inequality in the U.S. Similarly, we look for privately held companies that are actively seeking to invest in companies that provide access to education and training opportunities for everyone, regardless of socioeconomic status or race.

There are all sorts of other factors that we also consider within a racial equity framework, such as access to capital, good jobs, and so on. When it comes to climate change, we look at factors that stop the proliferation of greenhouse gas emissions through carbon capture and we look at renewable energy – in other words, our framework includes a variety of approaches that have been scientifically proven to make a positive impact on the environment. These issues are complex, and we believe investors have a right to know that the companies they are investing in are being vetted by asset managers and advisors for their actual impact on people and the planet.

Investors are seeking investments that produce a positive impact. Over the past year, there has been a significant rise in interest in investing to support social issues. These may take many forms including local and community investing to support local financial institutions providing small business community lending, mortgages, and offering financial services to underserved communities. Investors are seeking companies that have demonstrated a strong governance structure that addresses environmental and social risks. Addressing investor ESG requirements as well as ESG regulatory compliance is an area of growing responsibility for Boards and C-suites.

These issues are not limited to public companies. ESG strategy and implementation should be on minds of entrepreneurs and start-up companies. It is much more effective to build ESG into your culture rather than to bolt it on in the future. Incorporating ESG risk management at an early stage will make your organization more valuable in an acquisition, as the purchase multiple will not need to be discounted to reflect undisclosed ESG risk. Even if your organization doesn't access public markets for funding, major corporations are seeking information from their vendors and supply chain regarding ESG risk including performance, reporting, and remediation programs. Clients are requiring this information from professional service firms as well. As mentioned in the previous interview, fund managers are being asked about the diversity of their teams, ownership, and senior leadership. We have reached the tipping point where environmental and social justice must be part of core business strategy, operation, and reporting.

4.3 Inclusive Access to Capital

Access to capital for BIPOC, AAPI, and women entrepreneurs is a key piece of the puzzle that is missing to drive long-term systemic change. According to research from Cornerstone Capital, in 2018, the majority (80%) of venture capital funding went to White, predominately male, founders. Only 1% of venture capital dollars funded Black start-up founders, 1.8% went to Latino founders, and 17.7% went to Asian founders.[14] The divide of venture capital funding between female and male entrepreneurs is also staggering. Venture capitalist founders are predominately White males, and venture teams are 82% males.[15]

Research done by Crunchbase found that after analyzing data from 4500 investors over 42% of all venture capitalists come from 12 schools. Of those, the top five are Harvard, Stanford, UPenn, MIT, and Columbia. Over 25% of all money invested goes to those who have graduated from an Ivy League School. These are schools of power and privilege with significant barriers for entry for marginalized and underserved students despite affirmative action programs.

Investment return results indicate that venture founder teams which contain diversity of gender, race, and ethnicity of founders are more innovative, and their investments produce better financial outcomes. Without diversity of identity, perspective, and experience, it is difficult for venture investors to understand the opportunities and risks outside of their sphere of expertise. Most venture capitalists think they are contrarians and believe they are looking for the unicorn, but in practice, they look to patterns of past success to help identify future opportunities. As a result, their approach leaves out great swaths of society especially entrepreneurs from communities of color. Understanding new market opportunities requires diversity of thought and perspective, which doesn't come from a homogeneous-White, male, monolithic view. Venture capitalists with diversity in their funding group are more likely to invest in diverse founder teams. While top performing venture firms and angel investors groups have female investors, women only represent 12% of investors. With women-controlled wealth expected to reach $72 trillion, their representation is growing in venture capital (VC) firms.[16] Fewer than 10% of decision-makers are women so increasing the representation of women in senior roles at VC firms is crucial to drive impactful change.[17] VC partners that are women are twice as likely to invest in start-ups with at least one woman founder and three times as likely to invest in firms with a female CEO. PitchBook fund performance data shows that 69% of venture firms that scored a top-quartile fund between 2009 and 2018 had women in decision-making roles indicating a strong correlation between hiring female investors and generating strong returns.[18] The benefits of founder team and venture capital professional diversity has been demonstrated, but the investor community must accelerate transformation to improve equity of access and opportunity.

Some best practices recommendations include that Limited Partners (LPs), the investors in VC firms, request more than just fund performance information during VCs pitches. LPs should request diversity representation information from the VCs on the companies that they back such as gender identity, race, and ethnicity. As investors, LPs have a significant impact on distribution of funds across an ecosystem and focusing on their investment company's diversity will prioritize diversity and drive impact on inclusion. LPs can also compare the offerings from General Partners (GPs) company portfolios and choose GPs that reflect their J.E.D.I. value alignment. As a VC, consider allocating a percentage of pitch opportunities each month for pitch teams that include members from underrepresented groups. In addition to being the right thing to do, it allows VC professionals to learn more about opportunities in networks and communities outside of their own. Founders need to address J.E.D.I. issues as a core part of their strategic vision, and they should pitch it as a core strength of their business as a lever to minimize risk and maximize opportunity for investors.[19]

To dismantle industry-wide barriers in venture capital for women requires improving access to the male-dominated networks, increasing the number of female role models, and recruiting well-qualified women, who are available within existing talent pools and pipelines. The Wharton School at the University of Pennsylvania, a renowned business school, has reached gender equity with its MBA Class of 2023. Practices to improve representation within VC firms highlighting and elevating women as role models, investing in mentorship, sponsorship, and network expanding opportunities for women, and realigning VC firms' talent strategy for recruiting and developing women. Realigning their talent ecosystem requires reassessment of existing recruitment structures and process, hiring decisions, work assignments, and performance metrics and processes. In order to transform and create equitable access and opportunity, VC leadership must chose to make J.E.D.I. values part of their North Star strategy, and they must hold partners, principals, and associates accountable for their actions and behaviors including tracking metrics, reporting on goals, and tying results to compensation.[20]

A conversation hosted by the Wharton School Dean, Erika James on a Wharton Beyond Business Race and the Entrepreneur Webinar featured Josh Kopelman, Partner, First Round Capital, and Chris Bennett, CEO, Wonder School discussing ways in which to improve the venture ecosystem for entrepreneurs of color. Josh brings an investor perspective, while Chris provides perspective as entrepreneur and POC. Both stated that venture capitalists need to be more inclusive in terms of to whom they allocate funds and who they have on their teams. VC team diversity offers a wider lens through which to view start-up pitches providing different perspectives and experiences enabling a greater understanding of capabilities and outcomes especially from underrepresented entrepreneurs. Josh cited an example of a Black, female entrepreneur seeking seed money for her natural hair business. He stated that he didn't understand the product or the market opportunity. As a result, he planned to decline funding for the venture. Fortunately, a fellow VC partner was able to push back and challenge Josh's perceptions making him reevaluate his decision-making process, which revealed unconscious bias. As a result, the venture was funded. Chris highlighted the importance of building a robust ecosystem of networks, innovation spaces, and funders to support entrepreneurs of color.

In terms of the risks involved with being an entrepreneur both cited having a safety net as a factor in allowing entrepreneurs to take risks. Many people of color choose the safer pathway of a job over entrepreneurship, especially with top consulting firms and banks offering large salaries, because they don't have family wealth as a safety net. White students may have more options to take risks like being an entrepreneur. They may have graduated without student debt and have a family wealth safety net to protect them if they fail. This is an example of White privilege. Recognizing one's own privilege and using it to highlight someone without privilege can have meaningful impact on delivering a more equitable approach to access to capital.

Improving access to loans is another way to help improve access to capital for businesses that serve communities of color. Several large corporations have moved deposits to BIPOC community banks to support lending and lower barriers to capital in communities of color. Netflix moved $100 million in deposits to community of color banks to support institutions that make loans to BIPOC business owners and community members.[21] Supporting community business ownership and home ownership helps communities of color build wealth.

Access and opportunity for investor funding and loans need to improve for BIPOC, women, and other underrepresented entrepreneurs, business owners, and families in order to support community development, growth, and wealth accumulation. Without a meaningful financing pipeline to fund new ventures, community businesses, and innovations, underrepresented founders and business owners fight a losing battle. Achieving greater equity and access for enterprise funding requires a redesign in our capital allocation systems to make them more equitable for underserved entrepreneurs and business owners.

4.4 J.E.D.I. Maturity Continuum

To determine the most effective approach to achieving an organization's J.E.D.I. vision, we need to assess where our organization is on its own J.E.D.I. journey. Each organization is on its own path toward building a more just, inclusive and equitable organization. Moving forward on the J.E.D.I. journey requires assessing an organization's readiness in terms of culture, leadership capabilities, resources, systems, process and policies. To identify meaningful goals and KPIs as well as impactful programs and projects, leadership must determine organizational capabilities and capacity for change. One of the most common mistakes in the transformation process is trying to do too many change initiatives at one time or to launch an initiative that cannot be supported within current resources and organizational structures. As a leader, it is important to recognize your organizational capabilities, agility, and capacity for change. Figure 4.2 provides an overview of the stages of the journey toward becoming an inclusive and equitable organization – *Compliance, Awareness. Integration, Embedded, Systemic.* Each of the stages builds upon the previous level further integrating J.E.D.I. values into the organization's culture and operations.

Figure 4.2   J.E.D.I. Maturity Continuum.

Focus	Players	Actions	Outcome
D&I risk monitored to meet regulatory compliance and mitigate risk	HCM, Legal, D&I team Siloed	DEI policy development Process to deal with D&I risk and enforce policies Consequences are transparent and applied equally across the organization	Power dynamics and inappropriate behaviors are not tolerated Employees feel safe in reporting inappropriate behaviors

Figure 4.3   Compliance.

The first stage of the journey is *Compliance*, and the focus is on regulatory compliance and risk mitigation. Figure 4.3 highlights the focus, players, actions, and outcomes of this stage. The primary players are HCM, Legal, and perhaps a Diversity and Inclusion (DI) team or committee. Their efforts are siloed and focus on legal and regulatory compliance. The actions include developing DEI policies usually around prohibition of harassment and discriminatory actions. A process is usually developed to provide training, enforce policies, and to mitigate regulatory compliance risks. Employees are normally trained and informed about compliance requirements including the consequences of non-compliance. The desired outcomes are that the company avoids fines and legal challenges. As a company matures in this phase, power dynamics and inappropriate behaviors are less likely to be tolerated. A mechanism may be established for reporting inappropriate behavior, and employees are encouraged to report inappropriate behaviors. Consequences for lack of compliance are made transparent and are viewed as a risk factor across the organization. Since the focus is on legal compliance, leadership takes more of a minimum threshold strategic approach in this stage.

The 2nd phase is *Awareness* as highlighted in Figure 4.4. Change agents and select leaders begin ideating about the business and equity impacts of diversity, equity, and inclusion(DEI) programs and initiatives. But the process remains fragmented and

Focus	Players	Actions	Outcome
Improving Diversity, Programs, Business Case	HCM and DEI and Sustainability	Compliance plus ESG and DEI targets DEI metrics to measure impact Employee D&I recognition programs Leaders engaged	Power dynamics and inappropriate behaviors are not tolerated Employees feel safe in reporting inappropriate behaviors DEI programs and initiatives Leadership team engaged Employees included in the D&I initiative

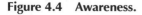

Figure 4.4   Awareness.

siloed. Actions include highlighting the importance of DEI, getting familiar with terminology, and gathering representational data to determine which groups are underrepresented. The focus is on improving organizational diversity representation, and one-off initiatives, pilots, and programs are being launched. The business case for DEI is starting to be socialized with the leadership team. Key players are HCM, DEI, and Sustainability teams. They are the change agents driving environmental and social justice initiatives internally. Part of their role is to engage leadership so that they begin to understand the business imperative of adopting a J.E.D.I. strategy including addressing stakeholder demands and addressing internal systemic issues around access and equity. Ad-hoc programming around unconscious bias training, events, conversations, town hall meetings, mentoring programs, and the creation of ERGs are the types of programming undertaken. Clients may be requesting information on your organization's social and environmental justice commitments further driving management focus on ESG and DEI reporting and compliance. Often the awareness stage is triggered by key customer requests for completion of supplier scorecards on an organization's ESG policies and practices. Outcomes include leadership and employee engagement around educations, awareness, and reporting on their current programs, policies, and initiatives. While environmental and social justice are gaining traction across the organization, the approach is fragmented rather than strategic.

As an organization moves forward in its J.E.D.I. journey, leadership's approach is focused less on program impact and more on strategy development that includes diversity and inclusion and expands to incorporate equity and improved access. In stage 3, we move into *Integration*, which is described in more detail in Figure 4.5. The focus is more strategic and prioritizes embedding J.E.D.I. values into an organization's operations such as improving representation within the talent ecosystem including recruitment, development, promotion, and succession planning. Initiatives may include capacity building such as unconscious bias training and awareness for leaders and people managers. J.E.D.I. champions expand to include the C-suite and senior leaders as change agents as they consider their goals and objectives and formulate a

Focus	**Players**	**Actions**	**Outcome**
DEI integrated into the operations	HCM, DEI and Sustainability Senior leadership lead, organization-wide	Compliance, Awareness plus	Power dynamics and inappropriate behaviors are not tolerated
Revise talent ecosystem strategy including talent pipeline	Cascading to managers and employees	Integration into recruitment, development, and advancement	Employees feel safe in reporting inappropriate behaviors
Consider organizational artifacts		Build relationship with more diverse institutions and groups	Leadership team models desired behaviors
Consider supplier diversity		Revise talent strategies	More diverse talent pool
		Assessment and metrics	More inclusive organization

Figure 4.5   Integration.

J.E.D.I. North Star vision. Leadership considers actions to integrate J.E.D.I. strategy across the organization by cascading vision and mission to managers and employees. Actions build on those of the previous stages integrating J.E.D.I. strategy into core operations including environmental impacts like emissions and waste intersection with community impacts. HCM revises their approach to talent recruitment, development, and advancement policies and processes to promote equity and inclusion to attract and retain talent from underrepresented groups. Part of the approach includes HCM leaders developing a broader talent pool by building relationships with more diverse institutions and community groups. Leaders develop and promote the organization's J.E.D.I. strategy and demonstrate their commitment through their behaviors and actions. Organizational artifacts such as artwork, marketing materials, and recruitment materials are reviewed through a lens of attracting and representing a diverse workforce. Procurement spending is assessed with an eye toward developing programs and resources to improve organizational supplier representation. The importance of inclusion and belonging moves to the forefront as managers realize that hiring diverse talent is only one step in the process. Transforming the organization's culture, policies, processes to make diverse employees welcome is a leadership priority. At this stage, leaders are evaluating organizational values, policies, procedures, and practices against their goals for progress on the J.E.D.I. strategic roadmap. J.E.D.I. goals are set across the organization and are supported by metrics to measure impact. Outcomes include engaging leadership in J.E.D.I. strategy development and modeling desired behaviors, cascading involvement of managers and employees in J.E.D.I. related initiatives, building a more diverse talent pool, creating a more inclusive culture, resetting talent strategy, and redesigning procurement to drive systemic change.

The 4th stage is *Embedded*, which is highlighted in Figure 4.6 and focuses on full operational integration and core business strategic alignment. An organization's board and C-suite are fully engaged in the visioning exercise. At this stage, the organization's J.E.D.I. values becomes an organizational pillar. Their strategic J.E.D.I.

Focus	**Players**	**Actions**	**Outcome**
Managers responsible for integrating D&I into functional areas, teams, and ecosystems. DEI as a strategic initiative	HCM, DEI and Sustainability Board, senior leadership, managers-organization wide	Compliance, Awareness, Integration plus Managers model inclusive behaviors ensuring that all are welcome and that teams reflect identity and cognitive diversity. Compensation tied to DEI Supplier DEI integration Audit and Assessment	J.E.D.I. strategic alignment Leadership team models desired behaviors More representative and inclusive organization Reporting Internal systemic changes

Figure 4.6   Embedded.

vision is embedded throughout organizational systems including strategic decisions-making, products and service offerings, product design, emission targets, locations of operation, pricing, market expansion, human capital strategies and policies, vendor selection, and support for creating opportunities for underserved members of their communities. The organization's J.E.D.I. North Star is a business imperative and part of every decision, process, project, and purchase. The full organization is engaged – board, C-suite, senior management, mid-level management, team leaders, and employees. Internal structures are created such as cross-functional committees to support this work and to embed it into operations. Everyone is aware and informed about the organization's J.E.D.I. North Star strategy. The J.E.D.I. strategy, roadmap, goals and performance metrics are a regular board agenda item, a priority for the C-suite, and on the agenda for departmental and team meetings. Leadership continues to spearhead the transformation, but the scope widens cascading the strategy implementation throughout the organization and engaging managers and team leaders. The focus is on embedding J.E.D.I. strategy into the culture of the organization and having these values demonstrated by employees through everyday behaviors, actions, and norms. The organization's J.E.D.I. strategic pillar is viewed as a valuable tool for innovation and market expansion, and it is embraced across the organization as a guiding principle. Actions include managers and team leaders modeling inclusive behaviors ensuring that all employees, customers, contractors, and suppliers are welcome and feel as if they belong and are able to bring their full selves to work for the organization. Teams are structured to promote identity, experiential, and cognitive diversity. Programming is systemic across the organization with feedback loops and real time reporting such as dashboards to support data driven decision-making by managers. Policies and work structures are designed to build an equitable culture addressing the individual needs of employees and focusing on flexibility and personal accommodation rather than standardization. Executive scorecards and compensation structures include J.E.D.I. goals and performance metrics. Procurement objectives are realign to support the organization's J.E.D.I. strategic roadmap. Supplier diversity programs include monitoring dollars spent with female, BIPOC, and AAPI vendors as well as outreach programs to engage and support underrepresented vendors. The procurement due diligence process includes a deeper dive into supply chain activities to promote, justice equity and inclusion in areas such as human rights, environmental impacts, representation and community business development. J.E.D.I. related questionaries are required from key suppliers describing their own goals, activities, outcomes. Based on these results, suppliers are ranked on scorecards with required action steps to remediate areas of concern. During this transformation process, the workforce reflects more diversity of identity, thought, and experience. The unifying culture of the organization is a shared vision of organizational purpose rather than a dominant culture. Outcomes include greater representation within the workforce, improved access and opportunity for underrepresented groups, improved employee engagement, and an equitable work culture. The focus is on building and supporting high-performing teams that value diversity. From a metrics perspective, success in this stage is often reflected in improved turnover ratios for diverse employees, higher employee engagement scores, improved rankings on 3rd party ranking sites such as Glassdoor. The organization has drilled deep within its systemic structures to revise policies, practices, and processes to embrace an equitable culture.

The 5th stage in the DEI Maturity Continuum represents *Systemic* ecosystem integration, which is depicted in Figure 4.7. This stage focuses on further embedding J.E.D.I. strategic vision within core operations and expanding engagement with external key stakeholders such as customers, regulators, community groups, and industry associations. An organization's J.E.D.I. North Star strategy is fully embedded into an organization's core strategy rather than being a separate strategy. It is part of all decisions and actions at all levels of the organization both internally and externally. This approach includes incorporating their J.E.D.I. organizational pillar into the brand strategy, product development, team dynamics, manager, and employee behaviors and actions, talent strategies, leadership development, procurement, industry, and community engagement. Players include the board, C-suite, managers, and employees but also expand to include a broad array of external stakeholders. Actions at this stage include industry engagement, industry leadership, community engagement, and a formalized stakeholder engagement plan. Organizational leaders actively and publicly champion their organization's J.E.D.I. vision addressing systemic barriers to justice, equity and inclusion both internally and externally. Organizational vision and mission are fully integrated into their business strategy, brand, operations, and people strategies. Leadership has a full set of integrated policies and processes to promote J.E.D.I. values within their organization that address the interconnectivity of environmental and social justice. They are seeking to influence their broader ecosystem acting as leaders and giving voice to raise issues that impact their organizations, industry, and community.. The organization publicly publishes targets and reports on goal progress with key metrics disclosing both positive and negative outcomes. To promote transparency, internal audits are supplemented by third-party racial equity or civil rights audits that are shared with both internal and external stakeholders.

While promoting supplier diversity was introduced earlier, at this stage an organization's supplier diversity program is more comprehensive and broader in scope. In addition to evaluating procurement allocations to diverse suppliers, it includes formalized

Focus	**Players**	**Actions**	**Outcome**
Engaging with key stakeholders to realize J.E.D.I. vision	HCM, DEI and Sustainability Internal and external stakeholders	Compliance, Awareness, Integration, Embedded, plus	J.E.D.I. strategic alignment Leadership team models desired
Further embed J.E.D.I. strategy into operations	Board, senior leadership, managers-organization wide	Ensuring that D&I is part of the firm's brand, platform, and agenda across the ecosystem	behaviors internally and externally More representative organization and inclusive organization
		Leadership serves as an ambassador for equity and inclusion	Internal and external systemic change
		Stakeholder engagement plan	Private-public partnerships
		External audit and reporting	Reporting transparency

Figure 4.7   Systemic.

programs such as partnering with various governmental and NGO agencies to support supplier events to extend their outreach to underrepresented suppliers. For key suppliers, requirements for action to supplement requests for information including scorecard ranking, remediation strategies within their own supply chain, and 3rd party audits. Organizations at this stage have fully formed goals, metrics, and reporting standards that they share publicly. Leaders often serve on boards and committees that address removing systemic barriers and often they are signatories to U. N. or other public policy commitments supporting social and environmental justice agendas.

Stakeholder engagement includes a robust plan for communication and feedback with key stakeholder groups. Community engagement reflects meaningful conversations around public-private partnerships to address issues such as access to education, living wages, and opportunities for underserved community members. As part of the stakeholder engagement process, leadership is engaging in conversations around establishing public-private partnerships to drive internal and external systemic change. J.E.D.I. values are fully aligned with core business strategy and are incorporated into the decision-making process and are reflected in actions and behaviors internally and externally. At this stage, an organization has reached J.E.D.I. maturity.

Understanding where your firm is on its journey on the J.E.D.I. Maturity Continuum informs strategy creation and roadmap development to guide implementation toward your organization's J.E.D.I. North Star vision. It is an important first step to determine your organizational commitment, capacity, and readiness for transformation. If J.E.D.I. champions try to launch programs and initiatives that are beyond their organization's capacity, they find that their efforts are unsuccessful. Selecting the best fit strategy is important for leadership and employee buy-in and adoption to support transformation. Even worse, leadership may be accused of "woke washing" because of lack of institutional alignment and action with professed intentions. Transformative change encompasses both vision and implementation which requires resources in terms of time, budget, and people. If the leadership team is not fully onboard, the J.E.D.I. change champion will find themselves with a lengthy list of goals and no means to implement projects and programs to achieve them. Senior leadership's commitment is crucial for overcoming organizational push back. If a J.E.D.I. strategy is a priority for the Board and C-suite, it will become a priority for senior and mid-level managers. Too often, J.E.D.I. champions are named but they are not given the support, authority, or resources to change hearts and minds. This challenge is most noticeable when transformations derail or are pushed to the back burner for "more pressing issues."

4.5 Summary

Developing a J.E.D.I. strategy is a business imperative to address investor, customer, employee, community, and other stakeholder demands. A J.E.D.I. North Star strategy aligns with organizational mission and vision to deliver on economic, environmental, and social impacts. Increasingly, stakeholders such as investors and financiers are demanding disclosure on ESG policies and practices to ensure environmental and social justice stewardship. The benefits of an integrated bottom line in terms of creating economic value through greater innovation, increased market access and opportunity, and risk mitigation are clear to the investment community.

Building equity and inclusion means creating opportunities for ownership and wealth accumulation. Improving access to capital for traditionally underrepresented entrepreneurs and business owners offers a pathway for impact. Significant changes are also needed to improve access to financing and loans for entrepreneurs that are women and POC. These changes include more inclusive practices by venture capital groups in terms of providing opportunities and access. They also involve increasing representation with the VC professional and investor communities. The solution includes offering more loans through financial institutions that support communities of color. Unless we drive systemic change within our financing systems, challenges such as closing the wealth and pay gaps will remain elusive.

As leadership steers its organization toward its J.E.D.I. vision, leveraging the J.E.D.I. Maturity Continuum provides guidance on organizational readiness and capacity to institute change. The J.E.D.I. journey is a continuous process with learnings adapted and applied to move toward the organization's J.E.D.I. North Star vision. As you move along the continuum on your transformational journey, it is important to build on successes and learn from failures as you travel toward your J.E.D.I. North Star.

Questions

1. If you are a J.E.D.I. champion seeking leadership support, what would be your approach to garnering approval and resources?
2. If you were tasked with aligning the organization's J.E.D.I. vision with its investment strategy, what questions might you ask your investment managers?
3. What J.E.D.I. policy and program changes would you most like to see in your organizations?
4. What barriers do you anticipate in trying to implement the changes selected above?
5. If you were a member of an underrepresented group and you were pitching a business proposal to a group of all White males, how might you feel?
6. If you were a VC professional, what recommendations would you make to your management team to improve diversity representation within your organization?
7. Have you ever been involved in a transformation project? If so, what were some organizational facilitators? Some barriers?
8. Where do you believe most organizations fall on the DEI Maturity Continuum? Why?
9. If you were assessing your organization's DEI maturity, where would you place it on the DEI Maturity Continuum?

10. Why do you believe that reaching the *Systemic* stage in the DEI Maturity Continuum is important?

Notes

1 OneTen, "Top Business Leaders Launch OneTen," accessed December 13, 2020, https://www.prnewswire.com/news-releases/top-business-leaders-launch-oneten-301190346.html.

2 "Small Business & Entrepreneurship Council," accessed January 11, 2021, https://sbecouncil.org/about-us/facts-and-data/.

3 "Delivering through Diversity," accessed December 14, 2020, https://www.mckinsey.com/business-functions/organization/our-insights/delivering-through-diversity.

4 "Why Diversity Matters," accessed December 14, 2020, https://www.mckinsey.com/business-functions/organization/our-insights/why-diversity-matters.

5 "How Diverse Leadership Teams Boost Innovation," U.S – EN, July 17, 2020, https://www.bcg.com/en-us/publications/2018/how-diverse-leadership-teams-boost-innovation.

6 "The Business Case for Diversity Is Now Overwhelming. Here's Why," *World Economic Forum*, accessed December 14, 2020, https://www.weforum.org/agenda/2019/04/business-case-for-diversity-in-the-workplace/.

7 "US SIF Trends Report 2020 Executive Summary.Pdf," accessed December 14, 2020, https://www.ussif.org/files/US%20SIF%20Trends%20Report%202020%20Executive%20Summary.pdf.

8 "US SIF Trends Report 2020 Executive Summary.Pdf."

9 PricewaterhouseCoopers, "New Human Capital Disclosure Rules: Getting Your Company Ready," *PwC*, accessed December 14, 2020, https://www.pwc.com/us/en/cfo-direct/publications/in-the-loop/sec-new-human-capital-disclosure-rules.html.

10 US SIF 2020 Trends Report

11 https://cornerstonecapinc.com/wp-content/uploads/Sacrifice-Nothing_A-Fresh-Look-at-Performance.pdf

12 https://www.morningstar.com/articles/994219/sustainable-funds-continue-to-rake-in-assets-during-the-second-quarter

13 "US SIF Trends Report 2020 Executive Summary.Pdf." accessed December 14, 2020, https://www.ussif.org/files/US%20SIF%20Trends%20Report%202020%20Executive%20Summary.pdf., p. 2

14 "Investing-to-Advance-Racial-Equity_Second-Edition.Pdf," accessed October 8, 2020, https://cornerstonecapinc.com/wp-content/uploads/Investing-to-Advance-Racial-Equity_Second-Edition.pdf.

15 "DiversityVC Report | Master - DiversityVCReport_Final.Pdf," accessed November 8, 2020, https://ratemyinvestor.com/pdfjs/full?file=%2FDiversityVCReport_Final.pdf.

16 "PitchBook-All Raise Report on Venture Financing in Female-Founded Startups Shows Progress, Yet Continued Gender Inequity," accessed June 16, 2021, https://pitchbook.com/media/press-releases/pitchbook-all-raise-report-on-venture-financing-in-female-founded-startups-shows-progress-yet-continued-gender-inequity.

17 Dan Primack, "Only 9.65% of Decision-Makers at U.S. Venture Capital Firms Are Women," *Axios*, accessed June 16, 2021, https://www.axios.com/venture-capital-women-tech-diversity-29c3f2f0-2d1e-4ec5-b542-7878ab149d45.html.
18 "PitchBook-All Raise Report on Venture Financing in Female-Founded Startups Shows Progress, Yet Continued Gender Inequity."
19 "DiversityVC Report | Master – DiversityVCReport_Final.Pdf."
20 "Venture Capital and Entrepreneurship," accessed June 16, 2021, https://wappp.hks.harvard.edu/venture-capital-and-entrepreneurship.
21 Joe Flint, "Netflix to Invest $100 Million in Black Community's Financial Institutions," *Wall Street Journal*, June 30, 2020, sec. Business, https://www.wsj.com/articles/netflix-to-invest-100-million-in-black-communitys-financial-institutions-11593517500.

Bibliography

"DiversityVC Report | Master - DiversityVCReport_Final.Pdf." Accessed November 8, 2020. https://ratemyinvestor.com/pdfjs/full?file=%2FDiversityVCReport_Final.pdf.

Flint, Joe. "Netflix to Invest $100 Million in Black Community's Financial Institutions." *Wall Street Journal*, June 30, 2020, sec. Business. https://www.wsj.com/articles/netflix-to-invest-100-million-in-black-communitys-financial-institutions-11593517500.

"Investing-to-Advance-Racial-Equity_Second-Edition.Pdf." Accessed October 8, 2020. https://cornerstonecapinc.com/wp-content/uploads/Investing-to-Advance-Racial-Equity_Second-Edition.pdf.

"PitchBook-All Raise Report on Venture Financing in Female-Founded Startups Shows Progress, Yet Continued Gender Inequity." Accessed June 16, 2021. https://pitchbook.com/media/press-releases/pitchbook-all-raise-report-on-venture-financing-in-female-founded-startups-shows-progress-yet-continued-gender-inequity.

PricewaterhouseCoopers. "New Human Capital Disclosure Rules: Getting Your Company Ready." *PwC*. Accessed December 14, 2020. https://www.pwc.com/us/en/cfodirect/publications/in-the-loop/sec-new-human-capital-disclosure-rules.html.

Primack, Dan. "Only 9.65% of Decision-Makers at U.S. Venture Capital Firms Are Women." *Axios*. Accessed June 16, 2021. https://www.axios.com/venture-capital-women-tech-diversity-29c3f2f0-2d1e-4ec5-b542-7878ab149d45.html.

"Small Business & Entrepreneurship Council." Accessed January 11, 2021. https://sbecouncil.org/about-us/facts-and-data/.

"US SIF Trends Report 2020 Executive Summary.Pdf." Accessed December 14, 2020. https://www.ussif.org/files/US%20SIF%20Trends%20Report%202020%20Executive%20Summary.pdf.

"Venture Capital and Entrepreneurship." Accessed June 16, 2021. https://wappp.hks.harvard.edu/venture-capital-and-entrepreneurship.

Chapter 5

Redesigning Systems for Impact

Both ecosystems and organizations are made up of systems, which are interdependent, impacting the other's inputs and outcomes. To create more just and equitable organizations, we need to understand how these interdependencies impact organizations and their broader ecosystems. Ecosystem inputs to organizations include societal norms and values, regulatory factors, competitive factors, market trends, suppliers, raw materials, demographics, labor markets, and stakeholder demands. Organizational response to these ecosystem inputs is reflected in its leadership strategy, roadmap for strategy implementation, agility in responding to changing dynamics such as societal norms and values, competitive pressures, and stakeholder demands. Internally, systems drive the operation of organizations, and they are impacted by their greater ecosystem including social norms and values being baked into organizational culture, policies, processes, and practices. In effect, systemic barriers such as racism, sexism, classism, ablism, etc. are incorporated into organizational systems and reflect our national levels of equity and inclusion represented in government, workplace, legal, and social systems. Outputs include achievement of an organization's North Star J.E.D.I. vision from an individual, team, and organizational level. Outputs also include the impacts of organizational actions on other stakeholders such as communities, competitors, and governmental agencies.

An example is corporate America's response to the broader societal response to police brutality and the horrific deaths of Black U.S. citizens. Organizational leaders issued statements of support with many backing these statements with financial commitment to drive change both internally and externally to address systemic racism. Understanding that organizations and their ecosystems have systemic barriers is the first step in the process to redesign our systems to drive just and equitable

DOI: 10.1201/9781003168072-6

outcomes. The focus of this chapter is to better understand societal, competitive, supplier, regulatory, and organizational systems and how they can both support and inhibit organizational justice, equity, and inclusion.

5.1 Organizational Systems Impact on J.E.D.I. Transformation

As with all meaningful change, the starting point is to understand your organization and its systems. The Causal Model of Organizational Performance and Change from Burke and Litwin provides a framework to consider how organizations receive and respond to external inputs and then process them through their internal systems to create outputs on an organizational, team and individual level.[1] We have adapted this model to create Figure 5.1 to better evaluate how an organization's interaction within its ecosystem and between its internal systems impacts its ability to create a more just and equitable outcome.

Using the Organization Impact Model (OIM), we consider how an organization operates internally and within its larger ecosystem. The OIM receives a variety of inputs as detailed in Table 5.1. Organizations operate in a VUCA world and are constantly receiving inputs from a variety of societal, economic, environmental, regulatory, competitive, community, technology, labor, etc. sources. Leadership develops a North Star J.E.D.I. strategy that includes environmental, social, and economic vision and goals. The implementation of the strategy includes addressing macro level demographic changes, operating in a competitive environment, obtaining raw materials, attracting investors and capital, attracting employees, complying with regulations, receiving customer feedback, addressing climate change, engaging communities, promoting social justice and negotiating with suppliers. Within this frame, organizations operate in a broader ecosystem of cultural and social norms, which include systemic barriers such as racism, sexism, heterosexism, ableism, ageism, and classism. An organization is part of its much larger ecosystem, and these factors become inputs to the organization impacting how it operates as well as the outputs produced.

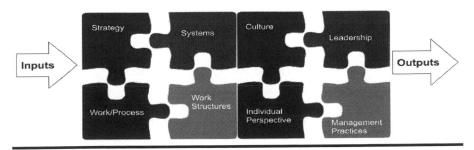

Figure 5.1 Organization Impact Model (OIM).

Table 5.1 Organization Impact Model Components

Input	Strategy	Leadership	Culture	Systems	Management Practices	Work/ Processes	Work Structures	Individual Needs	Output
Competitive Environment	Vision	Experience/ Education	Values	Decision-Making Process	Organizational Structure	Knowledge, Skills	Traditional	Talents, Knowledge, Skills	Organizational Performance
Customers	Mission	View of the Future	Beliefs	Financial Systems	Department Structure	Information Flows	Hybrid	Personal Experience	Achievement of J.E.D.I. Mission
Investors	Action Plan	People Strategy	Actions	Technology, AI	Team Structure	Rewards	Flexible	Bias	Team Contribution
Suppliers	KPIs	People Development	Behaviors	Rewards	Job Structure	Collaboration vs. Conflict	Teams	Ethnicity/ Background	Individual Contribution
Partners	Agility	Behaviors	Pillars	Benefits	Recruitment Practices	Work Location	Remote	Education	Stakeholder Engagement
Communities	Resiliency	Role Models	History	Learning & Development	Employee Engagement	Work Structures	Collaborative	Needs & Preferences	Competitive Standing
Government, Regulators	J.E.D.I.	Rewards	Story	Talent Recruitment	Feedback Process	Structures to Support Flexible/Hybrid Work	Cross-functional	Personalized Benefits	Political Activism-ESG Issues

(Continued)

Table 5.1 (Continued) Organization Impact Model Components

Input	Strategy	Leadership	Culture	Systems	Management Practices	Work/Processes	Work Structures	Individual Needs	Output
Societal Trends	ESG	Bias	Monoculture/Multicultural	Leadership Development	J.E.D.I. Requirements	Upskilling/Reskilling	Inclusive	Wellness and Well-being Programs	Community Engagement
Resources	Stakeholders	Ethnicity/Background	Inclusion/Belonging		Capacity Building	Benefits		Opportunities	Supplier Diversity
Societal Systems		Representation				Wellness/Well-being		Feeling of Belonging	Industry Influence Leadership Influence

Leadership's strategy includes responding to inputs in alignment with its J.E.D.I. vision and mission and impacts how the organization is viewed by both internal and external stakeholders. Leaders' ability to execute on their North Star J.E.D.I. vision is a function of their leadership, strategy, and organizational culture as well as the operating systems within their organization. Operating systems such as work structures, processes, work requirements, technology platforms, decision-making processes, and management practices must be realigned to support an organization's J.E.D.I. strategy. U.S. labor force statistics indicate that millennials comprise the largest generation in the workforce. While Gen Z is a recent addition to the workforce, there numbers will continue to grow. Millennials and Gen Z workers have different requirements than employees from prior generations. Organizational systems that were constructed to support a very homogeneous White male dominated workforce in the mid-20th century need to be revised to support the requirements of these new generations of workers. The millennial generation is more diverse with 44% identifying as minority.[2] In order to be reflective of their demographic identity representation, organizations need to rethink their systems around work processes and structures such as career advancement and leadership development as well as individual needs such as personalized benefits. Millennial and Gen Z generations are technology natives, and they expect that workplace technology will be able to support their work habits and requirements. Meeting this requirement may necessitate investment by organizations to upgrade technology devices and platforms. As an example, we have seen technology firms prioritizing human capital management digital transformation to better align internal processes with corporate mission and vision. Employees are expecting ease of use and automation throughout the organization, including managing their own human capital needs such as benefits, leave, and education. These generations approach work much more collaboratively making teamwork more the norm and team dynamics, structures, and collaboration support tools even more important. Workers in these newer generation are more highly educated, and they are seeking opportunities to align their values on environmental and social mission and their work. They also expect work structures to meet their requirements such as flexible hours and location flexibility. Organizations need to rethink work structures to offer hybrid models not as an exception but as a norm. To create a workplace that is welcoming to all, many workplace systems need to be reevaluated and changed to support the much more diverse requirements of the emerging workforce. Leaders with a mission to develop J.E.D.I. strategic alignment need to recognize the changes within their larger ecosystem and adapt their internal processes. Organizations operate in a VUCA world, and the rate of change is constantly accelerating. Leadership that is operating in the 21st century with a 20th century system design is at a competitive disadvantage.

Within the Burke and Litwin model, there are two major systemic categories transformational, which creates the framework and structure for organizational strategy, and transactional or operational, which implement this strategy. The transformational systems are high level such as strategy, mission, vision, culture, and leadership structure and style. These factors set the strategic vision for organization. From a transformational factor perspective, organizations that have clear cultural pillars around prioritizing people, promoting inclusion, and valuing diversity of identity, thought, and experience are better able to respond with agility to the VUCA world. They have a competitive advantage because their culture includes a clear set of guidelines for decision-making in alignment with their J.E.D.I. North Star vision. When the board and C-suite establish a strategic J.E.D.I. vision to build a culture of belonging promoting equity and inclusion as an organizational value, they are laying the foundation for transformational change. For this change to occur, it needs to be supported by leadership as evidenced by their actions, commitments, behaviors, and resource alignment. In effect, leadership needs to behave in alignment with the organization's J.E.D.I. vision both internally and externally. Through demonstrated actions, communication, prioritization, and resource alignment, the values that align with an organization's J.E.D.I. North Star mission and strategy begin to be rooted in organizational culture. Culture transformation requires time and resource commitment along with changes to policies, processes, and systems residing at the transactional level.

These operational systems impact how work is performed in the organization. They include management practices both written and unwritten, work assignments, recruitment, job descriptions, development opportunities and programs, performance management, technology, infrastructure/systems, internal processes, policies and procedures, individual worker's motivation and needs, and the structure of work groups and teams. Operational systems include both the formal systems such as policies and procedures and their often less formal application and usage. Within an organization, management practices on how fairly and equitably policies are applied, information is shared, and rewards and opportunities are allocated is known as organizational justice. Internally, organizational justice often varies across functions, departments, and teams. Much of the perceived organizational justice depends upon an employee's interaction with a manager. If managers are applying policies inconsistently based on biased perceptions, the outcomes will be inequitable. Ultimately, this creates a culture that lacks belonging and will result in competitive disadvantage. If managers and work structures aren't promoting inclusion by supporting psychological safety, flexibility, and valuing employees' contributions, their output is not going to align with an organization's J.E.D.I. vision. Consider if your management practices are inclusive and provide opportunities for all employees to demonstrate their talents and competencies. When evaluating work structures, are they designed for flexibility by offering hybrid work arrangements? Is the culture within your teams designed to promote psychological safety by encouraging team member to share their ideas without fear of retribution? Are your managers' performance goals aligned to the J.E.D.I. KPIs? Are your technology platforms and work structures able to support collaboration and hybrid work for both employees and managers? Are you meeting the needs of individuals to bring their true selves to work and to contribute fully? Taking the time evaluate your organizational systems using a lens that sheds light on a dominant monoculture, with bias baked in, facilitates redesigning systems to support the needs of a more diverse workforce, marketplace, and competitive environment.

Hybrid work is an example of a work policy, which intersects work structures/processes and individual needs. While remote work was far from the norm before 2020, the global pandemic necessitated that people work from home. Leaders rapidly established remote work structures including communication platforms, technology platforms to securely share work, new leadership tools to help managers manage remotely, new methods for recruiting, hiring, and onboarding remotely, and new ways for supporting workers remotely. While this change was enacted as a crisis response, leaders have an opportunity to broaden their perspectives and really consider the needs of their workforce in order to develop permanent hybrid models that meet workers' needs and desires for flexibility.

From an ecosystem perspective, where an organization operates can have a big impact on workers' experience with equity, inclusion, and belonging. If you are operating globally, laws and cultural norms may make working in those environments difficult or even life-threatening for some of your employees. Even in the U.S., different states have different rights for members of the LGBTQ+ community. Your organization's policies about transfers and requiring employees to work in locations that do not protect their rights or needs as individuals has a big impact on employee experience and even safety. Top talent will leave your organization if they are requested to relocate to a location where their personal and or family lives could be put at risk. Corporate decisions around communities, states, and countries for location of operations has an impact on the broader picture of equity, inclusion, and belonging.

Organizational outputs are normally thought of as products, services, or work deliverables, but they are much broader and include impacts to communities, society, the environment, education, health and wellness, and governmental systems. Each level of the organization – organization, team, individual – create its own impact. At the organizational level, an output may be the social and economic impact of delivering on its J.E.D.I. strategy, achieving its supplier diversity spending allocation goal, or its CEOs speaking out about their organization's environmental or social values and impacts. From a team perspective, an output may be delivering on a customer solution that offers a more inclusive tool such as a new technology for applying for mortgages in low-income neighborhoods, or a platform or service that improves accessibility. On an individual basis, the output may be serving as an ambassador, or perhaps a detractor, for the organization within the broader community. An individual's experience reflects their perceived organizational justice and whether their needs are being met. Each of these outputs impacts an organization's image, license to operate, access to talent, ability to serve and attract clients, community perception, and opportunity to develop collaborative partnerships.

Organizational outputs are positive, negative or even some combination. The following are several examples. An organization collaborates with a local NGO to design an outreach program encouraging underrepresented girls in their community to pursue technology-based careers. This program provides a more diverse talent pipeline for the company and provides quality jobs for these women, which addresses systemic challenges such as the wealth gap. An organization operates in a community, but there is no pathway to enhance education or skills to advance to better paying jobs for these community members. So, employees have jobs but no pathway to career advancement limiting their ability to move the needle on systemic inequities. A company provides a community well-paying job, but those jobs come with risks in terms of air pollution and the resulting health risks for community members. Too often, organizational leaders espouse a J.E.D.I. vision, but their organization's culture and operating systems act as barriers to its realization. If your systems are set up to support 20th century work structures, there is a strong likelihood that they require realignment.

5.2 Organizational Agility and Resilience

Organizations operate in a VUCA environment with the rate and scope of change coming ever faster. Change comes in many forms such as episodic, continuous, or disruptive. Responses to change depend upon the organization's objective. According to McCann and Selsky, the objectives are a function of the type of change. For episodic change, the goal is to control the impact by building buffers and redundancies. For continuous change to objective is to embrace change by removing barriers and building agility. For disruptive change, the preferred response is to prepare by building resiliency through planning for contingencies and building capabilities to recover.[3] From a J.E.D.I. transformation perspective, each of these types of change may be experienced. For transformation initiatives, we are focused on continuous change to support growth and maturation during an organization's J.E.D.I. journey. Given the social unrest and stakeholder demands for racial equity and justice during 2020, leaders experienced disruptive change with customers, employee, and communities calling for immediate change within social systems including within the business community. In response, many CEOs and executives issued statements in support of Black Lives Matter (BLM) and committed resources to drive internal and external change.

Leadership's ability to respond to and weather changing inputs reflects their organization's agility and resiliency (AR). To survive and thrive in a VUCA environment, organizations need both agility and resilience. An organization's responsiveness and ability to withstand ecosystem shocks are a function of its systems across all levels – ecosystem, organization, team, and individual. To better understand building organizational capacity to respond to change, McCann and Selsky developed the High AR model.

Table 5.2 Five High AR Capabilities

Capacity	Description
Purposefulness	Clear and positive self-identity, values, and beliefs that are demonstrated through behavior. Wellness both physically and psychologically
Awareness	Awareness of the environment developed through curiosity and active listening
Action Oriented	Open to change, being proactive or reactive, individually, or collaboratively
Resourcefulness	Creatively and innovatively using resources
Networked	Building and maintaining internal and external relationships

Source: Joseph McCann and John Selsky, *Mastering Turbulence* (San Francisco, CA: John Wiley & Sons, 2012).

The High AR Model recommends building five capacities across the individual, team, organization, and ecosystem levels. These five capacities – Purposefulness, Awareness, Action Oriented, Resourcefulness, and Networked – described in Table 5.2 are designed to promote high AR. Agility is the ability of an organization to response to change quickly and effectively. Resilience is the ability of an organization to withstand systemic shocks. For an organization to thrive, it must have high AR.

Purposefulness alignment is crucial for employees to feel engaged with their organization and its work. Leadership that aligns their mission and vision with an environmental, social, and governance (ESG) strategy have a platform based in environmental and social justice for engaging employees and other stakeholders across their ecosystem. *Purposefulness* also includes employee health and well-being. When an individual isn't able to fully engage and bring their authentic self to work, it impacts their health and wellness. Increasingly, organizations are aligning benefits and wellness programs to support a more diverse workforce with personalized offerings to meet individual requirements. *Awareness* and curiosity across all levels of the organization supports innovation and a growth mindset. It also supports interest in doing the work to learn one another's culture, history, and life experiences. Increasing the diversity of your workforce at all levels of the organization support building this key capability. Organizations that are *Action Oriented* are excited and energized including continuing on their J.E.D.I. journey to build more inclusive and equitable organizations and ecosystems. This includes designing products and services to promote equity and inclusion. *Resourcefulness* goes hand in hand with innovation allowing organizations to reinvent by reallocating resources and working with what is available to drive systemic change. Being *Networked* allows organizations to engage with internal and external stakeholders to create a more equitable an inclusive ecosystem. The call for greater board diversity representation is an example of building a more diverse network to improve organizational agility and resilience.

Their AR assessment tool (www.highAR.com) provides a valuable roadmap to assess your organization's perceptions about its environment, orientation toward change, and its capabilities to drive impact. The assessment identifies areas of strength and weakness across your organization by viewing its operation through both internal and external lens.

As organizational leaders, we have lived through a disruptive change experience in 2020 with COVID-19. Whole industries reinvented themselves, work structures changed, technology use adapted, new communication channels emerged, and managers found new ways to manage workers remotely. The capabilities in the High AR model were leveraged by many clients and colleagues. Empathetic leadership rose to the forefront as leaders adapted their own leadership styles demonstrating understanding and support for parents working remotely with children, employees caring for sick family members, and employees facing their own health challenges. Health and well-being were of great concern as the natural breaks between office and home blurred. Leaders became more aware of the needs of their communities, clients, and employees through active listening, and responding with newly designed solutions to meet their needs. Employers provided budgets for employees to upgrade internet speeds, lighting, and other equipment. Some even developed programs for employees' children to attend to give their employees uninterrupted work time. Commitments were made to support community development, lending, and education access. Partnerships were formed to create new models improving access and opportunities.

We also saw some significant inequities in organizations' responses to the pandemic. Some workers were considered essential workers and had to work in person, while others were able to work remotely. As societal support systems such as daycare facilities and schools were shutdown, women left the workforce in droves to serve as caregivers and educators for their children. Lisa Safarian, head of Bayer AGs North American crop-science business, is quoted as saying that she is very concerned that Bayer will begin to lose women with children, a demographic that organizationally they have focused on developing for the future of their business.[4] Women feel exhausted, burned out, and as if they are not doing either their jobs or parenting well. For women with caregiver responsibilities at the intersectionality of race, gender identity, and disabilities, the stress levels are even higher. These stress levels impact performance, wellness, and well-being. Gaining perspective on the lived experiences of your employees supports building organizational systems to support an equitable culture.

Using the OIM and the High AR models as assessment tools provides leadership with insight into their organizations' transformational and operational systems as well as their intersectionality with their broader ecosystems. The assessment highlights an organization's agility and resilience to lead and adapt to change. With this information, leadership is able to identify organizational systemic dynamics including facilitators and barriers to creating a more just and equitable organization

5.3 Organizational Culture

Organizational culture plays a significant role in determining vision, mission, goals, actions, and behaviors. Culture is both visible and invisible. It is a representation of an organization's vision, shared values, attitudes, and beliefs. Culture is reflected in a variety of ways such as work habits and structures, language, symbols, assumptions, power structures, decision-making processes, physical spaces, and even compensation structures. An organization's view of environmental and social justice reflects its cultural norms and values. Culture is apparent through the board and C-suite's actions, words, and deeds and the values that are codified as organizational pillars. An organization's point of view is reflected in how senior leaders represent their organization both internally to employees and colleagues and externally to peer organizations, community members, and other stakeholder groups. Fully integrating a culture that prioritizes environmental and social justice into business strategy gives leadership, managers, team leaders, and individuals a set of values and a framework through which to evaluate options and to make decisions in alignment with strategic pillars. Culture is represented throughout the organization in the language used, in the structure of meetings, in behaviors that are preferred, accepted, and even tolerated. In redesigning organizational systems for impact, we must look deeply within the organization to really understand how work is performed, what is valued, and what is rewarded.

Expanding workforce diversity representation requires creating a work environment of belonging that supports an equitable culture. Organizations that have expanded their talent sources and are seeking diverse talent are taking steps in the right direction. In order to keep diverse talent, we must promote a culture of belonging that welcomes and values individual identity. We must shift from a dominant culture with a singular set of values, beliefs, and attitudes to an equitable culture that values and integrates perspectives from a variety identities, cultures, and experiences into the organization's systems, processes, and policies. Employees bring an intersectionality of race, culture, experience, education, gender identity, and other identifiers to work. When building a culture for belonging, leaders must consider that employees don't fall into predefined groups; they are representatives of multiple groups. For example, a Black, cisgender female raised in an urban setting with a master's degree may have different priorities and requirements from an employer than a Black, transgender female from a rural background with a high school degree. Ensuring that your organization's culture supports a diverse workforce is crucial to the J.E.D.I. transformation process.

Understanding an organization's culture necessitates viewing the organization from both an internal and external perspective. The Cultural Assessment for Environmental and Social Impact found in Appendix 5A offers a series of questions to guide evaluating your organization in terms of its current mission, vision, strategy, goals, and internal and external systems. The objective is to assess where your organization's strengths and weaknesses are relative to embedding a J.E.D.I.

culture. These questions and their answers begin to paint a picture of an organization's commitment to environmental and social justice. This assessment provides an overview of organizational climate that can be utilized as a foundation by leaders tasked with strategic J.E.D.I. visioning and/or those seeking continuous improvement during the transformation process. The assessment can be given to J.E.D.I. committee members, focus groups, a select group of leaders, managers, and employees to shed light on their perceptions of the organization's social and environmental justice culture. It can even be modified and used with key external stakeholders. The organizational profile depicted from the assessment provides leadership with information on areas that are being addressed and areas for improvement in order to identify or refine strategic priorities.

5.4 Talent Systems

As we dive into internal systems and the role that they have in driving culture and creating more just and equitable organizations, we need to consider systems that impact access and opportunity for people within the organization. One area is the talent ecosystem around sourcing and recruiting talent, and retaining and developing talent. When we look for talent from the same sources, we find the same kind of talent. Recently, Charles Scharf, CEO of Wells Fargo blamed the lack of Black employees within senior levels of their organization on a limited pool of available talent. Yet, the total number of post-secondary degrees awarded to Black students rose by 63% from the 2000–2001 to the 2015–2016 academic year timeframe.[5] Clearly, it isn't a talent pool issue. Perhaps, the Wells Fargo human capital management team needs to redefine their recruitment criteria. Many organizations have a very specific set of schools or requirements that they use for recruiting talent. Broadening the pool of institutions can have a significant impact on generating qualified candidates. Tapping into historically black colleges and universities (HBCUs) is a source of diverse talent, but so are public universities and community colleges. Rethinking recruiting efforts and resource allocation has a significant impact on generating a more diverse talent pool. Partnering with community-based groups helps expand the talent pool and pipeline by encouraging underrepresented groups such as BIPOC or female students to pursue degrees in technology, data science, and coding by offering resources and programming like workshops, classes, tutoring, and internships.

Building a more diverse applicant and candidate pool is only the beginning. From a retention and development perspective, consider the structures that you have within your organization and how they make applicants, candidates and employees feel. The current DEI industrial complex with its check the box approach and mandatory DEI training isn't driving impact. Despite decades of DEI programs and initiatives, the number of senior level Black employees has not increased, it has declined. The percentage of senior level employees that identify as Black has fallen to 4.1% in 2018 from 8% in 2015.[6] Instead, we must focus on creating a culture of belonging, where employees can bring their full selves to work, contribute, and be valued and appreciated. The organizational climate needs to promote and encourage diversity of perspective, style, culture, and experience. As you evaluate your talent ecosystem, think about whether it supports a singular dominate culture or a multifaceted equitable culture.

Consider organizational artifacts such as media representation including branding and messaging. Artifacts should reflect an equitable culture in terms of language usage, image selection, and stories told. Both candidates and employees are assessing organizational artifacts to determine cultural fit and future opportunities. In addition, talents systems such as work assignments, development opportunities, performance evaluations and feedback all impact employees' perceived value and sense of belonging. Other operating systems like decision-making processes, team structure, manager roles, and resource allocation impact employees' experience and engagement. As outlined in the Cultural Assessment for Environmental and Social Impact, organizations must dissect their policies and processes to understand where bias is built into the system and its implementation.

Organizational systems impact how work is done, what is valued, and who is credited for outcomes. How fairly and consistently are policies and procedures implemented? Are certain individuals given a pass on adhering to standards for behavior, because they generate significant business? Unfortunately, policy implementation can vary by department and even team. If one manager agrees to a hybrid work arrangement and another does not, the employee experience is departmentally rather than organizationally dependent. Manager specific work norms such as requiring employees to work constantly without downtime results in employee burnout and lower productivity. To create equitable cultures, organizations must redesign their human resource policies to provide more support and flexibility as well as resources for both managers and employees. These enhancements may include revised paid time off policies, flexibility in hours, resource guides, and Employee Resource Groups (ERGs). Sharing a story from a member of an ERG, which was formed to support working parents, on the talent platform demonstrates to potential applicants that the organization values employees that need to manage work life integrations. This type of messaging allows people to identify with current employees and envision a future with the organization. The perceptions that employees have of an organization are reflected not only internally but also externally through their interactions with community and industry groups. As employees tell their stories and experiences with the firm, a picture is painted for the world. Employees can act both as ambassadors and detractors.

To gauge your employees' sentiment about their work experience, we have provided the following assessment. Responses to these types of questions begin to build a profile of your organizational climate from your employees' perspective.

EMPLOYEE SENTIMENT ASSESSMENT:

1. Are employees' individual needs being served?
2. Are their ideas and work valued?
3. Do they feel they belong?
4. Do they feel appropriately compensated?
5. Do their values align with those of the organization?
6. Is their team toxic or collaborative?
7. Are there barriers or obstacles for advancement?
8. Do they have opportunities to develop new skills?

Employees' responses identify how well their daily work experience aligns with an organization's J.E.D.I. vision. The details shared identify conditions for success as well as barriers to progress. Answers reflect the nature of your culture in terms of it being a single dominant culture or an equitable culture where a variety of styles, heritages, and experiences are supported. Often, answers to these questions vary depending upon location or manager. Even when the C-suite adopts a J.E.D.I. strategy, operational systems such as communication platforms, decision-making processes, reporting structures, people management, and work processes impact how this vision and mission is translated into people's daily work experience.

5.5 Procurement

Procurement is another operating system that can be leveraged to expand an organization's J.E.D.I. footprint. Through an organization's supply chain, suppliers provide inputs to organizations such as raw materials, component parts, or services which are then embedded into an organization's output, and its environmental and social justice impacts. In effect, an organization's ultimate output, whether it is a good or service, is impacted by the J.E.D.I. footprints of its vendors. When evaluating suppliers, organizations that are pursuing a J.E.D.I. strategy will want to purchase from a diverse group of suppliers as well as suppliers that have evaluated their own supply chain impacts. Some thoughts to consider:

1. Do we have a supplier diversity goal? What is it?
2. How can we support our supplier diversity goal while meeting the needs of our operation?
3. How is our procurement budget supporting or inhibiting our organization's J.E.D.I. vision?
4. How is diversity represented in our key supplier's supply chain?
5. How are our key suppliers managing environmental and social justice within their own operations?

6. What is their track record on human rights? Environmental impact? Social justice?
7. How are we tracking supplier performance?
8. What impact have our procurement policies had on our suppliers?

Suppliers are impacted by organizational outputs in terms of where and with whom dollars are spent on goods and services. Assessing your suppliers, vendors, and professional service providers to understand your diversity spend is a good starting point. Establish goals for sourcing with underrepresented groups and monitor your progress. Supplier diversity programs are an important tool in an organization's J.E.D.I. toolkit. Redirecting purchasing dollars to historically disadvantaged businesses can have a positive impact on breaking down long standing wealth gaps. Reallocating resources via the procurement process can have a significant impact on improving community health as well as racial and gender equity. Several organizations have established significant dollar targets to spend with minority and women owned businesses. One such group is the Billion Dollar Roundtable (https://www.billiondollarroundtable.org/). Founded in 2001, members of this group pledge to spend at least $1 billion dollars of their procurement budgets with minority and women owned businesses. Members include major companies such as Apple, IBM, Walmart, Ford, and Verizon. In addition to the spending commitment, the program promotes and shares best practices in creating supply chain diversity excellence. While most organizations won't be spending at this level, it is important to make a commitment and to follow through with a more equitable purchasing allocation.

To ensure that organizations have qualified minority, women, and veteran owned suppliers, procurement departments need to establish relationships with local business and community organizations such as chambers of commerce, women, or minority owned business certifying agencies and other minority supplier groups. Many organizations co-host diversity supplier events to meet diverse suppliers and to explain their own internal processes and requirements to do business with their organization. Coordinating with local certifying organizations and agencies is another great way to build a network. In addition, leveraging agency certification requirements is a useful guideline for establishing your own organization's diversity requirements. Certification as a women business enterprise, minority business enterprise, disabled owned, or service-disabled veteran owned business can come through state government programs, cities, or through national certifying councils such as WBENC, National Minority Supplier Development Council (NMSDC), and Disability:IN.

In order to promote women and minority owned business participation, consider the requirements that you are asking of women owned, minority owned, veteran owned, LGBTQ+ owned, disabled owned, or any other historically underrepresented business to meet. Creating training or support materials to build their capabilities to participate allows for greater access. Many large organizations utilize Enterprise Resource Planning (ERP) systems such as Ariba for procurement opportunities. Offering training or a resource guide to these types of systems can make bidding opportunities more accessible. When developing the request for proposal (RFP), it helps to provide clear guidelines including certifications and licensing requirements. Even if an underrepresented supplier isn't qualified to bid on a particular RFP, the skills and certification requirements provide information for future bidding opportunities.

Another supplier diversity tool is to create an RFP with minority, veteran, or women owned business carve outs. These require a certain percentage of the business to be allocated to suppliers from one of these groups. While this can be a useful tool in terms of reallocating dollars to underrepresented businesses, it needs to be constructed with great thought and care around objectives. If the winning RFP bid is also required to be the lowest price, this pricing condition may cause prime contractors to put price pressure on minority subcontractors having the opposite impact of promoting economic wealth distribution.

Supply chains also include professional services such as consultants, attorneys, and accountants. These services provide additional opportunities to allocate procurement dollars in alignment with an organization's J.E.D.I. strategic vision. Microsoft and Uber are among the firms requiring more diverse representation from their law firms. Others like Novartis have added a financial incentive to drive alignment. Novartis will withhold 15% of its legal fees if the law firm doesn't meet its diversity targets.[7] Their focus is to increase the representation of BIPOC attorneys in law firms, which remains low at less than 5% of attorneys and 2% of partners at U.S. firms.[8] While recruitment for BIPOC attorneys has improved, there are still systemic barriers to success within the firms themselves. Much of this lack of representation is attributed to the internal systems for work assignments within law firms. Attorneys that identify as Black say that they are not given sufficiently high-profile work to ensure a spot on the partner track. The way clients are distributed has also impacted their success. Perhaps, this new approach by clients to tie diversity, equity, and inclusion performance to contract offerings and billing rates will have a lasting impact.

Unfortunately, many supplier diversity programs have good intentions but poor configuration and structure. Over the years, I have attended organizations' supplier diversity outreach and procurement networking events. While these are good tools to help fill the procurement pipeline with minority vendors, the results of these events are often less beneficial to minority vendors than hoped. Many minority vendors have become disenfranchised as they have attended these events for years, followed up with contacts, and attempted to become a vendor without success. To drive impact, these supplier diversity events need to have clear goals and objectives in terms of delivering meaningful spending reallocations to impact an organization's supplier diversity goals and outcomes.

Taking supplier diversity goals a step further includes considering the vendors' own J.E.D.I. performance within their organizations and their supply chain. Mandating that suppliers complete questionnaires that include environmental and social justice questions provides procurement officers with actionable information.

Based on the data gathered and the actions steps taken, this approach offers a means of impacting equity and inclusion beyond the scope of your own organization. Answers to these surveys can help procurement develop a scorecard ranking suppliers' J.E.D.I. impacts to facilitate directing procurement dollars to support alignment with an organization's J.E.D.I. mission. Some organizations are going a step further and asking for their suppliers to assess their own supply chain on social, environmental, and economic justice issues. Once data is received, the suppliers are given a score and ranking based on their own supply chain impacts. Then, procurement professionals drill down into their key supplier rankings requesting details on remediation strategies and action plans that have been undertaken by key suppliers within their own supply chain. Those organizations that are pursing J.E.D.I. strategies are rewarded with contracts and additional business. The goal for supplier diversity programs is to remove barriers and to even the playing field for minority owned, women owned, LGBTQ+ owned, disabled owned, and veteran owned businesses and to improve outcomes in these traditionally underserved communities.

CASE: PENNSYLVANIA CONVENTION CENTER: DRIVING IMPACT THROUGH SUPPLIER DIVERSITY

By Erika L. White, CDE

Erika L. White, CDE is a Diversity Equity & Inclusion leader who currently serves as the first head of Diversity Equity and Inclusion for Pennoni Associates, a national Consulting Engineering firm headquartered in Philadelphia. Erika joins Pennoni from the Pennsylvania Convention Center, an ASM Global managed facility, where she served as the head of Diversity and Inclusion.

She is the co-founder of the networking group, The Philadelphia Diversity Professionals Consortium, and serves as a Board of Trustee for the Shipley School and Board of Director for the Center City Proprietors Association and ISM Philadelphia. Erika holds a Bachelor of Science in Business and Administration from Drexel University Lebow College of Business and has received her designation as a Certified Diversity Executive from the Institute for Diversity Certification.

THE PROGRAM

The Pennsylvania Convention Center/ASM Global (PCC) Purchasing Department is a partner with the local business community and seeks to obtain goods, services, and consultants that ensure the seamless operation of the Convention Center.

The PCC is committed to ensuring equal opportunity to economic opportunities available at the Center. Through its Diversity, Inclusion & Anti-Discrimination Policy and its staff, the Authority seeks to promote contractor, subcontractor, vendor and supplier opportunities for Minority, Women and Disadvantaged Business Enterprises, as well as for other underutilized persons. The PCC is committed to fostering an environment in which all businesses are free to contract with the PCC on an equitable basis, and without the impediments of discrimination. To that end, the PCC will employ all lawful programs at its disposal in any and all contracting opportunities at the Center.[9]

Supplier Diversity Program

The PCC is committed to the utilization of Minority/Women/Disabled Business Enterprises in all phases of contract opportunities to provide equal opportunity and access for all contractors, subcontractors, vendors, consultants, and suppliers to the economic benefits for contract opportunities generated by the PCC.

This Policy is intended to provide meaningful and substantial opportunity for all businesses and to prevent exclusionary and discriminatory business practices. The PCC is committed to fostering an environment in which all businesses are free to participate in business opportunities without the impediments of discrimination and are able to contract with the PCC on an equitable basis. To that end, the PCC will employ all lawful programs at its disposal in requests for proposals or invitations to bid on contracts.

REINVIGORATE THE PROGRAM

The mission of the PCC is to drive economic prosperity for the greater Philadelphia region, as a world class convention center. One of the ways that we seek to fulfill that mission is by partnering with stakeholders and strategic partners in the Commonwealth to maximize the business impact of the PCC, while maintaining a strong commitment to diversity and inclusion.

Our commitment to Diversity Equity and Inclusion is not new to the Center's history. Some key highlights are the $789 Million Dollar 2011 Expansion. It was the largest public works project taken on by the Commonwealth and had a 29% MWDBE participation. To reinvigorate the program, in 2017 we hosted a Diverse Vendor Outreach Day. Interested vendors signed up for the new vendor portal. Attendees enjoyed a panel discussion from current diverse vendors who had success working with the Convention Center. This was a great launch to the vendor portal. In order to breathe new life and vitality to the program, we hosted the Doing Business with the PA Convention Center event in 2019 and again virtually in 2020 that demystified the RFP/BID process.

STRATEGIC PLAN DEVELOPMENT

Through the evaluation and assessment of the current Diversity & Inclusion initiatives as the newly hired Diversity & Inclusion manager, I identified areas where we made strides in the first 6 months and where I felt our efforts can best be focused. I used the diversity and inclusion strategic plan to guide my efforts. The plan is inclusive of three key areas of focus as well as plans and recommendations for implementation for the following year.

Through the evaluation and assessment of the Supplier Diversity program and in light of our mission and focus on Diversity & Inclusion, we developed a strategy that includes a focus on three key elements:

Supplier Diversity
Workforce Development
Conventions/Conferences

Because each key element had a current assessment, a goal, and a recommendation for a way forward, when COVID-19 struck we were able to pivot while still maintaining our focus.

ENGAGEMENT OF BOARD OF DIRECTORS

The Board of Directors has a long history of supporting Diversity, Equity, and Inclusion so they were no strangers to being fully supportive. When the strategic plan was presented, they offered both feedback and support. During our Diversity, Equity, and Inclusion events, the leaders of the D&I Board Committee came and gave remarks and were active participants to ensure that we upheld our best and good faith efforts for all of our procurement outreach through RFPs and BIDs.

ENGAGEMENT OF SENIOR LEADERSHIP

The PCC leadership comprised of the President and Vice-President/General Counsel and on the operations side the General Managers. All members of the senior leadership were beyond supportive off all of the initiatives that I recommended. By clearly outlining the business case for our outreach and subsequent expansion of our supplier diversity program, the senior leaderships were fully onboard and committed to the success of the program. The senior leadership continually showed up to show support for my efforts on all levels and was a key component to our success.

COMMUNITY OUTREACH

As mentioned, we hosted the 1st Doing Business Event in 2019 as a community outreach tool. We welcomed over 150 vendors, suppliers, prime, and subcontractors to participate. We covered a variety of topics including Labor Relations, Rules of the Convention Center, Procurement Compliance, and Diversity and Inclusion.

Our Goals:
- To increase our vendor list of small and diverse businesses
- To demystify how business is conducted at the Center
- Share our upcoming opportunities

As a result of the event, we achieved all of our goals and increased our vendor contacts by 26.05%. In summary, the "Doing Business with the Convention Center" event achieved its goals by renewing our commitment to supplier diversity to the community, we increased our pool of outreach (MWBDE vendors) and let contractors, subcontractors, and other vendors know the process for securing a contract or doing business with the center overall.

Another important part to community outreach is supporting the organizations in the area that are committed to the advancement of diversity & inclusion as well as supplier diversity. These organizations include but are not limited to the following:

- PHL Diversity – Advisory Board member
- Pennsylvania Diversity Council
- Institute for Supply Management
- Women's Business Enterprise Center (WBEC) East
- Hispanic Chamber of Commerce – Greater Philadelphia Hispanic Chamber of Commerce (GPHCC)
- African American Chamber of Commerce – The African-American Chamber of Commerce of PA, NJ and DE (AACC)
- Asian Chamber of Commerce – Asian AACCGP
- The Philadelphia Tribune
- The Chinatown Development Corporation

I engaged with each of these organizations and others to fully communicate our goals and mission and play a key role in the furtherment of diversity & inclusion in the area.

A key area of outreach is the launch of the inaugural Pennsylvania Convention Center Diversity & Inclusion Champion Award. This award was granted to an individual, business, or organization that exemplifies The Pennsylvania Convention Center Authority's commitment to Diversity & Inclusion. For 2020, we granted The Pennsylvania Conference for Women with the award.

I also served as a member of the planning committee for the 2020 Diversity and Inclusion Conference Philadelphia. The conference is a leadership multi-industry and education summit dedicated to the exchange of insights and concepts about Diversity, Inclusion, and Equity best practices. Due to COVID-19, the Conference was canceled but The Philadelphia Diversity Professionals Consortium, which I co-founded, hosted a virtual preview panel discussion in collaboration with the 2020 Diversity and Inclusion Conference.

MEASURE IMPACT OF THE OUTREACH

Our efforts had a marked impact on our outreach. There was a 26% increase in our business network. To track and monitor our commitment and spend, the Diversity, Legal, and Compliance Departments developed contractual language and spearheaded the development of three key forms that actively collects contract and vendor spend as well as workforce utilization.

We use this data to track our supplier diversity commitment and spend. This will allow us to analyze our trends and set internal goals.

FULL ASSESSMENT

Working closely with the Legal and Compliance Department, an ongoing process for assessment was established to compare our diversity spend actual vs. projected. A full assessment of the program is done on a quarterly basis.

REPORT

A regular report is issued to the Diversity & Inclusion committee of the Board as well as the PCC's Senior Leadership. We learned through regular reporting that what gets measured gets attention, so regular reporting of the progress of our tracking of our spend as well as our community outreach allowed us to increase our supplier diversity outreach and participation commitment. Best practices are to regularly communicate with internal stakeholders and potential external vendors, suppliers, and contractors to share opportunities.

CONTINUED EFFORTS

Diversity & Inclusion continues to be a chief priority of the PCC. Through limited resources due to COVID-19, the in-person efforts have not been able to move forward but we have still committed to advancing the strategy originally established. We had a very successful virtual 2nd Annual "Doing Business with the Pennsylvania Convention Center" event in October of 2020. We held the event during The City of Philadelphia's 36th Annual Minority Enterprise Development (MED) Week. Our objective was to give a thorough explanation of our supplier diversity paperwork. Nearly 100 registrants received the information. When surveyed, we received very positive feedback. The event was rated overall excellent or very good as well as considered organized and was the right amount of time. Most of the respondents heard about the event through our email blast. We received comments that the event was very informative and to the point and attendees appreciated the contributions of the staff. There is interest in a business-to-business matching opportunity as well as a deeper understanding of how the diversity and inclusion factors into the decision-making process. At the conclusion of the event, we received a significant increase in registrants in the vendor portal.

LESSONS LEARNED

Having a clearly defined strategic plan was pivotal to both the execution of our supplier diversity program and the survival of our initiatives through the COVID-19 pandemic. Even though the hospitality industry was hit very hard by the pandemic because the Board and senior leadership of the PCC is committed to this work, we were able to continue with our strategy and effectively pivot and engage the community virtually.

5.6 External Organizations and Stakeholders

An organization's J.E.D.I. journey incorporates both internal and external stakeholder engagement. Competitive influences and industry associations impact organizational priorities and best practices. What is happening with peer organizations sets the bar on industry practice as well as topics and issues prioritized at industry gathering, forums, and events. Leading and sharing your organization's J.E.D.I. strategy, actions, investment priorities, and programs expands your organization's sphere of influence with peers. Encouraging your leadership team to speak at events on social justice issues such as racial and gender equity begins to change the conversation around justice, equity, diversity, and inclusion. Sharing projects and highlighting best practices and lessons learned facilitates growth and maturity for peer organizations and group members. Many policy changes have come about because of organizational peer pressure.

In the U.S., organizations belong to business groups such as their local chamber of commerce. While these groups are excellent for networking, obtaining resources, and gathering information, it is important to note that many of them advocate for legislative policy decisions as well. For example, the Philadelphia Chamber of Commerce initially supported a Pennsylvania Republican lead initiative against an increase in the minimum wage. Philadelphia is one of the poorest U.S. cities with 25% of Philadelphia residents living below the federal poverty rate.[10] While this policy position was eventually reversed, it is crucial, as a leader, to understand the impacts of organizations like chambers of commerce have on our communities. Part of your organization's dues go toward supporting policy initiatives with which you may not be aligned. In addition, information is increasingly transparent and stakeholders will expect answers as to why your organization is supporting, through your affiliation, legislation that is misaligned with your organizational values. Another area to consider is lobbying efforts and political action committee contributions. If you are messaging in one direction and funding in another direction, you run the risk of being identified as an organization that is "woke washing". Transparency and authenticity are crucial in demonstrating that organizational actions align with your mission.

Interactions with community, industry groups, and peer institutions are part of an organization's external systems, and they can have significant impact on how and organization is perceived. Communities have broad reaching impact on an organization's license to operate. Perception from community members drives an organization's ability to attract and retain employees. It also impacts their ability to partner with NGOs to offer programs designed to engage community members including underserved populations. An organization's reputation is impacted by its relationship with external stakeholders including regulators, community members, and competitors. Using social media, any group of stakeholders can share its views, positive or negative, on the organization. Management's stakeholder engagement plan defines community engagement and if and how community voices are incorporated into an organization's strategy vision.

From an investment perspective, we continue to see a rise in shareholder resolutions related to racial justice, diversity, inclusion, and equity as investors are seeking alignment between a company's J.E.D.I. strategy and internal actions for social justice issues such as BLM. The Interfaith Center on Corporate Responsibility, or ICCR, which is made up of over 300 member organizations, has filed 244 shareholder resolutions for the 2021 proxy season. Resolutions related to racial justice and diversity total 64 and represent a 50% increase from last year.[11] Stakeholders including shareholders are looking for authentic actions that align social justice actions with an organization's core mission and vision.

5.7 Designing for Organizational Impact

Designing an inclusive and equitable organization is a long-term strategy requiring board and senior management commitment. The process necessitates strategy development, resource alignment, and change management. While management may offer DEI lunch and learns, training initiatives, and a whole host of events, if creating an equitable and inclusive organization is not a core strategy, there will be no J.E.D.I. cultural transformation. Driving system change requires a J.E.D.I. roadmap to inform a transformational journey.

Figure 5.2 outlines a model to drive J.E.D.I. transformation deep within the systems of an organization. The process begins with engaging with key stakeholders to assess your organization's current state and to better understand internal and external stakeholder needs and requirements. Using this information to inform J.E.D.I. vision and strategy provides a roadmap for effective transformation and provides a North Star strategic focus for aligning organizational decisions. To realize this vision, the roadmap must highlight short- and long-term goals, resource allocation,

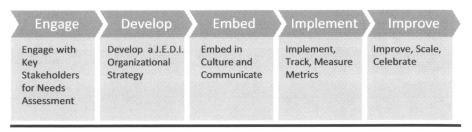

Figure 5.2   Designing an Inclusive & Equitable Organization.

and implementation plans. Effectively, the roadmap is the plan that bridges the gap between an organization's current state and its North Star vision. For an organization's J.E.D.I. vision to be impactful, it must be embedded into the culture and cascaded throughout the organization. Senior leadership must shift their own hearts and minds and be advocates and demonstrate their commitment in actions and behaviors. Otherwise, DEI programs that are offered but not really prioritized and valued will have little impact. The transformation process requires deep reflection on current norms, values, and beliefs as well as an assessment of current policies, processes, and procedures. In designing for J.E.D.I., we recommend a leadership development program that promotes understanding of key topics such as power and privilege, history of oppression, systemic racism, classism, sexism, ethnocentrism, and heterosexism. Gaining perspective and developing empathetic leaders is crucial to the process. Building a workplace that promotes psychological safety, proactively combats systems of privilege and racism, embraces approaches, styles, and perspective from a variety of identity groups, and promotes differences as an opportunity for learning and growth is key to the transformation. While senior leadership is vital to the success of transformational culture change so is engaging managers and employees. Creating two-way communication with clear messaging and a feedback mechanism for employees, teams, and managers provides a structure for input supporting continuous improvement. In the wake of the BLM movement, White leaders were making public statements of support, but many were unsure of what to say to Black colleagues. Opening a dialogue, acknowledging one's own pain and others, and authentically listening to people share their experiences lays the foundation for trust. Part of this transformation is being open and willing to listen to diverse perspectives and to seriously consider their merits for improving organizational outcomes and effectiveness. To be impactful, an organization's North Star J.E.D.I. vision must be effectively communicated across the organization so that it is embedded in people, policy, and processes becoming part of everyone's daily experience. Developing communication plans that encourage leadership to actively listen to a variety of voices ensures that they are hearing diversity of perspective. While the vision and the implementation will vary by the maturity phase of organization's J.E.D.I. journey, at all phases, authenticity is crucial for building trust, engagement, and breaking down silos and barriers that support bias and privilege. Training should focus on capacity building to support perspective taking, skill development, and new tool utilization. Core to the transformation is system redesign. Each area of the organization must be evaluated to breakdown discrimination, bias, and the resulting inequities built-in to policies, processes, and practices. This process includes identifying conditions for success as well as conditions that erect or maintain barriers.

As this process is undertaken, it is recommended that programs and projects are rolled out as pilots to allow for testing, modification, and then scaled across the organization. Program and projects should be prioritized based on alignment with strategic goals, expected impact, and capacity for success. To measure impact and communicate progress transparently, establish metrics, track them, and report on them regularly to key stakeholders. The goal is an integrated J.E.D.I. strategy that supports psychological safety, embraces differences, and values feedback creating a culture of belonging that drives innovation and new opportunities for organizational success.

The following case, which highlights the experience of Coke with their DEI programs and initiatives, highlights the need for designing for inclusion and equity. It highlights the need for fundamental change in leadership's hearts and minds as well as the value of listening, continuous improvement, and prioritization of a J.E.D.I. strategy as a guiding, North Star vision. Otherwise, your organizations may steer off course.

TWO DECADES OF DEI AT COKE: THE GAINS AND LOSSES

Coca-Cola Co. (Coke) has been actively addressing DEI for over 20 years. Their DEI initiatives were an outgrowth of a commitment made after losing a $192 million lawsuit for discriminating against their Black employees.[12] Ten years after their foray into creating a more just and equitable workplace for Black employees, Coke was generating impressive results. "By 2010, Black employees held 15% of executive roles in the U.S., up from 1.5% in 1998, shortly before the lawsuit was filed."[13] Unfortunately, within another 10 years, much of their progress was lost. In 2020, the number of Black employees in executive roles had fallen to 8%, and the representation of Black employees in salaried positions had fallen to 15%, which is actually lower than where they started when they began their initiative in 2000.[14] How did Coke's initial success turn to such failure in the subsequent decades?

During the first decade, Coke implemented new policies and practices supported by metrics and analytics. They initiated data analysis and people analytics to inform managers encouraging them to make data-driven employment decisions, including compensation, performance reviews, promotions, and layoffs. Through analytics, they identified disparities based on factors such as race in bonus or promotion recommendations. Compensation plans were redesigned tying executive pay to increasing diversity in the salaried workforce. HR expanded external recruiting and started an executive mentorship program designed to retain and promote Black employees. During layoffs in 2003, an adverse action report indicated that bias was creeping into the pool recommended for layoffs. Coke's leadership responded by improving the process with senior leadership agreeing to lower layoff targets and preserving more jobs, even though it meant missing several financial targets. In 2007, Coke was named the 4th most diverse organization in Diversity Inc's list of the top 50 most diverse organizations.

In the same year, gender equity was added as a priority to Coke's DEI goals. The decision to focus on women was sponsored by then CEO, Muhtar Kent. He realized that 70% of purchasing decisions were made by women; yet, women only accounted for 23% of Coke's leadership team.[15] Leadership initiatives for women were given top priority. In 2011, the data that Coke reported changed reflecting their broader definition of diversity; rather than reporting by race, they reported on multicultural employees. While the multicultural metrics show improving racial diversity at Coke, Black employee representation was actually declining. Other policies began to change, as well. They no longer tied executive compensation to diversity targets. Internally, employees believed that the issue impacting Black employee representation was a lack of inclusion and belonging rather than a diversity recruitment issue. While Black talent was being hired, they weren't staying because of lack of opportunity and speed of advancement.

Based on their current assessment, Coke's leadership team is reprioritizing Black employees especially at the executive level. They have created a new HR position focusing on diversity in executive recruitment. They are launching a 10-year internal and external talent-recruiting program for people of color with a focus on Black executives. In addition, they are focusing recruitment on selecting talent to develop for future career paths, and they are requiring leadership bias training. They are launching a training and development program modeled after their women's leadership council again with an emphasis on Black executives. The company has also pledged to disclose pay equity data, annually. Coke is setting goals for Black representation in executive roles based on the availability of candidates inside the company, the general labor pool, and on census data in markets where the company has large footprints. In Atlanta, where Coke was founded and headquartered, 51% of the population identifies as Black. So, there will need to be significant change and transformation to reach this goal.

The DEI story at Coke is a cautionary tale. It is a story where metrics and analytics masked a deepening problem of declining representation of Black employees within the ranks of executive and salaried employees. These are the levels in an organization that promote wealth accumulation and break down the systemic barriers of generational poverty, increase access to education, promote access to quality housing, and support mortgage lending. While tremendous progress was made in the first decade, backsliding because of a changing DEI vision more than offset those gains within the next decade. While Coke undertook many programs related to DEI, their story suggests that it never really became part of their culture. We will see if their transformative approach this time generates the long-term desired rebalancing of power and opportunity across their organization.

5.8 Summary

Taking a systems design view of an organization from and internal and external perspective allows us to begin the process of understanding of how these systems both promote and detract from creating just and equitable organizations. Using the OIM, we begin to trace both our transformational and operational systems to understand how these structures determine our organizational values, beliefs, and actions. These systems are impacted by societal trends, competition, resources, investors, access to capital, and communities. Outputs are generated on multiple levels – ecosystem, organization, team, and individual. Some outputs are more traditional like products and services, while others are less traditional like promoting supplier diversity. Organizational outputs might be positive like new services to promote more equitable access to capital and financing or negative like pollution, racism, and poverty. As leaders, we need to be cognizant of the impacts and outputs that our organizations have on our broader society.

Our decisions on vision, culture, organizational design, work environments, and processes, as well as the needs of individual employees impact our organization's long-term viability. Gone are the days of a single definer of success. Stakeholders including investors, employees, customers, and community members demand an integrated bottom-line which includes planet, people, and profit impacts in their measures of success. Ensuring that your business is agile and resilient includes being purposeful across all areas. Leading for success in the 21st century requires empathetic leaders who are open, listening, and considering the needs of their diverse workforce. Leadership skills for the 21st century include actively listening, scanning for changing trends, and being resourceful and dynamic in responding to changes. These include adapting and rebuilding internal systems to prioritize environmental and social justice internally and externally.

Designing an inclusive and equitable organization requires rethinking leadership's role as well as organizational policies, processes, and practices. All of our organizations have the "isms" embedded within them reflecting our larger social systemic biases and barriers. To drive impactful change, the J.E.D.I. strategy and roadmap must facilitate a fundamental shift in leadership's perspective as well as their modeled actions and behaviors. A crucial step is hearing from underrepresented stakeholders both internal and external to gain perspective on the systemic barriers faced by many employees within our organizations. Understanding the issues informs the strategy and allows for a redesign that supports and values a diverse workforce providing equal opportunity for success and advancement. The process is iterative and needs monitoring and reporting to support continued progress.

Questions

1 What are the megatrends that you see impacting your organization over the next 3 years?
2 How will issues around investor and community stakeholder requirements impact your operation?
3 What internal systems in your own organization enhance or create barriers for employees to bring their full selves to work?
4 What factors are impacting your organizations AR? What do you recommend to bolster organizational capabilities?
5 What are your ideas for improving supplier diversity?
6 How might you approach launching a supplier diversity program in your organization?
7 In the Coke case, what did you find most surprising about their J.E.D.I. journey?
8 Why do you think changing leaderships hearts and minds is crucial to designing for an equitable and inclusive organization?
9 What do you anticipate the most significant challenges to implementing a J.E.D.I. strategy to be for your organization?
10 What are your organization's priorities in terms of build a more inclusive organization?

Appendix 5A

Cultural Assessment for Environmental and Social Justice Impact

1. What is our organization's mission?
2. Are environmental and social justice organizational pillars included in our mission statement?
3. What are our ESG goals?
   a. How is success defined?
   b. How is progress measured?
4. What is our ESG strategy and is it aligned with our business strategy?
   a. Are we considering the intersectionality of environmental and social factors?

5. How are internal and external stakeholders engaged and informed about our environmental and social justice priorities, actions, and outcomes?
   a. Who is involved in the process?
   b. Who is responsible for external and internal communications?
   c. Is internal and external messaging consistent?
   d. How is stakeholder feedback incorporated into the decision-making process?
   e. How are they communicated?
6. Is the organization involved in private-public partnerships to drive environmental and social impact?
7. How is our organization supporting its ESG strategy?
   a. Is it on the board or C-suite agendas?
   b. Does the CEO speak frequently about our organization's mission to promote a more just and equitable society and organization?
   c. What budget has been designated to support initiatives both internally and externally?
   d. How is the vision of equity and inclusion cascaded to middle management?
   e. What type of organizational systems exists to promote cross-functional collaboration?
   f. Are ESG goals included as part of senior management performance management reviews and tied to compensation?
   g. Who are the champions and leaders of for J.E.D.I. transformation?
      i. What are their roles in the organization?
      ii. How are they involved?
   h. Who is in our supply chain and how is diversity represented in this process?
8. How are we engaging employees on environmental and social justice priorities?
   a. Is environmental and social impact part of everyone's job, or is it the job of one person such as Corporate Social Responsibility Officer or Diversity Equity Inclusion Officer?
   b. Are all employees given J.E.D.I. training?
   c. Is the expense for J.E.D.I. training and programming included in the annual budget allocation process?
   d. What protocols are in place to report harassment or bias?
   e. What tools or resources do we offer?
9. Is our employee diversity representation reflective of our community?
   a. How representative is our talent pipeline across our manager and leadership levels?
   b. What are our recruitment strategies?
   c. What are our retention strategies?

10. How are we tracking J.E.D.I. goals and measuring progress?
    a. How are goals allocated across the organization?
    b. What data are we tracking?
    c. How are we leveraging technology to facilitate data tracking and reporting?
    d. Is executive compensation tied to J.E.D.I. goals?
    e. How is this information being incorporated into the decision-making process?
11. What activities or programs are our employees involved with to support environmental stewardship or community investment?
    a. How aligned are these volunteer programs with your community's interests or requirements?
    b. Are these activities being performed in the name of the corporation?
    c. What types of resources does the corporation provide for volunteer activities and programs?
    d. How are initiatives promoted internally and externally?

Notes

1 W. Warner Burke and George H. Litwin, "A Causal Model of Organizational Performance and Change:," *Journal of Management*, June 30, 2016, https://doi.org/10.1177/014920639201800306.

2 William H. Frey, "The Millennial Generation: A Demographic Bridge to America's Diverse Future," *Brookings* (blog), January 24, 2018, https://www.brookings.edu/research/millennials/.

3 Joseph McCann and John Selsky, *Mastering Turbulence* (San Francisco, CA: John Wiley & Sons, 2012).

4 Kevin Sneader and Lareina Yee, "As Women Fight to Maintain Progress, Companies Need to Reimagine How They Operate," *Wall Street Journal*, September 30, 2020, sec. Business, https://www.wsj.com/articles/as-women-fight-to-maintain-progress-companies-need-to-reimagine-how-they-operate-11601434152.

5 "The NCES Fast Facts Tool Provides Quick Answers to Many Education Questions (National Center for Education Statistics)" (National Center for Education Statistics), accessed June 10, 2021, https://nces.ed.gov/fastfacts/display.asp?id=72.

6 Hamza Shaban, "Wells Fargo CEO Apologizes after Blaming Shortage of Black Talent for Bank's Lack of Diversity," *Washington Post*, accessed December 7, 2020, https://www.washingtonpost.com/business/2020/09/23/wells-fargo-ceo-black-employees/.

7 Sara Randazzo, "Law-Firm Clients Demand More Black Attorneys," *Wall Street Journal*, November 2, 2020, sec. Business, https://www.wsj.com/articles/law-firm-clients-demand-more-black-attorneys-11604313000.

8 Randazzo.

9 Pennsylvania Convention Center, "Diversity and Inclusion | Pennsylvania Convention Center," accessed April 6, 2021, https://www.paconvention.com/about/diversity-and-inclusion.

10 Christopher Wink / staff, "Philadelphia Is as Unequal as Colombia. Will a Minimum Wage Boost Help?," Technical.ly Philly, May 20, 2019, https://technical.ly/philly/2019/05/20/philadelphia-income-inequality-minimum-wage/.

11 "Companies Declared 'Black Lives Matter' Last Year, and Now They're Being Asked to Prove It - MarketWatch," accessed March 8, 2021, https://www.marketwatch.com/story/companies-declared-black-lives-matter-last-year-and-now-theyre-being-asked-to-prove-it-11614972986.

12 Betsy McKayStaff Reporter of The Wall StreetJournal, "Coke Agrees to Pay $192.5 Million To Settle a Bias Suit by Employees," *Wall Street Journal*, November 17, 2000, sec. Marketplace, https://www.wsj.com/articles/SB974396682804942184.

13 Jennifer Maloney and Lauren Weber, "Coke's Elusive Goal: Boosting Its Black Employees," *Wall Street Journal*, December 16, 2020, sec. Business, https://www.wsj.com/articles/coke-resets-goal-of-boosting-black-employees-after-20-year-effort-loses-ground-11608139999.

14 Weber.

15 Weber.

Bibliography

Burke, W. Warner, and George H. Litwin. "A Causal Model of Organizational Performance and Change:" *Journal of Management*, June 30, 2016. https://doi.org/10.1177/014920639201800306.

Center, Pennsylvania Convention. "Diversity and Inclusion | Pennsylvania Convention Center." Accessed April 6, 2021. https://www.paconvention.com/about/diversity-and-inclusion.

"Companies Declared 'Black Lives Matter' Last Year, and Now They're Being Asked to Prove It - MarketWatch." Accessed March 8, 2021. https://www.marketwatch.com/story/companies-declared-black-lives-matter-last-year-and-now-theyre-being-asked-to-prove-it-11614972986.

Frey, William H. "The Millennial Generation: A Demographic Bridge to America's Diverse Future." *Brookings* (blog), January 24, 2018. https://www.brookings.edu/research/millennials/.

Maloney, Jennifer and Lauren Weber. "Coke's Elusive Goal: Boosting Its Black Employees." *Wall Street Journal*, December 16, 2020, sec. Business. https://www.wsj.com/articles/coke-resets-goal-of-boosting-black-employees-after-20-year-effort-loses-ground-11608139999.

McCann, Joseph and John Selsky. *Mastering Turbulence*. San Francisco, CA: John Wiley & Sons, 2012.

Randazzo, Sara. "Law-Firm Clients Demand More Black Attorneys." *Wall Street Journal*, November 2, 2020, sec. Business. https://www.wsj.com/articles/law-firm-clients-demand-more-black-attorneys-11604313000.

Shaban, Hamza. "Wells Fargo CEO Apologizes after Blaming Shortage of Black Talent for Bank's Lack of Diversity." *Washington Post*. Accessed December 7, 2020. https://www.washingtonpost.com/business/2020/09/23/wells-fargo-ceo-black-employees/.

Sneader, Kevin and Lareina Yee. "As Women Fight to Maintain Progress, Companies Need to Reimagine How They Operate." *Wall Street Journal*, September 30, 2020, sec. Business. https://www.wsj.com/articles/as-women-fight-to-maintain-progress-companies-need-to-reimagine-how-they-operate-11601434152.

Staff, Christopher Wink/. "Philadelphia Is as Unequal as Colombia. Will a Minimum Wage Boost Help?" *Technical.ly Philly*, May 20, 2019. https://technical.ly/philly/2019/05/20/philadelphia-income-inequality-minimum-wage/.

StreetJournal, Betsy McKayStaff Reporter of The Wall. "Coke Agrees to Pay $192.5 Million To Settle a Bias Suit by Employees." *Wall Street Journal*, November 17, 2000, sec. Marketplace. https://www.wsj.com/articles/SB974396682804942184.

"The NCES Fast Facts Tool Provides Quick Answers to Many Education Questions (National Center for Education Statistics)." National Center for Education Statistics. Accessed June 10, 2021. https://nces.ed.gov/fastfacts/display.asp?id=72.

"Top 10 Best Practices for Mentors | Center for Mentoring Excellence." Accessed April 8, 2021. https://www.centerformentoring.com/top-10-best-practices-for-mentors.

Chapter 6

Chapter 6

Gaining Perspective

Creating a strategy to deliver on an organization's justice, equity, diversity, and inclusion (J.E.D.I.) vision requires understanding where your organization is on its journey along the J.E.D.I. Maturity Continuum. Factors such as organizational agility, capabilities, capacity for change, and resources all impact the implementation plan and execution. Mining your HCMS for data offers insights into employee representation which can be stratified by level, role, function, and location to provide information. Taking the temperature of your organization through an assessment such as the J.E.D.I. Framework provides management with and organizational profile as well as a baseline from which to design. It also offers a benchmark from which to measure progress moving forward. Assessments should be both quantitative and qualitative to provide meaningful insights. Once you have gathered your internal data, it is time to broaden your perspective through stakeholder engagement and assessment. Stakeholders include customers, employees, investors, suppliers, peers, unions, community groups, non-governmental organizations (NGOs), and governmental agencies. To gain valuable and impactful perspective, a carefully crafted stakeholder engagement plan needs to be developed and implemented for the various groups to engage and gather perspectives from a variety of voices. Driving systemic change requires diverse stakeholder engagement to provide a broader perspective and different lens through which to view an organization and its J.E.D.I. vision alignment. With this knowledge, leadership can collaborate with key stakeholders to build a more inclusive culture and better align resources to create a more equitable and just organization.

DOI: 10.1201/9781003168072-7

6.1 Organizational Justice, Equity, Diversity, and Inclusion Framework

In order to gain perspective and take the temperature of your organization, it is helpful to complete an assessment of your organization's justice, equity, diversity, and inclusion (J.E.D.I.) profile. This perspective is enhanced by gathering views from both internal and external stakeholders. Gathering the data and information highlighted in the Organizational J.E.D.I. Framework which appears in Appendix 6A provides a detailed profile of your organization's current state and areas of strength as well as opportunities for improvement. The J.E.D.I. Framework serves as a tool for J.E.D.I. committee leaders to gather information on stakeholders' perceptions about organizational culture and to drill into components such as norms, behaviors, actions and artifacts. Analyzing this information provides a lens to view perceived strategic alignment as well as quantitative data to inform strategic roadmap development, assessment, and refinement to move towards the organization's North Star J.E.D.I. vision. The J.E.D.I. Framework considers organizational culture, vision and strategy, work structure, board and management representation, employee representation, internal policies, performance metrics, talent ecosystem, leadership development, supplier policies, peer engagement, management practices, community engagement, customer engagement, tools and technologies to support J.E.D.I. goals, and the voice of the employee. It serves as a gathering framework to create a profile on the organization for its leaders on its current state, progress, and areas for improvement.

Focusing internally on culture, strategy, policies, processes, customer, and employee perceptions as well as externally on supplier requirements, community engagement, and the broader industry ecosystem, the J.E.D.I. Framework serves as a benchmarking and gap analysis tool. Response to assessment questions facilitates identification of an organization's perceived J.E.D.I. vision alignment as well as areas of focus to close strategic and functional gaps. Questions in the J.E.D.I. Framework are both qualitative and quantitative gathering data, information and key stakeholder perspectives. One of the main takeaways from this process is the understanding that integrating a J.E.D.I. strategic vision is a holistic and continuous process. As we addressed with the J.E.D.I. Maturity Continuum in Chapter 4, each organization is on its own J.E.D.I. journey and responses and quality of data will reflect their maturity along the continuum. Focusing on organizational priorities and creating or modifying a strategic roadmap to guide your organization on its journey is key to success. Most organizations begin their journey creating a DEI change agent or leadership role and then as the transformation is embraced more broadly by leadership, they create a cross-functional committee to drive the transformation. Best practice is to include a variety of functional roles and management levels on the committee to gather and share a cross section of perspectives and drive holistic impact.

6.2 Assessing Organizational Diversity Representation

Many leaders have a goal of increasing the diversity representation within their organizations. The process begins with gathering data on your workforce demographics to obtain a view of your organizational diversity representation. While aggregated diversity numbers are important, the greater impact comes from a clear picture of diversity by identity group across organizational levels, functions, and roles. If an organization claims to have equal gender representation (50% men and women), it sounds like they have a very diverse organization with equal opportunities for men and women. In reality, these numbers may skew toward women being in entry level and lower management positions while men are in the C-suite, senior leadership, or engineering and technical positions with higher pay, more power, and more opportunities. Understanding how diversity is represented across your organization is crucial to getting an accurate picture of its equity and inclusion profile. Using this data as a baseline provides a foundation to benchmark progress and measure impact.

As a first step, review your numbers relative to the configuration and structure of your organization as depicted in Table 6.1. This report configuration is a talent pipeline stratification and represents where underserved populations are represented within the leadership development pipeline.

Table 6.1 Diversity Representation by Organization Level

Organization Level	Employee Entry Level	Team Leader	1st Level Manager	Middle Manager	Senior Manager	C-Suite
Identifies as Male %						
Identifies as Female %						
Identifies as Gender Non-binary %						
Identifies as LGBTQ+ %						
Identifies as AAPI %						
Identifies as BIPOC %						
Identifies as Disabled %						

The first source of data for this analysis is an organization's human capital management system (HCMS). Some of the data may be available in an EEOC report that the organization prepare to comply with EEOC regulation in the U.S. While the data can be analyzed in its raw form, it can be a cumbersome process subject to data entry and calculation errors. Within the HCMS arena, many vendors provide delivered reports that can be run using business intelligence tools to extract data and report on talent pipeline configuration. If additional data is needed, it can be gathered via an employee survey or a shorter more targeted pulse survey from the employee population. The categories in Table 6.1 are a representative sample, but data points and organizational levels can be configured to meet the reporting needs of your organization.

McKinsey and Lean In have been tracking women's progress within the talent pipeline for several years. Their 2020 Women in the Workplace report shows a slow progression for women over the past six years, but it continues to highlight a phenomenon known as "broken rung," which represents the first step on the ladder to a management position. Their study shows that the first step in the managerial ranks continues to be a barrier to more women reaching the leadership ranks.[1] In effect, their research indicates that women fall behind at the initial stage of access to the leadership level.

Figure 6.1 is developed based on joint research by McKinsey & Company and Lean In. The data presented is from the beginning of 2020 and reflects responses from over 300 companies. The diagram represents the percentage representation of employees by race and gender at various levels ranging from manager through the C-suite within these aggregated organizations. Comparing the representation data for C-suite and SVP levels from these organizations to Entry Level employee

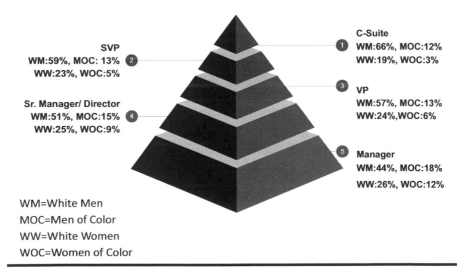

Figure 6.1 Representation of Organization Level by Gender and Race.[4]

representation data of White Men (WM) 35%, Men of Color 18%, White Women 29%, and Women of Color 18% gives a perspective on pipeline leakage.[2] As the diagram indicates, at each stage of management level advancement in the talent development pipeline, WM represent an increasingly disproportionate percentage. While WM represent 35% of the entry level positions, they represent 66% of the C-suite. This representation data highlights how ineffective current DEI initiatives and programs have been in driving meaningful change within organizations.

Since the Women in the Workplace study began six years ago, the most growth in opportunities for women have been in the senior management level. The percentage of women in the C-suite has grown from 17% to 21%, and in SVP roles the representation has grown from 23% to 28%.[3] Representation from Women of Color across all organizational levels remains alarmingly low and spotlights an area that needs leadership focus and resources. The lack of representation by women of color reflects that they are subject to more workplace barriers like microaggressions, microinequities, and discrimination than other groups. In order to recalibrate, leadership must take a deep look into their norms, values, accepted behaviors, policies, and practices. To make workplaces more inclusive for women, leaders must reset norms around flexibility, work policies, performance review processes, and increase their commitments to wellness and well-being. Key to success is that senior leadership embraces policies and practices that support all women in the workplace. In addition, managers and executives must model using these programs such as hybrid work options to demonstrate leadership acceptance of their usage. While this study reveals that women's percentage representation of the workforce has increased at every level of the organization, including rising approximately 20% at the senior levels, their representation remains well below women's 51% representation in the U.S. population. As highlighted earlier, the impact of the pandemic on women in the workforce has been disproportional. The exodus of women from the workforce during the pandemic reflects their traditional caregiver roles, the loss of supplemental support such as daycare and school, career salary differentials as well as their significant representation in hard hit industries such as the hospitality and retail sectors. In addition, the majority of frontline and essential workers are women creating greater health risks and subsequent job loss. As a result, we expect the gains for women cited in the Women in the Workplace 2020 report to be significantly diminished and even reversed in the coming years because of the impacts of the pandemic. Clearly, organizations and their leaders need to do more to create cultures of belonging where women and people of color can thrive.

Many organizations use the McKinsey and Lean In Representation of Corporate Pipeline by Gender and Race as a benchmarking tool for their own organization. While it serves as a good general benchmark, it is important to note that industries have different talent pipelines and different talent recruitment and retention challenges. Some industries such as engineering, technology, and IT services have challenges attracting women into entry level jobs. While others have challenges at the middle and senior management levels. As a result, the more specific your data is relative to the organization's industry, the better alignment for benchmarking. Fortunately, the Women in the Workplace 2020 report does include industry-specific talent pipelines. Other good benchmarking resources are available from industry groups, benchmarking services such as Mercer, and governmental demographic data for your region of operation.

In addition, further insights can be gained by gathering representation data based on functional areas. Mobility within organizations is based on experience, skills, jobs, and job families. Often, certain jobs and roles have greater upward mobility than others. Understanding representational data by function such as Customer Service, Sales, Operations, Marketing, IT, HR, Finance, etc. gives insight into where employees from underserved groups such as women and BIPOC categories are employed. For example, the HR function may be dominated by women while the IT function may be dominated by men. Gaining a perspective on employees representation across the organization gives insight into career pathing and leadership development. Thinking back to the role of organizational systems in determining how organizations function, an imbalance of diversity representation within functions creates barriers and inequity of opportunity for employees depending upon your management practices and leadership development pathway. Certain career paths lead to higher level positions and if BIPOC, LGBTQ+, or women are not represented in these functional roles, their avenues for career advancement may be severely limited. To better understand this issue, think about your own organization's succession planning. How are successors for senior positions identified? Certain skills, experiences, and organizational knowledge are usually required for consideration for leadership development and promotion. If diverse candidates are not given the opportunity to serve in the functions and roles required for career advancement or to develop the requisite skills, then the diversity representation within an organization's talent pipeline, especially at the more senior level, will not improve.

Table 6.2 provides a framework to gather data by functional area within an organization. The data in Table 6.2 can be modified to reflect your organization's functional requirements. Some organizations seek to disaggregate data further splitting out groups such as BIPOC into Black, Indigenous, or Latinx to track even more specific goals by identity group. Gathering the data is the first step in driving system change. Creating more access and opportunity requires a holistic approach to support the growth and development of underrepresented groups within an organization.

Looking at the data by operating unit or region of operation provides another layer of insight. Tracking diversity representation by geographic location, operating entity, or by facility provides another view of workforce representation. Power and privilege are often associated with a specific operating unit or with the headquarter location. For example, a banking organization had significant numbers of BIPOC employees, but they were predominately located in its community banking group. Internally, the community banking group was perceived as less skilled than the corporate lending group, which was predominately White. The pathway for the current senior leadership team was primarily through the corporate lending group. When selecting candidates

Table 6.2 Diversity Representation by Function

Organization Function	Production	Sales	Marketing	Finance	IT	HCM
Identifies as Male %						
Identifies as Female %						
Identifies as Gender Non-binary %						
Identifies as BIPOC %						
Identifies as AAPI%						
Identifies as LGBTQ+ %						
Identifies as Disabled %						

for future bank leaders, corporate lending has been the traditional feeder group for leadership talent development. As a result, there were few opportunities for BIPOC staff to rise within the company. Understanding departmental, functional, and even location diversity representation within an organization provides insights in how to address systemic barriers. Solutions include realigning group representation through recruitment, offering training to promote mobility, and altering the traditional pathway for advancement. In the bank's case, broadening the representation in the corporate lending group might drive impact, but that will require supporting recruitment efforts with culture changes to promote inclusion and belonging. Diversifying the representation without revising culture and systems will not be an effective solution. Another solution might be taking a hard look at the required skills for bank leaders. Perhaps the skills required are being developed in the community bank and using corporate lending as a leadership training ground is more of a policy and practice issue rather than a skills and experience issue. A wider set of skills and experience could be acquired through rotational positions, and cross-functional collaborations, as well as creation of other opportunities designed to engage and attract underrepresented employees to the leadership track. In order to gain actionable insights on the fundamental systemic issues, it is crucial to examine the data.

Inequity is also be found between roles at the headquarter location and satellite offices. Often, the power base is at the headquarter location where decisions are made, and careers are sponsored and advanced. A disproportionate representation of White males at the headquarter office can generate unintended consequences. Those employees who have exposure and interactions with senior leaders are often the ones to be included in the slate for promotions and other opportunities that advance careers. In effect, lack of exposure creates a dearth of opportunities for employees from underrepresented groups. While sponsorship programs can combat this issues, organizational leaders need to think deeply about how their employees are represented across the organization. Diving into the data and analyzing your employee representation on a variety of criteria provides insight into where groups of people are employed and how that might be impacting their future opportunities within the organization. In addition, senior level representation impacts the culture of your organization in terms of role models and opportunities that are evident to both internal and external stakeholders.

Benchmarking your organization's diversity numbers on both an aggregated and disaggregated basis is crucial for gaining meaningful and actionable insights. Too often, organizations track an aggregated "minority" representation figure. The minority category needs to be broken down into the underrepresented group that are reflective of your community of operation or another relevant representation standard to ensure attention and impact. As we saw in the Coke case, if data is being tracked only in the aggregate, the "minority" trend line may not provide an accurate representation relative to your organization's diversity goals. In the Coke example, their data showed that minorities were making progress at all levels of the organization, but when the data was disaggregated, the progress was being made by White women with other identity groups such as Black males falling behind. Digging into the data provides information and shines a spotlight on areas for adjustment, change, and impact.

6.3 Formalized Assessments

Formal assessments are used to gather employees' voices or perspective on organizational culture, work environment, organizational justice, and other organizational systems and factors. Engaging in a more formalized process provides data, sentiment analysis, and a baseline measurement from which to measure progress overtime. Questions are designed to measure trust, leadership, diversity, equity, fairness, psychological safety, opportunity, inclusion, and belonging. Leveraging information and insights from a formal assessment allows management to prioritize J.E.D.I. goals and to develop a strategic roadmap in alignment with their organization's DEI maturity, capacity for change, and resources. Assessment data provides actionable insights to share with management via dashboards impacting real-time decision-making.

If your organization is seeking a formal assessment, which is often undertaken by a professional service consultancy, the following discussion with Dr. Fiona Jamison, CEO of Spring International highlights the process and beneficial impacts. She shares best practices, lessons learned, techniques for sharing information, and informing data-driven decision-making. In addition, she shares her insights as leader of a technology and data company around the impact of data on refining J.E.D.I. strategy and the value of providing data to managers within the organization. Lastly, she offers her perspective on what is next for improving assessments and employee engagement (EE) as well as the importance of partnerships in creating more equitable and inclusive organizations.

GAINING DIVERSITY, EQUITY, AND INCLUSION PERSPECTIVE THROUGH ASSESSMENTS AND STAKEHOLDER ENGAGEMENT: SPRING INTERNATIONAL

Spring International, a woman owned business, is known for their customized research and people analytics providing insights into employees and other stakeholders. At Spring, the team is driven and passionate about gathering data to improve the employee experience. Their motto is "Your company succeeds when everyone has a great day at work!"

As CEO, Dr. Fiona Jamison brings more than 16 years' experience conducting research and providing solutions to both for-profit and non-profit organizations with specific expertise in EE, employee relations, change management, and human capital analytics.

Born and raised in Britain, Fiona has provided research and consultancy services in the U.K., Europe, and the U.S. This international experience adds a unique perspective to understanding organizational culture and communications. She is the author of numerous articles which focus on the impact of downsizing and understanding the role of line managers in organizational change.

The following is a conversation with Dr. Fiona Jamison, CEO on her experiences working with clients to improve diversity, equity, and inclusion outcomes through including the voice of the employee through assessments and leveraging data and information for impact.

How does your team leverage Spring International's research and assessment tools to help leaders reach their diversity, equity, and inclusion goals?

Many leaders are now focusing their energies and attention on diversity and inclusion, but they really don't know where to begin. Often, management is in a rush to respond and they launch a training program without aligning strategy and goals. The Spring International Assessment tool provides a baseline for management and helps them understand their organization's diversity and inclusion profile. With this information, leadership is able to identify issues, establish goals, track progress, and prioritize initiatives such as training to drive impact. Our assessment includes both a quantitative and qualitative analysis. We use both survey tools and interviews to gather data on diversity, equity, inclusion, engagement, and trust. We have many years of data from which we have built benchmarking indices for data analysis and comparison. So, we can help leaders understand how their organization compares to their peers. The interviews help us understand the leadership team's perspective allowing us to begin to build leadership alignment around a unified DEI strategy.

What are the most common lessons learned in this process?

There are four common lessons that we have learned through our DEI assessment process.

1. Initially, leadership is often not comfortable with this conversation. In addition, they frequently have different perspectives and are not aligned on their DEI strategic vision. In order to build a culture for inclusion, we need to get leadership unified and comfortable articulating on these topics.
2. The data explores differences of employee opinions based on their demographics – for some this is the first time they are looking at the data through this lens. For managers, they are often surprised by both the similarities and differences in survey responses.
3. Responses often vary based on small pockets or locations within an organization. You may find marked differences of opinions on the state of diversity, equity, and inclusion between roles, functions, or facilities. It is rare that every part of an organization has issues.
4. Change takes time. Management often wants to achieve their equity goals or hit their diversity targets quickly, but driving lasting change requires building trust and that is done over time. There is no quick fix.

How does an organization's maturity relative to its DEI strategy impact how they gather data and information from employees and other stakeholders?

We look at where an organization is in terms of its DEI maturity. Our model has five stages of maturity – Idea, Foundational, Emerging, Capacity Building, and Strategically Integrated.

Idea is the first stage where leadership begins thinking about DEI. Often the impetus for changes comes from the Board of Directors or the leadership team. Data comes from existing data sources such as HRIS data and EE surveys. Next is *Foundational*, which focuses on compliance. Additional data is gathered for developing an employee population profile. Leadership awareness and alignment grows. As an organization matures into the *Emerging* stage, the focus is on defining terms, mission, and DEI strategy. The assessment seeks to answer the questions of "What DEI issues matter to employees?" Actions at this stage include forming a DEI task force and developing specific programs such as Employee Resource Groups (ERGs), revising recruitment strategies, and developing mentoring programs. As an organization's maturity grows, they move into *Capacity Building* which includes assessment and feedback loops. Data is gathered from a variety of sources and integrated into the business process. An organization at this stage may have a Chief Diversity Officer with a variety of programs such as leadership development, learning and mentoring. DEI is baked into an organization's culture. The final stage of the journey is *Strategic Integration* in which DEI is core to business strategy and performance. Key performance indicators are tracked regularly across the organization and integrated into strategic planning. Data is aggregated and shared via dashboards. DEI is a cultural pillar – essential to the business.

How are organizations using assessments and analytics to engage with other stakeholders?

While assessments are less common outside of their internal operations, some organizations are using them to assess the DEI practices of their supply chain or to share trend results with key stakeholder groups. High level assessment results are shared selectively with community groups to demonstrate DEI commitments and opportunities as well as an organization's progress over time. Often these results are focused on sharing changes to recruitment strategies to promote diversity and/or progress that an organization has made in terms of improving the diversity profile of their employees. One client used the assessment to review their recruitment strategy and realized that by recruiting from three local universities that they were limiting their options for more diverse candidates. With this knowledge, they were able to add two additional colleges to improve their pipeline of qualified, diverse candidates.

How are leadership teams using the data collected to inform strategy and cascade the implementation throughout the organization?

We recommend that DEI assessment data is reviewed and analyzed at the strategic level. Because this information is sensitive, it is typically controlled by the C-suite, Legal, DEI, and HR. Our recommendation is that data is aggregated to protect confidentiality and be shared to the level of where action needs to happen. That level varies depending upon the organization but drilling down to the supervisory level is often not productive because they aren't empowered to act.

That said, we also strongly recommend thanking employees for their feedback. Sharing high level findings, insights, and providing information on major trends and planned actions is critical so that employees know that their voices have been heard.

What impact have you seen from having diversity numbers accessible in real time via dashboards?

In our experience, having information on data trends promotes more data-based decision-making which ultimately improves outcomes for employees. Providing access for managers to information in a more visual format, such as a dashboard, also helps them to better understand trends and impacts than just straight numbers. That said, data quality is important and employee data tends to have a great deal of noise so real-time dashboards can, if not set up correctly, provide misleading information. Getting a report in 2 days can be less effective than receiving accurate information in 2 weeks when you know the proper data quality issues have been addressed.

As a technology and consulting company, what do you see as next for improving assessments and engagement?

I see four major areas:

1. I anticipate that more organizations will be aligning across data sources so that data points can speak to one another and provide more meaningful information.
2. While many organizations are assessing their employee data, I expect to see more organizations leveraging external data to compare their demographic data to their community's demographic data. This insight will facilitate a better understanding of how their workforce matches the profile of their community. This data can also be leveraged to help determine the impact of a new site location on the diversity profile of an organization. For example, "Are there community members that can be hired that will allow us to meet our diversity goals?"
3. Using passive organizational network analysis (ONA) data, managers will be better informed about with whom they have been spending time, who has been invited to next level meetings, and other development opportunities to engage with employees. Getting access to opportunities is crucial for employee development.
4. As I work with clients, I also see the importance of partnerships between academia and business. We have a manufacturing client that has partnered with local schools and technical colleges to create job awareness opportunities and training pathways all the way down into middle schools.

Assessments are critical for gathering data to drive impact and supporting data-driven decisions. While an informal assessment gives you insights to inform early stage priorities and actions, a formal assessment provides actionable data for longer-term strategy development and baseline information from which to benchmark progress. To drive action and accountability, data should be incorporated into management information systems and shared via dashboards. Ongoing formalized assessments provide actionable insights into an organization's J.E.D.I. strategic impact as well as areas that are delivering on desired outcomes and those requiring realignment. Leveraging a formalized approach offers data insights that are measurable and comparable over time to track progress and to inform resource reallocation. For leaders who are committed to a J.E.D.I. transformation, undertaking a formal assessment provides an excellent foundation as well as a source of data to drive strategy prioritization.

6.4 Include Diverse Voices

For an effective engagement strategy, both internal and external stakeholders need to be part of the process. Ideally, the blend of voices should reflect the entirety of your ecosystem including organization, supply chain, customers, community, and peers. However, many organizations begin with gathering the voice of their employees and expand their stakeholder engagement as they mature in their DEI journey. Gathering and sharing information with your stakeholders helps to inform your strategy for improving just and equitable outcomes. Trust and commitment from all parties grows through this shared experience of ideas being heard and acted upon. As an organization's maturity with environmental impact and social justice evolves, these conversations and feedback loops become more integrated into strategy development and stakeholder engagement.

Let's begin with getting more insights from your employees. Moving beyond the numbers and getting a more qualitative assessment on your employees' knowledge of DEI topics and issues as well as how they feel about the organization's DEI practices provide valuable information. This type of survey is often referred to as an organizational climate survey, and it provides insights from key stakeholders on their attitudes toward and experiences with the organization's J.E.D.I. strategy and impacts. Some points to consider are:

1. Who is included in conversations? Is this a senior management and Board of Directors conversation? Or, are you reaching out to all levels of the organization to better understand issues throughout all layers of the organization?
2. Do you have Employee Resource or Affinity Groups? Are they part of the conversation?
3. Are you planning on surveying the entire employee population? Or are you using a sampling or focus group approach?
4. Will you be using a formal assessment process or are you developing the survey internally?
5. How much data is being gathered and does leveraging an artificial intelligence (AI)-based tool to analyze the data make sense?

6. What are you seeking information about-Diversity, Equity, Inclusion, Conditions for Success, Programs, Justice, Climate, etc.?

The information that you are seeking determines the focus and creation of your questions. The organizational justice climate relates to how employees perceive fairness in terms of compensation and policy enforcement, the team and interpersonal dynamics that are encouraged and those that are tolerated, and how information is shared and with whom. In terms of better understanding how employees feel about your organization's culture around diversity, equity, inclusion, and justice, the greater the number of voices, the better the profile for assessment. Surveying approaches include both sampling and census surveys depending on the scope of voices you wish to include. There are a wide variety of survey tools available depending upon your organization's size, resources, and budget. Survey tools include internally developed surveys such as those from Survey Monkey or Google Survey, professional surveys from third-party vendors, and survey vendors with SaaS artificial intelligence (AI) survey tools. Internally developed tools may be useful in the early stages of a J.E.D.I. journey for an initial project or for taking quick pulse surveys. Third-party survey vendors provide tools and often consulting resources as well as baselining and measuring progress overtime. SaaS AI survey tools leverage technology to provide benchmarking data and additional insights, but may require additional consulting support. Selecting the appropriate survey tool depends upon your project goals, budget, and other resources.

Survey question creation, and selection can be complex based on organizational objectives. The following Employee J.E.D.I. Survey questions are some examples of foundational survey questions to consider asking to gain perspective on your employees' understanding of DEI concepts, their experience within your organization, practices that support belonging, barriers that hinder belonging, as well as the climate of your organization.

EMPLOYEE J.E.D.I. SURVEY QUESTIONS

1. What does diversity mean to you?
2. What does inclusion mean to you?
3. What does equity mean to you?
4. What does a culture of belonging mean to you?
5. How well do you feel our organization does diversity, equity, and inclusion?
6. How do you feel when you come to work?
7. Do you feel you can bring your full self to work?
8. Have you ever felt marginalized or discriminated against in our workplace?

9. What could we do to improve our culture of belonging?
10. What challenges do you face in bringing your full self to work?
11. What practices and processes help you feel valued and welcome?
12. What practices or processes act as barriers to your work experience?
13. What practices promote distributive, procedural, interpersonal, and informational justice?
14. What practices deter distributive, procedural, interpersonal, and informational justice?

Employees' responses to these questions provide a starting point for developing an organizational profile from the employees' perspective. Their answers provide insight on their J.E.D.I. related knowledge, experiences, and practices helping to identify areas to build employee and manager awareness and skills as well as opportunities to redesign systems. The question focus might include employee perceptions on underserved group representation within the company, division or function, the organization's policies for reasonable accommodation, work life balance support systems, and team dynamics on promoting inclusion of diverse identities, thoughts, and experiences. Other information may highlight your organizational justice climate around issues such as rewards distribution, policy and process consistency, interpersonal and group dynamics for accepted behavior, and candor around information and information accessibility. The focus depends on the information sought by those leading the J.E.D.I. transformation including areas of excellence to be shared and scaled as well as opportunities for improvement. With this data on knowledge, perspective, and climate, an actionable plan can be crafted to drive impact in key areas.

Moving forward in your J.E.D.I. journey, the level of survey question granularity and sophistication increases as Chief Diversity and other J.E.D.I. leaders require more specific and actionable data to refine strategic plans for impact. The deeper the dive into organizational systems, the more specific and targeted the survey questions. Question structure and thematic considerations become more complex in order to gather specific and targeted data. As your organization's J.E.D.I. journey continues, selecting a formal assessment service allows for more complex analysis in terms of sentiment analysis, which illuminates leadership on employees' positive and negative views.

A pulse survey is a tool for quick check-ins with employees. These surveys tend to be shorter and focused on a key topic such as belonging, benefits, or engagement. It provides insights on how your employees feel about a specific topic within your organization at a point in time. Some organizations prefer to conduct a series of pulse surveys over the course of the year in order to focus on particular EE aspects and to then combine the findings to provide a holistic employee engagement profile.

Software as a Service (SaaS)survey tools have been developed to provide greater insights and data to promote leadership action. Several of these tools leverage AI based technology known as natural language processing (NLP) to analyze large amount of text data, to gain insights into employee sentiment measuring key themes and employee emotions to give timely and actionable insights to broaden perspectives and drive change. NLP uses programming and machine learning to understand and identify employee sentiment analysis based on responses including from survey text. As a result, these survey tools can ask open-ended questions to gather detailed information and analyze the data in a very short amount of time. Gone are the days of waiting months for employee survey results.

UKG's Employee Voice, a SaaS survey reporting and workforce insight tool, provides a view into the voice of your employees using NLP and machine learning combined with industrial-organizational psychology and survey expertise. The tool analyzes structured and unstructured responses and data to provide a sentiment analysis or a picture of EE or perception. In Table 6.3, there are several terms that are useful to become familiar with if you are interested in leveraging NLP-based tools to analyze employee sentiment.

These terms give a sense of what is being measured, the evaluation scale, and how data is being reported to managers to inform decision-making. Most SaaS survey reporting tools set minimum sample thresholds to protect individual employee's confidentiality while gathering and reporting on key metrics. It is important to protect anonymity of an individual's response to build trust and credibility. Providing senior leadership with actionable data via heatmaps that offer options to drill down

Table 6.3 Terms for NLP Assessment Tools

Branching Logic	Enables displaying a specific question to a respondent by linking the answer choice to a specific question page.
Detractor	Suggest dissatisfaction with an organization, service, or experience.
Emotional Promoter Score – EPS	Indicates employee sentiment.
Heatmap	Represents graphically with color tiles with favorable, average, or below average ratings.
Industry Organizational Psychology (I-O)	Study of human behavior in organizations and workplaces.
Net Promoter Scores – NPS	Indicator of employee satisfaction.
Promoter	Indicates satisfaction with an organization, service, or experience.
Sentiment	Identifies a response as positive, neutral, or negative.

into specific regions, departments, and managers provides insight for data driven decision-making. Employees are more willing to participate and to share their feelings and experiences on surveys when they see that demonstrable actions are being taken to address areas of concerns or to reward areas of excellence.

Leveraging an employee survey assessment tool as part of the process is very useful in benchmarking employees' perception of justice, equity and inclusion within the organization. The initial data serves as a baseline to measure progress against later surveys as projects and programs are implemented to drive systemic change. In traditional employee surveying, the cycle between launch and data is lengthy and data is usually aggregated returning a general profile but few specifics for actionable insights.. As a result, leadership knows there is a challenge, but they aren't sure if it is an organization wide issue or if it is specific to a region or department. Without detailed information, it is very difficult for management to take targeted strategic action to drive impact. Using NLP based survey tools provides timely information on key themes and sentiments allowing for targeted response. Sentiment analysis identifies systemic barriers requiring redesign as well as areas of success for replication such as manager training, benefits redesign, or developing hybrid work arrangements to meet employee needs. This type of AI-driven sensitivity analysis and employee sentiment solutions are very helpful in identifying managers, departments, regions, and business units with stronger and weaker performance allowing for targeted remediation and sharing of best practices. Gathering the voice of employees gives a foundation from which to measure impact and progress as management guides an organization on its J.E.D.I. journey.

LEVERAGING AI TO HEAR THE VOICE OF THE EMPLOYEE

UKG's Employee Voice, powered by Xander®, is an EE survey tool that leverages artificial intelligence (AI) using natural language processing (NLP) and machine learning technology, along with industrial-organizational (I-O) psychology and survey construction expertise. Using this technology, it analyzes both structured and unstructured data for a complete picture of EE.

The tool supports quantitative questions, such as multiple choice, rankings, and yes/no questions, and supplements them with context from open-ended comments. But it also allows qualitative questions. The engine is able to analyze both types of questions to give insights into employee emotions and key themes. "Themes summarize what the text is talking about (e.g., concepts like 'Cross-Team Collaboration'), and emotions describe how the author feels about that particular response (e.g., feelings like 'optimistic' or 'annoyed')."[5] The result is an emotional promoter score that is based on employee sentiment, themes, and key words. This analysis provides insights into employees' feelings, experiences, and top priorities on a number of topics and subjects including an organization's culture around inclusion. More importantly, this assessment tool provides timely, actionable data by further parsing data by manager, department, function, and region. The ability to assess and provide actionable data to drive strategy, programing, training, development, or even intervention demonstrates the impact of leveraging AI tools to better assess employee perception of your organization's culture as it relates to your J.E.D.I. vision.

A climate survey is another type of survey to gather quantitative and qualitative information on an organization's diversity, equity, and inclusion organizational climate. The survey gathers demographic and experiential data from a variety of stakeholders such as employees, customers, suppliers, and other stakeholders. In an academic setting, a climate survey may include students, faculty and staff, and alumni to paint a broad institutional profile of representation, experience and attitudes about justice, equity and belonging within the educational community.

In the Bard MBA in Sustainability program, one of our first actions as the Diversity Equity and Inclusion committee was to launch a community climate survey to better understand the students' demographics, perspectives and experiences within the program. The survey results provided a temperature check, or baseline, to assess our current state, measure future progress and inform the program's need for additional training, tools, and identify resources to support the shared vision for a J.E.D.I. community. We sought information on the following areas:

1. Demographic Information
2. Program Feedback
3. DEI Models, Strategy, and Topics Embed into Curriculum

With this information, the DEI committee was better able to make recommendations to faculty, administration and student leadership as well as offer programming recommendations to support existing and incoming students in support of strengthening our community culture. To develop our climate survey model and questions, we consulted resources from the University of Michigan, Stanford University, and the Higher Education Data Sharing Consortium. While the design of this climate survey was targeted to a higher education environment, these resources can be used to help inform climate surveys for other types of organizations. While the Bard MBA in Sustainability program continues its J.E.D.I. journey, the findings from the climate survey have supported new course offerings, curriculum revisions, adoption of a Diversity, Equity, Inclusion Code, and revisions to recruitment processes for students and faculty. The information gathered in the survey informed the institution's J.E.D.I. strategy and provided the foundation on which we developed our institutional transformation roadmap.

Assessing both quantitative and qualitative data is an important step in the journey toward building an organization with a J.E.D.I. mission. During the information gathering process, best practice focuses on including diverse voices to have a representational perspective for strategy and roadmap development. While most assessments begin with an inward focus, it is also important to understand how your organization is perceived by stakeholders in the community.

6.5 Identifying Stakeholders and Collecting Requirements

Engaging with a broad group of stakeholders facilitates gathering data to understand how your organization is perceived within its ecosystem. These stakeholders may include customers, suppliers, peer institutions, regulators, and community members. Community is a relative term and can mean a local community, but it can also mean how your organization is perceived by its global community. The scope of community is organizationally dependent and reflects its areas of operation and impact. This stakeholder gaze is the outside in view of the organization. How are you seen by customers, communities in which you operate, suppliers, regulators, and NGOs? Gaining perspective on how you are viewed internally and externally is a crucial step for leadership in prioritizing goals and initiative when developing a strategic plan to building a more just and equitable organization.

Engaging with a broad group of stakeholders provides leadership greater insight into their perceptions of your organization's brand, reputation, and culture-related J.E.D.I. issues. Gathering this information identifies risks and highlights opportunities. Risks include operational risk, loss of license to operate, brand devaluation, damage to your reputation, regulatory non-compliance, and loss of access to capital or debt markets. Any of these risks could be devastating to an organization's ability to operate. Engaging with stakeholders offers insights into new opportunities to expand markets, offer new products and services, and explore joint ventures. In addition, ecosystem feedback helps to identify opportunities for collaboration with partners, best practices for systemic realignment, and opportunities to engage with new talent pools. Each of these insights enhance brand and market value while supporting growth in an organization's J.E.D.I. maturity.

While engaging with stakeholders generates insights, it can also be a contentious process. Leadership must be prepared to listen and to enter into a dialogue that reframes issues, increases awareness, and perhaps creates some initial pain for the organization. Feedback from stakeholders is often not the reflection that organizational leaders would like to see in the mirror. The benefit is that from this engagement comes great opportunity to realign your strategy, programs, and policies to better meet stakeholder needs. Entering into the process openly and authentically yields impactful results. If the process is simply a check the box exercise, the impact will not be transformative and could be detrimental to stakeholder relations.

Engaging with stakeholders is crucial for understanding organizational perception. In addition, it creates potential new opportunities for collaboration on numerous levels including community advisory groups, private-public partnerships, community development and accessing new avenues for top talent. Maintaining open lines of communication and engagement with key stakeholders minimizes business disruption from strikes, protests, loss of operating license, and maximizes opportunities like being a preferred employer, where local community members value being employed, and employees serve as ambassadors within their communities. It also reduces the likelihood of being called out for "woke washing" as external messaging is more likely to be aligned with strategy and internal action. The bottom line is that stakeholder engagement on environmental and social issues creates organizational value.

STAKEHOLDER ENGAGEMENT ENHANCES MARKET VALUATION

Research conducted by professors from the Wharton School of the University of Pennsylvania, New York University, and the University of South Carolina found empirical evidence that stakeholder engagement improves the value of an organization. They analyzed 26 goldmines, owned by 19 publicly traded firms, and found that the market valuation discounted the firm's stock price up to 72% because of lack of stakeholder engagement disclosure. Uncertainties about the impact of governments, regulators, community leaders, and civil society on mine openings, continued operations, labor disruptions, and potential cost overruns were being built into the valuations. By tracking over 50,000 stakeholder engagement events through media sources, the researchers created an algorithm to predict the degree of stakeholder conflict or cooperation at these mines. Introducing stakeholder engagement measures into a market capitalization analysis, they were able to reduce the discount placed on these mining firms between 13% and 37%. Two mines with the same gold deposits, cost of extraction, and global gold prices varied in valuation because the more valuable mine engaged with local stakeholders.[6] Key to the successful organization was its engagement with local community members and leaders as well as its transparency on reporting its stakeholder engagement plan and outcomes.

Identifying stakeholders is a process that evolves over time as your leadership team grows in experience and expertise during its J.E.D.I. journey. Stakeholder engagement should begin with those who have the most impact on your organization. Consider the following questions:

1. Which stakeholders impact our organization?
2. How do they impact us?
3. Who represents this group?
4. How do we envision engaging with this group?

As indicated in Figure 6.2, there is an inner ring of stakeholders such as employees, suppliers, investors, and customers that have the most immediate impact on an organization. In addition, there is an outer ring of stakeholders such as community organizations, trade associations, NGOs, government agencies, business associations, and unions that may not be involved daily but provide the most long-term opportunities and risk. Each business will have slightly different groups of stakeholders depending upon their scope of operation, location, industry and market. If your organization does not have a robust stakeholder engagement plan, begin with your inner stakeholders. As you gain experience with this engagement process, initiate an engagement strategy for the outer stakeholder.

As you begin to develop the engagement plan, remember that it is important to both listen to stakeholders and to share information. The engagement must be authentic and transparent. In order to be effective, organizations must share their information transparently, meaning the full story needs to be told and stakeholder concerns must be heard, and thoughtful responses provided. As the process evolves, sharing the impact that stakeholder concerns or ideas have on company's plans is an effective way to promote authenticity, transparency, and engagement. A framework for developing an action plan is highlighted in Table 6.4.

Creating a more equitable and just organization requires engaging with both inner and outer stakeholders. The scope, size, and nature of the program or project will help to inform who should be included on specific initiatives. Best practice suggests that all stakeholders are included in strategy and information sessions on a regular basis. Some organizations hold annual forums to which they invite their stakeholders to communicate key initiatives and to gather support and feedback from their stakeholder partners. Engagement strategies vary depending upon the

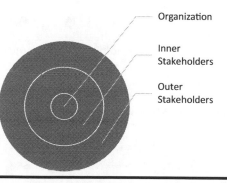

Figure 6.2   Stakeholder Identification.

Table 6.4 Stakeholder Engagement Plan[7]

Plan	What are the issues on which we are seeking feedback? Which stakeholder groups should be included? How will stakeholders be evaluated for initial and ongoing inclusion? How will we rank stakeholders on impact and influence? What is our objective for stakeholder engagement? How are we defining the objective? What type of engagement format will best suit our objective? Who is accountable for the engagement process? How will we measure success? What metrics will be used?
Do	How and when should the invitation be extended to stakeholders for engagement? What are the ground rules for engagement? What issues/objectives might be good starting points? What format should be used for the engagement sessions? Who is the best fit to be assigned to manage the various stakeholders? What resources, materials, training are needed in this process? Is a third-party facilitator needed? Is third-party verification or audit required?
Check	What are the results? Did we meet our objectives? Do we need additional sessions? Was the process helpful or are changes needed? Do we have the correct stakeholders in the room? Is the right person assigned to own and manage each stakeholder relationship? Are our metrics effectively measuring the desired outcomes?
Act	How will the stakeholder requirements be communicated to key decision-makers? How will the impact of stakeholders' contributions be demonstrated to them? How will ongoing stakeholder engagements be modified to maximize effectiveness? What is the best frequency and form of ongoing communication for each of the stakeholder groups? Do we need to realign any stakeholder relationships?

Table 6.5 Stakeholder Engagement Strategy

Stakeholder Tier	Action	Steps
Tier 1	Engage	Engage in Regular Dialogue Include as Advisory Committee Member Invite to All Stakeholder Meetings Share Key Data and Information Listen and Respond to Feedback
Tier 2	Communicate	Engage in Dialogue Invite to Annual Stakeholder Meetings, Workshops, or Forums Provide Access to Company via Communication Portal Offer Interaction Over Social Media Platforms
Tier 3	Inform	Provide Access to CSR Information – Reports, Publications, Blogs, Press Releases Engage via Social Media – Twitter, Facebook, LinkedIn

stakeholder tier. As indicated in Table 6.5, it makes sense to break stakeholders into groups for engagement based on their tier. Tier 1 or inner stakeholders that have high impact on the organization and high potential for engagement. The Tier 1 group of stakeholders requires regular, honest, and open dialogue on key issues. They may be asked to join a senior level advisory committee to help leadership formulate and give feedback on strategic J.E.D.I. initiatives. The outer stakeholder group includes Tier 2 and Tier 3 stakeholders. Tier 2 stakeholders are still influential, and they wish to be kept informed and to have access to information for regular updates. They want to be part of the process but not to necessarily play an active role like Tier 1 stakeholders. Members of the Tier 2 group might be effectively engaged in raising of issues around justice, equity, and inclusion that impact their group members. They still want to be heard and to have their input reflected in an organization's J.E.D.I. action plan. Tier 3 stakeholders are really seeking to be informed through Impact or Corporate Social Responsibility Reports, company blogs, social media, and publications. Social media such as Twitter, Facebook, and LinkedIn can be used to communicate, track responses, and measure impact via analytics with this group on J.E.D.I. progress, programs, and impacts.

Engaging with stakeholders provides meaningful information and insights but it requires a significant commitment from management in terms of time and resources. Including a wide variety of stakeholders gives management insight into barriers and opportunities to create a more inclusive and welcoming organization with opportunities for all. Managing relationships, gathering data, incorporating findings into organizational norms, behaviors and actions, and then, reporting back to stakeholders on outcomes is a significant commitment. Gaining this perspective provides important information for leadership as they navigate their organization on its J.E.D.I. journey. Looking at situations through a different lens offers new and often better solutions.

As the process begins for stakeholder engagement, topics and questions might include:

1. Do our organization's Corporate Social Responsibility (CSR) initiatives align with your group's needs or requirements?
2. Do our CSR initiatives represent the diverse perspectives of our stakeholders?
3. How might we better support your group's requirements with community outreach, programming, or collaborations?
4. Do members of your group feel as if they do or would belong within our company as employees?
5. What internal changes do your group members suggest that our company incorporates to make members of your group feel welcome and as if they belong as part of our community?
6. How can we support your group's workforce development to increase the number of opportunities for them in our industry and firm?
7. What do you need from our organization to support your group's goals?
8. How can we collaborate to solve …?
9. Do our J.E.D.I. initiatives recognize systemic issues and support redistributing power and privilege in meaningful ways? Please highlight areas of success or areas for improvement.
10. Do our J.E.D.I. initiatives support marginalized and disadvantaged groups? Please highlight areas of success or areas for improvement.
11. How can our organization leverage its power to make our community a more equitable and just ecosystem?

In Table 6.6 some best practices for maximizing the benefits of stakeholder engagement are indicated. I developed the acronym ENGAGE to help remember the steps for effective engagement with stakeholders.

One of the most beneficial aspects of stakeholder engagement is gaining perspectives. To really understand someone's journey, you need to take the time to listen to their story. Once you understand a stakeholder's perspective, it is crucial to acknowledge that you have heard the feedback and that you will incorporate it into the organization's decision-making process. While it will not be possible to address all stakeholder feedback immediately, keeping them informed on where their issues stand relative to the overall plan can be very impactful. As mentioned in the ENGAGE model, the strategy for communication will vary depending on the

Table 6.6 ENGAGE: Guidelines for Stakeholder Engagement

E	Encourage	Involvement and promote inclusion All interested groups An environment of tolerance and respect Diverse participants to gain a variety of perspectives
N	Navigate	Group dynamics to facilitate an environment to allow all issues to be heard Dynamics to create open sharing of strategy, goals, actions, and limitations Formats to create an environment for an open exchange of ideas Areas of impact and focus on the future Relationships to promote authenticity to build trust
G	Generate	Impact by focusing on relevant issues in a timely manner Impact on decisions and actions Perspective by listening and gathering feedback Recommendations based on a cocreation model
A	Act	In a timely manner to provide stakeholder responses On how stakeholder impact will be incorporated into organizational thinking On issues by incorporating requirements, ideas, and concerns into strategy development On building credibility by demonstrating corporate actions based on prior stakeholder input
G	Give	Clear objectives with metrics and timelines A communication plan including mode, frequency, and channel for conveying and receiving information Stakeholders' forums for gaining information on process and progress for providing feedback
E	Excite	Stakeholders by authentically including them in the process Tier 1 stakeholder by including them in events and forums designed for senior level engagement Tier 2 stakeholders by inviting them to industry association events focusing on J.E.D.I. issues Tier 3 stakeholders by including them in outreach initiatives with other stakeholder groups

stakeholder tier, but keeping stakeholders informed is a crucial part of the stakeholder engagement process. Being authentic with stakeholders and creating an environment for inclusion builds sound long-term relationships that benefit both the organization and its key stakeholder groups.

6.6 Communication Plan

Once we have engaged with stakeholders and have identified challenges and opportunities that are priorities, a communication plan facilitates an effective launch and rollout. Developing a communication strategy is an important part of effectively engaging stakeholders. Developing a communication strategy using the questions highlighted in Table 6.7 identifies the goals or objectives of the communication campaign. A communication strategy is also a useful tool for targeting the audience, fine tuning messaging, and allocating resources. When developing a communication strategy, it is important to consider how you will be measuring success. Of course, communication needs to be two way, so including a feedback loop is also important.

Of vital importance is internal and external messaging consistency especially around J.E.D.I. impact issues. As highlighted in the "woke washing" example in Chapter 1, inconsistent messaging can lead to leadership being accused of "greenwashing" or "woke washing," which damages an organization's brand and image with customers, employees and other stakeholders.

In Table 6.8, there is an example of an internal communication plan announcing the launch of Allies for People with Disabilities, a new employee resource group (ERG) for employees with disabilities. In this example, we chose the name for the ERG based on some best practices from Diversity Inc. While many organizations try to select cute names or acronyms, research indicates that including the name of the group that they ERG is formed to impact in the title helps to drive engagement and participation. The name sends a message to employees around the group's focus and intention.

Table 6.7 Communication Strategy

- What is our goal?
- What is the message(s) that we want to deliver?
- What outcome are we seeking?
- Who can help deliver the message?
- What is our budget?
- What is our action plan and timeline?
- Which communication channels will be most effective?
- How are we going to measure impact?
- How will we gather feedback from our audience?
- How will we inform senior management about stakeholder feedback?
- How will we keep stakeholders informed about the impact of their feedback?

Table 6.8 Communication Plan

Message	Date	Channels	Audience	Purpose	Owner	Metric	Approver
Launching a New ERG: Allies for People with Disabilities	1/15	Internal Newsletter	All Employees	Inform and Engage Interested Employees	ERG Leader	Newsletter Analytics – Open Rate	ERG Executive Sponsor
Same	1/22	Cafeteria Presence	H. Q. Employees	Same	Same	Number of People Visiting	Same
Same	1/15-1/31	ERG Meetings	ERG Group Participants	Same	Other ERG Group Leaders	Group Registration	ERG Leader
Feedback Loop	2/27	ERG Registration Portal	All Employees	Identify and Engage Interested Employees	ERG Group Lead	Number of Registrations	ERG Group Lead

In the communication plan, we designated the ERG leaders as the owners of the communication that they will be posting in the firm's regular employee newsletter. Leveraging newsletter analytics, they will be able to gauge how popular the story was with employees by analyzing the click through rate. Other forms of communication to consider for this launch might be a program to engage the other ERGs to let their group members know of the new ERG's existence, and its goals and priorities. If you have a cafeteria, the Allies for People with Disabilities ERG leaders might want to set up a table during lunch to engage with employees and make them aware of the group. A feedback mechanism is important to both measure the impact of your communication and to move the ERG programming and initiatives forward.

Depending upon the project or program, communication plans vary in level of complexity. Plans often involve multiple organizational levels and stakeholder groups. Communication channels include websites, newsletters, and posters as well as roadshows, kick-off meetings, town hall meetings, staff meetings, videos, and webinars. Events are crafted to be informational, educational, and to gather input and feedback. Trainings are often part of a communication plan designed to support a change initiative. For example, an organization that is rolling out a new diversity, equity, and inclusion plan often has an employee training to cover foundational topics and a separate manager training to help managers understand their additional goals and requirements as people leaders. Whether you are engaging with internal stakeholders, external stakeholders, or both, a communication plan is a valuable and impactful tool.

PEPSICO'S RACIAL EQUITY JOURNEY

In response to the global call for social justice for George Floyd, Ahmaud Arbey, Breonna Taylor, Rayshard Brooks, and countless others, Ramon Laguarta, PepsiCo's CEO, shares their commitment to invest $400 million over 5 years to uplift Black communities and increase Black representation within PepsiCo. He acknowledges that the struggles for equity exist in many forms including religious freedom, gender equity, indigenous people's rights, LGBTQ+ rights, Latino rights in the U.S., and other racial and ethnic discrimination. While he highlights PepsiCo's history with their first Black sales team dating back to 1947 and their ongoing contributions to the NAACP Legal Defense Fund, he admits that "the promise of our journey remains unfulfilled," and that they have much work to do.[8] He also acknowledges hearing from a long-time PepsiCo associate, who spoke of Black American's struggles and called upon PepsiCo to walk along-side their Black employees and communities to address the many challenges that too many in the Black community face each day. It is clear from his statement, that Mr. Laguarta, has spent time engaging with stakeholders and gaining perspective from his listening journey with Black Community leaders and with MOSAIC, their African American employee resource group (ERG).

From a people policy perspective, PepsiCo committed to increasing their Black managers by 30%, implementing unconscious bias and inclusion training, expanding recruitment with historically black colleges and universities (HBCUs), increasing partnerships with diverse organizations at their core recruitment schools, adding 100 Black associates to their executive ranks, and establishing a $25 million scholarship fund to support students transitioning from 2- to 4-year programs. In addition, these scholarship funds are available to support trade and certificate programs as well as 2-year degrees from community colleges.[9] While these actions represent a strong commitment, it is important to recognize that PepsiCo is on a journey, and that they will need to continue to peel back the layers and look deeply at their organizational justice, culture, internal policies and processes, and vendor management to drive systemic change. Through stakeholder engagement, the journey will be refined and enhanced.

From a business perspective, they are more than doubling their spending commitment with Black-owned vendors and suppliers. Their goal is an incremental increase in spending of $350 million with these vendor groups. In addition, they are investing $50 million over the next 5 years in Black-owned small businesses. They are also committing to incorporate more Black voices in creating marketing content. For communities, they have established $6.5 million in community impact grants designed to address systemic racism. In addition, they have launched a $5 million Community Leader Fellowship Program.[10]

To drive change, these are some best practices recommended by Merary Simeon, North American VP of Diversity and Engagement at PepsiCo:

1. Set goals along with an implementation plan
2. Leadership must walk the talk
3. Engage with the broader community
4. Allocate resources to provide support for underrepresented employees[11]

In order to meet their pledges, a taskforce made up of Black employees, primarily executives, meets monthly to assess and report on the progress PepsiCo is making on its commitments. This taskforce ensures transparency and accountability. Transformation begins with the C-suite and their support both internally and externally is crucial, but these commitments must cascade to middle managers and first-level supervisors to ensure that systemic change is being achieved. In terms of community commitments, leveraging employees' community knowledge and empowering them drives impact in their communities. Take a close look at your community investment strategy, who is involved, and how local businesses and suppliers are being engaged and included.[12]

The equity picture shared in Figure P2 Equitable Support in the Diversity Primer demonstrates the need for varying levels of support to bring people to the same level of advantage. Since we all begin from different starting points, the level of resources and support required to drive equity varies. As a leader, it is important to provide resources to underrepresented employees to help close these systemic gaps. In addition, it is not the responsibility of underserved employees to carry the burden of educating non-diverse co-workers, friends, and others. It is important that organizations provide ongoing justice, equity, and inclusion education for their workforce to gain perspective on other members of the community's lived experiences. Gaining perspective is crucial to driving systemic change and creating a culture of inclusion and belonging.

6.7 Summary

Gaining perspective is an ongoing journey. A key component is to lay down preconceived ideas and to truly listen to internal and external stakeholders. The process of gaining perspective includes gathering quantitative and qualitative data through data mining, analytics, and surveys. Data can be gathered through either formal or informal assessments that provide information to develop a strategic roadmap, prioritize issues, allocate resources, and implement programs. Numerous survey tools including AI based NPL-driven assessment tools are available to gather and leverage insights for impact. A key to successful transformation is to understand your organization's maturity on the J.E.D.I. Maturity Continuum, its capacity for change, and your organizational goals. Trying to launch programs and initiatives that are not in alignment creates challenges and obstacles that may derail your organization's J.E.D.I. journey.

Gathering key data on your organization's diversity representation that includes disaggregated DEI data by demographics across levels and roles provides insights on pathways and blockages within the organization. These details provide a roadmap to look at processes and policies within the organization such as talent policies, vendor policies, communication policies, and their implementation that are inhibiting or facilitating progress with J.E.D.I. goals. Engaging a broad range of stakeholders is crucial to gathering diverse voices to inform strategy and program initiatives and priorities. As we saw in the PepsiCo case, taking the time to truly listen allows leadership to make significant commitments to partnership with its community to address systemic barriers especially in underserved communities.

Two-way communication is a key to gaining perspective. Communications include listening, sharing information, and maintaining a feedback loop for adjustment and refinement of messaging. Developing a stakeholder engagement communication strategy and plan as well as a program/project communication plan is crucial for effective engagement and implementation. Communication begins with listening, which is foundational to gaining perspective and driving impact.

Questions

1. How does gathering and sharing employee data by organization level impacts leadership perspective?
2. How do you think technology supports better J.E.D.I. outcomes?
3. Complete the J.E.D.I. Framework in Appendix 6A for your organization.
   a. What is your organization doing well?
   b. Where do you need improvement?
   c. What organizational capabilities or capacity might be leveraged?
   d. What action might you recommend based on this assessment?
   e. How does your organization rank in terms of its DEI maturity?
   f. What would you recommend as organizational priorities?
4. Take the Employee J.E.D.I. Survey Questions.
   a. How well do you think your organization addresses DEI?
   b. Do you feel that your organization is welcoming to all employees?
   c. What changes might you recommend in order to create or strengthen a culture of belonging?
5. If you were tasked with performing a J.E.D.I. assessment which survey approach, might you recommend? Why?
6. Consider your organization's ecosystem, who are your Tier 1, Tier 2, and Tier 3 stakeholders?
7. How might you use the ENGAGE model and/or the Stakeholder Engagement Plan to engage with Tier 1 stakeholders?
8. How might you leverage the Communication Strategy to further this engagement?
9. In reading the PepsiCo case, are there programs or initiatives that were not highlighted that you believe would improve their J.E.D.I. strategy and impact?
10. How might you use the Communication Plan to engage with employees at PepsiCo regarding the recommendations you made in Q. 9?

Appendix 6A

Organizational Justice, Equity, Diversity, and Inclusion (J.E.D.I.) Framework

1. How is our organizational culture described by the following stakeholders?
   a. Board/C-suite
   b. Managers
   c. Employees
   d. Suppliers
   e. Community
   f. Other Stakeholders

2. How are J.E.D.I. values reflected in our organizational pillars?
   a. Vision
   b. Goals
   c. Priorities
   d. Strategy
3. How are J.E.D.I. principals reflected in our culture and operations?
   a. Values
   b. Norms
   c. Shared Beliefs
   d. Role Models
   e. Resource Allocation
   f. Behaviors and Actions
   g. Artifacts
4. How is DEI reflected in our organization's performance goals?
   a. Internal
      i. C-suite Scorecard
      ii. Senior Manager Goals
      iii. Middle Manager Goals
      iv. Team Goals
      v. Individual Goals
   b. External
      i. Supplier Goals
      ii. Community Goals
5. What is the diversity representation of our …?
   a. Board of Directors
   b. C-suite
   c. Senior Management
   d. Middle Management
   e. Employees
6. How effective are our internal policies, processes, and systems in promoting our J.E.D.I. vision?
   a. How do they promote an inclusive culture?
   b. How do they act as barriers to an inclusive culture?
   c. Where are we doing well?
   d. Are we considering both internal and external impacts?
   e. How do we compare to our industry peers?
   f. Are our leaders serving as role models in policy adoption and execution externally?
   g. Where do we need help?

7. How are our people management systems impacting the J.E.D.I. goals?
   a. What are our recruitment and talent acquisition diversity metrics?
   b. What development opportunities are being offered to support awareness and understanding of the culture, history, and experience of underrepresented communities?
   c. How are we managing our career development?
   d. What are the diversity metrics for our leadership program?
   e. What are the diversity metrics for our high potential employees?
   f. How are we recommending and delivering talent development?
   g. What tools are we offering to support employees' needs for work life balance?
   h. What are our community-based talent interactions?
   i. How reflective of our community is our workforce representation?
8. What are our talent recruitment strategies?
   a. How do we recruit talent?
   b. Where do we recruit talent?
   c. Are we recruiting from diverse sources?
   d. What is the diversity of our talent recruitment pipeline?
   e. What language(s) do we use in job postings?
   f. How are we addressing unconscious bias in the hiring process?
9. What are our talent retention strategies?
   a. How reflective of our community is our talent diversity representation?
   b. How are new opportunities shared?
   c. How is talent developed?
   d. How do we define meritocracy?
   e. How do we demonstrate that we value employees?
   f. What are our turnover rates? By category?
   g. How do we compare to our peers?
   h. What do our employee engagement (EE) surveys reflect?
   i. How are promotions and raises determined?
   j. Who is eligible for leadership development?
   k. Are we auditing talent policies and processes for conversion and retention leakages?
10. How do we develop leaders?
   a. What core competencies do we identify and prioritize?
   b. Who sponsors employees for selection in leadership development programs?
   c. How transparent is this process?
   d. How diverse is our leadership pipeline?
   e. What curriculum is included in leadership development to support J.E.D.I. capacity building in future leaders?

11. How do we engage with middle managers on topics related to J.E.D.I. initiatives and priorities?
    a. What training and development is given to middle managers?
    b. How are outcomes measured?
    c. What is the impact on middle managers performance scorecard?
    d. What expectations do we have of managers?
12. How are teams designed?
    a. Do teams reflect diversity of identity, experience, thought?
    b. Do we promote psychological safety?
    c. Do we promote inclusive norms?
    d. Do we avoid tokenism?
13. What tools are available to build capacity and support J.E.D.I. goals?
    a. Training
    b. Development
    c. Mentoring, Reverse Mentoring, Shadowing
    d. Allyship
    e. Sponsorship
    f. Storytelling
    g. Employee Resource Groups-ERGs
    h. Town Halls
    i. Flexible Work Policies
    j. Metrics and Reporting
14. What technologies allow for scaling of solutions across the organization?
    a. Process improvement
    b. Workflow automation
    c. Data-based decision-making
    d. Artificial Intelligence tools
    e. Reporting
    f. Communication
15. What are our J.E.D.I. standards for procurements and suppliers?
    a. Percentage spent with BIPOC-owned businesses?
    b. Percentage spent with AAPI-owned businesses?
    c. Percentage spent women-owned businesses?
    d. Percentage spent with LGBTQ+-owned businesses?
    e. Are we including professional service firms?
    f. Do we have a supply chain J.E.D.I. questionnaire?
    g. Do we request remediation plans from suppliers?
    h. Do we have an outreach program to support underrepresented businesses?
    i. Is a supplier scorecard used?
    j. Do we maintain a supplier ranking matrix based on scorecard performance?

16. How are our J.E.D.I. commitments reflected in our community outreach?
    a. How do we define our community?
    b. What are the demographics of the communities in which we operate?
    c. How do we engage our community? (CSR outreach)
    d. How do our philanthropic beneficiaries align with community demographics?
    e. What programs and outreach are we engaged with in the communities?
    f. Which community members are included on advisory boards?
    g. What employee volunteer programs are we supporting as an organization?
    h. Where are our employees choosing to spend their volunteer time?
    i. How well does our community feel our CSR initiatives support a culture of belonging and inclusion?
17. How do we hear the voices of our employees on J.E.D.I. issues?
    a. How often do we conduct employee engagement surveys?
    b. Are survey results shared? If so, how?
    c. What is done with the information?
    d. How is this information translated into action?
    e. What is the timeframe for actions or remediations?
18. How do customers perceive our organization's J.E.D.I. strategy?
    a. How is our J.E.D.I. strategy reflected in our branding and image?
    b. How are we receiving feedback from customers?
    c. What are our marketplace J.E.D.I. commitments?
    d. Is there alignment between external messaging and internal actions?
19. How do we engage with industry associations and peer organizations?
    a. Who attends these events from our organization?
    b. Who leads the J.E.D.I. agenda in these groups?
    c. What roles do our out leaders play in these organizations?
    d. How active is our CEO in championing J.E.D.I. issues within this ecosystem?

Notes

1 "Women-in-the-Workplace-2020.Pdf," accessed October 6, 2020, https://www.mckinsey.com/~/media/McKinsey/Featured%20Insights/Diversity%20and%20Inclusion/Women%20in%20the%20Workplace%202020/Women-in-the-Workplace-2020.pdf.
2 Ibid.
3 Ibid.
4 Ibid.
5 Ultimate Software, "The Promise of Unstructured Data" (Ultimate Software Group, Inc., n.d.).

6 Witold J. Henisz, Sinziana Dorobantu, and Lite J. Nartey, "Spinning Gold: The Financial Returns to Stakeholder Engagement," *Strategic Management Journal* 35, no. 12 (2014): 1727–48, https://doi.org/10.1002/smj.2180.

7 Kristina Kohl, *Becoming a Sustainable Organization: A Project and Portfolio Management Approach* (Boca Raton, FL: CRC Press, 2016).

8 "PepsiCo's Racial Equality Journey: Black Initiative," PepsiCo, Inc. Official Website, accessed May 6, 2021, http://www.pepsico.com/about/diversity-and-engagement/racial-equality-journey-black-initiative.

9 "PepsiCo's Racial Equality Journey."

10 Ibid.

11 "How PepsiCo Is Reinvesting in Diversity and Inclusion," MIT Sloan, accessed April 28, 2021, https://mitsloan.mit.edu/ideas-made-to-matter/how-pepsico-reinvesting-diversity-and-inclusion.

12 "How PepsiCo Is Reinvesting in Diversity and Inclusion."

Bibliography

Henisz, Witold J., Sinziana Dorobantu, and Lite J. Nartey. "Spinning Gold: The Financial Returns to Stakeholder Engagement." *Strategic Management Journal* 35, no. 12 (2014): 1727–48. https://doi.org/10.1002/smj.2180.

Kohl, Kristina. *Becoming a Sustainable Organization: A Project and Portfolio Management Approach.* Boca Raton, FL: CRC Press, 2016.

MIT Sloan. "How PepsiCo Is Reinvesting in Diversity and Inclusion." Accessed April 28, 2021. https://mitsloan.mit.edu/ideas-made-to-matter/how-pepsico-reinvesting-diversity-and-inclusion.

PepsiCo, Inc. Official Website. "PepsiCo's Racial Equality Journey: Black Initiative." Accessed May 6, 2021. http://www.pepsico.com/about/diversity-and-engagement/racial-equality-journey-black-initiative.

Ultimate Software. "The Promise of Unstructured Data." Ultimate Software Group, Inc., n.d.

"Women-in-the-Workplace-2020.Pdf." Accessed October 6, 2020. https://www.mckinsey.com/~/media/McKinsey/Featured%20Insights/Diversity%20and%20Inclusion/Women%20in%20the%20Workplace%202020/Women-in-the-Workplace-2020.pdf.

Chapter 7

Creating a Culture of Belonging

Creating a culture of belonging is crucial to ensuring that your workforce believes that they are welcome, supported, and valued by your organization. Driving a J.E.D.I. transformation requires leadership to look deeply into their own culture and to understand who sets the standards for norms, values, attitudes, and beliefs. Leadership must ask themselves if they expect employees and other stakeholders to assimilate into their dominant culture or if they are building an equitable culture that values and supports a variety of perspectives, identities, cultures, and styles. So often, leaders focus their strategy on increasing the diversity representation of their talent pool, but they don't fully appreciate the importance of creating a culture where diversity is appreciated, valued, and rewarded. Creating a culture of belonging means changing how organizations operate including board representation, leadership competencies, leadership development, recruiting practices, supplier practices, talent development practices, and team norms. Transforming into a J.E.D.I. organization requires drilling deep into organizational systems to understand root causes and systemic barriers built into the operating foundation.

7.1 Leadership Competencies for Belonging

Creating a culture of belonging is different from creating an inclusive culture. Inviting someone and including them implies that the person is joining an already existing group with its own culture. Often this is exemplified by the dominant culture of an organization, and employees must adapt to the organizational culture in order to be accepted, valued, and promoted. It implies that the employee is joining

DOI: 10.1201/9781003168072-8

an existing work environment with work structures, team dynamics, and policies based on a particular cultural paradigm. Inclusion assumes that the new employee will adapt to the existing culture. In reality, creating a diverse workforce means that the work environment and work structures need to change in order to allow for different work requirements, structures, and practices. It requires establishing a culture where a variety of perspectives, experiences, styles, and backgrounds are valued and supported. Policies, practices, and processes need to be evaluated and redesigned to support a culture of belonging. While reasonable accommodation, modification, or adjustment of the work environment, may be the most visible of these adaptations, it is certainly not the only one. Team dynamics require reevaluation so that the loudest voice doesn't dictate decisions and that all team members feel comfortable contributing. Working parents especially women, may require flexible work arrangements. Culturally diverse workers may require different accommodation for different holiday schedules. Creating a culture of belonging means welcoming and celebrating differences. An organization's culture and policies must reflect the diverse needs of its workforce, customers, and community.

The need to create a culture of belonging goes even deeper. It requires looking at what behaviors and contributions are valued by an organization and its leadership. Are certain university degrees valued over others? Do you require new hires to have experience with certain organizations? Valuing certain degrees or work experiences in the recruitment process and hiring based on those criteria create a culture with affinity bias. In effect, the process values hiring people that are like the existing workforce and leadership over others that have the required skills but reflect a different education background or work experience. Internally, there are biases for pathways to promotion and leadership, as well. Often, the leadership path requires experience with departments or functions within the organization. Consider the following questions to evaluate your organization:

1. Within the organization, are underrepresented groups more predominately represented in a certain division?
2. If so, is this division's contribution to the organization valued in the same way as a predominately White division?
3. Which divisions serve as the talent pipeline training ground for the leadership track?
4. What has been the career path for your existing leadership team?
5. How might the organization need to redesign its leadership development track to promote a culture of belonging?

As organizations seek to promote diversity, equity, and inclusion (DEI), we see that within organizations, there is a great deal of variance in terms of roles and responsibilities and perceived value across the organization. In order to retain a diverse workforce, an organization must create a culture of belonging that includes career development and advancement opportunities that reflect valuing workforce diversity. In order to manage, develop, and effectively engage a diverse workforce, new skills and competencies need to be developed for leaders and managers. To drive impact, we suggest moving from training to capacity building. In addition to offering training, educate on discrimination, fairness, access, and legitimacy, and focus on building leadership competencies to improve people management at the individual, team, department, and organizational level.

In order to instill diversity of identity, thought, and experience within an organization, consider your organization's board level diversity representation. Role models at the board level are crucial to ensure that employees, customers, and communities feel that there is someone at the board level with whom they identify. Figure 7.1 highlights performing a GAP analysis of the current board's diversity representation and comparing that to the organization's J.E.D.I. mission and vision.

As part of the process, consider the ecosystem in which your organization operates including employees, customers, suppliers, and communities.

1. What is the representation of these key stakeholder groups?
2. How does your board representation align with the diversity of identity, thought, and experience of these key stakeholders?
3. What are the gaps between the representation in the current slate of board mebers and the organization's board representation goals?

A list of diversity factors is provided in Figure 7.1 to facilitate the Gap Analysis, but additional factors may need to be added depending upon the requirements of an organization. Using this approach, identify the perspectives that are represented by your current board and those that need to be developed to better match the representation of your stakeholders. Consider the current as well as future needs of your organization. While understanding the strengths and weaknesses of your current board is crucial to the process, it is also imperative to consider the future direction of

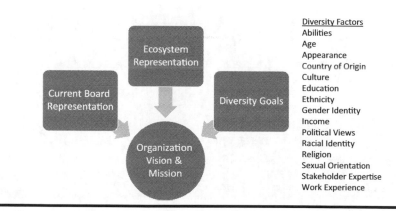

Figure 7.1   Board GAP Analysis.

your organization. As part of the Gap Analysis, consider the additional perspectives as well as business experience and subject matter expertise needed to support future growth and market expansion. Once you understand your board's representation gaps, then the Board of Directors can begin the process of recruiting board members that are able to contribute those needed perspectives.

While recruiting diverse board members is a critical step, the process of building a representational board requires changes beyond board recruitment. A board governance review should be undertaken. Factors to consider include by-laws, board size, make-up, responsibilities, recruitment practices, and compensation. Just as with organizations as a whole, boards need to review their policies, practices, and culture to ensure that diversity of perspective is valued, and that space is made for contributions by all board members. The goal is to create a board that is able to develop meaningful relationships with your diverse stakeholder groups and to provide unique and impactful insights to board leadership. Board tokenism, which is the practice of making a symbolic board appointment from an underserved group to create the appearance of diversity, should be consciously avoided. The benefits of board diversity are significant and include innovation, improved stakeholder engagement, enhanced organizational reputation, and expanded networks. Achieving board level diversity is crucial as it creates new organizational opportunities and minimizes risks.

Driving systemic change at the C-suite and executive level of the organization requires reviewing leadership competencies. Creating a more equitable and inclusive organization, necessitates reviewing leadership's role as well as the skills and competencies needed to promote a culture of belonging. As indicated in Figure 7.2, leadership competencies for a Social Impact Leader include focusing on people, acting as a credible role model, leading vision and strategy, and effectively implementing that strategy.

Taking a *People Focus*, leaders must engage and listen to internal and external stakeholders in order to create an authentic culture of belonging. Stakeholder

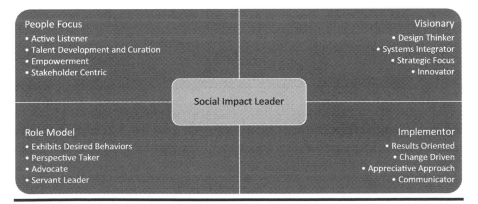

Figure 7.2 Social Impact Leadership Model.

engagement must be authentic with feedback loops so that employees, customers, and community members feel heard and that impacts of their inputs are demonstrated by the organization. One of the most important actions and behaviors is listening to diverse voices in order to gain perspective. After the year of social upheaval in 2020, many CEOs began the process of truly listening to their BIPOC community leaders. For many, it was the first time that they really gained perspective on BIPOC community issues and concerns. Gaining perspective creates the opportunity for change. It also helps to define the role of a servant leader, one who focuses on the growth and well-being of their employees and community members, by informing the leader's role as a facilitator and supporter of their people and other stakeholders. As a social impact leader, it is important to promote change internally as well as externally. Organizations exist within communities and societies, and we see that systemic barriers cross our public, private, and community sectors. Stakeholders including employees are expecting more from their leadership. Leaders are speaking out about voting rights, immigrant rights, LGBTQ+ rights, and other issues of importance to their key stakeholders. Advocacy is a competency that is becoming increasingly important with CEO activism on the rise. Being a J.E.D.I. organization means reaching beyond the boundaries of your own organization to influence regulation, policy, and practices in the broader ecosystem.

Listening helps leaders understand where and how employees, especially underrepresented employees, are facing blockages or barriers. Frequent and open communication between leadership and employees is one of the most effective tools in building resiliency for employees. In order to allow employees to speak truth to power, open lines of communication must be developed and actively utilized. Empowering managers, team leaders, and employees is crucial to cascading environmental and social justice throughout the organizations and for providing authentic feedback loops.

Transformation requires talent development and curation to fill the leadership pipeline with highly qualified candidates that represent the diversity of your organization's community. Leaders need to think about succession planning and best practices around leadership development in terms of experiential training, formalized training, and self-development. Some best people practices include:

1. Consider the workforce requirements to meet strategic goals including succession planning.
2. Leverage both internal and external data to understand organizational impacts and employee trends.
3. Support career development and opportunities for all employees.
4. Find and develop diverse talent for the future.
5. Facilitate networks both internally and externally to support growth and collaboration.
6. Evaluate traditional pathways to leadership and redesign systems to provide more opportunities for underrepresented groups.

Leaders have a responsibility to support employees' growth and development as part of their own core competencies. This role is especially important as organizations seek to engage and retain underrepresented groups at all levels of their organization. Rather than a single monolithic culture in which everyone must conform to a single standard, effective leaders support a culture that promotes belonging and welcomes and supports a variety of attitudes, beliefs, and values. A manager has the ability to create conditions for success through their people management and development. Capacity building at the leadership level begins with developing manager's people development and management skills to promote a culture of belonging.

Leaders must be *Role Models* in order to drive transformative organizational change. They need to exhibit the desired actions and behaviors within their organization, the community, as well as broader industry groups. If senior leadership is only giving lip service rather than implementing meaningful changes within their areas of responsibility, the organizational impact will be derailed. It is crucial for leaders to set the standards for actions and behaviors internally and to support and advocate for equity and justice externally.

The *Visionary* leadership competency focuses on an organization's long-term mission ensuring strategic alignment between mission and vision, and its environmental and social justice goals. Understanding that their organization is part of larger social, political, community, and environmental systems is foundational to the role of a visionary leader. The cascading impacts of strategic vision, goals, and policies within and across organizational systems must be harnessed and leveraged to drive meaningful change. The visionary focus needs to be holistic and encompass all stakeholder views including customers, employees, investors, suppliers, and community members. Board diversity representation of identity, thought, and experience impacts leaderships' ability to transform an organization's vision and mission. Encouraging innovative new approaches and leveraging tools such as people-centered design allows for a conversation around what is possible. Leaders must listen and learn from their broad stakeholders to develop an innovative roadmap to promote equitable and just organizations.

As an *Implementor*, it is incumbent upon leaders to navigate paradoxes and to support resource alignment with organizational vision and mission. The issues of access and legitimacy are often a consideration as organizational priorities are selected, and project funding is approved. Leadership competencies around recognizing strategic direction and workforce diversity alignment for the future is an important component in terms of building long-term and equitable workforce diversity. Effectively, funding and project prioritization must be aligned with these goals as well. It is in the implementation phase where strategic alignment and change happen. Crucial to the success of implementation is building an organizational culture where diversity of identity, thought, and experience are valued by all. Taking an appreciative approach and scaling practices that are working and driving impact accelerate the change process and deliver on results. Digital solutions are a helpful tool in supporting meaningful and inclusive change as they support data-driven decision-making and keep information centered in leaders' decision-making processes. Selecting key performance indicators (KPIs) to measure progress focuses attention on results and ensures accountability.

Companies in the U.S. are looking for candidates to fill recently reinvigorated or newly created Chief Diversity Officer (CDO) positions. In fact, according to Phenom People, a talent platform software firm, this role was one of the hottest jobs in 2021. A CDO is an experienced business leader with deep expertise in equity, diversity, and inclusion. In this role, the CDO is responsible for an organization's J.E.D.I. vision, strategy, and implementation including developing an organization-wide J.E.D.I. strategic plan, developing training and capacity building for employees, managers, and leaders, representing the organization on J.E.D.I. issues with internal and external stakeholders, and acting as a partner to other leaders in the organization to collaborate on delivering on the organization's J.E.D.I. vision. Developing and implementing an organization's J.E.D.I. strategy is complex with multiple dimensions and intersectionalities. Each organization is on its own J.E.D.I. journey, which means that the CDO role will vary by organization in terms of organizational capacity, programs, partnerships, and resources. Appendix 7A contains an example of a CDO's duties and responsibilities. As the job description indicates, the role is cross-functional, strategic, and tactical, which requires board and CEO support and active advocacy in order to drive transformation toward a J.E.D.I. culture. Reflecting on the competencies for a Social Impact Leaders, these requirements – *People Focused, Role Model, Visionary, and Implementor* – are the core competencies required in the CDO role. As we build J.E.D.I. organizations, these leadership competencies are crucial across leadership roles.

THE VIEW FROM WITHIN: THE SUSTAINABILITY LEADER'S RELATIONSHIP TO THE SYSTEM

By Gilles Mesrobian

Gilles Mesrobian, is the Managing Director of The Red Queen Group as well as a Senior Associate at the Support Center for Nonprofit Management. His credentials include over 26 years of senior management experience in the non-profit arena, with nearly 20 years as an Executive Director. His consulting experience covers a broad range of organizational work in the non-profit and philanthropic sector, including executive leadership transition and executive search. Gilles is also a Certified Governance trainer through BoardSource as well as a faculty member of Bard's MBA in Sustainability where he teaches leadership development in Sustainability. He is a member of the national training faculty for NeighborWorks America and facilitates several leadership training programs including the New York Foundation for the Arts' Emerging Leaders program, a yearlong cohort-learning program for senior non-profit professionals.

We live in perhaps the most parlous of times. Human history has demonstrated again and again that it is our innate ability to lead and be led that determines whether we will vanish, endure, or thrive as a species. Sustainability mandates transformative change to overcome the challenges that stand between the present and a flourishing and sustainable world. In order to herald such change in others and within the organizations they lead, sustainability leaders must be open to transformative change within their own leadership practice.

The drive to create an environmentally sustainable and socially just world, mandates a passion and vision that is very different from those of traditional business leaders. Sustainability leaders recognize that while our society has benefited from the unparalleled prosperity and innovation of the last century, much of that benefit is unequally distributed and has come at the price of a changing climate, increasing income inequality, and many other social and environmental challenges.

SUSTAINABILITY LEADERS SHARE A UNIQUE WORLDVIEW

At the core of this different worldview, lies a fundamental difference in the leader's personal relationship to the system – whether it be their communities, organizations or the very ecosystems in which they live. While the traditional leader may imagine themselves above and in command of the system, the sustainability leader sees themselves embedded within the system. Unable to distance or separate themselves from the events and forces that occur around them, these leaders experience the system in a completely different manner.

The sustainability leader recognizes that, like other inhabitants and participants, they are permeable in some regards so that the system itself has a more immediate influence upon them. They cannot separate their health, their well-being and their success from the health, well-being and success of the system in which they exist. The two are indistinguishable.

In this manner, this most basic leadership relationship is entirely different from the way we have defined leadership in the past. The leader's relationship to the larger system is motivated by a different worldview, one that is informed by the way they experience the world around them, their immediate interactions within those systems as well as their vision of the role of the leader.

We are witnessing this fundamental redefinition of what it means to lead through the leaders we witness around us today. In the process our expectations of leadership are changing – in terms of what we aspire to as leaders, and what we respond to as followers.

As a result, a new generation of leaders is emerging with a different vision of leadership. They see their role as in service to society and the environment as opposed to the traditional leadership view of being in command of society and the environment. As such they imagine and are drawn to business models that are not only financially profitable but able to improve social conditions while being responsible environmental stewards. In addition, their vision of the world, as well as their role in it, is driven by their desire for a more just and civil society.

THE LEADER'S RELATIONSHIP WITH GROWTH

While the Sustainability leader's relationship with the system is informed by their world view and vision, this perspective also influences the leader's fundamental interpretation of many core business concepts. Let us examine the leader's relationship with one of the fundamental goals of business – growth. The basic recipe for sustainability begins with learning to do more with less. From lifestyles to industries, society can – and must – increase our efficiency in all aspects. Doing this is not simple given our traditional interpretation of change and growth. However, when one redefines growth to emphasize quality over quantity, it is inherently in our best interest to be efficient.

Assuming that all leaders are motivated by growth we must acknowledge that all of us experience growth differently. For some, growth is expansive and is measured horizontally often in terms of numbers, dollars, units delivered, or individuals influenced by our products and services. For others, growth is interpreted vertically, in terms of depth or quality of product, service or experience or its long-term impact upon the individual. While growth can be calculated as the average across a wide range or across the entire system, it can also be calculated on an individual basis.

One's relationship with the system profoundly impacts our perceptions of growth and in the process our definition of sustainable growth. From a distance we may witness the growth of an entire system and may not see the inconsistency of how the system grows. The traditional leader, experiencing growth from above, rather than embedded in the system may form an unbalanced view. They may see a growing or changing system but not recognize that the system, while growing and benefiting some individuals, does so at the detriment of others. It is this distorted view of change and growth that we are witnessing today. Traditional leaders, who view the system from a position of command are unable or unwilling to recognize that dramatic inequity and imbalance between how different individuals experience growth can exist even while the larger system is experiencing exponential growth. In this way, the experience of growth is very different based on the leader's relationship with the system and even more by their position and role in the larger system.

The same can be said for how leaders interpret other key business concepts such as communications or risk. A sustainability leader, embedded within a changing system, has a more immediate relationship with the system. The effectiveness of communications is impacted by the removal of barriers between the leader and those around them when they see themselves as part of the system rather than removed from it. This not only improves their ability to understand, listen, and communicate effectively, but it also ensures that the leader is able to communicate through the lens of a "lived" experience as opposed to an "observed" experience. The "lived" experience that comes from being within the system also contributes to a more flexible and adaptable leadership style as sustainability leaders are more attuned and permeable to changes occurring around them.

THE LEADER'S RELATIONSHIP WITH OPPOSING VIEWS

This is particularly important in the leader's ability to balance opposing views. We live in a period of increasing polarization which threatens to undermine our society and the economic models on which we rely. At the heart of the increasing resentment against social justice and the equitable systems that it mandates, is a fundamental division between how individuals experience the system. It is for this reason that we need leaders who are able to experience the injustices that are inherent in the system firsthand – through a "lived" rather than an "observed" experience. The leader positioned above the system may experience growth and success but cannot see the imbalance and equity that exists within, and as such cannot begin to understand what is needed to correct the historic harm against members of society. And worse, the traditional leader may see the goals of social justice as threatening or damaging rather than necessary for a truly sustainable business model, economy, society, and environment.

Key Takeaways:

- Sustainability leaders have a fundamentally different world view from traditional leaders – one that informs their relationship to the system and the way they do business.
- This different worldview positions sustainability leaders as embedded within the system rather than above and in command of the system.
- A more direct relationship with the system causes them to interpret key business concepts such as growth, change, communications, risk, i.e., very differently than traditional leaders.
- As a result, their leadership practices support more balanced, inclusive, equitable, and sustainable business models.

7.2 Roadmap to Belonging

Driving systemic change, holding leadership accountable, and embedding J.E.D.I. across all operational aspects of an organization are complex and require significant commitment and resources. In order to provide a framework for the process that

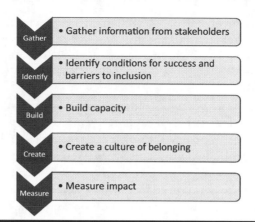

Figure 7.3   Driving Toward Belonging.

can be leveraged for large, complex organizations, middle market companies, and smaller family-owned business, Figure 7.3 shares five best practices for driving organizational change to create a culture of belonging.

It all begins with gathering information from stakeholders using an appreciative rather than a deficit-based approach. Gathering stakeholder information provides examples of where and when employees felt that they could fully contribute and bring their full selves to work. It also provides insights as to when community members felt heard. The process identifies conditions for success as well as barriers to belonging. The key questions are:

1. When did it work well?
2. What conditions were at play?

With this information, team dynamics, work rules, dress codes, promotion requirements, and other policies and procedures can be reevaluated to focus on what is working to support diverse employees. In the case of community members, gathering this feedback helps to redesign engagement and impact programs to better align them with community needs.

Build capacity by giving people information and tools to improve outcomes. From a leadership perspective, it means reframing the J.E.D.I. conversation as a business imperative and providing resources to build cultures of belonging. Capacity building promotes education, awareness, skills, and other management tools. Best practices include creating J.E.D.I. cross-functional committees to share initiatives, best practices, and lessons learned across the organization. It includes creating a board advisory committee for community stakeholders to provide perspectives and insights on effective engagements especially around meeting the needs of marginalized groups. Including both successes and failures in these conversations promotes transparency, authenticity, and meaningful impact. Capacity building includes training and development, but training programs must include resources and tools to go beyond compliance requirements. Trainings should include materials that help people do the work of learning others' perspectives and history, and may include resources on Black history, Asian culture, or selected readings by BIPOC authors.

As work structures, processes, and policies change, leadership's capacities must be retooled and bolstered to support a work environment that promotes equity and inclusion. Through looking deeply at existing habits, behaviors, and norms, we begin building capacity to reposition new organizational priorities that promote a culture of belonging. The cycle is iterative, and measuring impact along the journey is crucial to ensure systemic and long-lasting change. To measure progress, establish a baseline and measure impact along the journey. Selecting key metrics that align with goals and sharing data, metrics, and results across the organization creates a common language, measurement of progress, and accountability.

7.3 Taking an Appreciative Approach

Key to building a culture for belonging is continuous improvement. This approach to driving change and learning from experience of success is the foundation of Appreciative Inquiry. The origins of Appreciative Inquiry come from David Cooperrider's research at Case Western University in the 1980s and his approach to modeling and driving transformative change. Traditional change management takes a problem-centric approach in which we identify a problem, analyze the causes, propose solutions, and solve a problem. The frame for this approach is a deficit-based model. Instead, Appreciative Inquiry focuses on what is working and leverages successes to drive impact. The model is described in Table 7.1.

Table 7.1 Appreciative Inquiry Organizational Change Model

Phases	Actions
Discover	Discover the best scenario or example
Dream	Imagine the possibilities
Design	Engage others to co-create
Destiny	Drive transformation

Source: Bernard J. Mohr and Jane Magruder Watkins, *The Essentials of Appreciative Inquiry: A Roadmap for Creating Positive Futures* (Waltham, MA: Pegasus Communications, Inc., 2002).

This model begins with inviting stakeholders to imagine building an organization and community in which they would like to work and live. Appreciative Inquiry is based on collaborative discovery around making organizations more effective environmentally, socially, and economically. In effect, it incorporates an integrated bottom-line approach in its foundational ethos. In order to drive organizational change, stakeholders weave new knowledge and techniques in to the existing formal and informal organizational systems.

An example of leveraging Appreciative Inquiry to address equity and inclusion in an organization comes from former CEO of Xerox, Ursula Burns sharing her perspective on racism and sexism. "One of the things that I learned as a senior executive is that the '-isms' of sexism and racism are like air. They're everywhere."[1] Her advice is to not ask the question of have you experienced racism and sexism, but rather, under what set of conditions have you not experienced racism and sexism. In terms of society and norms, we need to collectively redefine our societal definition of normal, making it more inclusive. Being a Black, female CEO should not be seen as an anomaly, but rather as the norm. Her perspective and approach to driving systemic change on issues of sexism and racism dovetails with Appreciative Inquiry in terms of using a collective approach that focuses on when environmental factors and reaffirming behaviors supported equity and inclusion promoting a culture of belonging.

Appreciative Inquiry follows five process steps as outlined in Figure 7.4. The first step is to adopt a line of inquiry focusing on the positive. As this may be the first time that key stakeholders such as leadership, employees, and other groups are using this approach, it is imperative that time be spent on educating them about the Appreciative Inquiry philosophy, approach, and process steps. In order for this methodology to work, it is important that key stakeholders buy-in to the process. They need to be able to envision the approach being used in their organization. Once

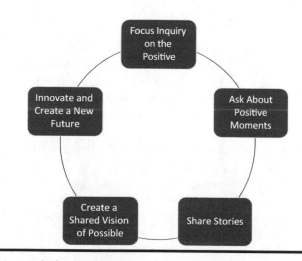

Figure 7.4 Appreciative Inquiry Process Steps.[2]

there is support and agreement on the Appreciative Inquiry methodology, research needs to be done on an organization's exceptional moments. This stage is about collecting organizational stories of excellence. Asking about positive moments can be done via interviews, surveys, or even asking employees to share their stories of organizational excellence via an internal portal designed for collecting stories. The focus of the inquiry is asking people to share their best experiences either at work, within the community, or in their personal life. Ask them to reflect on this best experience and to identify when they felt the most alive or excited by their involvement. Probe to better understand the specifics that made the experience exciting and who was involved with the event. Next, focus your questions on their values. Ask them to consider what they value most about themselves, their work, organization, or community. Taking a page from the agility and resiliency discussion in Chapter 5, drill into what gives an organization its resiliency and agility to adapt and transcend challenges. Embedded within this answer is usually an organization's core life-giving factor. If this core life-giving factor did not exist in this organization, how would it change the organization? The final question focuses on an individual's wishes for the future of the organization or community. This line of questioning helps identify stakeholders' desires for their organizations and communities to make them more vibrant and effective places to work, live, and to drive impact.

The objective of the Appreciative Inquiry approach is to get people telling stories about when they were most engaged and alive, to identify a core driver of organizational culture, and what they wish for the organization's future. With this information, a transformational vision and plan of action begins to take shape. Since the approach is collaborative, the next step in the process involves sharing the gathered stories so that as many stakeholders as possible can collectively review the data and identify learnings about the organization's and or community's positive core values and the conditions that support shared stories. Taking these learnings and overlaying the wish list begins the process of developing the list of what is needed to transform the organization. Digital surveying tools can be leveraged to assist in the data gathering process.

Next, participants share a vision of the preferred state for their organization. At this stage, we are inviting participants to share in the development of an organization's J.E.D.I. mission. The vision statement includes how the organization wishes the world to view its contribution and the strategy to implement this vision. Implementation includes structures, processes, systems, policies, work environments, and technologies that need to be interwoven into existing formal and informal systems to realize this vision. This step focuses on innovation and designing for their shared vision to create a culture of belonging.

The final phase involves engaging with stakeholders and bringing this shared vision into reality. This action step involves making a commitment to the vision transformation. Stakeholder commitments may be strategic support or represent a specific offer of a resource – money, time, or talent. As with change management in general, committing to continuous improvement is a best practice to sustain momentum.

Leveraging Appreciative Inquiry to design a culture of belonging creates a positively focused transformation plan that encourages all stakeholders to participate and share their voices in creating a J.E.D.I. organization. Rather than focus on diversity numbers, Appreciative Inquiry encourages capacity building and collaboration by focusing organizational resources on what is possible and building consensus for a unified vision. It provides both a vision and a pathway forward to creating a more just and equitable organization. Focusing on capacity building and creating a set of conditions for success, this model allows organizations to both imagine and design for a culture of belonging.

Aim2 Flourish (https://aim2flourish.com/) is an initiative of the Fowler Center for Business as an Agent of World Benefit at the Weatherhead School of Management, Case Western Reserve University. Under the leadership of higher education professors, students from around the world contribute stories using an Appreciative Inquiry approach to highlight businesses focused on innovative solutions to achieving the U.N. Sustainable Development Goals. (Outlined in Chapter 1) This resource provides thousands of stories and cases of businesses acting on their shared vision of improving the well-being of the world. One of the submissions by a group of students is a French company, Andyamo, whose mission is to make movement easier for people with mobility issues. One of the founders became disabled after a skiing accident. As a result, they became very aware of the limitations in terms of access and accessibility within France for people with limited mobility. Through its app, Andyamo provides users with GPS information designed to determine if a route is wheelchair accessible, or if someone with a walker can gain access to a facility, as well as many other mobility challenges.[3] Focusing on what is possible, creates opportunity for innovation while addressing core societal challenges.

Another story, written by one of my Bard MBA students highlights the transformative impact of B Lab "calling in" organizational leaders to leverage B Lab's tools and resources to develop a shared vision that promotes environmental and social justice. (https://aim2flourish.com/innovations/b-lab-pioneers-of-better-business) Their approach is to provide tools to leaders to support capacity building. These AIM2Flourish stories leverage Appreciative Inquiry to share innovations, sustainability as flourishing organizations, and leadership practices that highlight mindfulness and focus on employee well-being. This resource repository highlights and shares best practices of organizations that are working to address some of our most pressing global, social, and environmental challenges.

7.4 Creating Conditions for Success

When building a culture to support belonging, the presence of role models plays an important role in making people feel that they have a welcoming environment that understands and appreciates them. People who self-identify as members of underserved groups need to see leaders with whom they can identify. In addition, diversity

Increase	Review	Develop	Train	Promote	Engage
• Increase percentage of diverse people in leadership and on boards	• Review who is being depicted in artwork, ads, recruiting and training materials	• Develop leadership programs to support leadership diversity	• Train managers to manage diverse workforces. • Model desired leadership behaviors	• Promote mentorship and sponsorship	• Engage with the community to promote a more diverse talent pipeline

Figure 7.5   Creating Role Models.

representation in leadership is important for authentic and meaningful engagement with customers, investors, communities, employees, and candidates. All of these stakeholder groups want to feel that your organization is a place that they belong and will be welcome, supported, respected, and valued. As indicated in Figure 7.5, there are many ways to reflect your organization's J.E.D.I. commitment and to ensure that you have authentic representation of underrepresented groups in leadership positions. Building your employer brand image to demonstrate your employees' diversity representation and authentic experiences has a significant impact in attracting underrepresented candidates. Ensure that the communication, media, and office artifacts depict your organization's J.E.D.I. values. Review your artwork, advertisements, social media sites, employee information portals, benefits brochures, newsletters, and blogs to ensure that you are authentically representing community diversity.. Equally important is authentically representing your J.E.D.I. values when engaging with candidates for employment. When creating a talent platform, it is important to demonstrate to candidates that a variety of perspectives, styles, and cultures are welcome and encouraged to apply. Talent experience platforms that promote the candidate experience such as Phenom (https://www.phenom.com/) allow for customizing candidate's talent journey and highlighting employee stories and career experiences to attract top diverse talent. Leveraging technology tools helps highlight organizational role model stories through videos, blog posts, and other storytelling programs to attract and engage talent from underrepresented groups.

Role models are essential at all levels of the organization including the board and C-suite. One group that is tackling the lack of women and other minorities in the board room and C-suite is the 30% Club. They believe that, "Only those organizations that foster truly inclusive cultures – cultures that embrace women who look, act and, importantly, think differently – can reach their full potential to positively impact their people, their markets and their communities."[4] This global network has identified the lack of network connections and access to sitting board members as a critical barrier to women being appointed to boards. In order to provide women better access to board members, who have influence over whom is nominated and appointed for director seats, the 30% Club has partnered with the Catalyst Women on Board program, which facilitates access for women to this crucial board member network. Catalyst pairs CEOs and board chairs with women board candidates to act as mentor-sponsors providing guidance and access to their networks.[5] The results have been impressive with 66% of alumnae being appointed to a corporate board.

Modeling programs after the Catalyst program for other underrepresented groups is an effective tool to increase board representation numbers. While board level representation is crucial, building networks, and providing mentorship and sponsorship is critical at all levels of the organization. Employees with mentors and sponsors have more professional opportunities. Mentorship is important for supporting employee self-development and growth. Sponsorship is vital for changing the trajectory of careers, creating stretch opportunities, and opening new pathways. Leveraging these tools supports leadership growth and development expanding the representation diversity within the leadership talent pipeline. When managed effectively, these programs give opportunities, advice, and introductions allowing underrepresented leaders to join the career pathway toward CEO and other C-suite roles. In order to include more diverse candidates in the leadership pipeline, leadership development and the process to be eligible for leadership development must be made transparent. Facilitating network building through allyship programs, where those in power use their power and privilege to support employees who are members of underrepresented communities, broadens the pool of eligible candidates by shining a light on these talented but perhaps overlooked candidates.

Ebony Beckwith, Chief Philanthropy Officer of Salesforce and CEO, Salesforce Foundation shares the impact that sponsors and mentors had on her career growth and development as a woman of color. She is the highest-ranking Black executive at Salesforce. From an early age, she had a supportive network including a San Francisco municipal employee, who was a camp counselor, at a summer camp she attended. A former Salesforce executive and boss, Kirsten Wolberg, suggested that Ebony find the courage to request assistance on a project as asking for help shows "strength, self-awareness, and confidence." She also stressed the importance of building a network with other women executives at Salesforce. Robin Washington, the first Black director for Salesforce, served as a role model by modeling the leadership behaviors that are crucial to success. In addition, she coached Ms. Beckwith on future skills that she might require for advancement and served as a sounding board. When Salesforce was wrestling with its response to the murder of George Floyd, Amy Weaver, CFO of Salesforce, suggested creating a taskforce on racial equity and justice and that Ms. Beckwith lead it. It was an opportunity for Ms. Beckwith to provide invaluable leadership and guidance for Salesforce to develop a plan of action to dismantle systemic racism.[6]

Developing leadership programs and sharing more transparently the pathway to leadership generate results. We are well into the 21st century, yet many of our leadership programs and practices remain rooted in the past century. The process of identifying high potential employees (HiPos) who are the rising stars in organizations needs to be revisited. These are the candidates identified based on potential, ability, and aspiration to hold successive leadership positions within the company.

These are the cadre of individuals who are funneled into leadership development training and are slated to succeed current leadership. As with many other processes, the selection of HiPos is subject to bias. The most frequently used HiPo assessment processes are performance ratings, manager nominations, formal talent reviews, 360-degree assessments, and interviews with senior executives. Unfortunately, each of these assessments has potential for bias to be baked into their creation and implementation. In order to transform the leadership diversity representation, it is crucial to fully unpack your organization's leadership development pipeline and program.

Many well-intentioned leaders have tried to train their organization out of their diversity problem. While training has its place in the process, it can only take an organization so far on their J.E.D.I. North Star journey. Often, employees and managers feel that they are being told to fix themselves with DEI training. As we know from the lack of progress over the past several decades, training alone doesn't drive transformation. Instead, reorient your focus to capacity building programs that support leaders with information, tools, and models to drive change. Awareness is a first step but driving systemic change requires heavy lifting, and it means transferring platitudes into actionable practices. Reevaluating processes, providing tools, and reframing issues as business challenges all drive impact. An organization's DEI maturity impacts the types of capacity building programs and projects selected and the rate at which these initiatives become fully embedded within organizational culture. In order for J.E.D.I. transformative change to flourish, leadership needs to create an environment for diversity equity and inclusion to thrive. Creating a culture of belonging needs to be a value pillar for the organizations, and it must be part of everyone's job. While this transformation starts with the board and senior leadership team, all people managers and leaders within the organization need to be supported and held accountable. Invest the time and resources to help future leaders understand unconscious bias and its impact on decision-making. Include trainings that focus on building collective intelligence such as psychological safety and the importance of managing group dynamics and norms. Leverage behavioral design techniques to redesign processes focusing on planning, goals setting, and feedback to drive systemic change. Highlight the benefits of data-driven decisions and develop skills to interpret actionable data. Leverage people analytics to remove unconscious bias and better inform just and equitable decision-making.

7.5 Conditions for Organizational Intelligence

Identifying conditions when you felt most alive, engaged, valued, and empowered begins the process of creating these conditions and scaling them across the organization. In Figure 7.6, we look at some best practices for building collective intelligence within an organization. While designating a DEI leader such as a CDO with a team and resources is a crucial step in building an actionable DEI program; it will only take an organization so far on their journey. In order to drive transformative change,

Figure 7.6 Embed Conditions for Organizational Intelligence.

J.E.D.I. must be embedded into the organization and be part of everyone's job. Otherwise, the initiative becomes siloed and the CDO becomes increasingly frustrated by their lack of senior cross-functional support, resources, and impact. Much like human resources, DEI leadership can act as the architect to create structures to support J.E.D.I. goals, but systemic change requires engagement, buy-in, and full participation at all levels of the organization to transform into an organization that promotes J.E.D.I. values, actions, and behaviors throughout its ecosystem.

Redesigning talent process around recruitment, onboarding, development, engagement, and performance assessment provides an opportunity to adapt processes to support an equitable culture. We are all susceptible to unconscious bias including confirmation bias, which causes us to search for information that confirms our viewpoint and affinity bias, which causes us to prefer people most similar to ourselves. Removing human bias from the process by leveraging tools such as assessment tests, predictive indicators, and structured interviews substantially reduces errors in the prediction of employee success and promotes greater representation within the workforce. Unfortunately, Human Resource professionals report that they perceive unstructured interviews as the most effective means for selecting employees despite research to the contrary.[7] In many cases, introducing structured interviews as a preferred process requires behavior change.

To conduct a structured interview, plan out your interview process including developing questions, following your process, avoiding group interview panels, and assigning scores to candidates immediately following the interview. Best practice includes establishing a set of questions to be asked to each candidate as well as following the same set of questions and protocols in each interview. According to Iris Bohnet's research, it is crucial to score candidates immediately to avoid the halo effect, which causes information shared by one candidate to be attributed to another candidate. After the interviews, it is important to compare questions across candidates one at a time using preassigned weights. All scores should be submitted to a designated person to tabulate results. If there are controversial candidates, Bohnet recommends meeting as a group to discuss the candidates and breaking down into sub-groups for high-profile positions. Establishing and following these practices will improve the opportunities for candidates from a variety of identity groups to join and excel within your organization.[8]

As most work is performed by teams, ensuring that team dynamics support psychological safety is crucial in creating an environment that supports and empowers all team members. Consider team norms and practices to welcome and encourage diverse perspectives. Construct teams to promote diversity of identity, thought, and experience. Ensure that teams include critical mass of any sub-groups to avoid tokenism. While team composition should be reflective of your community, the rule of 3 has been shown to be the tipping point to empower members from underrepresented groups. For example, with three BIPOC members on a team, there begins to be psychological safety and empowerment for these team members. The goal is to avoid anyone being the only representative of a particular group.

Create and empower Employee Resource Groups (ERGs) to drive impact both internally and externally. ERGs are voluntary, employee-led groups organized based on a common characteristic such as gender, race, ethnicity, lifestyle, or interest. Their purpose is to promote a diverse, equitable, and inclusive workplace in alignment with organizational J.E.D.I. values. ERGs provide a safe space for meaningful conversations, bringing your full self to work as well as personal growth and career development. ERGs are present in 90% of Fortune 500 companies.[9] Empowering ERGs and giving members access to senior leadership drives impact including addressing organizational challenges, raising issues, bringing employees together in a safe environment to share, improving the physical work environment, improving the work environment for marginalized employees, and identifying and developing leaders. ERGs can be leveraged to help leadership identify gaps in their business strategy as organizations seek to expand their business with new customers and communities. They can be instrumental in identifying gaps in an organization's recruitment and development strategies. They can also be a valuable partner in welcoming and assisting with the new employee onboarding process. Key to success is organizational leadership involvement, listening, engagement, and feedback.

Gather, track, and analyze data to better understand patterns and trends within organizational decision processes including in the talent ecosystem of your organization. Even in the 21st century, a significant number of managerial decisions are made based on intuition rather than data. Most organizations are able to pull the employee data from their human resource information systems and many of these platforms offer business intelligence and report writing functionality to facilitate gathering and analyzing data. From a human capital management perspective, DEI data is a business necessity. Data needs to be accurate and accessible in real time in order to impact decision-making. Transparency of use of information and process is crucial for building credibility.

7.6 Talent Integration

While recruitment from diverse sources is one of the first steps that most organizations take when seeking to increase diversity in their workforce, creating a culture of belonging requires an analysis across an organization's talent ecosystem. The talent ecosystem as described in Figure 7.7 reflects the experience of your employees, gig workers, and contractors throughout their life cycle with your organization. The phases include talent acquisition, motivation, growth, and mobility for your own employees. The talent ecosystem also includes contractors, outsourced service

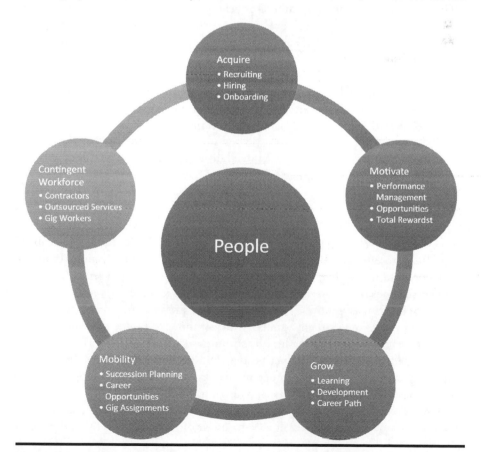

Figure 7.7   Talent Ecosystem.

providers, and gig workers that also need to be part of your J.E.D.I. strategy. At each phase of the talent ecosystem there is an opportunity to improve your organization's policies and processes to better support equity and inclusion. While managers may have good intentions in terms of hiring and promoting employees from underrepresented groups, it takes more than good intentions to succeed. Progress requires a thoughtfully developed plan that reflects the voices of the diverse stakeholders and provides room for continuous learning and adaptation within the talent ecosystem. Too often, good intentions lead to poor work and team environments because of a lack of communication, appreciation, and understanding. These dynamics lead to acrimonious conversations stemming from strategies founded on the principles of discrimination and fairness as well as access and legitimacy. The discrimination and fairness principle focuses on the moral imperative for a diverse workforce to ensure societal fairness. The access and legitimacy principle focuses on the value creation benefits of diversity through alignment between your workforce and marketplace. While both principles must be addressed in an organization's J.E.D.I. talent strategy, each lacks depth in creating a culture of belonging to effectively manage and support the needs of a diverse workforce. To drive change within the talent ecosystem, managers must consider their roles as talent developers and curators. Some of the best practices include:

1. Create a work environment that promotes belonging
2. Establish effective channels of communication including listening
3. Collaborate cross-functionally to promote organizational agility and alignment
4. Provide feedback to foster growth and development
5. Support resource alignment and opportunities for all employees

In order to ensure that employees feel valued and appreciated, current practices around development opportunities and promotion need to be evaluated and most likely modified. When seeking to incorporate access to senior leadership for employees, ERGs are effective forums to engage in two-way communication. Programs such as reverse mentoring, where more junior staff mentor more senior staff, help to open the lines of communication across levels of the organization and allow for sharing of diverse perspectives. Penn Medicine has a reverse mentoring program for senior staff that requires them to meet with community health practitioners on a regular basis at the community health location not in the C-suite. The point is to hear and understand a different perspective that can be used as a lens for decision-making. Traditional mentorship programs are also useful to help employees identify career goals, learning opportunities, and develop networks.

Employees that are exposed to stretch assignments and opportunities that give them visibility to higher levels in the organization are the ones that are considered when it is time for promotion. To effectively promote a culture of belonging, leaders have to take steps to ensure that a representational slate of candidates get these opportunities. While many organizations require a balanced slate of candidates be considered for promotions, there is a big difference between being on the slate and having experience working with the people who are making the decision. Sponsorship provides a formalized program for a more senior person in the organization to actively advise and promote a more junior person's career development. Having a sponsor, who knows the candidate and their capabilities, at the decision-making table is an effective tool for promoting and supporting a more diverse selection of candidates.

Breaking down the talent ecosystem further, we dive into the talent recruitment process. In Figure 7.8, we look at the talent acquisition cycle in detail. It begins with defining your talent pool and ensuring that you are engaging with a variety of sources that will offer a pool of diverse candidates. In order to improve recruitment outcomes for underrepresented candidates, Lincoln Financial created two dedicated recruiter positions – one focused on entry level talent and the other focused on executive talent. In addition, they redesigned hiring practices to address unconscious bias. Internally, every position at the assistant vice president level and above must have a balanced slate of candidates requiring at least one woman and one BIPOC candidate or other underrepresented group member to be included in the interview process.

If your organization is still hiring only from a handful of colleges and universities, it is time to expand the pool to include Historically Black Colleges and Universities (HSBCU), public universities, and community colleges to expand the diversity of the talent pool. If your firm hires for positions that do not require degrees, consider partnering with community–labor coalitions and work centers that are designed to improve outcomes for underserved populations. Partnering with NGOs to create opportunities for quality life-sustaining jobs with career pathways moves the needle on pay and wealth gaps. Opportunities are available to invest in developing a more representative future talent pipeline by getting involved with programs such as Girls Who Code, which is improving the diversity of representation and thought in the tech sector. Through its programs, they are preparing the next generation for good quality jobs that build wealth and a better standard of living. Consider working with public schools to share opportunities with local youth and promote apprenticeship programs in order to build skill levels for future workers.

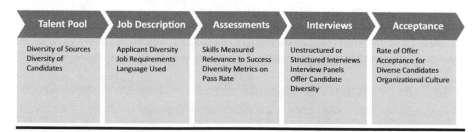

Figure 7.8 Assessing Attrition for Diverse Candidates at Each Stage of Recruitment.

Candidates from underrepresented groups may not be selecting an organization for employment based upon their perceived job fit. Review job descriptions to ensure that the requirements listed are essential for the job. Engage the hiring manager and review the requirements to ensure that the education, experience, and skill requirements are merited and that they are considering skills needed for next 3–5 years. Often, job descriptions are written with an ideal candidate in mind rather than current and future competency requirements. Skill requirements have expanded and include categories and career tracks that are technical or managerial in focus. As part of this process, we see more workers seeking higher credentialing through degree, certification, and other training programs in order to differentiate themselves in the labor market. Increasingly, the labor market is relying on credentialing as a means of measuring candidates' knowledge and capabilities. As a result, many positions require credentialing, such as a college degree or 10 years of experience in a role, which may not really be necessary to perform the job function. These requirements may deter well-qualified applicants from applying for positions resulting in a less diverse applicant pool. Evaluating job descriptions to ensure that the credentialing requirements are valid is an important step in increasing accessibility to a more diverse pool of candidates. Research has shown that men tend to apply for a job when they meet 60% of the requirements and women tend to apply if they meet 100% of the requirements.[10] Women tend to be less aggressive and confident when applying to jobs often eliminating options through self-screening. When an organization is overloading its job descriptions, the result may be a more homogenous pool of candidates because candidates are self-selecting out of applying.

Job description language is another area that can create attrition especially with diverse candidates. Job data has consistently shown that the top paying jobs have a male association while the lowest paying jobs have a female association bias. In crafting job descriptions, we tend to use words that have gender associations that reinforce these gender role biases. As a result, the language used in the job description may be attracting or repelling candidates based on their self-identified gender. In the Silicon Valley, job descriptions often include "bro speak", such as "ninja" or "world class", that can be off-putting to candidates that don't identify with these experiences. As a best practice, review job description language including pronouns. Select gender neutral titles to allow a broader array of candidates to identify themselves within the role.

In order to reduce bias, organizations are using testing and other assessments to try to find the best candidates for their positions. While testing, assignments, and assessments may reduce human bias, it is important to track the outcomes of these tools across identity groups to identify any trends that suggest tool bias. As a first step, your human capital management leadership needs to invest the time in determining which assessments are effective in terms of predicting job performance. In addition, they must ensure that the assessments are measuring the job related skills and capabilities. While testing removes the human bias in the candidate interview and screening process, it may create an unintended consequence of weeding out BIPOC, female, and other underrepresented applicants because of bias in assessment design. Tracking diversity metrics against assessment pass rates and scores provides additional insights and may suggest opportunities for improvements in assessment protocols. As part of the talent recruitment process, it is important to track data on your talent conversion process and to identify leakages in the pipeline.

Consider the interview process and tools and techniques that reduce bias and improve outcomes for diverse candidates. In the 1970s, 95% of the musicians in top performing orchestras were men. Today, women make up 35% of the musicians in these orchestras. In order to drive change and improve the gender balance, the Boston Symphony Orchestra began holding blind auditions. They had musicians audition from behind a screen. As a result, the probability that a female musician would advance to the next round of auditions rose by 50%.[11] By acknowledging bias in the process and creating a blind audition to address the bias, this change in audition protocol had a significant impact on outcomes.

Leveraging this idea of blinding the selection process, some firms have begun anonymizing the applicants' personal identifiable information such as name, photo, address, etc., before interviewers see the resumes to reduce first impression biases like the halo effect and the beauty premium. "In the United States, for example, better-looking men earn up to 5 percent more and worse-looking men earn up to 13 percent less that average-looking men, controlling for their education and experience."[12] Debiasing the selection process improves outcomes.

The interview process is susceptible to bias as well. In evaluating your interview practices consider the process itself including the structure of the interview. The following are some best practices to consider during the interview process:

1. Acknowledge that you have unconscious biases
2. Invest the time to learn about how members of underrepresented communities experience work
3. Consider where bias might enter the hiring decision process
4. Avoid group thinking
5. Apply the "Flip it to test"[13]
6. Hire for culture addition not culture fit

Even if you are a member of an underrepresented group, you have biases that impact your recruitment decisions. Hiring decisions are extremely susceptible to affinity bias, which is favoring someone who looks, speaks, and acts like us. Just think about an organization's proclivity to hire alumni from the CEO's university. Some practices that reduce hiring bias are developing a learning program to help yourself and others learn about the experiences of underrepresented groups (Several resources are recommended in Table 8.1) Ensuring that the interview process allows for individual evaluation and that hiring managers decisions are not influenced by other reviewers. Using device like the "flip it to test," which means substituting an underrepresented group candidate with a more traditional candidate and asking the question of yourself if you would have the same reaction or ask the same question. Avoiding falling into the hiring for "culture fit" trap. If your objective is to have a more heterogeneous workforce, start hiring for cultural addition. This approach drives diversity of thought and experience facilitating innovation and new opportunities. Addressing bias in the interview process requires being present and reflecting on the recruitment process and areas for improvement to level the playing field for candidates from underrepresented groups.

7.7 Reshaping Norms and Promoting Transparency

Figure 7.9 highlights some best practices to create a culture of belonging. *Ensure* that J.E.D.I. strategy is a regular agenda item for both the board and C-suite with ongoing goals and strategic priorities. While an organization may have a CDO position, making J.E.D.I. initiatives and progress toward goals a regular part of all meeting agendas makes it a priority for all senior leadership. Linking leadership compensation metrics and scorecards to J.E.D.I. goals further supports prioritization and resource alignment. By holding leadership accountable, J.E.D.I. priorities are cascaded throughout the organization creating further alignment and resource allocation. Leadership's commitment to change from a monolithic culture to a culture that promotes belonging permeates J.E.D.I. norms across the organization. Encouraging leaders to act as role models assures that these norms are visible throughout the organization and that J.E.D.I. focused programs such as flexible work are viable options for all employees.

Use rules, codes, policies, and practices to express new norms and embed them into operations. One of the major obstacles for an inclusive workforce has been flexibility of work location and hours. The pandemic forced many women from the workplace to assume unpaid caregiver roles to children, parents, and other family members. Much has been written about the "Mommy Track," in which women take part-time, shared jobs, or lesser roles in order to accommodate both work and family demands. Another barrier is the motherhood tax and a fatherhood bonus. Researchers have tracked that women earn less for each child they have while fathers earn more. While offering workplace flexibility in terms of remote work, flexible hours, and compressed work weeks provides a tool to help bridge the gender gap in pay and career advancement, using these programs is often viewed with a

Ensure	Use	Give	Redefine	Align	Promote
Ensure J.E.D.I. strategy is on the board and C-suite agendas	Use rules, laws, and codes of conduct to express norms	Give managers new tools	Redefine work and team norms	Align compensation with J.E.D.I. goals and objectives	Promote data driven decisions

Figure 7.9 Reshaping Norm.

negative stigma. Research suggests that temporal flexibility, in the form of control over work hours and ease of taking time off during the day, positively increases promotion aspirations, especially for women.[14] Gaining control over your work requirements serves as a work resource for employees improving productivity and performance. Employees' work demands create burnout and stress whereas work resources support motivation and engagement. In response to women's perceptions about work demands of certain roles, they are self-selecting out of jobs and career tracks. Research suggests that their self-censoring may be related to anticipating work-family conflicts relating to types of positions or career tracks. As a result, this perception reduces their likelihood to pursue promotions, opportunities, or even career paths that they believe may create this conflict. Flexible work arrangements have been found to encourage promotional aspirations especially for women with children. It should be noted that men are also experiencing the work/family paradox and their reporting of this conflict has been growing quickly over the past few decades. In fact, 63% of fathers report spending too little time with their children primarily because of work obligations.[15] The research clearly indicates establishing flexible work arrangements as part of organizational norms offers an impactful tool to improve the gender diversity especially at the more senior levels.

Post-pandemic, there has been a great deal of discussion about organization's offering flexible and hybrid work options to accommodate the needs of all employees for work-life integration. Organizations are redesigning work policies in support of hybrid work allowing employee choice around returning to in person work, remaining remote, or a combination. Companies like J.P. Morgan Chase are allowing workers on certain teams to schedule a work from home day. Firms are finding that top talent especially those with highly sought after technical and engineering skills are insisting on the flexibility to work from home. According to a recent survey of 9,000 workers by Accenture, 83% responded that they felt that a hybrid work structure was optimal.[16] Perhaps, organizations have reached the tipping point and flexible work arrangements are becoming truly ingrained in organizational culture.

Give managers new tools to help them manage based on deliverables and outcomes rather than on facetime in the office. Digital tools that support feedback and encourage development support managers' continued commitment to developing remote employees and employees with a variety of personal and professional requirements. These may include new collaboration tools, pulse surveys, feedback tools, and flexible work arrangements. Designing flexible work arrangements requires planning, education, manager buy-in, and communication. In order to offer effective flexible work arrangements to employees, consider the following best practices:

1. Clearly communicate the flexible work arrangement to employees and empower them request options that work for them and their team.
2. Identify requirements for remote work such as internet speed, workspace, data protocols, safety and privacy, and offer a stipend to cover costs of setting up and operating a home office.

3. Ensure that the programs are offered consistently across the organization.
4. Identify and communicate how performance and productivity will be measured.
5. Fully disclose the use of performance monitoring software ("Tattleware").
6. Educate managers on flexible work policies and remote work management and encourage them to act as role models.
7. Support flexible work with a technology-based platform to allow for ease of application and tracking of approvals and declinations.
8. Provide collaboration tools and communication platforms to integrate in person and remote workers.
9. Ensure that performance ratings, promotions, and career paths are tracked for both in person and remote workers to ensure that all are given opportunities for growth and advancement.
10. Establish communication protocols allowing for blackout times to reduce stress and burnout.

Additionally, managers can drive impact by advocating for forums for employees to discuss non-work-related topics to share passions and perspectives.[17] As a manager, understanding the organization's programs and policies allows you to be an advocate and guide for your people helping them to get the support and resources to thrive at work. Acting as role models by exhibiting respectful behavior and addressing situations where behavior is not acceptable, even with top performers, demonstrates personal and organizational commitment to a culture of belonging.

Redefine work and team norms to support building a J.E.D.I. culture. Work structures need to be realigned to support an equitable culture. To promote flexible work arrangements, we find that team norms need to be redefined to support a variety of work structures such as hybrid or virtual meetings. For example, a moderator may need to be appointed during meetings to ensure that all team members have an opportunity to contribute to the conversation. To drive belonging, practices around sharing opportunities and identifying candidates for stretch assignments, new projects, or promotions need to be more transparent and accessible. Supporting mentoring and sponsorship programs and encouraging participation make these tools more acceptable and mainstream for employees. *Align* total rewards for leadership and employees with an organization's J.E.D.I. mission to drive impact. Tying compensation to these J.E.D.I. KPIs ensures employee and resource alignment across the organization encouraging a cross-functional solution development approach. *Promote* data-driven decisions by sharing data especially around J.E.D.I. goals and KPIs. Ensure that information is accessible and available so that it is incorporated into management's decision-making process. Driving systemic change requires a culture shift necessitating transformation around beliefs, values, and norms.

A crucial part of driving transformation is aligning with strategic vision and promoting transparency of process and outcomes. In Figure 7.10, we highlight some best practices for achieving this objective. *Establish* meaningful short- and long-term

Establish Goals	Establish both short- and long-term goals
Analyze	Analyze data using digital tools such as people analytics and dashboards
Report	Report information and metrics that are relevant and comparable
Socialize	Socialize the J.E.D.I. goals by integrating into meetings at all levels of the organization
Accountability	Promote accountability across the organization

Figure 7.10 Promote Transparency.

J.E.D.I. goals that are supported by metrics to measure progress. Ensuring that goals are clearly identified, and that metrics have been identified to promote authenticity and improves outcomes. *Analyze* data by leveraging digital tools to gather, sort, aggregate, and share information. There are a number of people analytics tools such as Visier (visier.com) and dashboarding tools such as Tableau (tableau.com) to facilitate transforming data into meaningful and actionable information. *Report* information to all key stakeholders based on agreed upon metrics that are relevant and comparable. This data becomes the foundation for information reporting on progress, improving decision-making, and improving outcomes. *Socialize* the organization's J.E.D.I. mission, vision, and strategy by discussing it regularly at senior levels and in department or team meetings. Ensure that your group or team understands the business imperative of the J.E.D.I. strategy and the implications for their roles and responsibilities to create *Accountability*. Cascading this information into the organization promotes transparency of process and creates opportunities to innovate and mitigate risk in alignment with the strategic J.E.D.I. vision.

7.8 Building Belonging

Simply, belonging means that everyone is welcome to bring their full selves to work and that they feel empowered, valued, and appreciated. As neuroscience tells us, the need to belong in the workplace is second only to the need to belong at home.[18] In order to meet this employee need, employers must better understand the conditions that exist that make employees feel marginalized and address those conditions. In addition, they must proactively support conditions for belonging and build organizational intelligence around these ideas. While HCM or DEI groups might lead these initiatives, in order to drive impact, the whole organization must be involved and engaged. Ensure that your values are clearly stated and communicated across the organization and that behaviors and actions that are aligned with these values are the ones being rewarded. Table 7.2 highlights some practices to build a culture of belonging within your organization. Mentorship and sponsorship are crucial to giving equal opportunities for career advancement. Leveraging your ERGs to create programs that encourage employees from underrepresented groups to seek mentors and sponsors begins the process of leveling the playing field. Offer ongoing trainings and education for employees, managers, and leaders to promote practices that value shared vision, purpose, and employee value and belonging.

While ERGs can be impactful groups they must be supported and resourced to thrive. Best practice includes an executive sponsor and budgetary funding. ERGs that are truly engaged across the organization to support business strategy are most effective. The following are some examples and suggestions for ERGs to drive impact:

1. Include ERG representation on J.E.D.I. councils
2. Include ERG representation on board advisory councils
3. Invite ERGs to speak at onboarding sessions
4. Encourage ERGs to recommend and engage in community stakeholder events
5. Empower ERGs to recommend and participate in volunteer opportunities
6. Leverage ERGs to act as change agents and ambassadors for J.E.D.I. programs
7. Encourage ERGs to offer programming, events, and speakers to highlight awareness and perspective building
8. Encourage ERG programs supporting mentorship and sponsorship

As with the J.E.D.I. journey, each organization's ERGs are on their own maturity continuum. The programs, roles, responsibilities, and impacts will develop over time as ERG leaders grow in their experience and employees and leadership become more engaged and familiar with various ERGs' functions and impacts. At Comcast, an ERG focused on accessibility came up with idea for the voice activated remote to improve accessibility to cable programming. It was not only a great idea to solve an accessibility challenge, but also a market differentiator for all customers giving Comcast a competitive advantage in the marketplace. ERGs that are incorporated into core business strategy and give employees a voice are extremely effective.

ERGs are a good resource to leverage for employees interested in mentorship either as a mentee or a mentor. Best practices for mentors include:

1. Take the time to get to know your mentee
2. Agree on the purpose and rules of your arrangement
3. Focus on learning goals
4. Take a balanced approach to speaking and listening
5. Encourage questions rather than just give advice
6. Encourage meaningful conversation including experiences of success and failure
7. Question assumptions

Table 7.2 Tools to Promote Belonging

Allyship	Allyship is when a person of privilege seeks to operate in solidarity with an underrepresented or marginalized group. It is a continuous, active, and arduous practice of listening, learning, and reevaluating. Allyship requires genuine interest in challenging systemic power structures by leveraging our own privilege for the benefit of people in an underrepresented or marginalized group.
ERGs	ERGs are voluntary, employee-led groups organized based on a common characteristic such as gender, race, ethnicity, lifestyle, or interest. Their purpose is to promote a diverse, equitable, and inclusive workplace in alignment with organizational J.E.D.I. values.
Mentorship	Influencing, guiding, and advising mentees to support growth and development. It can be anyone who has experience at the organization. ERGs can be a good source of mentors for employees. Reverse mentoring encourages senior staff to learn from and gain perspective from junior staff.
Sponsorship	Engaging with a senior person, normally not a direct boss, in order to advance one's skills, experience, and career. The role includes giving advice and recommendations as well as advocating for an individual for promotion or advancement. ERG groups are a good resource for sponsors for employees especially from underrepresented groups.
Storytelling	Sharing authentic experiences of when you felt most engaged, alive, or that you really belonged in a situation, on a team, or in an organization. Stories shared by employees from underrepresented groups are especially impactful in creating a feeling of belonging for candidates and employees that identify with underrepresented groups.
Town Hall Meetings	These meetings can offer a safe space to build empathy and understanding as well as serve as a tool to educate. This platform supports listening and perspective building. Action items to improve belonging may come from these events. These meetings can be conducted in person, virtually, or as a hybrid event.
Capacity Building	Leadership and manager training on perspective taking, inclusive practices, feedback, and communication. Employee education and development. Opportunities to engage with underrepresented communities.

8. Both support and challenge
9. Encourage two-way feedback
10. Meet regularly to stay on track[19]

For mentees, here are some best practices as well:

1. Focus on achieving clearly defined learning goals
2. Take charge of the mentoring relationship and ask for what you need
3. Be authentic and open to facilitate growth and development
4. Prepare for your mentoring meetings
5. Be willing to stretch and take on new opportunities or challenges
6. Ask for and provide specific feedback
7. Keep your focus on the future
8. Keep track of your journey through a journal

In a mentoring relationship, it is crucial that both sides value one another's time and goals in order to facilitate growth and to develop future opportunities.

LINKEDIN DRIVES BELONGING: THE DIBS INDEX.

Pat Wadors, former SVP of LinkedIn's Global Talent Organization, shared a story of how she coined the term "DIBs," which stands for diversity, inclusion, and belonging. Over the past decade, technology companies and their leaders have launched numerous diversity and inclusion programs to address equity and inclusion challenges within their industry. Despite all of these initiatives, they failed to drive meaningful impact. In reflecting upon the situation, Pat shared that, "What I really wanted was those moments when I feel that I belong to a team, I matter, and I'm able to be my authentic self."[20] It was from this self-reflection that she came up with the missing piece in the DEI paradigm – belonging.

Using the DIBs index, which LinkedIn developed as an annual survey to measure engagement, they found that the answer to the following questions that center on belonging accounted for 91% of employee engagement.

1. I make an effort to help others feel like they belong at LinkedIn.
2. Even when something negative happens, I feel like I belong at LinkedIn.
3. I feel comfortable being myself at work.
4. Someone at work cares about me as a person.[21]

According to Gallup, disengagement costs U.S. employers over $350 billion per year. Building belonging and engagement adds economic value to organizations effectively creating a self-funding budgetary pool to support J.E.D.I. programs.

Neuroscience research supports that our brains are wired toward social connections and belonging. In fact, research indicates that for some employees belonging and attachment to coworkers can be a better motivator than monetary rewards.[22] Research performed by a group from Stanford suggests that interventions to mitigate persistent worries about belonging improve outcomes for underrepresented groups like Black Americans.[23]

Here are some actionable steps that were developed by LinkedIn to create belonging:

1. Make introductions and use language of belonging such as "our" to promote the team feeling.
2. Ask and listen.
3. Seek input and opinions during meetings.
4. Delegate by giving meeting agenda items to someone on your team.
5. Pay attention and be fully present. Show respect for everyone. Put away devices during meetings.
6. Storytelling. Share stories that highlight human connection and show your vulnerability include both failures and successes. If you are a member of an underrepresented group, sharing your stories may have even more impact.[24]

There are many moments that can either encourage or discourage belonging for candidates and employees. Being cognizant and aware that individual, team, and organizational actions and behaviors influence a candidate's or employee's sense of belonging begins the transformation process.

7.9 Summary

Creating a culture of belonging begins with senior leadership. At the board level this means taking the time to conduct a self-analysis and truly consider board level requirements for an organization that values J.E.D.I. principles. Expanding board diversity representation is crucial to developing better networks, stakeholder engagement, role models for current and future employees, new opportunities, and mitigating risks. As organizations move forward on their J.E.D.I. journey, the skills and competencies required to support this transformation have evolved. Leaders must develop competencies to be social impact and sustainability leaders. Embarking on the journey is really the beginning of a continuous improvement cycle. Using an appreciative approach allows stakeholders to develop a shared vision for organizational purpose and impact. This approach focuses on identifying and replicating conditions for success to build more just and equitable organizations. In order to promote a J.E.D.I. vision, we focus on creating conditions for organizational intelligence and success such as creating role models, building organizational capacity, redesigning systems, setting goals, and measuring impacts. It requires drilling into organizational systems and redesigning the talent ecosystem, training and development especially leadership development, and reshaping norms to focus on belonging and psychological safety.

Drilling deeper into the talent ecosystem provides insights on the employee life cycle and the points at which talent strategy, policy, and process can enhance or detract from creating a J.E.D.I. culture. Reviewing organizational culture through a J.E.D.I. lens allows for a reshaping of norms such as how can work be restructured to support a diverse workforce. The process involves redesigning policies, codes, and guidelines to consider how dominant culture may be impacting underrepresented employees.

Gathering and sharing information with stakeholders establishes authentic engagement and credibility. Promoting transparency by sharing information and reporting on meaningful metrics supports socializing goals and reinforces focus and accountability. Creating a culture of belonging to support a just and equitable organization gives an organization a competitive advantage on multiple levels. It is the right thing to do and economically beneficial.

Questions

1. Using the Board Gap Analysis tool, evaluate your organization's board composition. What areas are needed in terms of representation, skills, experiences, education, and stakeholder expertise?
2. Using the Social Impact Leadership Model as a guide, evaluate your own leadership style. What are your areas of strength and what areas need improvement?
3. What are some opportunities that you may have to create conditions for organizational intelligence or success?
4. What recommendations would you make to improve representation within your organization?
5. In thinking about your experience as a candidate applying for jobs, what action would you recommend to organizations to increase the feeling of belonging?
6. In thinking about your own talent ecosystem, are there changes that you would recommend to achieve J.E.D.I. goals?
7. How might you leverage the principals of Appreciative Inquiry to drive transformative change within your organization?
8. Do you agree or disagree with taking an appreciative approach to change? What do you feel are some benefits and pitfalls?
9. What are some of the best practices within your organization to drive toward J.E.D.I.?
10. What barriers remain to be overcome?

Appendix 7A

Chief Diversity Officer Job Description

The CDO will:

- Form and lead the J.E.D.I. Committee to plan and implement an organization's J.E.D.I. initiatives and activities.
- Serve as a subject matter expert in providing J.E.D.I. resources, best practices, training and development, and leadership development.
- Model behavior and action that reflect a commitment to the organization's J.E.D.I. goals and objectives.
- Establish and work with the organization's bias incident response team to respond and investigate bias-related incidents, and make strategic and proactive recommendations based on outcomes.
- Facilitate opportunities for workforce training, collaborate with human resources to enhance recruitment, hiring, promotion and retention of diverse candidates and employees and provide support to employees with diverse experiences and backgrounds.
- Build and maintain knowledge on current and emerging J.E.D.I. developments/trends, assess the impact, and collaborate with senior management to incorporate new trends and developments in current and future strategies.
- Direct and enhance organizational J.E.D.I. initiatives by positively influencing and supporting change management initiatives.
- Collaborate with senior leaders to develop and implement specific enterprise diversity objectives, and business plans to align inclusion initiatives with business strategies and metrics focusing on the workplace, workforce, marketplace, and community.
- Ensure J.E.D.I. programs and outcomes are reflected in the workforce/workplace and in business activities, including marketing materials, suppliers/vendors, and community-facing efforts.
- Build relationships with leaders, stakeholders, and colleagues to formulate a communication plan to drive diversity-related messages throughout the organization.
- Educate, partner, consult, and collaborate with business functions to effectively build, incorporate, and manage J.E.D.I. initiatives.
- Partner with Procurement to initiate the development of supplier diversity strategies and support implementation of initiatives. Collaborate to establish supplier diversity goals. Monitor and report supplier diversity program performance and trends. Develop and implement best practices for J.E.D.I. action planning within procurement.
- Identify, develop, and build relationships with key external stakeholder groups including community leaders, J.E.D.I. thought leaders, partners, and vendors.

- Design and implement metrics, ensure regulatory compliance, create monitoring and reporting systems to effectively benchmark organizational progress on J.E.D.I. goals, monitor and assess the impact of initiatives, report on program effectiveness, and make recommendations for enhancement and improvement.
- Collaborate with senior leadership in designing and implementing institution-wide changes to ensure a culture of belonging.
- Lead strategic, innovative initiatives that institutionalize J.E.D.I. across the organization.
- Advocate for and provides executive oversite of J.E.D.I. spheres of influence such as diversity councils, employee resource groups (ERGS), and stakeholder advisory councils and ensures their voices are heard to drive strategic impact on organizational systems.
- Collaborate with leadership to develop and maintain strategic partnerships with community organizations and other entities as appropriate. Represent the organization in J.E.D.I.-related groups, roles, and functions.[25]

Notes

1 "'The '-Isms' of Sexism And Racism Are Like Air. They're Everywhere.' | LinkedIn," accessed October 22, 2020, https://www.linkedin.com/pulse/isms-sexism-racism-like-air-theyre-everywhere-adam-bryant/?trackingId=.
2 Mohr and Watkins, *The Essentials of Appreciative Inquiry*.
3 "A GPS for People with Reduced Mobility," *AIM2Flourish*, 2, accessed January 20, 2021, https://aim2flourish.com/innovations/a-gps-for-people-with-reduced-mobility.
4 "30% Club," accessed February 23, 2021, https://30percentclub.org/.
5 "Catalyst Women On Board™," *Catalyst* (blog), accessed February 23, 2021, https://www.catalyst.org/catalyst-women-on-board/.
6 Joann S. Lublin, "The Executive Who Helps Salesforce Stay True to Its Founders' Philanthropic Pledge," *Wall Street Journal*, June 19, 2021, sec. Management, https://www.wsj.com/articles/the-executive-who-helps-salesforce-stay-true-to-its-founders-philanthropic-pledge-11624075202.
7 Iris Bohnet, *What Works* (U.S.: First Harvard University Press, 2018).
8 Iris Bohnet.
9 "What Are Employee Resource Groups (ERGs)? | Great Place to Work®," accessed May 25, 2021, https://www.greatplacetowork.com/resources/blog/what-are-employee-resource-groups-ergs.
10 A. B. C. News, "Women Are Less Aggressive than Men When Applying for Jobs, despite Getting Hired More Frequently: LinkedIn," *ABC News*, accessed May 26, 2021, https://abcnews.go.com/Business/women-aggressive-men-applying-jobs-hired-frequently-linkedin/story?id=61531741.
11 Iris Bohnet, *What Works*.
12 Iris Bohnet.

13 Ruchika Tulshyan, "How to Reduce Personal Bias When Hiring," *Harvard Business Review*, June 28, 2019, https://hbr.org/2019/06/how-to-reduce-personal-bias-when-hiring.

14 Julia B. Bear, "Forget the 'Mommy Track': Temporal Flexibility Increases Promotion Aspirations for Women and REduces GEnder Gaps," *Psychology of Women Quarterly* 1–14 (2021), https://doi.org/10.1177/03616843211003070.

15 Julia B. Bear.

16 "If You Thought Working From Home Was Messy, Here Comes Hybrid Work – WSJ," accessed May 26, 2021, https://www.wsj.com/articles/if-you-thought-working-from-home-was-messy-here-comes-hybrid-work-11621935000?st=7809jfec5zsbzpz&reflink=article_email_share.

17 Research and North America, "How Middle Managers Can Help Make a More Equitable Workplace," Knowledge@Wharton, accessed June 30, 2021, https://knowledge.wharton.upenn.edu/article/middle-managers-can-help-make-equitable-workplace/.

18 Holly Althof and Holly Althof, "Viewpoint: Belonging Is the Missing Piece in the Fight for Inclusion," *SHRM*, August 21, 2020, https://www.shrm.org/resourcesandtools/hr-topics/behavioral-competencies/global-and-cultural-effectiveness/pages/viewpoint-belonging-is-the-missing-piece-in-the-fight-for-inclusion.aspx.

19 "Top 10 Best Practices for Mentors | Center for Mentoring Excellence," accessed April 8, 2021, https://www.centerformentoring.com/top-10-best-practices-for-mentors.

20 Pat Wadors, "Diversity Efforts Fall Short Unless Employees Feel That They Belong," *Harvard Business Review*, August 10, 2016, https://hbr.org/2016/08/diversity-efforts-fall-short-unless-employees-feel-that-they-belong.

21 Chris Kang, "DIBs – Diversity, Inclusion & Belonging by Pat Wadors," https://www.slideshare.net/misschriskang/dibs-diversity-inclusion-belonging-by-pat-wadors-67307975.

22 Wadors, "Diversity Efforts Fall Short Unless Employees Feel That They Belong."

23 Shannon T. Brady et al., "A Brief Social-Belonging Intervention in College Improves Adult Outcomes for Black Americans," *Science Advances* 6, no. 18 (May 2020): eaay3689, https://doi.org/10.1126/sciadv.aay3689.

24 Wadors, "Diversity Efforts Fall Short Unless Employees Feel That They Belong."

25 Jess Man, "Chief Diversity Officer Is Both the Hottest and Toughest Job in 2021," accessed May 29, 2021, https://diversity.social/chief-diversity-officer/.

Bibliography

"30% Club." Accessed February 23, 2021. https://30percentclub.org/.

AIM2Flourish. "A GPS for People with Reduced Mobility." Accessed January 20, 2021. https://aim2flourish.com/innovations/a-gps-for-people-with-reduced-mobility.

Althof, Holly, and Holly Althof. "Viewpoint: Belonging Is the Missing Piece in the Fight for Inclusion." *SHRM*, August 21, 2020. https://www.shrm.org/resourcesandtools/hr-topics/behavioral-competencies/global-and-cultural-effectiveness/pages/viewpoint-belonging-is-the-missing-piece-in-the-fight-for-inclusion.aspx.

Bear, Julia B. "Forget the 'Mommy Track': Temporal Flexibility Increases Promotion Aspirations for Women and REduces GEnder Gaps." *Psychology of Women Quarterly* 1–14 (2021). https://doi.org/10.1177/03616843211003070.

Bohnet, Iris. *What Works. U.S.: First* Harvard University Press, 2018.

Brady, Shannon T., Geoffrey L. Cohen, Shoshana N. Jarvis, and Gregory M. Walton. "A Brief Social-Belonging Intervention in College Improves Adult Outcomes for Black Americans." *Science Advances* 6, no. 18 (May 2020): eaay3689. https://doi.org/10.1126/sciadv.aay3689.

Catalyst. "Catalyst Women On Board™." Accessed February 23, 2021. https://www.catalyst.org/catalyst-women-on-board/.

"If You Thought Working From Home Was Messy, Here Comes Hybrid Work - WSJ." Accessed May 26, 2021. https://www.wsj.com/articles/if-you-thought-working-from-home-was-messy-here-comes-hybrid-work-11621935000?st=7809jfec5zsbzpz&reflink=article_email_share.

Kang, Chris. "DIBs – Diversity, Inclusion & Belonging by Pat Wadors." 19:02:31 UTC. https://www.slideshare.net/misschriskang/dibs-diversity-inclusion-belonging-by-pat-wadors-67307975.

Lublin, Joann S. "The Executive Who Helps Salesforce Stay True to Its Founders' Philanthropic Pledge." *Wall Street Journal*, June 19, 2021, sec. Management. https://www.wsj.com/articles/the-executive-who-helps-salesforce-stay-true-to-its-founders-philanthropic-pledge-11624075202.

Man, Jess. "Chief Diversity Officer Is Both the Hottest and Toughest Job in 2021." Accessed May 29, 2021. https://diversity.social/chief-diversity-officer/.

Mohr, Bernard J., and Jane Magruder Watkins. *The Essentials of Appreciative Inquiry: A Roadmap for Creating Positive Futures*. Waltham, MA: Pegasus Communications, Inc., 2002.

News, A. B. C. "Women Are Less Aggressive than Men When Applying for Jobs, despite Getting Hired More Frequently: LinkedIn." *ABC News*. Accessed May 26, 2021. https://abcnews.go.com/Business/women-aggressive-men-applying-jobs-hired-frequently-linkedin/story?id=61531741.

Research, and North America. "How Middle Managers Can Help Make a More Equitable Workplace." *Knowledge@Wharton*. Accessed June 30, 2021. https://knowledge.wharton.upenn.edu/article/middle-managers-can-help-make-equitable-workplace/.

"'The '-Isms' of Sexism And Racism Are Like Air. They're Everywhere.' | LinkedIn." Accessed October 22, 2020. https://www.linkedin.com/pulse/isms-sexism-racism-like-air-theyre-everywhere-adam-bryant/?trackingId=.

"Top 10 Best Practices for Mentors | Center for Mentoring Excellence." Accessed April 8, 2021. https://www.centerformentoring.com/top-10-best-practices-for-mentors.

Tulshyan, Ruchika. "How to Reduce Personal Bias When Hiring." *Harvard Business Review*, June 28, 2019. https://hbr.org/2019/06/how-to-reduce-personal-bias-when-hiring.

Wadors, Pat. "Diversity Efforts Fall Short Unless Employees Feel That They Belong." *Harvard Business Review*, August 10, 2016. https://hbr.org/2016/08/diversity-efforts-fall-short-unless-employees-feel-that-they-belong.

"What Are Employee Resource Groups (ERGs)? | Great Place to Work®." Accessed May 25, 2021. https://www.greatplacetowork.com/resources/blog/what-are-employee-resource-groups-ergs.

Chapter 8

Understanding and Addressing Bias

Bias is a tricky topic because much of bias is implicit or unconscious. We aren't aware that our brains are taking short cuts in its decision-making process based on centuries of conditioning. Neuroscience and behavioral research have identified that the brain processes massive amounts of information simultaneously and relies on a sorting mechanism to make instantaneous decisions based on instincts.[1] While most people believe that their decisions are rational, research indicates that most decisions are emotional. If you feel a situation makes you feel uncomfortable or fearful, your brain has already activated your response system before you even have time to think about the situation. Human survival has been based on immediate response to these "fight or flight" decisions. This hardwired pattern of responding to the world is our unconscious bias at work. In effect, we have filters that impact what we see and how we interpret information and situations. Unconscious bias impacts our lives daily on both a personal and professional level.

8.1 Unconscious Bias

Unconscious bias represents our hidden beliefs, attitudes, and people preferences that have been formed by our own lived experiences. Often, these unconscious biases do not align with our own self story and stated beliefs. Research indicates that we all tend to have unconscious bias that favors our own in-group. As a result, unconscious bias impacts our assumptions about people and perceptions of situations. We are incorporating these unconscious biases into our daily decision-making on both a personal and professional level.

DOI: 10.1201/9781003168072-9

There are approximately 150 types of biases with the top 10 cognitive biases indicated in Figure 8.1. These biases impact how we receive and process information which in turn impacts our personal and professional decision-making processes. Confirmation bias means we tend to listen to input that most closely aligns with our own opinions. Hindsight bias is our tendency to suggest that we can predict outcomes of even random events. Anchoring bias is being overly impacted by the first information received. The misinformation bias is having a memory of an event be impacted by events that occurred well after the event. The actor-observer bias is our tendency to attribute our own failure to outside influences and to attribute others' failures to internal factors. The false consensus effect is when we believe others agree with our views, behaviors, and actions. The halo effect is also known as the physical attractiveness stereotype. We tend to allow our first impression influence our overall impression of a person. Self-serving bias is giving ourselves credit for successes and lay blame for failures on outside factors. The availability heuristic reflects our tendency to elevate the probability of an event based on the number of examples we can recall. The optimism bias is overestimating the probability of a positive outcome.[2] These are just a handful of the most common biases that enter into our evaluation and decision-making processes.

The Institute of Neuroscience groups the most common types of cognitive biases that impact decision-making into five categories: safety, expedience, experience, distance, and similarity.[4] In effect, these are mental short cuts to allow the brain to multitask and give different decisions varying levels of consideration. Sometimes these short cuts help us in decision-making such as a flight response saving our lives from a vehicle about to strike us, and other times they cause us to make decisions that hurt us and others because of these biases. Decisions that focus on safety tend to be conservative in order to protect our existing status rather than to accept risk to achieve gains. Our tendency for expediency results in making decisions quickly rather than gathering additional information and reflecting upon the decision. Expedience bias incorporates several of the aforementioned biases, such as confirmation bias, halo effect, and anchoring bias, but also includes belief bias and representative bias. Our

- Confirmation
- Hindsight
- Anchoring
- Misinformation
- Actor-Observer
- False-Consensus
- Halo Effect
- Self-Serving
- Availability
- Optimism

Figure 8.1 Types of bias.[3]

experience biases means that we perceive that all of our experiences are an accurate reflection of events and facts. To gain perspective on just how wrong we are, view this clip to see what your experience bias reflects – The Monkey Business Illusion – https://youtu.be/IGQmdoK_ZfY

After viewing the video consider the following questions:

1. What did you see as a firsthand observer?
2. Can you understand why eyewitnesses to events often see the event differently?
3. Does this clip make you reconsider an observable truth?
4. How does awareness of bias make us reconsider our own behavior in meetings?

As a result of our bias, we often come to our own conclusion and tune out all other input. Our biases impact what we see, what we focus on, and what we don't see. Understanding the impact of our biases on our decision-making process is the first step in making changes to our own behavior.

Distance bias reflects our preference for what is closer rather than what is farther away. Many organizations have seen this reflected in headquarter vs. satellite location tensions in terms of inclusion of remote voices, representation of issues, and allocation of resources. Similarity bias means that we prefer people, places, and things that are similar to what we know. It is often referred to as "in group out group" bias. This is the types of bias that we all tend to exhibit. These types of biases are dangerous in organizations when dealing with people strategy decisions around talent recruitment, development, and promotion. These types of biases lead to high caliber candidates being excluded because of their diversity. Similarity bias also inhibits an organization's opportunities for innovation and market expansion as these require valuing diversity of identity, thought, and experience. Hopefully, you now agree that we all have biases and that these impact on how we interpret events, evaluate people, and make decisions.

Unconscious bias impacts decisions made across organizations. We see it in recruitment, hiring, role designations, advancement, and performance appraisal decisions. We see it in who is invited to a meeting, given a stretch project, or even allowed to contribute input during a meeting. Unconscious bias leads to actions, behaviors, and decisions that are often bias against certain genders, races, nationalities, ages, and other groups.

If you have not taken an unconscious or an implicit bias assessment, this is a tool to give you a baseline. Harvard offers a free assessment known as the Implicit Association Test (IAT) available at https://implicit.harvard.edu/implicit/takeatest.html. The IAT measures people's attitudes and beliefs that they may be unable or unwilling to report. This information often reveals attitudes and biases of which you are unaware, yet, they impact your decision-making, perceptions, and beliefs. The results can provide insight to the taker on their perceptions relative to certain groups of people.

In *The New York Times* Bestseller, *The Blind Spot*, authors, Mahzarin R. Banaji and Anthony G. Greenwald, use the term blind spot as a metaphor for the psychological and social blind spots to biases that unconsciously impact our behaviors, thoughts, and actions. They identify "mindbugs" that influence how we perceive, remember, reason, and even make decisions particularly related to race, gender, ethnicity, or other group identifiers. Because of these "mindbugs," we make decisions without realizing the existence of these biases that may adversely impact others. These biases begin very early in life. In-group preference has been found in young children's preferences for those that look and sound like their primary caregivers. The IAT test data indicates that 70–80% of test takers indicate implicit racial preferences for people identified as White over people identified as BIPOC or AAPI and stereotypes associating men over women with careers, science, and leadership.[5] The first step to correcting unconscious biases or "mindbugs" is to identify them and be consciously aware of them. Since our unconscious bias is reinforced in our everyday experiences, taking the time to consciously identify bias is an important first step. Many people believe that they do not have a conscious race preference, but the IAT research shows that even self-identifying egalitarians do have an unconscious White racial preference. As we saw in the earlier chapters, there is much evidence supporting BIPOC disadvantage in our society. There are several variations of the IAT to measure unconscious bias from which to choose, and you may take as many as you wish. As you consider your IAT results, it may be helpful to consider these IAT reflection questions:

1. What is your initial reaction to the test results?
2. Are the results aligned with your self-perception? Are they misaligned?
3. Does this alignment create acceptance or resistance to the results?
4. Are you able to identify any experiences or interactions that may inform these results?
5. How might these unconscious biases impact your interaction in your personal or professional life?
6. How might these biases impact your role as a leader?
7. How might these biases impact designing organizational systems around hiring, promotion, compensation, and opportunities?
8. How might these biases impact team member relationships and dynamics?
9. How might these biases impact vendor or contractor selection?
10. How might these biases impact who is selected as a high potential employee or future leader?

The key takeaway is that we all have biases, and we are all susceptible to bias. It is difficult to manage bias when you are in the decision-making process. A better approach is to develop practices and processes in advance so that you have a strategy to draw upon when making decisions. These include building cultural competency, slowing down the decision-making process, redesigning talent ecosystem processes, redesigning procurement processes, and promoting data driven decisions (see Chapters 5 and 7 for more detailed actions).

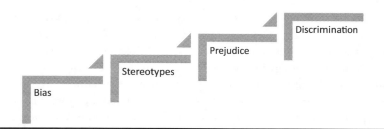

Figure 8.2 Bias versus discrimination.

The good news is that biases do not equate to discrimination. As indicated in Figure 8.2, biases can be a building block for discrimination, but we have an opportunity to intervene and break this sequencing. Bias informs our assumptions about people, and left unchecked, assumptions can lead to stereotyping. As a result, we begin to make decisions and take actions that are based on our stereotyping of people. This thought process results in prejudice actions, behaviors, policies, and institutions. The decisions, policies, and legislation that are created based upon these assumptions, stereotyping, and prejudice lead to systemic discrimination and societal barriers. In order to break this cycle, we need to slow our complex brains and recognize that we are reacting to a variety of stimulants and are making decisions based on assumptions. Acknowledging our biases and developing our own list of checks to reduce our biases is a good start. Creating a self-action strategy supports individual decision-making, but bias, stereotyping, and prejudice is baked into our organizational and societal systems.

As an individual, evaluate your own assumptions, expectations, and "mindbugs." Think about how you treat people and your communication style. Create a plan of action for yourself to modify your own behavior to better serve the needs of your customers, employees, team members, and colleagues. Language matters and how something is said has a big impact. Microaggressions occur daily, and it is imperative that we all check our assumptions and language to avoid committing them. One of the best ways to break this cycle is to increase your cultural competency by exposing yourself to different groups of people. It means doing the work to check your biases and assumptions in order to change how you perceive and interpret all of the stimuli flowing into your brain. It also means expanding your own experiences to develop a broader frame of reference. Lastly, it requires developing a strategy to check your own biases and to create a process to improve decision-making and actions.

8.2 Bias in the C-Suite and Leadership

An area of growing research known as behavioral corporate finance focuses on management bias and the implications for their organizations. This research has begun to dismantle traditional economic devices such as selection, learning, and market discipline that support the rational-manager paradigm.[6] During selection, the rational-manager model assumes that managers that are well educated and intelligent will be able to rise above susceptibility biases present in others such as consumers and investors. It also assumes that managers learn from their mistakes and incorporate their learnings into future decision-making. During a leader's tenure, the market discipline component of the paradigm suggests that through close monitoring by boards and the market, organizations are able to limit bias-driven errors.[7] Given the level of systemic racism, sexism, ableism, etc. in our society and organizations, we see that this paradigm is a fallacy.

Research in the field of behavioral corporate finance identifies how decisions made by even the most educated and influential decision-makers such as board members and CEOs are influenced by bias. The findings reinforce how unconscious bias is hardwired into decision-making even at the most senior levels of an organization. This bias is reinforced through lack of diversity in the most senior levels. During the selection process for senior roles, certain characteristics such as high levels of confidence outweigh other competency considerations. Certain demographic groups such as White males tend to exhibit much more confidence than other groups. Overconfident individuals often are willing to take risks to generate greater rewards leading them to be on the slate of potential candidates for the CEO spot. Senior leaders reinforce their selection of a male candidate over a female candidate citing the male's willingness to take risks. As a result, overconfident individuals are funneled to the top of organizations rather than filtered out.[8] Taking the time to develop a set of competencies for a senior role and standardizing the interview process helps to remove this type of bias that often gets incorporated into decision-making when intuition is valued over data.

Often, CEOs bring their prior team with them to replace the existing C-suite. While this team hire approach may have benefits in terms of team dynamics, it may also suffer from group think, where participants are susceptible to the loudest voice in the group. If the team was not constructed to ensure diversity of identity, thought, and experience, decision outcomes might not accurately address both opportunities and risks. Major decisions around corporate strategy including mergers, acquisitions, and divestitures (M&A) may not receive adequate vetting for both opportunity and risk assessment in terms of impacts on key stakeholders such as customers, employees, investors, and communities. In addition, overconfidence can lead to valuation models based on perceived synergies that are improbable or overestimated. The research suggests that the infrequency of major events such as a M&A event make it difficult for a CEO to learn from past mistakes and incorporate those learnings into current actions. Building diversity of representation in C-suite leadership mitigates bias and encourages holistic reflection on opportunities and risks for the benefit of the organization and its stakeholders.

Board of Directors regularly exhibit "In group" bias in selecting CEOs. Research indicates that boards select CEOs based on gender, similarity of cultural backgrounds, education, or a certain career or experience path[9]. Board governance procedures for recruitment, evaluation, selection, compensation, and retention of CEOs need to be reviewed to ensure that processes are in place to reduce bias. Building and maintaining board member diversity provides an inherent structure to minimize bias. Since bias is present at every level of the organization, it is crucial to create conditions for success such as inclusive leadership development, governance structures to keep power in check, requiring candidate slate diversity, and alignment between compensation and decision-making outcomes. Research indicates that S&P companies with above median gender diversity on their boards experience a 15% higher ROE.[10] Being aware of these biases allows organizations to design processes and systems that support greater CEO diversity.

8.3 Cultural Competency

Understanding our own cultural norms and preferences offers a first step in building cultural competency. Often our cultural values and beliefs are so deeply rooted in our beings that we don't consider that we have learned these beliefs over time based upon our experiences. For most of us, cultural values and norms were learned at a young age and have been reinforced daily throughout our lives. These cultural norms guide us in determining acceptable actions and behaviors in a variety of situations. In a global work community, not everyone was raised with the same cultural values and norms. Lack of understanding of others' cultural norms and values can create tension, misunderstanding, and even project team breakdowns and poor productivity. I recall a story of a female project manager from India who was working in the U.S. on a project. A male colleague extended his hand in greeting and instead of shaking his hand, she formed the Namaste sign as a form of greeting. In her region in India, it was unheard of for a man to touch a woman to whom he was not married. While the business custom of shaking of hands between genders is a common practice in western civilization, in other parts of the globe this practice is seen as inappropriate. It is crucial to understand cultural norms and to not make judgments based on your own deeply ingrained cultural norms.

Cultural norms and values impact business conduct including how projects are run, presentations are structured, meetings are scheduled, and a whole host of other best practices that may differ from your own culture's business values and norms. Understanding that personal and professional attitudes, norms, and behaviors are different in different cultures around the world is the first step in acceptance and behavior modification. Differences can include communication styles, work habits, beliefs, attitudes, relationships, expression of emotions, social distance, decision-making, conflict resolution, time orientation, and even social traits such as making eye contact, shaking hands, greeting styles, and many other cultural norms. Expats and other global travelers may be more in tune to cultural differences and the need to build cultural competency, but we all need to develop these skills. When interacting with people from other cultures, it is important to check our own attitudes and stereotypes to ensure that unconscious bias is not impacting our behaviors, actions, and decision-making. A useful tool to understand cultural differences in the workplace is What's Your Cultural Profile (https://hbr.org/2014/08/whats-your-cultural-profile).

Understanding how your own country's business cultural norms compare to those of another country provides foundational knowledge around fundamental differences in priorities, styles, and preferences. This assessment is based on eight components of culture including communication, evaluation, persuasion, leadership structure, decision-making, basis of trust, disagreement resolution, and adherence to schedules. As an example, in some countries, such as the U.S., we prefer a low context communication style meaning that messaging is clear and concise. Other countries, such as India, prefer a high context communication style meaning there is nuance and layering and messaging requires interpretation. From a leadership perspective, some cultures are more hierarchical such as China, Russia, and Japan while others prefer a more egalitarian approach such as Scandinavia and Israel. In the U.S., we tend to build trust through work and demonstrated competency. In other part of the world, such as Brazil and India, trust is based on relationships and time spent together.[11] Expanding your cultural competency and taking the time to learn another's culture and their business norms, customs, and perspectives is crucial to managing global teams and projects.

The Power Distance Index (PDI) is an indicator of where national cultures fall on the power distribution continuum from centrally controlled to shared. If the PDI is high, a country is more hierarchical. When it is low, people believe that power and authority should be shared. Another indicator is Individualism vs. Collectivism (IDV). Countries with a high IDV have employees that operate in a manner to thrive and excel as individuals. These countries tend to value individual performance and recognition over team contributions. Countries such as the U.S., the U.K., the Netherlands fall into the high IDV category. Lower IDV scores indicate more focus on team goals and performance than individual achievements. Uncertainty Avoidance Index (UAI) suggests the appetite for leaders and employees to take on risk. Countries with a high UAI such as Greece and Portugal are very risk adverse, may require more time and effort to obtain strategic buy-in than countries with lower UAI such as Singapore and Denmark.[12] Operating globally highlights cultural competence as a necessity, but cultural competency is also crucial when operating domestically.

As a manager, bias can impact your assumptions around work performance. Ensure that you are aware that employees' work style, personality traits, communication styles, and other work habits may differ from yours or others in your group. Consider if your assessment of your employees is based on work output rather than assumptions and personal preferences. As a manager, it is crucial to check your bias and to consider strategies and devices to short-circuit "mindbugs" to ensure that you are promoting a climate of organizational justice supporting equity and belonging.

Some best practices to reduce unconscious bias and to promote cultural competency include:

1. Slowdown and evaluate your actions, behavior, and decisions.
2. Create opportunities to promote cultural understanding and appreciation of other cultures.
3. Ask questions about your own beliefs and your organization's attitudes and beliefs. Are the organizations' core values, attitudes, and acceptable behaviors identified and broadly shared?
4. Build your own cultural competencies in order to value diversity of ethnicity, race, culture, ability, gender, experience, thought, and all of the 40+ attributes of diversity.
5. Ensure that the organization's values on diversity, equity, and inclusion are clearly communicated to all employees.
6. Review your policies around holidays, flexible time, and other accommodations to meet the needs of a diverse workforce.
7. Evaluate who is depicted in your organizational artifacts such as artwork, advertisements, recruitment material, etc.
8. Consider how community, national, or even global events are impacting your workforce.

As you consider these points, think about how these issues may be impacting the culture of your organization as well as the impact on employees and their ability to bringing their full selves to work.

Suggestions to improve your cultural competency include:

1. Seek a mentor, advisor, or coach to help build your cultural competencies.
2. Encourage your organization to provide cultural competency training.
3. Seek volunteer opportunities that give you exposure to people from different cultures, backgrounds, races, and experiences. These can be either international or local volunteer opportunities as long as they provide exposure to different cultures and perspectives.
4. Seek global assignments that expose you to new cultures and people. These can be in the form of being a member of a global project team or an assignment in another country.
5. Expose yourself to art, music, and literature from different cultures.
6. Actively seek to spend time with people from different cultures and those with different beliefs, and backgrounds.

Assessing your own cultural competency and working on expanding your exposure to and awareness of different cultures both globally and locally begins the journey in checking your bias around acceptable norms for behavior, actions, work habits, and work structures. From an organizational perspective, offering resources and training to support employees in building their cultural competencies is a vital component of "doing the work." It is important to remember that it is not incumbent on members of underrepresented groups to educate others on their lived experience. It is up to all of us to "do the work" and organizations that are aligned with a J.E.D.I. vision need to support this work with programs to promote cultural education and understanding.

8.4 Stereotypes, Model Minorities, and Microaggressions

Stereotypes are a short-hand categorization of someone into a group based generally on identity factors such as race, culture, gender, class, etc. Instead of getting to know an individual, we make assumptions based on stereotypes. These assumptions impact how we treat an individual, the opportunities they may receive, the stretch assignments given, and the opportunities for handling high profile projects. Racial stereotyping is prevalent, and we have already given many examples in this book such as police stopping Black drivers, store clerks following Black customers around the store, and Black youth arrest rates. These stereotypes follow us into our organizations and impact how we view situations and make decisions. Assumptions that we make based on stereotypes impact how we view job candidates, where we recruit candidates, how we distribute opportunities and recognize performance. In addition, these stereotypes impact who is given entrepreneurial opportunities, as they impact who gets funding from banks and venture capitalists. They also impact who is selected in terms of vendors or partners.

But stereotyping can be much more subtle and even well intentioned. When creating a slate of candidates for a global position, a manager excludes a high performing female candidate from this opportunity because she had small children. While the employee may make the choice to decline the opportunity for a variety of reasons including having small children, it is up to the employee to decline the opportunity not for the manager to make an assumption about their employee's answer. The manager is in effect stereotyping women as primary caregivers. In fact, many women with small children have accepted global assignments as they believe that the experience and exposure will further their careers. Making assumptions based on stereotypes further embeds bias into our systems and processes.

Stereotyping is also done based on age. For example, recent research in Europe indicates that age discrimination is the most widely experienced discrimination reported in Europe. Older workers are perceived as less motivated, less willing to engage in training and development, resistant to change, less trusting, more likely to experience health issues, and more impacted by work–family conflicts.[13] Interviews with older employees indicated that their work experience actually runs counter to these stereotypes. Not surprisingly, the advice for organizations to counter these negative stereotypes of older workers is to:

1. Engage workers with meaningful and stimulating work.
2. Provide opportunities to have some autonomy in their own work design.

3. Offer opportunities for flexible work structures to promote health and well-being.
4. Offer opportunities to socialize with colleagues.
5. Offer equal access to formal and informal development and training.
6. Establish mentoring and other programs to transfer knowledge to younger colleagues.
7. Offer competitive compensation and benefit packages.[14]

Interestingly, these recommendations focus on autonomy, use of skill, and influence, which stands in conflict to the previous described stereotype of older workers. Clearly, members of older generations in the workplace want to make a contribution and a difference, but they are being sidelined by harmful stereotyping.

Model minorities take stereotyping a step further. For example, the stereotype of Asian Americans is that as a group they are hardworking, academically high achieving, and progressively financially successful. If we think about it, we know that this stereotype is not true. Asian Americans encompass a large group of people, countries, and cultures. Asian Americans include people from Japan, China, and Singapore but also people from Cambodia, Vietnam, Myanmar, and many other countries. Many Asian Americans are newly arrived immigrants and others are people fleeing war, conflicts, economic, or environmental disasters.

> Originally coined in 1966 by sociologist William Peterson to profile the socioeconomic success of Japanese Americans, the myth of the 'model minority' has become a collection of stereotypes about Asian Americans, presenting them as an 'ideal minority group' in the eyes of White Supremacy.[15]

Asian teens have shared stories of extremely high pressure from parents to excel academically impacting their well-being and health. Despite the "model minority" stereotype, cultural ignorance and lack of cultural competency have led to hate crimes against Asian Americans especially people from South Asia. As we have seen in recent months, hate crimes against Asian American are on the rise because of attribution of COVID-19 origins to China. We have seen similar hate based actions such as attacks on people from Muslim and Hindi faiths around the time of 9/11 terrorist attacks. This kind of stereotyping creates many adverse impacts for members of the stereotyped group.

While more subtle than hate based actions, microaggressions have negative impacts for the recipients. Microaggressions are comments, behaviors, or actions that insult or denigrate someone in a marginalized group. The perpetrator of the microaggression may not intend to insult the other person, but intentional or not, their comments or actions have done just that. These microaggressions may be explained by the perpetrator as unintended or as a misunderstanding. But the reality is that to the recipient, they hurt, and the cumulative impact of microaggressions is significant, even debilitating over time. Often, microaggressions impact the recipient's ability to function fully at work and may impact their health and well-being. Stereotyping and microaggression often go hand in hand. In order to better understand microaggressions and their impact on people, here is a link to "Killing Me Softly" by Fobazi M. Ettarh, a simulation that allows the player to walk in the shoes of someone who experiences microaggressions on a daily basis and the significant impact of this experience on their health and well-being (http://fobettarh. github.io/Killing-Me-Softly/).

Microaggressions are really anything that another person perceives as such. Combatting microaggressions requires individuals to be open to learning about others' perceptions and lived experiences.

If you are being called out/in for a microaggression, here are some points to consider:

- Apologize and admit your mistake. Even if it was a joke, it hurt the other person.
- Acknowledge the other person's experience. Don't invalidate it.
- Once a person has shared their experience, don't compare it to the experience of another marginalized group.
- Be aware that words and expressions can send a subtle or not so subtle message to another.

If you are a victim of a microaggression, here are some points to consider:

- You can choose whether or not to respond, and how you wish to respond.
- Assertive responses involve engaging the person in a conversation about what made the comment hurtful.
- If you are feeling vulnerable, hurt, or angry, seek support from friends, family, or a professional. It is not up to you to address every microaggression. Ensuring your own safety is the priority.

Developing a diversity, equity, and inclusion statement for your organization that lays out expectations for calling in/out is a useful tool to facilitate employees navigating this territory. Educating employees on microaggressions and on best practices for addressing them provides both parties with a framework in which to have a productive conversation. If you find that you have committed a microaggression, PAUSE and use the technique described in Figure 8.3 to reflect on the situation, your assumptions, and the impact of your words or actions.

Stop and *Pay* attention to your situation. If you have hurt someone either intentionally or unintentionally, *Acknowledge* the impact that your words or actions had on that individual. Take the time to *Understand* the other person's perspective and reaction, and listen to their experience. *Search* for the most beneficial and productive way in which to address the situation. It is about healing and moving forward. Sometimes your actions can be corrected by small adjustments; other times

P-Pay Attention
A-Acknowledge
U-Understand the other person's reaction
S-Search for the most productive way to address the situation
E-Execute an intentional plan

Figure 8.3   PAUSE technique.

Understand Microaggressions	Become Comfortable in Discussing Microaggressions	Gain Happier Employees and a Profitable Company
By identifying microaggressions, we can all try to understand how our words and actions can impact others	Microaggressions can cause underlying tension in any setting, professional or personal	The more we understand our impact, the better our companies will function

Figure 8.4   Impact of mitigating microaggressions.

the solution needs to be systemic to correct the issue. Create a plan of action, and *Execute* the plan to revise actions and behaviors. Plans can include training, a personal checklist for conversations, or even an outreach to gain a better understanding of the cultures and practices of a particular community or group. Addressing microaggressions is important for personal relationships, but it is also important for organizational dynamics between co-workers, team members, and leadership. As outlined in Figure 8.4, we follow the road map of understanding and discussing microaggressions and the outcome of this process which is happier employees and more productive organizations. Making people aware of microaggressions and their impact on the health and well-being of others is a first step. Words and behaviors impact an employee's sense of belonging and directly affect their ability to come to work and contribute fully.

Allowing microaggressions in the workplace results in underlying interpersonal tensions that impact your employees' ability to bring their full and authentic selves to work. Microaggressions have a cumulative impact and have a detrimental impact on those directly involved as well as the broader work environment. Creating a plan to proactively address and mitigate microaggressions builds a more inclusive workplace in which there is greater appreciation and understanding of diversity of identity, experience, and thought.

In her TEDx Talk, "How to have a Voice and Lean Into A Conversation About Race," Dr. Amanda Kemp, author and professor, advises us to "Hold space for transformation." According to Dr. Kemp, approaching challenging conversations in this manner requires holding space for unconditional love and acceptance. These conversations are not about agreement, but rather a journey of discovery focused on shining a light on blind spots, making connections, and building compassion. For the person holding this space, Dr. Kemp suggests a self-check to determine if you are in a good place to have a conversation about race. The most common barriers to having a conversation about race are that people of color are exhausted by these conversations, and White people are afraid of saying the wrong thing. Holding space for transformation is a big ask. If we can create these spaces and share our authentic stories, we have an opportunity to change hearts and minds.[16]

As we reflect on our own attitudes and behaviors, it is time to take a deeper look into our own biases as a starting point for better understanding and accepting others. The neuro research indicates that none of us are free of bias and that we need to create an active plan to check and intercede in our decision-making processes in order to avoid bias. Building our cultural competencies gives us a broader tool kit with which to engage colleagues, customers, and teammates. Through gaining a broader perspective, we are able to break our pattern of making assumptions based on stereotypes. Reflecting on our language and the impact our words have on others, begins our transformation to mitigate biases, stereotyping and microaggressions. Building our personal ability to address bias supports our organizational ability to address bias. Bias is pervasive throughout our organizations. It isn't just confined to the shop floor. It is present at the most senior levels of our organizations. It pervades our client interactions, procurement decisions, talent acquisition and management practices, performance evaluations, promotion decisions, and even team interactions.

8.5 Doing the Work

Building your personal learning about underrepresented groups and their history and experiences in society and business is what is referred to as "doing the work." In order to facilitate your perspective taking capabilities, we are providing this list of resources These foundational readings will allow you to reframe your thinking and to begin to understand the significant biases and inequities baked into our daily lives. Many of these topics were introduced in Chapter 3, but to gain deep perspective and knowledge on the experiences of historically underrepresented groups in the U.S., the books listed in Table 8.1 are excellent resources.

As you begin or continue your journey, consider you daily interactions to identify ways that you as an individual can build your own perspective, competencies, and capacity to promote J.E.D.I. values and beliefs. Here are a few suggestions:

1. Identify practices to expand your cultural competency through exposing your-self to different cultures – attending cultural events, traveling, reading, engaging with people from different cultural backgrounds. An example might be setting up series of lunch and learns offering the opportunity for people to

Table 8.1 Perspective-Gaining Resource List

Author	Title
Ijeoma Oluo	*So You Want to Talk about Race*
Ibram Kendi	*How To Be an Antiracist*
Iris Bohnet	*What Works*
Edgar Villanueva	*Decolonizing Wealth*
Rhodes Perry	*Belonging At Work*

    share their cultural history with colleagues. A user-friendly resource for Black culture and history is BlackFacts (https://www.blackfacts.com/), which gives a fact minute for the day delivered in a short video.

2. Use inclusive language. When introducing yourself, share your pronouns and ask others to share their pronouns. Ensure that you are addressing colleagues and others in the way they wish to be addressed. Don't assume. Refrain from using acronyms that others might not know or define the acronyms. Think about the generational and cultural frame of phrases and expressions. Avoid gender or exclusive terms such as grandfathered, which originated based on practices in Southern U.S. states in the late 1800s as a way to circumvent the 15th Amendment and prevent Black citizens from voting.[17] Consider using legacy instead.

3. Listen. Truly listen and be open to hearing others' opinions and perspectives.

4. Consider with whom you spend time and expand your network to include people from underrepresented groups. Get to know people as individuals in order to minimize stereotyping.

5. Practice humility. If you are a member of the White privilege group, reflect on the advantages that you and your ancestors have had in creating your place in life and your current opportunities. Consider using your privilege to extend a hand to a member of an underserved group.

6. Speak up. If you see actions and behaviors being exhibited within your organization that are not in alignment with its J.E.D.I. vision and value, address the disparity. Using the Giving Voice to Values (GVV) model is a helpful tool for raising these concerns and issues.

7. Cultivate a growth mindset. Take the time to "do the work" to research and learn about other cultures, their history, and their practices

Each of us needs to invest in learning better ways to be inclusive and create an environment that promotes belonging. If someone is using a term that feels wrong, take the time to research the term and use your findings to support switching a term for future meetings. If someone is personally offended by a term, stop using it. Feel free to share your findings and to educate others as you learn. For example, someone outside your organization might ask about a change in term usage and you can explain the reasons, which will hopefully catalyze a change in their usage of the terms as well. When you know better, do better. Meetings can be started with sharing of names and preferred pronouns so that all group members can be referred to in a manner that they prefer. Modeling and normalizing inclusive behavior make it part of organizational culture.

Beyond pronouns, language needs to be inclusive. To promote the use of inclusive language consider substituting the terms as suggested in Table 8.2. Best practices include focusing on people as individuals, using gender neutral language, and using universal terms and phrases not idioms, jargons, and acronyms.

Early on in this book, we called out racism baked into capitalism. This relationship is apparent through our common use of terms in business that have racist origins. Table 8.3 highlights some common business jargon and outlines its problematic history. Eliminating these phrases from our workplaces promotes inclusion. Some of these terms can be microaggressions for some employees and they experience a negative impact every time the term is used. Image the debilitating impact of hearing this jargon continuously. In addition, research shows that the words that you use most often tend to shape your view of the world. Eliminating these terms has a broader impact of reframing perspectives which facilitates growth in your own and your organization's J.E.D.I. maturity.

Table 8.2 More Inclusive Terms

Instead of	Try
Guys	Folks, people, teammates
Girls	Women
Manpower, man hours	Workforce, personnel, team
Chairman	Chairperson
Husband, wife	Spouse, partner
Mothering, fathering	Parenting
Salesman, saleswoman	Man on our sales team, woman on our sales team
Females	Women
Housekeeping	Maintenance
Handicap	Disabled
American Indian	Native American

Table 8.3 Business Jargon with Racist Origins

Open the Kimono	A euphemism for transparency. Sexist synonym for revealing the inner workings of a project or company.
Chop-chop	This phrase is a pidgin English translation meaning to make haste. It is most often used by someone who has power and privilege over the person to whom it is said.
Grandfathered	The term originates from practices in Southern U.S. states in the late 1800s designed to circumvent the 15th Amendment and prevent Black citizens from voting.
No Can Do	This phrase is a pidgin English translation and originates from the mid-19th to the early 20th century, a time of racist attitudes toward the Chinese.
Long Time No See	Another form of pidgin English, which was adapted from Native American origins.
Master/Slave	Term used to define a machine data sharing relationship that is based on the history of slavery in the U.S.
Man	The term is used as a synonym for work. Man-hours or man the booth. It is an unnecessarily gendered language use.
Meritocracy	The belief that hard work and talent are the sole determinants of success. The concept excludes the impacts of privilege, bias, and systemic inequities on determining success.

8.6 Acting Upon Your Values

In order to drive systemic change, we need to speak up when we see actions, behaviors, and decisions that do not support J.E.D.I. values alignment. Decisions related to assignment of preferential projects, new opportunities, and promotions are often made behind closed doors with little transparency. For those with the privilege of being at the table and having those discussions comes the responsibility of acting in accordance with organizational and personal values. Speaking up is not always easy and may come with personal risk, but to drive meaningful change, we must question, push back on stereotypes, and ensure that adequate and fair consideration is given to all candidates. I have been in meetings when objections have been raised against certain candidates for reasons such as "culture fit" with a group or team. For women, I've heard, "She is too aggressive and assertive." In order to change this dynamic, those in the room need to find their voice and speak up to question assumptions or ask for examples. Of course, speaking up is hard, but the following model will help.

Giving Voice to Values (GVV) is a methodology developed by Mary Gentile that facilitates raising concerns when your values are misaligned with policies, actions, and behaviors within your organization. The model provides tools for acting on one's values in a particular situation by preparing for the conversation in advance. Often, we find ourselves in situations where we don't agree with what is happening, and we feel that it is unjust or inequitable, but we find it difficult to speak up. The GVV model helps us practice for these conversations, teaches us techniques for unpacking and reasoning through common arguments levied against just and equitable behavior, and helps us create a strategy for speaking our values. The first step is to identify your own values and to consider how they align with your organization's values. As part of this self-discovery process, you gain insights on your own risk orientation, preferred communication style, locus of loyalty, self-image, and purpose. As part of the organization's assessment, you consider factors such as the definition of a well-run organization, colleagues' views on environmental, social, governance, and ethical issues, and conflict areas for you within the organization such as downsizing, inequitable hiring practices, lack of diversity in leadership ranks, natural resource exploration, or supplier negotiations. Then you consider the impact of these value conflicts on you as an individual. The objective is to develop a self-story that allows you to act upon your values in these conflicted situations. The approach identifies enablers such as allies, framing, gathering information, asking questions, selecting and sequencing of your audiences, and understanding the audience perspective that supports acting on your values. For example, approaching a mentor or sponsor within the organization to solicit feedback on an idea or an approach to a conflict resolution is an example of leveraging the "allies" enabler. Asking questions may help reframe the issues or clarify the concerns being expressed especially in a situation when decisions are being made about opportunities for an underrepresented candidate's advancement. If your group has been given a slate of candidates to consider and they have all been vetted for competence, question quick decisions to eliminate candidates. If someone's objection is vague, ask, for an example of objectionable behavior exhibited by that candidate. Sometimes, it boils down to what is at stake for the individual raising the objection. Well posed questions can shed light and spotlight inequities. Reframing the situation and identifying the risk of not promoting a diverse candidate to the organization is another technique to leverage. Conflicts within organizations are normal, and we must anticipate that they will occur. We need to have a toolkit to act in accordance with our personal and organizational values and to serve as an ally for underrepresented groups.

From an organizational perspective, there are several enablers that can promote acting in accordance with J.E.D.I. values such as:

1. Clearly define your organizational values
2. Draft a policy statement that aligns with organizational values

3. Promote a culture of openness and transparency
4. Encourage a culture of conversation and debate

Creating an organization with clearly stated and communicated J.E.D.I. values allows for a clear framework against which to measure decisions and actions. In addition, a culture that values debate and openness promotes equal access and sharing of information and minimizes power dynamics that suppress ideas and thoughts. These organizational enablers are in line with the recommendations that have been made throughout the book to build equitable and just organizations.

As part of the preparation to facilitate speaking up, consider common arguments or rationalizations that are used in your organization to justify certain behaviors that are in conflict with stated J.E.D.I. values. Common ones include:

1. Expected or standard practice
2. Not material
3. Not my responsibility
4. My loyalty lies with …

I'm sure we have all heard these reasons for why a colleague is acting in a particular way when their actions are not in alignment with our values. To have a plan to speak up and address inequities, we have the GVV framework highlighted in Figure 8.5. The model provides a series of steps to facilitate speaking up against issues of injustice or inequity. It is a tool that we can each use to engage in difficult conversations when we see policies, processes, actions, behaviors, and decisions that do not align with our organizational vision of justice, equity, diversity, and inclusion.

- Values
    - Appeal to shared values
- Choice
    - Believe that you have choice
- Normalcy
    - Expect values conflicts
- Purpose
    - Clear understanding of objective
- Alignment with Self
    - Acting in a manner that is consistent with your own values
- Voice
    - Practice with respected peers and invite coaching and feedback
- Reasons and Rationalizations
    - Anticipate typical rationalizations

Figure 8.5   GVV checklist.[18]

Crucial to the process is playing to one's own strengths and creating conditions for success. Experience plays to your strength. Having addressed a situation once gives you strength to address it in similar situations in the future. Positive reinforcement is another strength builder. Speaking up even if the outcome doesn't change gives us confidence to express our own views and to bring our authentic selves to the conversation. In organizations, we will all find ourselves in situations that require us to question the status quo and to speak up. Practicing this behavior and having a plan of action to deal with common rationalizations allows us to act in accordance with our values and to encourage our colleagues to act in accordance with our organization's value pillars around justice, equity, and inclusion.

8.7 Summary

We are all subject to bias. Awareness is the first step in minimizing the impacts of biases when making decisions and creating policies, processes, and systems. There are numerous kinds of biases and they impact our perceptions, recollections, preferences, and ultimately our decision-making. To drive change, we need to debug our "mind-bugs" by slowing down our decision-making and reflecting upon our own behaviors, actions, communication style, and expedience shortcuts. Consider how these biases are baked into our organization's talent ecosystems, procurement systems, and even client management systems. Bias is present throughout the organization, even at the most senior levels. As you embark on your organizations' J.E.D.I. journey, the roadmap must consider that bias is present in every system throughout the organization.

In order to mitigate our biases, we need to "do the work" to build our cultural competence through exposure to different cultures, groups, and people. Having a growth mindset is crucial to engaging in "doing the work" to become more aware of other peoples' perspectives, cultures, practices, and beliefs. From an organizational perspective, it is crucial that resources are allocated to encourage employees to embark on this learning journey. Stereotyping results in inequitable decisions being made about individuals based on perceived group norms. People are individuals and decision must be made on individual competencies and capabilities. Microaggressions occur daily in the workplace. Developing a statement or protocol for calling people in to address microaggressions and to PAUSE and develop a pathway forward creates a condition for success. There are a variety of practices and techniques to improve your inclusion practices including using more inclusive language.

In order to drive systemic organizational change, we must find our voice and speak up when we see actions and behaviors that are not in alignment with our personal and organizational values. Engaging in difficult conversation is not easy but using the techniques outlined in the GVV model and routinely practicing speaking up creates a culture that supports and values diversity, equity, and inclusion. Transforming an organization requires both organizational and individual work to build competencies and capacity that promote J.E.D.I. values and strategy.

Questions

1. Take an IAT Implicit Bias test. What key learnings are you taking away from the process of taking the test and reflecting on the suggested questions in Section 8.1?
2. In what ways might lack of diversity in senior leadership result in poor outcomes for the organization?
3. What steps might be taken to improve diversity in the leadership ranks?
4. What steps might you undertake to improve your cultural competency?
5. How might the PAUSE technique be integrated into your organization to mitigate microaggressions and improve belonging?
6. What language is used within your organization that might not be inclusive?
7. How might you approach someone who is using language that is not inclusive?
8. What might be some fun ways to change language usage in your organization?
9. What conditions have supported your being able to speak up when a situation, action, decision doesn't align with your values?
10. What conditions have detracted from your being able to speak up when a situation, action, decision doesn't align with your values?

Notes

1 Chireda Cotman says, "Brain Stuff: The Neuroscience Behind Implicit Bias," *Spectra Diversity* (blog), December 27, 2017, https://www.spectradiversity.com/2017/12/27/unconscious-bias/.
2 Facebook and Twitter, "Types of Cognitive Biases That Distort How You Think," Verywell Mind, accessed March 18, 2021, https://www.verywellmind.com/cognitive-biases-distort-thinking-2794763.
3 Ibid.
4 "The 5 Biggest Biases That Affect Decision-Making."
5 "Blindspot," accessed February 24, 2021, https://blindspot.fas.harvard.edu/.
6 Marius Guenzel and Ulrike Malmendier, "Behavioral Corporate Finance: The Life Cycle of a CEO Career" (National Bureau of Economic Research, August 10, 2020), https://doi.org/10.3386/w27635.
7 Podcasts et al., "How Biases Influence CEOs Throughout Their Careers," *Knowledge@Wharton*, accessed February 24, 2021, https://knowledge.wharton.upenn.edu/article/how-biases-influence-ceos-throughout-their-careers/.
8 Ibid.
9 Guenzel and Malmendier, "Behavioral Corporate Finance."
10 Vicky McKeever, "BofA Says Companies with Greater Diversity Produce Higher Returns – Here's a List of Stocks to Watch," *CNBC*, March 9, 2021, https://www.cnbc.com/2021/03/09/bofa-stocks-with-the-greatest-diversity.html.
11 Erin Meyer, "What's Your Cultural Profile?", *Harvard Business Review*, August 14, 2014, https://hbr.org/2014/08/whats-your-cultural-profile.
12 Rich Maltzman and Jim Stewart, *How to Facilitate Productive Project Planning* (Maven House, 2018).

13 "Older Workers Need to Stop Believing Stereotypes About Themselves," *Harvard Business Review*, June 20, 2016, https://hbr.org/2016/06/older-workers-need-to-stop-believing-stereotypes-about-themselves.

14 Ibid.

15 Ijeoma Oluo, *So You Want to Talk about Race* (New York, NY: Seal Press, 2019).

16 TEDx Talks, *How to Have a Voice and Lean Into Conversations About Race | Amanda Kemp | TEDxWilmington*, 2017, https://www.youtube.com/watch?v=IF--2vGj7Tg.

17 Nehemiah Green, "70 Inclusive Language Principles That Will Make You A More Successful Recruiter (Part 1)," Medium, August 20, 2018, https://medium.com/diversity-together/70-inclusive-language-principles-that-will-make-you-a-more-successful-recruiter-part-1-79b7342a0923.

18 Mary C. Gentile, *Giving Voice to Values: How to Speak Your Mind When You Know What's Right*, 2010.

Bibliography

"Blindspot." Accessed February 24, 2021. https://blindspot.fas.harvard.edu/.

says, Cotman, Chireda. "Brain Stuff: The Neuroscience Behind Implicit Bias." *Spectra Diversity* (blog), December 27, 2017. https://www.spectradiversity.com/2017/12/27/unconscious-bias/.

Facebook, and Twitter. "Types of Cognitive Biases That Distort How You Think." *Verywell Mind*. Accessed March 18, 2021. https://www.verywellmind.com/cognitive-biases-distort-thinking-2794763.

Gentile, Mary C. *Giving Voice to Values: How to Speak Your Mind When You Know What's Right*, 2010.

Green, Nehemiah. "70 Inclusive Language Principles That Will Make You A More Successful Recruiter (Part 1)." *Medium*, August 20, 2018. https://medium.com/diversity-together/70-inclusive-language-principles-that-will-make-you-a-more-successful-recruiter-part-1-79b7342a0923.

Guenzel, Marius, and Ulrike Malmendier. "Behavioral Corporate Finance: The Life Cycle of a CEO Career." National Bureau of Economic Research, August 10, 2020. https://doi.org/10.3386/w27635.

Maltzman, Rich, and Jim Stewart. *How to Facilitate Productive Project Planning*. Maven House, 2018.

McKeever, Vicky. "BofA Says Companies with Greater Diversity Produce Higher Returns — Here's a List of Stocks to Watch." *CNBC*, March 9, 2021. https://www.cnbc.com/2021/03/09/bofa-stocks-with-the-greatest-diversity.html.

Meyer, Erin. "What's Your Cultural Profile?" *Harvard Business Review*, August 14, 2014. https://hbr.org/2014/08/whats-your-cultural-profile.

NeuroLeadership Institute. "The 5 Biggest Biases That Affect Decision-Making," April 9, 2019. https://neuroleadership.com/your-brain-at-work/seeds-model-biases-affect-decision-making/.

"Older Workers Need to Stop Believing Stereotypes About Themselves." *Harvard Business Review*, June 20, 2016. https://hbr.org/2016/06/older-workers-need-to-stop-believing-stereotypes-about-themselves.

Olua, Ijeoma. *So You Want to Talk about Race*. New York, NY: Seal Press, 2019.

Podcasts, Research, Wharton Business Daily, and North America. "How Biases Influence CEOs Throughout Their Careers." *Knowledge@Wharton*. Accessed February 24, 2021. https://knowledge.wharton.upenn.edu/article/how-biases-influence-ceos-throughout-their-careers/.

TEDx Talks. *How to Have a Voice and Lean Into Conversations About Race | Amanda Kemp | TEDxWilmington*, 2017. https://www.youtube.com/watch?v=IF--2vGj7Tg.

Chapter 9

Strategies for Building Workplaces of Belonging

Creating a culture to promote equity, inclusion, and belonging relies on leadership and stakeholders to inform and cocreate a shared vision and purpose that translates into the lived experience of all employees in their workplace environment. Cascading justice, equity, and inclusion throughout an organization requires engaging middle managers, team leaders, and employees by communicating vision and goals, building capacity, and providing resources. Capacity building in the form of J.E.D.I. development, tools, and resources for middle managers and team leaders is crucial to embedding shared vision. The saying goes, "Employees don't leave companies; they leave bad managers." Crucial to the J.E.D.I. transformation process is making your people feel that they belong every single day. It requires investing in training, tools, and process redesign to build a culture of belonging. Shared vision includes the lived experience of your employees which directly impacts the culture of your organization. Designing teams based on people-centered design helps to promote team norms and practices that value and focus on equity, inclusion, and belonging.

9.1 Team Norms

In today's work environment, most work is performed in teams; so, ensuring that we raise the collective J.E.D.I. capabilities of team leaders and team members is crucial. The impacts begin with team formation and team members acquisition practices. Team norms around processes, protocols, and dynamics also have an impact. Teams are comprised of people with different personalities, expertise, experiences, education, gender identity, gender expression, and work/life balance requirements. Often,

DOI: 10.1201/9781003168072-10

the team norms reflect the leader's requirements and preferences rather than those of the team members. A strong servant leader considers the needs of the team and creates an environment that facilitates team members thriving and growing. Creating a team dynamic that respects and welcomes diverse voices is crucial to promoting a team culture that embraces J.E.D.I. values

To better understand the attributes of an effective team, Google conducted research known as Project Aristotle. Their findings are of interest because the most effective teams aren't the ones comprised of the top performers or superstars. Instead, Google found that the most effective teams had team dynamics that promote belonging, which included the following characteristics:

1. Psychological safety
2. Dependability
3. Structure and clarity
4. Purpose
5. Impact[1]

Team psychological safety is described as creating a team environment where members feel that it is safe to take risks, ask questions, raise new ideas, or admit mistakes. Since members do not fear retribution or embarrassment from fellow teammates, they were free to bring their whole and true selves to team meetings. As a result, they contribute fully, which improves productivity and results. Through promoting psychological safety in the team norms, diversity of thought is expressed and valued. Team members thrive when they can depend upon one another for timely, accurate, and quality work. Clarity of project goals and one's individual role relative to the overall project helps individual contributors understand their role on the team. Google uses Objectives and Key Results (OKRs) to define project short- and long-term goals and to measure results. Finding purpose at work is also important for effective team dynamics. It can be a purpose related to environmental and social justice or it can be more personal such as providing for their family or engaging in a passion project. Team members thrive when they have alignment between work and purpose. Purpose goes hand in hand with impact. Team members want to understand how their work is contributing and making a difference in outcomes, which can be broader societal or organizational impacts. Effective teams want to feel that their contributions matter. In the end, researchers concluded that the effectiveness of teams related more to how they worked than who was on them. Effective teams are not that way because of superstar members; they are effective because of team norms and their alignment with supporting organizational culture that values justice, equity, and inclusion.

As we think about creating norms for teams to drive equity and inclusion, consider these questions to identify the norms of your own team.

1. Do you set the agenda ahead of time to allow for team feedback and topic prioritization?

2. Are there meeting guidelines to facilitate hearing all voices? Too often, the loudest voice in the room prevails!
3. Are you considering the needs of different personality types in your meetings? For example, extroverts vs. introverts.
4. Where are meetings held? If it is in person, how is the room set up? Is the room designed to reinforce a power dynamic or an exchange of equals?
5. Who takes notes? Does it rotate?
6. How are team roles and assignments distributed and shared?
7. Is the team structure static or dynamic?
8. Is time allocated to discuss project goals, team norms, and best practices to ensure team members' awareness and alignment?

As a team leader, consider the impact of team norms and dynamics on your team members. Think about ways that you may be able to improve their experience through adjustments to meeting structures, team representation, and role assignments. They also need to consider their team's dynamic and atmosphere, and whether it encourages contributions and feedback from team members. Figure 9.1 highlights some questions to consider that shed light on the team dynamic around input and feedback. Creating a team dynamic in which all team members feel empowered and valued is crucial for driving diversity of thought. Practicing open listening and respectful perspective taking as a team leader sets the example. Team leaders should be receptive to hearing constructive feedback. In fact, they should encourage and model this behavior by asking questions and encouraging thoughtful answers that may push back on assumptions. If a team member offers an opposing view, team leaders need to truly listen. Acknowledge team members' views, listen to their comments, and incorporate them into the decision-making process. Avoid tuning team members out, or worse, shutting them down. Creating an environment where the group feels safe suggesting new ideas, making some mistakes, and truly sharing their perspectives drives belonging and ultimately innovation. As a team leader, encourage investigation, collaboration, and conversation to drive impact.

Best practices include setting and communicating expectations for team members' work outputs as well as team meeting participation. Co-creating the agenda and sharing it ahead of time allows team members to raise issues and prioritize meeting

Figure 9.1 Creating a team environment for impact.

topics to meet their needs. It also allows them to consider the topics and be prepared to contribute to the conversation. Ensure that all team members understand that they have been invited to the meeting to contribute and that their insights and perspectives are valued. Consider the roles and responsibilities of the team members and ensure that the members have opportunities to grow and develop by assuming different roles and responsibilities. Some teams are agile with people coming together for a project and others are static with the core unit working on projects as a team or in collaboration with other groups/teams. Consider how teams are formed and which project teams get the high-profile assignments. If the perceived superstar team is given all the "Goldilocks" assignments, then they are going to be the team members given the best opportunity for advancement and career development. A manager and team leader have a great deal of impact around team members' access, equity, and inclusion in the workplace. These dynamics impact who within the organization is given opportunities that lead to advancement within the organization. As the McKinsey and Lean In research indicates, it is the first step of the managerial ladder, which begins the differentiation process for underrepresented groups.

Setting the ground rules for team dynamics is useful in creating J.E.D.I.-centric teams. Best practice includes developing a diversity, equity, and inclusion (DEI) statement to govern interactions. This DEI statement should be grounded in organizational vision, goals, and guidelines, but it should also reflect some details on how the team will function. In Appendix 9A is a DEI statement that I drafted for my course in the Bard MBA in Sustainability program to promote a group culture that aligns with our institutional J.E.D.I. vision and provides concrete action to support a group dynamic to promote equity and belonging. This DEI statement provides the group with a standard and a protocol to enter difficult conversation. It references the organization's code of conduct which focuses on respectful engagement including "Calling In" when possible. "Calling In" is an approach to respond to a microaggression made by another based on addressing the issues privately with a focus on shared learning and bridging the divide. "Calling Out" is most often done when the comment or statement is hurtful or harmful. In effect, it is hitting the pause button to allow for a reset in the conversation. The DEI statement provides action steps and escalation steps if a group member experiences discomfort or offense. Best practice to introduce and use a DEI statement is to discuss it as a group, and then vote on accepting it. Requesting all group members sign in acknowledgment of the DEI statement reinforces the group's mutual commitment to one another.

In Table 9.1, we share some best practices to adopt during team meetings to foster equity and inclusion and to promote a culture of belonging. As a best practice, draft your own team norms or guidelines that include shared commitments for communication within the team and with others, responsibility, and accountability. If you find that you need to redesign your systems and processes to build inclusive teams, read on.

Table 9.1 Ground Rules for Inclusive Meetings

Listen actively	Respect others when they are speaking. Listen to their perspective.
Speak from your own experience	Avoid generalizing or stereotyping.
Be on time	Practice timely attendance to demonstrate respect for others.
Respectfully challenge others	Challenge other team members by asking questions, focus on ideas not personal attacks.
Engage and participate	Come to meetings prepared to contribute to the team. Share your voice, perspective, and ideas.
Share your own experience	Don't invalidate another's experience.
The goal is not to agree	The goal is to listen and explore different perspectives and ideas. Brainstorm and diverge to generate ideas.
Consider body language	Much of communication is non-verbal. Be aware of your body language to ensure that it too is respectful.
Recognize the speaker and give the speaker the floor	Ensure that each person is given the opportunity to speak, and that full attention is paid to that person when speaking. Avoid conducting sidebar conversations.
Treat others as you wish to be treated	Keeping this fundamental rule in mind will focus your intentions and actions on inclusive behavior.

9.2 People-Centered Design

One of the ways to redesign systems and processes such as the talent ecosystem or team dynamics is to use a people-centered design approach combining principles from human-centered design with Appreciative Inquiry, which is discussed in detail in Chapter 7. In the first phase of the people-centered design as depicted in Figure 9.2, we engage our project team in dreaming about what is possible. We consider what we wish for our organization more broadly and our team more specifically. Then we consider what might be possible. This approach to dream gathering may include an organization-wide gathering or it may be more focused on a specific group or team.

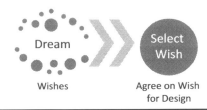

Figure 9.2 People-centered design.

Each member of the project team receives two votes to select the wish that will be chosen by the group on which to focus. The wish with the most votes wins. Voting can be done individually with an x, ., or another agreed upon mark to ensure that all voices are heard and equally valued in the voting process.

Figure 9.3 Wish selection process.

Through this process, the team gathers hopes and wishes for their organization or team. Next, they go through a brainstorming exercise as depicted in Figure 9.3. Post-it notes or a digital tool such as Google's Jamboard can be used for gathering ideas. Once the ideas have been gathered use a voting mechanism that provides all group members with an equal voice in selecting priorities. We recommend using a voting scheme where each participate receiving two votes to cast for their top two wishes. Through this process, the group identifies a mutually identified wish to focus their efforts on achieving. Once the votes are counted, the wish with the most votes moves forward to the design phase. Using this approach allows for brainstorming of diverse ideas and for each group members to share their wishes without group dynamics impacting the outcome of wish selection. In this example, the wish selected is to increase the percentage of underrepresented groups in the candidate talent pipeline.

The design stage, as depicted in Figure 9.4, considers what conditions have supported the desired outcome or wish in the past. The design phase is an opportunity to hear a variety or perspectives and experiences on the conditions that supported this outcome. These might be practices experienced at other organizations, ideas from an industry event, or even something done by another group or team.

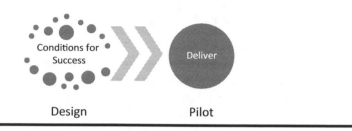

Figure 9.4   People-centered design: Phase 2.

Create a pilot program based on conditions for success that support designing a better process for increasing the pipeline for diverse talent.

Figure 9.5   Design a pilot for recruiting more diverse candidates.

This phase is a second brainstorming session, and creativity and innovation should be encouraged. In this example, the group considers what conditions contribute to promoting underrepresented candidates to apply for new positions or promotions. The conditions for success include those listed in Figure 9.5.

The ideas appearing on the post-it notes include ideas such as expanding sources of talent to include institutions that traditionally have higher levels of diverse candidates, reviewing job descriptions for language and requirements, reviewing websites and talent platforms to ensure that organizational diversity is authentically represented, and evaluating the data from assessment tools to determine if these assessments are more favorable to certain groups of people. Once the team agrees on a design focus, they develop a pilot or a program to test within the organization to test the impact on improving candidate diversity within its talent recruitment pipeline.

People-centered design is a tool that can be leveraged to promote a team dynamic that values diversity of identity, experience, and thought. In addition, the structure and process encourage all voices to be heard and valued, not just the strongest voices. It also allows for team members to weigh the ideas individually, which reduces group think, and encourages innovation. Implementing people-centered design takes time and commitment, but the outcomes generated are impactful and lead to meaningful change. As a result, team buy-in and engagement is significantly higher and better aligned with an organization's J.E.D.I. strategy.

9.3 Inclusive Benefits, Wellness, and Well-Being

In the U.S., millennials indicate that they are looking for a position within an organization that offers healthcare benefits. In many countries around the world, adequate healthcare is a universal right, but in the U.S., it is not. Yet, the number one reason for personal bankruptcies is medical bills.[2] Deductibles and surprise medical bills are the most often cited affordability problems.[3] In order to achieve an organization's J.E.D.I. vision, healthcare and benefits access must be part of the conversation. Lower incomes, higher deductibles, and chronic conditions are all associated with affordability challenges for healthcare. Low-income and marginalized communities are disproportionally impacted by these challenges and often forego or delay care. Our most vulnerable citizens run the greatest risk of becoming ill and not having adequate insurance. Or they have no insurance because of falling behind on premiums due to loss of work, illness or another disruptive event. Even being burdened with long-term, continuous, often rising health insurance costs can create an unmanageable burden for low-income workers and underserved communities. Without a more holistic safeguard for healthcare, medical emergency financial shocks will continue to disrupt earning streams and wealth accumulation. As a result, closing the wealth gap will be impossible. From a wellness and well-being perspective, offering adequate health insurance coverage, educating employees on plan options, and providing a resource for covering premiums in the event of loss of work is crucial. Consider creating a self-funded reserve fund where employees pay in a small premium to have limited premium coverage. While Health Savings Accounts (HSAs) under IRS code do allow for paying healthcare continuation coverage such as COBRA for coverage during unemployment, there is not a safety net to cover the gap when someone is still employed but unable to work for several weeks. HSAs also require supplemental employee contributions which may not be possible for low-income workers. Addressing the healthcare gap is crucial for addressing the wealth gap. As an employer, consider your role in offering benefits to employees and structuring work to allow them to be eligible for benefits. Unfortunately, in the U.S. healthcare costs continue to consume a significant portion of employers' benefits budgets and employees' salaries.

Benefit offerings must be designed or redesigned to appeal to a multigenerational workforce. As millennials and Gen Z workers representation in the workforce rises, their needs are further shaping employee benefit requirements and employer benefits offerings. Workers from these generations are interested in employers contributing to their student loan payments. The 2019 Society for Human Resource Management Benefits Survey indicates that company-paid employee student loan benefits are being offered by 8% of the organizations surveyed – a 100% increase from 2018. As part of the coronavirus stimulus package, employers are allowed to contribute up to $5,520 toward their worker's student loans on a tax-free basis.[4] Because of the growing percentage of workers from the millennial and Gen Z generations, we expect to see the demand for this type of benefit rise. To support new parents, lactation/caregivers' rooms are offered by over 50% of companies surveyed, which is a significant increase from 2015.[5] Family leave policies above the required federal Family and Medical Leave Act have been rising. The percentage of respondents offering paid leave for new fathers has been on the rise moving much closer to the percentage of respondents offering paid leave for new mothers.

If much of your workforce is baby boomers, consider adding benefits to support aging parents such as caregiving benefits and flexible work policies to support mental health and work-life balance. Organizations such as Homethrive (https://www. homethrive.com/) are offering elder care benefits solutions that combine access to a network of social workers and a digital platform to support home caregiving for aging parents. This type of benefit targets employees, who are working later into their lives and need support with aging parents. Women continue to bear a disproportional burden of caregiving. As we saw during the pandemic, women left the workforce to serve as caregivers at disproportionate levels. To address the needs of women at work, the full lifecycle of caregiver requirements needs to be considered-new parents, school age children, health related caregiving, and aging parents.

Many benefits have inequities in terms of availability, access, and cost. Employers need to consider the inequities that may be embedded into their benefit offerings, and with the input of key stakeholder groups begin to make benefits more equitable across the organization. Consider solutions to promote health and wellness in every employee including time off for doctor's visits, drop-in day care, and additional support systems to ensure that the most vulnerable employees have access to these benefits. The following are some benefits that have been identified for promoting equity and inclusion for workers in the LGBTQ+ community:

1. Paid parental leave and family building support
2. Paid sick leave
3. Professional development opportunities
4. Student loan repayment
5. Reimbursement for fertility treatment
6. Paid volunteer time
7. Retirement plans[6]

For LGBTQ+ community members having access to paid parental leave is necessary to support raising a family. For families that use family building approaches such as adoption or fertility treatments, having access to family building benefits helps them with the burden of these expenses. Paid sick time encourages all employees to make their health a priority, but for members of the LGBTQ+ community, finding a healthcare facility and professional who acknowledges and supports their identities is especially difficult and time-consuming. This benefit is especially important to members of the LGBTQ+ community as they often face discrimination, lack of knowledge, and other obstacles when seeking healthcare. The National LGBTQ Task Force reports that 19% of transgender and non-conforming people have been refused care because of their identity.[7] In addition, 28% of respondents report deferring care when sick or injured because of having experienced discrimination or disrespect within healthcare systems.[8] Professional support through networking, mentoring, and sponsorship all foster career growth and advancement. The LGBTQ+ community has additional support needs to navigate issues such as discussing gender identity at the office, knowing their legal rights and employer obligations, transitioning in the workplace, and networking with LGBTQ+ colleagues and allies. Members of the LGBTQ+ community report feeling concerned about their level of student loans. For transgender employees who are transitioning, employers should consider benefits such as prescription benefits for hormone therapy, medical visits and lab procedures related to hormone therapy, gender-affirming surgical procedures, and long-term leave for surgical procedures.

Respondents to a Student Loan Hero survey indicate that LGBTQ+ students have $112,607 in student debt on average compared to the general population average of $96,211.[9] This statistic reflects that many LGBTQ+ youth have been denied support by their families and have had to manage their living and educational expenses on their own. Fertility benefits defray the cost of treatments. Fertility treatments are expensive with the average lifetime amount of U.S. fertility coverage benefit at $36,000. Many LGBTQ+ families use fertility treatments to build their families. Paid time off to volunteer allows employees to select the organizations to whom they wish to contribute their time and resources. For those organizations supporting the LGBTQ+ community, this benefit can broaden their impact and community support. A recent survey reports that only 47% of LGBTQ+ people have retirement savings compared to 56% of the general population.[10] Part of this differential is a result of earnings levels, job insecurity, and discrimination that depress lifetime earning capabilities. As a result, LGBTQ+ community members' ability to support themselves in retirement is challenging so retirement benefit programs add a safety net of support.

Providing 401K and other retirement investment options allows employees to plan and save for retirement. The investment options should include funds with ESG investments allowing individuals to choose to align their retirement investments with their values around environmental, social, and governance issues. While fund investment methodologies vary their positive and negative screens for impact, it is possible to gather information on investments that relate to both internal and external ESG impact. Including ESG funds in the mix of 401K investment options for employees better aligns investment strategies with their personal values.

Wellness and well-being programs have become a standard for organizations seeking to attract and retain top talent. Research indicates that 80% of employees with robust health and wellness programs report feeling engaged and appreciated by their employers. To develop and implement a successful wellness program, an organization must consider the design process as highlighted in Figure 9.6. The initial step requires gathering information from your employees to better understand their needs. Consider that needs may differ by generation, income level, and

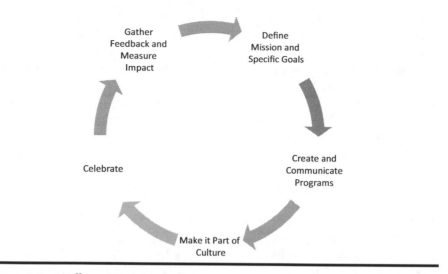

Figure 9.6 Wellness program design.

other identity factors. It is important to survey your employees, understand their needs, and treat them as individuals using benefits and wellness programs as tools to help customize the work environment for the individual. Revising benefits to be reflective of the needs of a diverse workforce is an impactful part of moving from a dominant to an equitable culture. Major categories for wellness programs include:

- Nutrition and healthy living
- Group activities and fitness
- Fitness challenges, competitions, and contests
- Rejuvenation
- Perks and fun activities
- Productivity enhancers
- Mental health
- Personal growth[11]

Programs can be both impactful and fun such as improving healthy eating habits by bringing in a chef either in person or virtually to teach people some healthy and quick recipes to make at home. If you have a location with a company cafeteria, consider offering dinner to go options for employees and their families. During team meetings, taking the time to acknowledge team efforts and to share gratefulness reduces burnout. Financial health workshops guide employees in budgeting and saving as well as financial literacy. Offering flexible work, even one day a week, accommodates work/life integrations and boosts productivity. Promote environmental justice by rewarding employees who drive EVs with designated EV parking. Offer employer matches for employee contribution to not for profits to enhance the impact of their contributions to preferred charitable organizations. Another option is giving employees time from workdays that can be allocated to volunteering. These are just a few wellness and well-being ideas. The key is to offer what is of value to your organization's employees and to create a selection of engaging programs that appeals and supports the diversity of your workforce.

As with all projects, it is crucial to ensure leadership support in terms of resource allocation but also in terms of program advocacy and usage. If senior leadership accesses and utilizes the programs, it is acceptable for others to do so as well. Establishing goals for wellness helps to ensure that programs have meaningful targets, which should be supported by metrics to measure impact. Sharing the mission and reporting on progress with employees drives transparency and engagement. Promote employee participation by establishing clear wellness and health data use policies that are shared and monitored for compliance.

Develop a communication plan to inform employees and other key stakeholders about your organization's wellness and well-being programs. In many organizations, some of their most interesting wellness and well-being offerings are, unfortunately, their best kept secrets. If your employees don't know of these programs existence and how to access them, they aren't benefitting either the employees or the organization. Consider your communication plan and channels for push and pull communications. Letting employees know once about a program isn't sufficient. Use regular announcements as well as a resource guide to support ongoing engagement. When designing programs, make participating convenient for employees. In addition, develop an engagement plan for managers to educate them on the programs as well as the benefits for employee health, well-being, engagement, and productivity. Prioritizing employee health, wellness, and well-being must be part of organizational culture to be authentic and to promote participation and managerial support.

Celebrate successes by showing employees you appreciate their investment in their physical and mental health and well-being. For contests, competitions, and challenges, use company swag and gift cards to fun activities or healthy restaurants as prizes. If individual employees reach a personal health goal, offer incentives, such as a discount on health insurance premiums. Celebrate reaching a health and wellness organizational goal by giving everyone an extra ½ day off. Or just celebrate the individual by giving them their birthday off. There are many ways to celebrate. The important point is to track and recognize both individual and organizational achievements. The key to just, equitable and inclusive wellness and well-being programs is to keep your people at the center of your design.

9.4 Inclusive Work Structures

While flexible work arrangement in terms of both location and time were an anomaly before the pandemic, they are much more mainstream today. Building a hybrid work model that accommodates both individuals and the organization requires getting creative and thinking outside of the box. The benefit of hybrid work is a more purposeful, agile, flexible, and productive work structure. In Figure 9.7, we view work flexibility on a time (hours) and place (location) matrix. As the figure suggests, we have four basic designs for hybrid work based on the needs of the employee and organization. Organizations can offer employees more flexibility on where they work, when they work, or both. During the pandemic, many workers had flexibility in their work location with some working from home, parent's houses, and even vacation locations. Others had flexibility in both location and hours worked. Others had to be onsite, but hours were more flexible, which helped with caregiving, reduced virus exposure, and lessened stress. Many workers such as healthcare, warehouse, and factory workers were required to be on location for normal shifts despite the pandemic. A common stressor reported during the pandemic was that workers felt they were constantly at work because their work hours morphed to much longer hours than normal office hours. Employers need to care if an employee works extra hours as it can impact employer obligations such as overtime or benefits eligibility as well as cause employee burnout. Thoughtfully constructing hybrid work structures is an important tool to better meet the work-life integrations of both employees and organizations. From an equity and inclusion perspective, hybrid work allows work flexibility for caregiving, accessibility challenges, religious requirements, health concerns, and mental health, as well as environmental justice by reducing traffic congestion, emissions, and real estate footprint.

Effectively structuring and managing a hybrid workforce requires significant change from a manager's perspective. In a hybrid work structure program that HRcomputes designed, a primary focus was on manager awareness, education, and adoption. The recommendation was that all roles should be constructed to offer hybrid work, as a norm rather than an exception, using formats like flexible hours, flexible location, compressed work weeks, and remote work options. While managers were given the right to approve requests for flexible work arrangement,

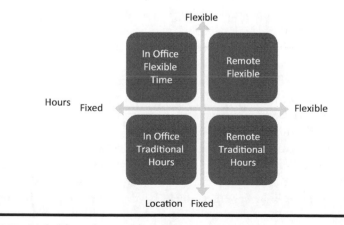

Figure 9.7   Hybrid work structures.[12]

the program was supported by a technology platform that allowed flexible work arrangements to be reviewed and approved by the next level of the organization to ensure equity, fairness and consistency across the organization.

When allowing workers to adopt a hybrid work structure, managers need to consider jobs and tasks, employee preference, projects and workflows, inclusion, and fairness.[13] Each job has a different combination of requirements consisting of focus, cooperation, collaboration, and productivity. The key is to develop a combination of offerings and resources to support hybrid work and allow each of these requirements to be met while minimizing the downside of tradeoffs for organizational impacts. As a best practice, include a diverse selection of employees on the workstream tasked with developing hybrid work solutions. This group should hold "listening" sessions to gather feedback from across the organizations. The client's hybrid work program leveraged a self-assessment tool designed to help employees identify their own preferences, capabilities, and requirements to select a best fit flexible work arrangement. This approach encouraged both employee and manager acceptance and prepared both groups for what to expect under a hybrid work arrangement.

Hiroki Hiramatsu, the Global Head of HR at Fujitsu, a Japanese company, realized that out of the great remote work experiment during the pandemic that organizations have an opportunity to redefine work-life balance for both employees and organizations. To make hybrid work more effective, Fujitsu created an ecosystem of workspaces that they called the borderless office using hubs, satellites, and shared offices. Hubs, which are in major cities with an open floor plan layout are designed for cross-functional collaboration. These locations include collaboration tools and technologies to support team building, brainstorming, and innovation. Hubs are used to collaborate with customers and partners as well. The satellite locations are designed to support collaboration and cooperation for project teams working on a shared project. These locations allow for both in-person and virtual meetings with the support of video conferencing facilities and secure networks. Shared offices are located all over Japan at convenient locations such as near train stations for ease of access. They are used by employees traveling to visit customers or as an alternative to working from home. They are designed as quiet spaces to support focused work.[14] Organizations are redesigning workspaces to support a variety of work styles, structures and objectives. Some areas support small team collaborations and individual focused work; others offer open areas furnished with coffee bars, tables, and couches to promote casual conversations and serendipitous gatherings. Workplace design needs to be people centered and align with the organization's J.E.D.I. culture and vision to support organizational justice.

In addition, tools and resources must be provided for managers to manage a workforce with differing work structures. In response to sudden plant and facility closures, managers leveraged new tools such as robotic devises to facilitate inspections allowing data to be reviewed remotely by team members. Other managers are revising workflows, workloads, work projections, and deliverable timeliness to better align with hybrid work models. Reviewing transactional processes and leveraging process automation and artificial intelligence supports hybrid work structures. Training managers to embrace managing virtually is part of the transformation. Managers need to promote thinking differently about work requirements and encourage employees to schedule time and space for collaboration and conversation, and even fun events like Gratitude Friday, Wellness Wednesday, etc. Managerial skills and knowledge around hybrid work need to be developed. They must be conversant in hybrid work and act as roles models in terms of using the work structure and making time for interactions with employees. Crucial to this process is ensuring that all employees are included in meetings and team events and that workers that work remotely don't become second-class citizens. As part of the transition, managers must develop new metrics to meaningfully measure productivity. Face time will no longer be the metric for productivity. While technology-based tools can help, planning and communication are key to successful management of employees and workflows in hybrid work structures.

9.5 Designing for Accessibility

Disabilities impact over 26% of adults in the U.S.[15] As we live our lives, we are all at risk of developing disabilities. Any type of accident can leave someone disabled. Falling while hiking can leave someone blind or an automobile accident can leave someone with a physical disability. Becoming disabled can happen to anyone and a person's ability to be gainfully employed should not be impacted by a disability. To address disabilities, which are experienced by a significant portion of the labor market, employers need to develop an inclusive strategy to support workers with disabilities and to ensure that they feel welcome and valued in our workplaces. Focusing on designing for accessibility necessitates taking an appreciative approach by asking questions such as:

1. What are we trying to achieve?
2. How do we want to be perceived by both external and internal stakeholders including people with disabilities?
3. Who should be included in the development of the plan?
4. Who can we partner with to achieve our goals?
5. How will we define and measure success?

Designing a workplace for accessibility and inclusion requires creating a work environment that is flexible to meet employees' needs to create a work environment that supports belonging. Inclusive design includes three principles: accessible, usable, and universal. Accessible design considers the accessibility of products, services, and facilities to people with disabilities. These include considerations such as curb cuts, door handles, adjustable desks, handicapped accessible washrooms, Braille signage, and color-contrast setting on device screens. When designing for accessibility, ensure that diverse voices, including those of people with disabilities, are part of the planning and design. Leverage survey tools to gather feedback from employees on what creates a culture of belonging, and leverage focus groups to test prototypes and designs to promote inclusion. The design phase needs to think about usability of products, tools, and other resources. Areas to consider include organizational technology support such as software to support screen readers for the visually impaired and creating ADA compliant websites. Creating a culture of belonging for people with disabilities goes beyond designing physical space and requires looking deeply at programs, processes, and policies. To design and implement effective solutions to support employees with disabilities, consider people and partners who can provide resources, support, and guidance during the journey. Often solutions that were originally developed for people with disabilities become universal design as the idea enhances everyone's lives. Examples include texting, originally designed for people with hearing loss, and automatic door openers, originally designed for people with mobility limitations.

There are several free resources to help through the process of recruiting and supporting a workforce that includes people with disabilities. The Vocational Rehabilitation and the National Employment Team support employers in building inclusion plans and implementing programs for recruitment, hiring advancement, and retention. In addition, these organizations provide support to the candidates to better help them meet the needs of the employers in terms of setting career expectations and developing marketable skills. Their Talent Acquisition Portal provides resource for employers seeking candidates with disabilities and job seekers with disabilities looking for employment.

Talent Acquisition Portal (TAP) is a collaboration between the council of State Administrators of Vocational Rehabilitation, the National Employment Teams, and disABLEDperson, Inc., a not-for-profit organization. TAP is an online database that includes a national talent pool of Vocational Rehabilitation approved agency candidates seeking employment as well as a job posting board for businesses seeking applicants with disabilities. The process is facilitated by agencies and teams supporting applicants. Candidate and employer services include pre-employment, recruitment and retention support, staff training on disability awareness and labor laws, DEI strategy, consultation, financial support, and employee assistance. (https://tapability.org/employer-overview)

The pandemic has disproportionately impacted employees with disabilities. Approximately, one fifth of people with disabilities have lost their job compared to one seventh in the general population.[16] In addition, many people with disabilities rely on the workplace for social interactions and service delivery. The abrupt shift to working from home significantly impacted their lives and access to support services. In order to bridge the gap for employees with intellectual disabilities making the transition to remote work, Bank of America's team prioritized offering support to facilitate the transition. Mark Feinour, support services executive director, assumed the task of guiding his employees through the work from home transition. He set up personalized trainings to get employees familiar with new technology and organized programs to help with personal issues like medication refills and flu shots. To retain a sense of community, he focused on promoting connections and communication with a weekly mailing to employees that included cards, newsletters, and games. They even collaborated on a fun project by collecting recipes to create a quarantine cookbook that was shared with community members. Appreciating and valuing people with intellectual disabilities has been a major talent win for Bank of America.[17]

From an accessibility perspective, hybrid work options can open the world of employment opportunities for people with physical disabilities as well as people with neurodiversity. Neurodiversity is defined as the range of differences in individual brain function and behavioral traits. By normalizing hybrid work for all, the work environment becomes more inclusive for those that don't thrive in a typical office setting. For people who are introverted and prefer to process information before responding, remote work helps to even the playing field. For neurodiverse people, using technology and digital tools to contribute moves from being the exception to being the norm. Hybrid work structures such as distributed teams, flexible hours, and remote locations are redefining the nature of work making economic viability and prosperity much more accessible for people with neurodiversity or disabilities.

DESIGNING A PLAYBOOK TO BUILD A CULTURE OF BELONGING FOR PEOPLE OF ALL ABILITIES

The following is a conversation with Cara Pelletier, a diversity, equity and belonging leader, who served as the first Sr. Director Diversity, Equity, & Belonging at Ultimate Software until late 2020. Ultimate Software is now part of UKG, a leading cloud-based human capital software organization formed by combining Ultimate Software and Kronos. At UKG, their purpose is people.

Cara holds a master's degree in Organizational Leadership from Gonzaga University and a Certificate in Public Leadership from Harvard Kennedy School. For the last 13 years, Cara worked at Ultimate Software where she led the teams that built Ultimate's leadership development and diversity and inclusion programs from the ground, up. She was recently named one of North America's Most Influential D&I Leaders 2020 by Hive Learning and has appeared in the New York Times, Forbes, Fast Company, HR Dive and other publications.

IDEATION

At Ultimate, we want to be an employer of choice for people with disabilities. We set this goal after doing some research on our employee population, the greater labor pool, and our competitive marketplace. We found that employee data indicated that about 20% of our employees identified that they had some type of disability. Because we have such long tenure for employees, we believed this figure would rise as our employee population aged. We also learned that many of our employees who do not have disabilities have family members who do or are friends or caregivers to people with disabilities. Creating a more inclusive work environment for people with disabilities was important for both attraction and retention of talent.

We also took a look at our talent pool, which we know was very tight prior to the pandemic. According to the U.S. Bureau of Labor Statistics, in 2019, 30.9% of the employment population ages 16–64 reported being disabled and the employment ratio for this group was only 19.3% compared to 66.3% for those without disabilities.[18] From a talent pool perspective, there are a great many talented people with disabilities who are not being attracted and retained by employers. Research published by Harvard Business Review reminds us of the organizational value created through creating a culture of belonging – 56% increase in job performance. We felt it was a competitive advantage to create a culture of inclusion for people with disabilities to attract top talent to our organization.

In addition, we took a look at organizations that rank companies on their performance relative to creating a culture of inclusion for people with disabilities such as Disability:IN with its Disability Equity Index. We realized that most of our competitors were not addressing this issue in terms of culture and leadership, enterprise-wide access, employment practices, community engagement, and supplier diversity. Again, we saw this as an opportunity for competitive advantage.

At Ultimate, we had undertaken an initiative to build our software with accessibility in mind. Our then CIO, Adam Rogers, saw accessibility for people with disabilities as a business imperative. We began building software from the ground up to meet the needs of people with disabilities including the visually impaired and those who use screen readers and other assistive technologies. Our approach was both the right thing to do and made good business sense. In the fourth quarter of 2020, news broke that one of our major competitors, ADP, was being sued because of complaint filed by LightHouse for the Blind and Visually Impaired, a not-for-profit organization. The complaint states that the ADP payroll and human capital management cloud services are not accessible to people who need to use screen readers to translate digital text into synthesized speech. Using our "People First" pillar as our lens, we were able to leverage our technology platform to both serve people and improve our business outcome.

THE 5 P FRAMEWORK

We used the framework highlighted in Figure 9.8 to drive this initiative forward in a meaningful way within a short timeframe of only 12 months. We were able to achieve our goals despite being a small group of two with limited resources by being strategic with our budget and by engaging other groups in the organization and inviting them to be part of the transformation. Providing information and resources for others allowed them to run with their own ideas for driving impact across the organization.

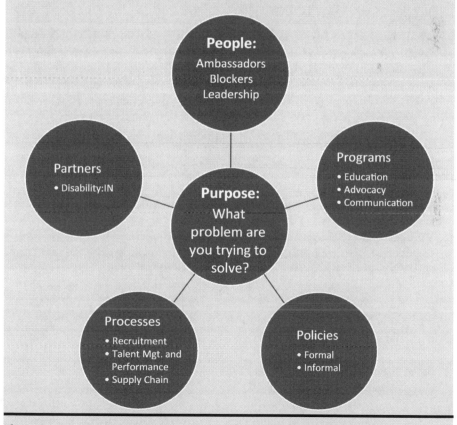

Figure 9.8   The 5 P framework.

PEOPLE

Starting with people, we identified an executive sponsor, former chief people officer, Vivian Maza. She was instrumental in being a champion for the initiative and for removing obstacles and barriers. We spent time thinking about who in our organization would be strong champions because they were personally interested and involved with promoting opportunities for people with disabilities. We also thought about who might serve as barriers or obstacles during this transformation. The main objections that we received were concerns about how people could deliver on their own job requirements and performance metrics while incorporating changes to build a more inclusive culture for people with disabilities. Once we were able to address these concerns with viable solutions, most people were onboard with the mission to build a culture of disability inclusion.

PROGRAMS

We developed a variety of programs from foundational to really transformational. We focused on advocacy and education. We had traditional classroom training and online learning options to cover some of the basics on engaging with people with disabilities. We helped people overcome being uncomfortable about saying or doing the wrong thing. We brought in a variety of speakers to share their own advocacy stories. Speakers included Haben Girma, a disability activist, and the first deaf and blind graduate of Harvard Law School and Alice Wong, a disability activist, who writes and produces the Disability Visibility Project, which shares stories of amazing disabled people. We hosted events to raise global accessibility awareness and offered workshops to share with participants what it is like to use a screen reader and Braille interpretation with our software.

Communication was a significant part of our programming initiative, and we developed a communication plan to educate, inform, engage, and update our people on programs and progress. We used our "All About Us" newsletter to highlight stories about people with disabilities. One of the most popular stories was one that focused on a guide dog used by a manager in our Atlanta office to ensure that his diabetes was kept under control. Everyone loved the dog! The goal of the communication plan was to infuse a culture of belonging for people with disabilities in a systematic and meaningful way and to normalize the conversation about disability as a regular and accepted part of everyday work life.

Other programming developed more organically. We had an intern, who was on the autism spectrum, and they developed a panel discussion in partnership with other employees who either have autism or have children with autism. Their program focused on what autism looks like at work and how can we create a work environment that is sensitive and welcoming to autistic employees. It was a huge success and it involved people from across the organization.

POLICIES

We reviewed our human resource and benefits policies to ensure that we weren't creating unintentional barriers for people with disabilities. Specifically, we looked at our disclosure and request for reasonable accommodation policies with an eye toward facilitating accommodation requests. We reviewed our flexible work arrangement and flexible hours policies to ensure that they considered the needs of the disabled community. We even considered employee handbook items like dress code to ensure that they met the needs of people with disabilities especially those with mobility issues who may be using wheelchairs or other adaptive equipment.

We also reviewed our facilities to ensure that we are both ADA compliant and are providing welcoming access. Often these are not the same; there can be a considerable difference between adhering to the letter of the law and providing a workspace that is both compliant and truly supports the unique lived work experience of disabled employees. Our facilities and campus operations team believe that our buildings should be more than just buildings. They should reflect our values and welcome all our employees home. In order to review our physical space, we hired a consultant who visited several of our buildings in their wheelchair to see how welcoming the workspace is for people with a mobility disability. I invited our facilities manager and their team to join us for the facilities review. They were so engaged with the project that they immediately began coming up with no- and low-cost ideas to improve accessibility. One of the ideas was so simple but so impactful. It involved asking your beverage vending machine vendor to fill the racks vertically rather than horizontally, so that a person in a wheelchair could access the full offering of beverages.

PROCESSES

We began this process with an imagining meeting. What could we do to create a welcoming workplace for people with disabilities? We invited a cross-functional team as we were looking to drive transformative change across the organization. We offered to pay for team members' flights if their manager would give them the time to attend this initial summit. By allocating our budget to support partnering, we were able to move the project forward in an impactful way.

At the imagine meeting, we included representatives from facilities, learning, talent acquisition, product development, human capital, etc. We began the process of reimagining the talent acquisition process, interviewer training, employee training, manager training, and the performance management processes as well as our facilities layouts and supplier diversity. When you consider what we accomplished in 12 months, it really is transformational.

We know that we needed training for our recruiters. Our partner, Disability:IN, offered a program for our recruiters to interview college students with severe disabilities so that they would become accustomed to interviewing people with disabilities. It was a great success and helped our recruiters hone their skills while also providing valuable career feedback to talented students. Today, several of our people serve as mentors for these college students as they begin the process of launching their own careers. We've also offered paid internships to several students as well.

PARTNERS

Finding the right partner was crucial in allowing us to deliver an award-winning program within a year. We partnered with Disability:IN, a leading non-profit resource for business disability inclusion worldwide. Their goal is to create an inclusive global economy where people with disabilities participate fully and meaningfully. They are amazing partners and provided toolkits, guidance, and resources. Some helpful resources included an RFP guideline for vendors to complete relative to their own actions to support people with disabilities, a list of suppliers with disability-owned businesses, and language for our website to promote inclusion for people with disabilities. Leveraging partnerships is key to making change that is both impactful and timely.

OUTCOME

We are honored to have earned 100% from the Disability Equality Index for our inclusion of people with disabilities especially in the areas of culture and leadership, enterprise-wide access, employment practices, community engagement, and supplier diversity. While the award was fantastic, the most meaningful impact was much more personal.

Our employee resource group for employees with disabilities is called ADAPT: Accessibility and Disability Allies Partnering Together. The ADAPT EERG Executive Sponsor, John Mc Gregor, CIO, joined our National Disability Awareness Month event in October. John has a special interest in ADAPT as it is our ERG for people with disabilities and John has a close relationship with a person who is deaf. For this special event, Mandy Harvey, a renowned singer and songwriter known for her America's Got Talent performance who is also deaf, was our headliner. As I watched Mandy and John backstage, they were having a conversation by signing to one another. For me, it was humbling to see the humanity of the moment and to see the impact that DEI work has on making the world a better, more welcoming place for everyone, even our C-level executives.

On a more macro level, our organization created a program called Kids Kamps to help support our employees who are parents working remotely with school-aged children during COVID-19. As with many organizations, we had employees doing triple duty as employees, parents, and teachers simultaneously. When we released the program, I received an email from a parent asking why there wasn't a Kids Kamp for her son with autism. We had done such a good job messaging about our commitment to building a culture of belonging for people with disabilities that she felt comfortable asking for this level of support. While the Kids Kamp initiative was not a DEI program, we quickly raised her concerns and were able to facilitate a solution.

WHAT IS NEXT?

While I am moving on to a new opportunity with Moderna, the next area of focus for DEI at UKG is building a culture of allyship. Many of us are well-intentioned White people. We ask questions like: What can I do? And how can I show up to support BIPOC colleagues? When we look at systemic barriers, we need to consider privilege, which comes in a variety of forms. Privilege can mean race, education, socioeconomic status, safety, food security, and a whole host of other privileges. Allyship is using your privilege to help those who are less privileged. It can take many forms and fundamentally asks whose voice is missing from a conversation, meeting, project, etc. and how can I facilitate inclusion of that voice. In order to really drive equity and inclusion, we all need to better understand our own bias and privilege and work to take actions to actively change our behaviors.

9.6 New Ideas

In order to allow employees to express their voices, consider creating a new type of affinity group of activists that is established with employer structure and governance but directed by employees. The idea is the creation of an employee impact group (EIG) that is an ERG and volunteer program hybrid. This structure allows employees to fund group selected passion projects through payroll withholding, volunteer hours, and business skills and expertise. To qualify, the values, mission, and vision of the EIG must align with the organization's J.E.D.I. mission. The organization provides guidance through establishing a framework to support these employee lead initiatives including a set of governance standards for oversight and operation. Here are several use cases for EIGs:

1. Employees form a group and provide funding with the purpose of making charitable contributions to community not-for-profit organizations selected by the group. Funding is contributed by employees and funds are directed by the group's grant making committee. This structure is similar to community-based organizations such as Impact 100 (https://impact100global.org/), an organization that transforms communities through collective philanthropic giving empowered by women, lead local chapters.
2. Employees form a group to provide volunteer hours, business expertise, and funding to one or a select group of community-based not-for-profit organizations. Employees can donate time, skills, or money to support selected charitable organization in alignment with the EIG's shared values and goals.
3. Employees form a group with a vision of making local investments to support community organizations, local development, artists, and small businesses. In effect, they act like an investment group making direct investments or providing loans. The Maryland Neighborhood Exchange is an example of a resource to identify local businesses including BIPOC-owned businesses seeking community investment. (https://www.communitywealthbuilders.org/md-exchange.html.)

Establishing EIGs empowers employees, supports their initiatives with corporate guidance, and allows them to harness the power of their collective voices to drive change and impact by extending community-based giving beyond corporate philanthropy.

Another idea is to include an employee representative as a member of the organizations board of directors. Including workforce representation at the board level offers a realistic perspective of an organization's policies and practices as they relate to organizational justice and equity and inclusion. Despite the SEC requiring disclosure on CEO compensation and more recently the CEO pay ratio, CEO median pay has continued to rise. The fact that CEO pay rose in 2020 during the pandemic when so many lost their livelihoods is disturbing. From an equity and justice perspective, board members really need to reevaluate their executive compensation practices. Including a worker's perspective when the board is voting on compensation packages would put pressure on those voting for stratospheric CEO pay packages. Reducing CEO performance pay and reallocating performance-based pay across the organization would have a significant impact on rebalancing social and racial wealth in the U.S., and it would begin to chip away at the widening pay and wealth gaps.

While unions have been marginalized in the U.S., in Europe, they remain strong and impactful. Germany has works councils, and as few as five workers in an organization may vote for the formation of a works council. Like a union, the works council represents employees excluding managing directors, managing boards, or senior staff members. Members of the works council have protection against dismissal. Works councils generally meet weekly during work hours in private to discuss concerns of the works council. They also hold assembly style meetings for employees during working hours several times a year. During these meetings, the works council discusses environmental, social, or economic policies with all employees. The cost of the work council is born by the employer.[19] Work councils are in addition to trade unions and are often independent of the trade unions. Their role is representing workers of a company. Imagine if workers had a voice with organizational leadership to raise issues related to environmental, social, and economic justice through a structure like works councils in the U.S. Conversations around worker compensation, benefits, training, and healthcare would change dramatically. Issues such as whether organizations or individuals should bear the cost of workforce reskilling and upskilling to meet changing market dynamics, and CEO compensation formulas and levels would be substantially reframed. The absence of workers' voices in organizational leadership creates inequity in policies, processes, and practices, which are further widening pay and wealth gaps.

9.7 Summary

Designing inclusive workplaces that promote belonging as a core tenant requires going deep within an organization's people, policies, and processes. While organizational vision and leadership is crucial to creating a culture of belonging so is embedding a culture of belonging deep within the organization so that it becomes part of daily activities. With most work occurring within teams, evaluating teams' formation, structure, norms, policies and protocols is crucial to building equity and inclusion. Redesigning work through a J.E.D.I. lens requires gathering diverse perspectives and voices to share ideas that support conditions for success as outlined in the people-centered design model. Supporting a diverse workforce means offering benefits, wellness, and well-being programs that meet the needs of individual employees rather than the dominate culture. Employers need to provide hybrid work options as the norm not the exception to encourage utilization of this option. Institutional resources and knowledge need to be developed and disseminated so that managers have the tools and resources to support hybrid work while meeting the needs of the organization and their customers. An organization cannot be inclusive without providing accessibility to all. The 5 P approach serves as a model to drive accessibility equity. To continue to drive J.E.D.I. transformation, we need to empower employees and provide access for them to impact leaders and organizational direction to ensure that societally we are addressing wealth, education, health, and pay inequities.

Questions

1. What team norms would you like to see adopted by your team?
2. How might you incorporate a DEI statement into your team's norms?

3. What appeals to you about people-centered design? What doesn't appeal to you?
4. How might people-centered design be used to drive impact within your organization?
5. What benefits would you like to see adopted by your employer? Why?
6. What role do you believe benefits play in promoting a culture of belonging?
7. What are some wellness or well-being programs you would enjoy?
8. What type of hybrid work structure would you prefer? Why?
9. How might your workplace be redesigned to improve accessibility?
10. What new ideas do you have to build a more inclusive and equitable workplace culture?

Appendix 9A

Diversity, Equity, and Inclusion Statement

In this course, it is my intention to align course objectives, structures, and classroom interactions with the Program DEI Vision statement.

Program DEI Vision Statement:

> A program that transcends the distinction of diversity, seeks to practice equity and inclusion, and allows students, alumni, and faculty members of all abilities, backgrounds, races/ethnicities, socioeconomic backgrounds, sexual orientations, and gender expressions to feel welcome and have access to the tools necessary for success.

Acknowledgment:

> We acknowledge the imbalance of power and privilege within our social systems often based on race, gender, gender identity, socioeconomic status, ability, language, religion, ethnicity, nationality, culture, and other tangible and intangible human characteristics that serve to create an uneven playing field and uphold White supremacy, power, and privilege while marginalizing other groups and individuals.

Goal:

> It is my intention that students from all backgrounds and perspectives be well-served by this course, that students' learning needs be addressed both in and out of class, and that the diversity that the students bring to this class be viewed as a resource, strength, and benefit. It is my intent

to present materials and activities that are respectful of diversity: gender identity, sexuality, disability, age, socioeconomic status, ethnicity, race, nationality, and culture. Your suggestions are encouraged and appreciated. Please let me know ways to improve the effectiveness of the course for you personally, or for other students or student groups.

I intend to foster an environment in which each class member can hear and respect each other. It is critical that each class member show respect for all worldviews expressed in class.

Please let me know if something said or done in the classroom, by either myself or other students, causes discomfort or offense. If and when this occurs, there are several ways to alleviate some of the discomfort or hurt you may experience:

1. Discuss the situation privately with me. I am open to listening to students' experiences and want to work with students to find acceptable ways to process and address the issue.
2. Discuss the situation with the class. Chances are there is at least one other student in the class who had a similar response to the material. Discussion enhances the ability for all class participants to have a fuller understanding of context and impact of course material and class discussions.
3. Notify me of the issue through another source such as your academic advisor, a trusted faculty member, or a peer. If for any reason you do not feel comfortable discussing the issue directly with me, I encourage you to seek out another, more comfortable avenue to address the issue.

In our dealings with peers, faculty, and others both inside and outside of the classroom setting, we plan to follow the Bard MBA Code of Conduct as highlighted below and fully outlined in the linked resource. Our goal is to promote a culture of belonging in which all class participants can bring their full selves to the conversation, while being respectful of others.

Community Code of Conduct

The purpose of the code of conduct is to facilitate respectful dialogue within all conversations in the community and ensure all members feel welcome and encouraged to participate in discussion.

1. Listen actively first, then respond.
2. Speak with respect toward others and your community.
3. Speak from your own experiences instead of generalizing ("I" instead of "you," "we" instead of "they").
4. Welcome diverse perspectives: the goal is not to agree, it is to gain a deeper understanding.

5. Do not be afraid to respectfully challenge one another by asking questions but refrain from personal attacks. Focus on ideas.
6. If a member of the community speaks disrespectfully, politely ask them to rephrase their statement or question (call in not call out).
   a. Take a moment to explain the impact of the statement or question and why you are asking them to rephrase the question.
   b. If someone asks you to rephrase your statement or question, calmly do so.
7. Be conscious of the space you are taking up (step up/step back).

In virtual conversations, use chat or physically raise your hand on video to speak next. (Turn your video on whenever possible to be fully present).

Notes

1 "Re:Work," accessed March 11, 2021, https://rework.withgoogle.com/print/guides/5721312655835136/.
2 Full Bio Follow LinkedIn Kimberly Amadeo is an expert on U.S. et al., "Do Medical Bills Really Bankrupt America's Families?," The Balance, accessed May 30, 2021, https://www.thebalance.com/medical-bankruptcy-statistics-4154729.
3 Liz Hamel, Cailey Muñana, and Mollyann Brodie, "Kaiser Family Foundation / LA Times Survey Of Adults With Employer-Sponsored Health Insurance," n.d., 36.
4 "More Employers Are Starting to Offer Student Loan Repayment Assistance," accessed June 1, 2021, https://news.yahoo.com/employers-student-loan-repayment-123755707.html.
5 "SHRM 2019 Employee Benefits Survey: Student Loan Repayment, Paternity Leave, Standing Desks and Telemedicine All Ticking Upward," *SHRM*, June 25, 2019, https://www.shrm.org/about-shrm/press-room/press-releases/pages/2019-shrm-employee-benefits-survey.aspx.
6 "7 Employee Benefits Your Company Needs to Be Truly LGBT Inclusive," Ladders | Business News & Career Advice, accessed June 2, 2021, https://www.theladders.com:443/career-advice/7-employee-benefits-your-company-needs-to-be-truly-lgbt-inclusive.
7 "New Report Reveals Rampant Discrimination against Transgender People by Health Providers, High HIV Rates and Widespread Lack of Access to Necessary Care," *National LGBTQ Task Force* (blog), October 13, 2010, https://www.thetaskforce.org/new-report-reveals-rampant-discrimination-against-transgender-people-by-health-providers-high-hiv-rates-and-widespread-lack-of-access-to-necessary-care-2/.
8 "New Report Reveals Rampant Discrimination against Transgender People by Health Providers, High HIV Rates and Widespread Lack of Access to Necessary Care."
9 "7 Employee Benefits Your Company Needs to Be Truly LGBT Inclusive."
10 Miranda Marquit, "Survey: Student Loans and the LGBTQ Community," *Student Loan Hero*, December 3, 2018, https://studentloanhero.com/featured/survey-lgbtq-student-borrowers-regret-loans/.
11 "121 Employee Wellness Program Ideas Your Team Will Love," *SnackNation* (blog), May 7, 2021, https://snacknation.com/blog/employee-wellness-program-ideas/.

12 Lynda Gratton, "How to Do Hybrid Right," *Harvard Business Review*, May 1, 2021, https://hbr.org/2021/05/how-to-do-hybrid-right.

13 Gratton.

14 Ibid.

15 CDC, "Disability and Health Overview | CDC," Centers for Disease Control and Prevention, September 15, 2020, https://www.cdc.gov/ncbddd/disabilityandhealth/disability.html.

16 "Bank of America Gets Creative in Supporting Employees with Disabilities," *Employee Benefit News*, April 13, 2021, https://www.benefitnews.com/news/bank-of-america-gets-creative-in-supporting-employees-with-disabilities.

17 "Bank of America Gets Creative in Supporting Employees with Disabilities."

18 Ibid.

19 "Dealing_with_german_works_councils.Pdf," accessed June 2, 2021, https://www.squirepattonboggs.com/-/media/files/insights/events/2011/10/works-councils-in-germany-confrontation-or-colla__/files/dealing-with-works-councils-tip-sheet/fileattachment/dealing_with_german_works_councils.pdf.

Bibliography

CDC. "Disability and Health Overview | CDC." Centers for Disease Control and Prevention, September 15, 2020. https://www.cdc.gov/ncbddd/disabilityandhealth/disability.html.

"Dealing_with_german_works_councils.Pdf." Accessed June 2, 2021. https://www.squirepattonboggs.com/-/media/files/insights/events/2011/10/works-councils-in-germany-confrontation-or-colla__/files/dealing-with-works-councils-tip-sheet/fileattachment/dealing_with_german_works_councils.pdf.

Employee Benefit News. "Bank of America Gets Creative in Supporting Employees with Disabilities," April 13, 2021. https://www.benefitnews.com/news/bank-of-america-gets-creative-in-supporting-employees-with-disabilities.

Gratton, Lynda. "How to Do Hybrid Right." *Harvard Business Review*, May 1, 2021. https://hbr.org/2021/05/how-to-do-hybrid-right.

Hamel, Liz, Cailey Muñana, and Mollyann Brodie. "Kaiser Family Foundation / LA Times Survey Of Adults With Employer-Sponsored Health Insurance," n.d., 36.

Ladders | Business News & Career Advice. "7 Employee Benefits Your Company Needs to Be Truly LGBT Inclusive." Accessed June 2, 2021. https://www.theladders.com:443/career-advice/7-employee-benefits-your-company-needs-to-be-truly-lgbt-inclusive.

Miranda Marquit. "Survey: Student Loans and the LGBTQ Community." *Student Loan Hero*, December 3, 2018. https://studentloanhero.com/featured/survey-lgbtq-student-borrowers-regret-loans/.

"More Employers Are Starting to Offer Student Loan Repayment Assistance." Accessed June 1, 2021. https://news.yahoo.com/employers-student-loan-repayment-123755707.html.

National LGBTQ Task Force. "New Report Reveals Rampant Discrimination against Transgender People by Health Providers, High HIV Rates and Widespread Lack of Access to Necessary Care," October 13, 2010. https://www.thetaskforce.org/new-report-reveals-rampant-discrimination-against-transgender-people-by-health-providers-high-hiv-rates-and-widespread-lack-of-access-to-necessary-care-2/.

"Persons with a Disability: Labor Force Characteristics Summary." Accessed October 26, 2020. https://www.bls.gov/news.release/disabl.nr0.htm.

"Re:Work." Accessed March 11, 2021. https://rework.withgoogle.com/print/guides/5721312655835136/.

SHRM. "SHRM 2019 Employee Benefits Survey: Student Loan Repayment, Paternity Leave, Standing Desks and Telemedicine All Ticking Upward," June 25, 2019. https://www.shrm.org/about-shrm/press-room/press-releases/pages/2019-shrm-employee-benefits-survey.aspx.

SnackNation. "121 Employee Wellness Program Ideas Your Team Will Love," May 7, 2021. https://snacknation.com/blog/employee-wellness-program-ideas/.

U.S., Full Bio Follow Linkedin Kimberly Amadeo is an expert on, World Economies, investing, With Over 20 Years of Experience in Economic Analysis, and business strategy She is the President of the economic website World Money Watch Read The Balance's editorial policies Kimberly Amadeo. "Do Medical Bills Really Bankrupt America's Families?" *The Balance*. Accessed May 30, 2021. https://www.thebalance.com/medical-bankruptcy-statistics-4154729.

Chapter 10

Driving Data-Driven Decisions

One of the most impactful ways that data-driven decisions improve equity is by reducing manager biases in the decision-making process. As we have learned, we all have biases and moving to data-driven decision making improves outcomes and minimizes instinctive decision-making. Data-driven decisions are based on tangible, measurable outcomes, and or feedback from a variety of contributors rather than based solely on managers' perceptions. Perception based decisions often reflect unconscious bias rather than actual employee performance or organizational outcomes. Using an instinctive approach, candidates in marginalized racial and ethnic groups are often identified by hiring managers as not a good culture fit for a job, not ready for a promotion, or that their communication style doesn't meet company expectations. Most managers believe that they are hiring and promoting fairly, but they are not.[1] Unconscious bias is creeping into their decision-making processes. In an effort to counter decision-making bias, organizations are looking to people analytics to encourage data-based decision-making. The objective is to improve transparency, objectivity, and credibility. Through integrating data-driven decision-making into organizational processes, bias is reduced and equity and inclusion are enhanced.

While data is an important tool for managers, we must remember that data alone does not provide information. Data needs to be gathered and reported on in an informative format to support managerial decision-making. The data must be accurate and reported in a manner that provide meaningful information and key metrics for business units and managers. The first step in the process is to analyze the data for quality and completeness.

For data to be useful, ensure that data quality is analyzed including its source, effective representation, and accuracy. Next, take the time to understand how data

DOI: 10.1201/9781003168072-11

will be analyzed to determine trends and patterns including which tools and models are being utilized. It is crucial to fully comprehend the models and any assumptions that are being made to avoid creating unintended consequences. Artificial Intelligence (AI) is defined as the ability of a machine to perform cognitive functions that we associate with human minds such as learning, reasoning, perceiving, and problem solving. AI is both algorithms and machine learning. AI is embedded in people analytic models through algorithms and machine learning to predict outcomes. Both the data set being used, and the model must be vetted for bias. Best practice is for management to establish codes of conduct for AI, which include clear intention of data process and usage of information. In addition, employees, whose data is being analyzed and used to predict outcomes, should be informed and allowed to opt out of the process. Data usage, AI functionality, and the intended use of this information should be shared transparently with employees and other key stakeholders.

A recent survey indicates that while information is highly valued by leadership for decision-making, less than 25% of executives and managers are using data to inform their decisions. There is a gap between leadership's aspirations around decision-making and the realities of the decision-making process today. Some of the obstacles include lack of a digital ready culture, insufficient data, and poor data quality. Other challenges include lack of integrated human capital data platforms and digital tools as well as limited digital skills and competencies in the executive and management levels.

10.1 Connecting Data to Desired Outcomes

Gathering meaningful, accurate and representational data is crucial to creating a decision-making culture which values and rewards data-driven decisions. Identifying the sources and location of the data that will provide information is vital to the process. Thinking back to the J.E.D.I. Maturity Continuum, organizations have different levels of data resources, technology capabilities, and analytics expertise. Understanding the organization's current capacity for moving to a culture of data driven decision-making it a crucial first step.

Clearly defining the purpose of gathering the data and data usage objectives facilitates the data collection process. As part of defining the objectives of the project and the data that will be utilized, define what success will look like and select metrics, KPIs, or other measures to identify success and to measure progress. Taking this approach ensures greater organizational alignment and leadership support to provide the digital transformation team credibility to drive change and access to data, especially if data is siloed. Data comes from a variety of sources, different organizational databases, web-driven feedback forms, even internal chat, or social media. Approximately, 80% of a data analyst's time is spent on cleaning and organizing data.[2] The data gathering phase includes scanning data for accuracy, reviewing it with key stakeholders for relevance, ensuring that it is representational, and correcting errors. Our recommendation is to include diverse, cross-functional team members on the transformation team to ensure multiple perspectives and voices throughout the process. Once the data is cleaned and organized, the statistical analysis tool, or model is run to create information for data driven decision-making. Analytics provide information based on patterns and trends from historical and current data and predictive analytics use algorithmic functions to suggest future outcomes. Information is presented in a variety of formats and frequencies including reports on KPIs, standard reports, ad hoc reporting, and dashboards. For many managers, working with data is a new process, and they need support to analyze and interpret the information in a meaningful and actionable manner. In addition, expertise may be required to support advanced technologies and to deliver tools such as configurable reporting, dashboards, and drill down capabilities which offer managers more granular insights. As the culture of the organization matures in the data decision-making process, managers will become more adept with integrating data informed decisions into their decision-making processes.

Information is an important tool in promoting equity and inclusion for an organization's people strategy by providing the board, leadership, and managers with a baseline from which to benchmark progress. Selecting and tracking key metrics aligned with J.E.D.I. goals provide insight into areas of success and areas for improvement. Key performance indicators (KPIs) track actionable metrics for managers to use in their decision-making processes. Managers that are making decisions on allocating client relationships or new opportunities to team members have data to determine who is the best choice rather than just intuition. Holding managers responsible for KPIs such as diversity representation goals both within their department and in the candidates recommended for promotion drives accountability.

Gathering data on an organization's talent ecosystem provides insights around equity and inclusion to promote workforce diversity. Aggregated data analysis provides a holistic view of the talent ecosystem allowing for an assessment of J.E.D.I. enablers and barriers in various stages of talent acquisition such as recruitment, screening, interviewing, and acceptance. Once candidates become employees, data analysis highlights J.E.D.I. challenges in onboarding, engagement, development, and career pathing. People strategy equity and inclusion issues are complex and multilayered. Challenges are present from both an organizational and individual perspective. It is a pipeline problem and a conversion problem, but it is also a self-selection and a belonging problem. Gathering and analyzing data improves accountability, objectivity, and credibility in the people strategy decision-making process.

Human Capital Management (HCM)) systems house people data including employee demographics, jobs, divisions, locations, and pay providing a wealth of data for people analytics. Many HCM SaaS solutions incorporate people analytics capabilities into their platforms allowing configuration of standard and custom reports based on a set of data available in modules. Standard reports can be created, accessed by, and distributed to managers with relative ease. Custom reports that use data from more than one module or data source often require customization, which usually necessitate additional configuration and expense. Our recommendation is to investigate the extensive library of pre delivered reporting options available in HCM SaaS solutions as a first step in the reporting and analysis process. Information can be shared with management in a variety of formats such as regularly scheduled reports that are automatically distributed, or a visualized format such as a preconfigured dashboard that is updated on a predetermined schedule, or for the more advances a real time interactive dashboard that support ad hoc query, custom views, and granular drilling capabilities. Increasingly, leadership is demanding people analytics to better manage their business, meet compliance requirements, minimize risk, and hold managers accountable. In Table 10.1, several top-rated HCM software vendors are listed that offer a full suite of integrated products including data analytics and reporting. Insights can be provided on KPIs, retention, attrition, diversity, inclusion, hiring, talent, and performance.

While these platforms function differently, they all offer data query or reporting functionality with some HCM solutions leveraging machine learning or predictive analytics to provide additional insights. Workday People Analytics uses augmented analytics to identify top risks related to the organization's workforce and highlights these risks to leaders allowing for faster and better data-driven people decisions. This analytics tool leverages machine learning, algorithms and natural language reading to develop and convey metrics, and trends for actionable insights to management. SAP SuccessFactors People Analytics offers a business intelligence tool for query and reporting combined with planning and predictive capabilities. It leverages data pattern analysis through machine learning, supports data blending from multiple sources, and provides opportunities for collaboration and team input for planning. Oracle Analytics comes with prebuilt KPIs and dashboard library for human capital

Table 10.1 HCM Vendors

Vendor	Website	People Analytics Tool
Workday	https://www.workday.com/	Workday People Analytics
SAP SuccessFactors	https://www.sap.com/products/human-resources-hcm.html	SAP SuccessFactors People Analytics
Oracle Human Capital Management	https://www.oracle.com/human-capital-management/	Oracle Analytics for HR
UKG Pro	https://www.ukg.com/	UKG People Analytics

professionals to leverage such as workforce demographics, turnover, retention, performance talent ratios, and diversity statistics and trends. UKG's People Analytics allows for data queries, reporting, filtering, and sorting using multiple data packages within UKG. A variety of formats including reports and dashboards are available. While all these vendors provide reporting tools to help with gathering, reporting, and dispersing information, the tools have varying degrees of complexity and capabilities especially in terms of highlighting risks. As with all technology platforms, there needs to be training, resource, and a budget dedicated to effectively support delivering meaningful information to management to drive J.E.D.I. transformation.

In addition, HCM SaaS platforms include modules supporting talent development and performance management. These can be leveraged to personalize the experience for employees in terms of their achieving goals, receiving feedback, career pathing, aligning compensation, identifying skill areas for development, and mapping out training modules and programs. Leveraging technology to provide transparency, accountability, and resources empowers managers and employees making organizations more just, equitable and inclusive. These leading HCM platform vendors integrate with a variety of tools usually found within their marketplaces to enhance and customize functionality, data tracking, and reporting options.

Leveraging data from your HCM system is a good starting point to better understand your organization's diversity representation composition. Leadership needs a clear view on with whom and where there are gaps in representation. Using data aggregation provides high-level foundational information on the organization at a point in time documenting a baseline from which to measure progress as an organization moves forward on its J.E.D.I. journey. Aggregated organizational data is useful for measuring overall trendlines and can help identify high-level priorities to improve equity and inclusion in an organization's people strategy. However, aggregated data doesn't always provide a clear and transparent picture in order to identify areas of strength and weakness across the organization. As outlined in Chapter 6, further stratification of data by function, role, level, and location provides insights on challenges and opportunities within a leaders span of control and influence. It is necessary to dive more deeply into the data to understand which areas of the organization do and do not have representational equity based on aggregated numbers. The aggregated data may provide a picture of gender equity because it indicates 50/50 representation of employees equally divided between men and women. If women are predominately represented in low paying customer service jobs and men are primarily represented in the executive suite or other professional positions, an organization does not have gender equity.

Decisions on presenting information such as categories and aggregation impact how information is interpreted. Aggregating all underrepresented groups into a minority category to track can generate unintended consequences as each of these groups have their own representation within an organizations community, and priorities and programs impact underrepresented groups differently as we saw in the Coca Cola case. Moving from a dominant to an equitable culture requires digging into to data to understand underrepresented groups and the intersectionalities of the group members.

In addition to the HCM systems people data, you want to incorporate data from other sources and organizational systems such as manager feedback tools, pulse reviews, project deliverable data, and even sales data to better understand and assess your internal people policies and processes. To support a digital J.E.D.I. transformation, a checklist is provided in Table 10.2.

The questions in this checklist are designed to drill down into the data gathering process. Issues such as data access and control often arise as this process is undertaken. It is crucial to have senior support to promote cross-functional collaboration as the required data may be housed in different units with access controlled by various department heads. Access to data may be limited because of data privacy regulations. Once the data is gathered, decisions must be made around providing information to management and leadership including type, detail, format, and frequency. Selecting metrics that measure impact and align with strategic priorities is an important step to track progress and promote accountability. As the J.E.D.I. digital transformation team undertakes the transformation to promote data-driven decisions to improve equity, access, and belonging, other issues and challenges will surface. Organizations often bring in consultants to help facilitate the transformation to data-driven decision to supplement data, technical, communication, and change management resource capabilities. Moving to data-driven decision-making is a transformation requiring dedication of time, money, and resources to drive impact and adoption.

Tracking and presenting data to organizational leaders promotes awareness and begins the transformation process. Providing data reshapes the decision-making process by minimizing instincts and focusing instead on actionable information. As the process evolves and managers become more adept at leveraging data to support strategic decision-making, the culture of the organization changes so that data-driven decisions become the norm. Building organizational capacity in terms of data acumen requires engagement and training of people managers. Vendor or internal trainings provide foundational information, but gaining acumen requires practices and customized training. Sharing best practices via internal communications and highlighting success stories further supports learning and adoption. Of course, senior leadership acting as role models by practicing data-driven decision making has a significant impact on adoption and usage.

10.2 Leveraging Technology and People Analytics

Ensuring technology and business strategy alignment is an important first step in selecting a solution that supports organizational goals. Garnering support for technology-based tools is much more effective if you have a C-suite champion

Table 10.2 Data-Driven J.E.D.I. Transformation Checklist

Do we have senior leadership support? Who from senior leadership is our champion?	
Who needs to be on the team?	
What information are we seeking, and what data are we trying to gather?	
Who will be using this data, and how will they be using it?	
Where is data located? Is it in a single system or multiple systems?	
How can we access the data?	
Do we need technical expertise on an ongoing basis to leverage this technology?	
Who needs to authorize data access?	
Is use of the data protected by regulations such as the General Data Protection Regulation (GDPR), California Privacy Rights Act (CPRA), or others? If so, what compliance actions are required?	
What tools are available to support the process of gathering data and then reporting and sharing information? Do we need a new tool?	
What information and metrics will be reported?	
Will we offer periodic reporting, dashboards, or system driven reports?	
How will the new tool or dashboard be socialized with leadership and managers to promote data-driven decision?	
Will leadership need training and support to incorporate data-driven decision-making?	
How will the culture change toward data-driven decisions be socialized with employees?	
How will managers be held accountable for decisions that impact achievement of J.E.D.I. goals as measured by metrics and KPI?	
What behaviors, policies, and procedures need to be changed to drive J.E.D.I. impact?	

supporting your equity and inclusion driven mission. While managers will be responsible for making data-driven decisions that impact their peoples' strategy and the related J.E.D.I. outcomes, employee data is often managed and maintained by the HCM function. A cross-functional team that includes HCM, IT, Operations, Sales, Finance builds collaboration, engagement, and adoption across the functional areas of the organization.

Selecting an HCM systems platform, people analytics tool, or other AI-based tool are important steps in the transformation process and necessitates an assessment of your organization's requirements. Spend time with stakeholders to understand both their current and future requirements. Ensure that a diversity of voices is included in the requirements gathering session. Too often, technology solution purchases are based on reasons other than business requirements such as buying the industry leading solution, or the solution used by a competitor, or even the solution used at the last place a decision-maker worked. There are many components to the software and tool selection process such as product functionality, vendor support, ongoing system and upgrade management, and the resource commitment for maintaining the system and leveraging the reporting functionality. Digital transformation team members tasked with this responsibility can utilized online ranking tools and rating reports to gain insights into functional capabilities. However, a deeper dive into functional, ease of use, and data accessibility is required to make the best choice for your organization. HCM SaaS solution highlighted in industry ranking sources such as Gartner Magic Quadrant may make sense for your organization or they may not depend upon your needs, capabilities, digital acumen, resources and even countries of operation. In order to ensure that you are selecting the best tools for your organization, develop your requirements using a broad selection of stakeholders. Ensure that diverse voices are represented in requirements gathering and in the HCM platform or tool selection process. Incorporating a variety of perspectives encourages a full and complete vetting of software solutions and their functionality to meet the needs of your diverse workforce. When selecting a tool, ensure that you understand the technologies being leveraged by a vendor's HCM SaaS platform or tool and that it is a viable solution for your organization. Viability includes the tool capabilities as well as the organization's capabilities to incorporate the tool usage into operations in a meaningful and useful manner. If an organization is not ready for machine learning, process automation, or predictive analytics, buying and implementing these tools will not be an effective solution. It is crucial that decisions are made based on organizational goals, platform or tool functionality, technical expertise, and support requirements. Avoid the "shiny new thing" trap as there are no silver bullets for moving forward on the J.E.D.I. data-driven decision-making transformation process.

When budgeting for your digital human capital transformation, plan on budgeting for change management and adoption to ensure that integration and adoption is a success. Survey results from companies with successful AI implementations indicate that 90% of the organizations spent more than half of their budget on activities to drive adoption, such as change management, workflow redesign, communication, and training.[3] MIT Sloan School of Management professors, Andrew McAfee and Erik Brynjolfsson, performed a study in conjunction with the MIT Center for Digital Business. In this study, they discovered that among the companies surveyed, the ones that were primarily data driven benefited from 4% higher productivity as well as 6% higher profits. Benefits accrue from better decision making, increased agility, improved productivity, innovation, and improved employee engagement.

Best practice in tool selection and adoption includes thinking about how people work, productivity measures, manager roles, and how these processes may be impacted or need to be redefined in order to effectively integrate a data driven approach. Utilizing a subject matter expert (SME) to provide expertise, guidance, and support will improve the probability of success. The money spent on a consultant will more than offset the savings delivered via a successful transformation.

Figure 10.1, depicts a technology adoption and people analytics path for organizations on their HCM digital transformation journey from stewardship through organizational agility to continuous strategy. The impetus for undertaking a HCM digital transformation varies depending on the organization's maturity on the J.E.D.I. Maturity Continuum. In early stages, leadership is seeking improved access to data and information to create a baseline profile. In later stages, they are seeking to automate transactions and processes to enhance access to information and resources and to promote equitable outcomes. In addition, managers are required to respond more quickly as they navigate their organizations in a VUCA environment. Leaders require information to respond rapidly to changing requirements from clients, competitive dynamics, investors, and other stakeholders, and at the same time they need to ensure that their actions promote the J.E.D.I. values of the organization. Data and insights are crucial for minimizing managers' bias for expedience when solving problems. Competitive demands require agility and responsiveness and stakeholder demands require a more thoughtful approach focused on improving organizational environmental and social

Stewardship	Organizational Agility	Continuous Strategy
Automate Transactions	Process Automation	Data in Real Time
Provide Employee Information	Machine Learning Replaces	Accurate Predictions
Data is Siloed	Humans for Routine Functions	Augmented Insights
Compliance	Data Provides Insights	Data Driven Decisions
	Active Planning Based on	Actionable Information
	Data	

Figure 10.1 HCM AI Journey.

justice. Managers need accurate data and timely access to information to navigate this paradox between agility and equity.

In order to gain insights into people data, leaders need information to be delivered in a usable and actionable format. To reach this stage, most organizations need to undertake a HCM digital transformation. The initial stage, *Stewardship*, is often characterized by awareness that data is needed but it is fragmented and hard to gather. Data resides in silos with a variety of different gatekeepers. There is limited data to inform management's people strategy. From an employee perspective, obtaining information such as benefits, training programs, and education reimbursements may be fraught with access and accuracy challenges. If the process is to contact HR, your employees and human capital staff are spending time on transactional rather than value-added related tasks. At this stage, organizations are often using HCM service centers to field employee questions and Excel spreadsheets to gather, aggregate, and analyze data. Data access is limited because of data silos. Management is seeking to improve data accessibility, reduce resources assigned to routine transactions, and provide better information to managers and employees. At this early stage of adoption, it remains difficult to provide meaningful data to report on J.E.D.I. goal progress as data often remain siloed. As a result, it is difficult to report on organizational J.E.D.I. designated KPIs and to measure progress or outcomes. To enhance digital capabilities and functionality, the organization must move forward on its journey.

The next phase is *Organizational Agility*, where HCM's roles and responsibilities are better aligned with an organization's strategic vision including its J.E.D.I. mission. At this stage, AI-based tools are introduced primarily for machine learning to automate processes relieving employees from routine transactional work allowing them to focus on more impactful endeavors. This work includes leveraging AI tools to gather data, report on information and KPIs, and provide data insights for management. Planning and decision-making are based on data insights. This stage requires cross-functional collaboration and data sharing to support data gathering from multiple sources. New skills and knowledge are required to utilize the technology and to analyze the information, so training and development are important for analysts as well as managers and leaders. In order to support socialization of data-driven decision-making, a change management plan is launched to encourage adoption and utilization of AI-based tools.

When an organization reaches the *Continuous Strategy* stage, leadership seeks to drive organizational value through aligning J.E.D.I. and business strategies for impact. In order to realize its environmental and social mission, people strategy, policies, technologies, and capabilities are fully aligned. At this stage in the transformation, AI incorporates machine learning and algorithmic models to transform data into business insights. These include both augmented insights that aggregate data from multiple data sources and predictive insights, such as predicting employees at risk for leaving. The objective is to share actionable information to support data-driven decisions. Management will require training on the tool usage as well as the practice of making data-driven decision. Data must be accurate, transparent, and timely. Sharing key metrics and trends via dashboards drives real-time decision-making. In order to drive manager behavior change, training, communication, and senior support are crucial. To support a digital transformation, best practice is to have a project management plan which includes an organizational change management plan. In order to drive continuous improvement, align management's performance metrics and compensation with J.E.D.I. designated KPI's to reinforce accountability.

Data-driven decisions have a significant impact on removing bias from the routine people decisions that managers make around access and opportunity. These include distributing assignments, offering opportunities for team leadership, and designating stretch opportunities as well as hiring, giving promotions, and even designating high-performance employee. As we have learned, unconscious bias is present in all these managerial decisions. Moving people strategy from intuition to data-driven decisions, which are based on skills, credentials, assessments, peer and colleagues' reviews, project ratings, and other tangible factors, results in less decision-making bias and more equitable outcomes.

While many organizations are focusing on equity and access issues in their talent ecosystem, organizations further along in their HCM AI journey, such as Johnson & Johnson, have redesigned their talent recruitment process leveraging data to inform them about both stickiness and leakages in their hiring process for diverse talent. This recruitment redesign allows them to apply tactical adjustments to improve outcomes throughout the talent recruitment process. "In the past, we would post jobs, then kind of wait and see where we came out on the other side, because we didn't have complete visibility into how we'd gotten there," explains Scott Montemurno, Global Head of Talent Acquisition and Mobility at Johnson & Johnson.[4]

> Now, armed with data that shows us what's happening at each moment in the hiring process, we're able to approach our DE&I strategy not only holistically, but also very, very tactically. We can see how DE&I is pulling through at each step, from the application stage all the way through to offer acceptance.[5]

Their use of data has helped them to identify actionable points within the talent recruitment process to apply changes and resources to improve their DEI talent outcomes in a meaningful and impactful manner.

Recruiting diverse talent isn't just a sourcing challenge, there are leakages throughout the recruitment process for underrepresented group members. Tools that provide insight into where leakages occur enable human capital leaders to apply targeted solutions to address specific challenges for underserved groups during the talent recruitment, interview, and onboarding process. For example, one organization was having challenges attracting candidates from an underrepresented group because the language used in the job description was a deterrent to members of that group. For another company, it was an assessment tool that appears to be neutral, but was actually screening out members of an underrepresented group.

As an organization grows in its sophistication with data, reporting tools are available to provide key information to managers on their talent pipeline performance through analytics such as a hiring funnel analytic report. This type of reports visually identifies leakage spots across the talent conversion pipeline identifying targeted areas for change. Providing people managers with dashboards and analytics facilitates focusing on high level metric trend lines, but also allows for drilling into information to identify targeted actions. In addition to providing data, creating a decision-making culture that requires data and tying managers' performance scorecards to J.E.D.I. metrics focuses attention and drives behavior change.

Figure 10.2 includes metrics that HRComputes shares with clients that are looking for greater insight into their J.E.D.I. performance. These recommended metrics focus on representation, grievance or legal action, retention, recruitment, selection, promotion, development, performance, pay equity, employee engagement, supplier diversity, turnover, and comparisons of employee representation data to community demographics. Gathering this type of information begins the process of identifying barriers and highlighting equity and/or disparity within an organization. Sharing people metrics widely via KPIs and dashboards begins the process of embedding these data points into organizational decision-making systems. To determine the

- Assessment
  - % IG by Organization Level
  - Number of Lawsuits, Fines. Grievances
- Retention
  - IG Turnover Compared to Average Turnover
  - IG Pay Equity Analysis
- Recruitment
  - % of Applicant from IG
  - Employee referrals of Friends and Family
- Selection
  - % of Chosen Applicant from IG
- Promotion
  - IG% of in the Pipeline
  - IG % Promoted
  - IG = Indentity Group

- Development Opportunities
  - IG #High Profile Assignments
  - IG #Key Clients
  - IG # Access to Leadership
  - IG # Leadership Training
- Exit Interviews
  - Reported experience
- Ambassador
  - Employee Survey Results
- Comparison of Employee Demographics with
  - Customer Demographics
  - Community Demographics
  - Competitor Demographics

Figure 10.2   Metrics by Identified Group.

root cause of inequity and underrepresentation, we need to drill deeper into the data as well as engage with key stakeholders to better understand sentiments and perceptions.

As discussed in Chapter 6, driving systemic change begins with an assessment, which include a variety of techniques including stakeholder surveys, one on one conversations, and focus groups to better understand company culture, decision-making processes, work processes and policies. Next, review historical data trends and organizational policies to understanding the gap between written policy and daily actions. This organizational climate gap analysis provides an assessment of current state verses written policies and sheds light on inconsistencies in managerial policy implementation and perceived equities by employees. Delving into data around employee and stakeholder sentiment provides information to either redesign people policies or to restructure the checks and balances on how they are implemented. Employee engagement and sentiment data provide actionable insights to leadership teams to identify system-wide equity and inclusion challenges versus department of manager specific challenges. Best practices include garnering senior leadership support, providing transparency around the process, reporting on outcomes, and providing a safe space for sharing perceptions related to organizational culture, values, and beliefs. The goal is to peel back the layers of an organization to truly understand how work is done. Once current organizational systems, processes, and policies are understood, the redesign process begins to remove both written and unwritten barriers to equity and inclusion.

We find that engaging with a broad array of stakeholders early on in the digital transformation has a significant impact on adoption and ultimate success. Understanding who might be early adopters and ambassadors is crucial to spreading acceptance and effective utilization. Likewise, understanding who your blockers, even saboteurs, might be allows for early listening and engagement in order to begin the process of changing hearts and minds. Over the years, we have turned some of our initial detractors into advocates for digital transformation through this approach.

One of the most frequent challenges to moving toward data-driven decision making is leading the transformational change required. Often, organizations want to save budget, and insufficient resources are allocated to the change management processes to promote digital tool adoption, utilization, and behavior change. Tools are introduced without sufficient information and training for managers to promote adoption. Tools designed to facilitate managing people working hybrid schedules such as productivity tracking software, which use AI to track employee activity and to offer engagement, nudge tools, which remind managers to check-in with employees or identify data falling outside of normal ranges, and continuous feedback tools, which encourage capturing real-time feedback to improve relevance and information, require managers to change their own behaviors. For some organizations, the transformation requires prioritizing people management. For many leaders, people management responsibilities are often pushed to the when I have time list, and the never-ending list of deliverables pushes it to the I never have time list. A solution is to have senior leaders model the people management behaviors they wish their managers to emulate. For other organizations, managers need to be given training and support to develop new habits, norms, and practices. Organizations spend millions on new technology only to find that their employees are not adopting the new tool. If organizations truly want to create more equitable playing fields and deliver on a culture of belonging, resources must be allocated to digital transformation to provide the data and tools needed for systemic redesign.

10.3 Platforms to Engage Diverse Talent

A growing portion of the workforce identifies as a gender other than male or female. Members of Gen Z are more likely than millennials to say that they know someone who prefers that others use gender-neutral pronouns to refer to them (35%) and that gender identity options other than male, or female should be options on forms (60%).[6] (Pronouns are included in the J.E.D.I. Primer.) Organizations that seek to attract and retain top talent must create a gender inclusive environment. For example, the HCM SaaS provider UKG Pro has updated its Core HR and Payroll products to capture employee's preferred name and gender identity to support client requirements for data systems that promote a gender inclusive culture. As we build technology driven tools, it is crucial to consider the needs of diverse populations in their design and functionality. In certain states, such as NY and California, capturing preferred name and gender identity is a legal requirement. When embarking on a digital transformation, it is imperative to inquire about the capabilities of a platform to support the requirements of a diverse workforce.

In Table 10.3, there are several technology platforms and consulting tools to support building a more inclusive workforce. *Higher*, a collaboration between Rhodes Perry Consulting and Diver Collective, focuses on building gender inclusive organizations. Using a software called the Higher Audit, they assess an organization's culture, systems, and policies around gender inclusion by asking stakeholders to respond to a series of questions. Based on this information and their own insights, the tool provides a baseline to understand an organization's current status and offers a strategy to build better outcomes as well as to benchmark against standards and to measure progress. In addition, organizations that use Higher Audit receive access to a pipeline of high potential transgender and non-binary talent who expect to work with gender inclusive organizations.

Jopwell, founded by Porter Braswell, a BIPOC entrepreneur, provides a data-driven approach to hiring more diverse talent. The site offers a technology platform to match candidates and jobs as well as provides networking and resource support for candidates. Jopwell works with a wide variety of partner organizations such as UBS, Spotify, and American Express. In addition, they have direct relationships with recruiters within their partner organizations to promote job opportunities to

Table 10.3 Technology-Driven Tools to Promote Workforce Diversity

Organization	Website	Impact
Higher	http://hellohigher.com/	Building gender inclusive organizations.
Jopwell	https://www.jopwell.com/	Job board for Black, Latinx, and Native American students and professionals.
Meytier	https://meytier.com/	AI-based tool for women to better assess skills and a job board for women.
Apres Group	https://apresgroup.com/	Job board for women returning to the workforce after a gap in their careers.
People of Color in Tech	https://www.pocitjobs.com/	Recruitment platform for people of color in technology.

their community members. Jopwell team members provide support and advice to candidates throughout the candidate and recruitment process.

Jopwell partnered with the PGA on their journey to build a more diverse and inclusive organization. They began the process by leveraging their platform membership to assess their perception of the golf industry as a possible career including barriers to entry, general awareness of opportunities, and thoughts around requirements. Based on the findings from this assessment, the PGA made some changes to their candidate experience and community outreach processes. They featured their PGAWORKS fellowship, internships, scholarship, and career opportunities and events more prominently on social media to improve exposure and access. In addition, they centralized job postings to gather data better. They dedicated resources to expanding their networks and outreach to underserved communities. Their goals included making diverse candidates aware of opportunities for employment within the PGA and reaching members of these communities in an authentic manner. Their approach included sharing stories from current diverse employees about their career experience with the PGA and increasing visual representation of BIPOC community members in golf careers. They partnered with organizations such as Black Enterprise and *Sports Business Journal.* They also launched the PGA Works Collegiate Championship for students from 200 HBCUs and Hispanic-serving institutions to support student athletes in this golf competition. Their strategy was to better connect with underserved communities through a variety of outreach and informational programs.[7]

In addition, leadership looked inwardly at their senior leadership team's diversity and began the process of improving their representation of underrepresented groups.

As part of their inward evaluation, they looked at creating systems of accountability around process change to drive a culture of belonging. Overall goals for recruitment of BIPOC candidates were developed and shared with management. The talent recruitment process was reviewed including standardize candidate review timelines and a process to redirect candidates toward other possible roles. Data on activities and outcomes relative to goals was tracked and reported upon to management. Using data, the PGA drove impact on their DEI goals.[8]

Meytier's Founder and CEO, Rena Nigam, developed its AI & analytics-based technology and platform to offset bias in candidate screening in order to create more opportunities for success for women. Leveraging technology and consulting services, the Meytier team guides organizations in strengthening their diversity efforts and hiring more qualified women. Their Meytier Score supports organizations in filling their talent pipeline with qualified women. A tool helps women candidates identify and translate their skills using Natural Language Processing (NLP) to terms that better match current industry terminology. In addition, Meytier offers a curated job board for women that is open to candidates with career breaks such as women returning to the workforce after taking time off for raising children. There are many platforms and resources available to fill candidate pipelines with diverse talent. While this process is a journey, filling the pipeline and offering opportunities to members of underserved communities are the first steps in the transformation. Think of the amazing talent pool that these tools help organizations access.

Other tools such as chatbots, workflow, and process automation tools provide improved access to information and resources for all employees, especially underserved employees. Leveraging chatbots to answer questions ensures that employees get a consistent and accurate answer. Human bias in terms of who within the organization is given access to tuition reimbursement information or hybrid work opportunities is greatly reduced if the process is automated. Workflow and process automation can speed and improve organizational readiness to welcome new employees. Many people have experienced an onboarding process where you arrive for your first day and nothing has been set up for you. Imagine being a member of an underrepresented group and arriving at the office with existing apprehensions to find that you have no desk, computer, or phone. No one has been assigned to act as a first week guide, and you don't even know where the cafeteria is located for lunch. Any employee would feel completely unwelcome and perhaps already planning for their exit strategy from the organization. Although an onboarding breakdown is detrimental to all employees, it can be especially detrimental in making new hires from underrepresented groups feel welcome and valued. Leveraging tools like process automation allow for necessary documentation, forms, and requisitions to be processed with minimal human intervention. As a result, your new employees arrive to a desk, computer, phone, onboarding session, first day guide, and maybe even a mentor. Using digital tools to automate onboarding processes remove these transactional processes from managers' email inboxes making them much more seamless and ultimately leading to new hires feeling welcomed and valued. The added benefit of this process automation is that it eliminates transactional tasks, and frees managers to focus on more value-added activities such as coaching and developing their people. Automating people processes improves the experience for employees and promotes a culture of belonging in your organization.

Process automation goes beyond onboarding and requisitioning. It can be used to guide employees to benefits, volunteer opportunities, even employee resource groups (ERGs). For large complex organizations with multiple locations, the system can be configured to provide the correct information to an employee based on their level or location. For example, if an employee is looking for information on their tuition reimbursement plan, the process automation platform selects the information pertinent to that employee, based on a variety of factors, to display. Additional people management processes such as regulatory compliance and reporting are also improved using document retention and report automation. The whole process makes information and resources transparently available to all employees removing dependence on a manager or someone in HR to share important employee benefit or resource information. In effect, this unfettered access to information promotes equity by facilitating access for all employees to crucial information for their organizational success as well as their personal health and well-being. Automation removes gate keepers that often contribute to lack of access and equity.

10.4 Pay Equity and Racial Equity Audits

The field of people analytics is shedding light on systemic barriers to equity and inclusion for underrepresented groups. The Ascend Foundation published research on Silicon Valley leadership diversity using an Executive Parity Index (EPI), a tool which can be used by an organization to measure its leadership diversity. The EPI is the ratio of one group's representation at the executive level vs. its representation at the professional level.[9]

$$\text{Executive Pay Parity} = \text{Percentage of Executives} / \text{Percentage of Professionals}$$

Utilizing this formula, the Ascend Foundation analyzed EEOC data from Google, Hewlett-Packard, Intel, LinkedIn, and Yahoo to compare South and East Asians in their leadership pipelines. Here are some of their findings:

- While both race and gender are factors contributing to a glass ceiling, for the Asian workforce, the negative impact of race is 3.7 times more significant than the impact of gender.
- White men are 42% more likely than White women, but 149% more likely than Asian men and 260% more likely than Asian women to be at the executive level.[10]

While the formula is a simple calculation from a people analytics perspective, the insight for both employees and employers gained from this data assessment is valuable. It provides clear data that pushes back on the stereotype of the model minority often associated with Asians. The stereotype is that Asians are very successful and that many already work in technology companies such as the ones in the data sample. Based on this analysis, the Asian leadership gap in Silicon Valley remains an issue, and it needs to be addressed. People analytics that analyzes industry and sector data on underrepresented groups provide insights around industry talent trends that are often masked without this type of industry aggregated data. For organizations seeking to improve their own J.E.D.I. outcomes, this type of industry insight provides a foundation and framework to consider what is happening to employees in underrepresented groups in terms of promotions and leadership opportunities not only in your own firm but also throughout your industry.

Organizations use assessments such as racial equity or civil rights audits to better understand their internal and external impacts on key stakeholders including issues around pay equity. Increasingly, organizations such as Starbucks, Facebook, and Black Rock have undertaken or have announced that they will undertake a third party racial equity audit to ensure independence and accountability. The purpose of the audit is to review the impact of policies and practices on key stakeholders such as employees, customers, and communities in order to identify changes that may make the organization more accessible and equitable. In addition, the audit confirms that governance systems are in place to ensure racial equity. Both Amazon and J&J have received shareholder proposal requesting a civil rights audit for the 2021 proxy seasons. These audits evaluate employee EEOC data, human capital strategies, product and service impacts on underserved communities, community impacts, and supplier diversity data. Audits include testing policies for a concept known as disparate or adverse impact. While disparate or adverse treatment is intentional, discrimination, or disparate; adverse impact is often referred to as unintentional discrimination. Disparate impact arises because policies, practices, and other systemic rules, which appear to be neutral, have a disproportional impact on protected groups. Hiring assessment tools that appear to be neutral but are failing a disproportionate number of BIPOC candidates is an example. Federal law prohibits both disparate treatment and disparate impact discrimination. Institutions must assess their policies, technologies, and practices to determine both intent and impact. If algorithms and machine learning are found to generate disparate impact, remediation strategies need to be undertaken to address these inequities. From an investor, board, and C-suite perspective, these audits are not only essential to address racial inequity, but also offer insights to mitigate risk factors that are crucial to an organization's license to operate. These are 3rd part audit of organizational justice that can be compared to a company's own analysis for independent verification of results and used to inform required change.

One of the people analytics tools used to drive data-driven decisions is a pay equity analysis, which is commonly used to identify employees that require pay remediation, but also sheds a light on more systemic challenges. Taking a deeper dive into pay equity begins the process of closing the pay and wealth gaps. Moving the pay discussion from an individual negotiation to an organizational mandate to ensure pay equity in roles across the organization drives deep systemic pay changes in salary and stock options. Pay equity analysis can be performed on a variety of factors such as gender, ethnicity, race, or other demographic factors. Figure 10.3 outlines the steps that HRComputes follows when undertaking a pay equity analysis.

Pay equity means eliminating differences in pay that cannot be explained by a bonified reason such as role, tenure, location, performance, education, etc. Here are some definitions to explain pay gap:

- Overall Pay Gap – percentage difference in average salary for whole population of female/male or other groups identified for comparison.
- Defined Pay Gap – percentage difference in average salary for whole population of female/male or other identified groups that can be explained based on occupations, education, labor market experience, or tenure.
- Real Pay Gap – percentage difference in average salary for whole population of female/male or other identified groups that are not explainable by reasonable and justifiable criteria.

As a starting point, it is crucial to understand the impetus for the pay equity analysis. Some organizations approach pay equity from a compliance perspective to meet shareholder, regulatory requirements, or customer demands. Other leadership teams are truly interested in achieving pay equity. For example, GM closed the overall gender pay gap throughout the company as well as achieved pay equity across the top, middle, and lower bands in 2018.[11] They are a clear example of a company committed to gender pay equity. Intention around pay equity matters as regression analysis assumptions as well as banding ranges can all have an impact on results.

Next, review workforce and compensation data for quality and completeness. Reviewing pay policies and practices as well as looking at workforce data analytics allows for identification of comparability metrics to determine comparison bands.

- Verify and Establish Pay Equity Analysis Goals
- Review Pay Policies and Practices
- Collect Data Leveraging Workforce Data and Analytics
- Determine Comparability Metrics for Jobs, Bands, and Levels
- Identify Analysis Plan and Perform Pay Equity Analysis
- Assess Results and Provide Recommendations
- Develop Remediation and Governance Strategy
- Recommend Reporting, Key Metrics, and Dashboarding
- Support Communication, Change Management, and Training

Figure 10.3   Pay Equity Analysis Approach.

The pay equity assessment is based on comparable jobs. While job titles and descriptions are useful in creating cohorts for comparison, this data needs to be carefully examined for skill levels, responsibilities, and other variables such as work location and working conditions when determining comparability. Understanding the federal, state, and even municipal guidelines for comparability is also important. Using regression analysis, the consultant performs an analysis of pay and a series of explanatory variables that indicate compensation such as role, location, experience, etc. This analysis includes establishing a control variable such as job level as well as an independent variable that indicates gender, race, or other areas of interest to test for a relationship between this variable and the dependent variable-pay. If there is a discernable impact from the independent variable, there is a possibility that there is either a systemic or local pay equity issues. Once outliers are identified, the process of investigation and conversation begins. It may be beneficial to run several variations of the model to generate the necessary pay equity insights.

When conducting a pay equity audit, for the first time especially, leadership must be prepared for compensation budget adjustments. Part of the process is identifying what range or standard deviation is acceptable to determine impacted employees. For example, setting the range at 80% will increase the number of employees that need salary adjustments compared to setting the range at 95%. In the U.S., prescriptive action is often based on the original intent of the pay equity analysis and on who is asking the questions (HR, Compensation Committee, Regulators or Investors). On average, pay equity adjustments impact 5% of the employee populations with pay adjustments of 4–6%. From a budget perspective, the impact is usually .1% to .3% of the total annual payroll.[12] For a $100,000,000 payroll, a reasonable payroll adjustment to anticipate is an impact in the $100,000 to $300,000 range.

Remediation and ongoing governance to ensure pay equity is a crucial step. In the event that no systemic pay equity bias has been identified, the approach to remediation may be to adjust the outliers. This approach is highly visible and transparent. Other organizations wait until the next merit pay cycle and apply adjustments to impacted employees without providing the managers or HR leaders with explanation. Adjusting pay with or without explanation can generate unintended consequences in terms or morale and engagement especially if this is a first time pay equity analysis. The second approach is much less transparent. Both of these scenarios address pay equity symptoms rather than root causes.

While the monetary component of pay equity disparities must be addressed, there are usually root cause issues that need to be identified and addressed as well. The pay equity analysis is a tool to shed light and provide direction. Discussing the pay equity audit information with senior leadership begins the process of sharing findings, discussing alternatives, and developing a course of action. Data may indicate either racial or gender disparities in certain roles, levels, departments, or regions within the organization. While a pay adjustment may address a one-off issue, addressing root cause challenges requires deeper systemic work. Solutions to these challenges relate to human capital strategies within the talent ecosystem such as recruitment, retention, development, and promotion. Focusing on capacity building for people managers to better understand their own biases and offering tools and resources to drive more equitable outcomes are part of the recommended process. Pay equity analysis gives a statistical analysis of pay equity in an organization, but other assessment tools that give workforce insights are often very useful in identifying trends, pockets of best practice, or areas that need improvement.

10.5 Pros and Cons of Algorithms

When using AI based solutions that leverage algorithms and machine learning, there are several ethical considerations including data quality and representation as well as disclosure around transparency of use, including compliance with data privacy requirements as indicated in Figure 10.4. The purpose and use of the AI tool should be clear and explainable to leadership, employees, and other stakeholders. Data that is being used to create an algorithm should be reviewed for inherent bias such as using a data set that includes a pool of past successful candidate that most likely includes biased data. Data that is used to develop and then train the algorithm needs to be screened to ensure diversity of representation. The project team developing the algorithm should reflect diversity of identity, experience, and thought, and members must be fully cognizant of their role in impacting outcomes for others based on their decisions. Their process must be transparent, and explainable, not a mysterious algorithm with an opaque process. Stakeholders including employees and customers are increasingly demanding transparency on tools leveraging AI to analyze and predict outcomes. Organizations are being required to undergo equity audits to demonstrate that algorithmic tools are not resulting in discriminatory outcomes.

AI based tools are leveraged to inform talent ecosystem decisions such as recruitment, hiring, promotion, development, and termination. They also provide information to people managers to better understand employee engagement, sentiment, and organizational justice views. An important consideration is whether the tool being utilized benefits or harms employees. In evaluating the tool, consider if the use of the tool is to support employee growth and opportunity or to deliver punitive

| DATA QUALITY, SOURCING, AND TRANSPARENCY | UNINTENDED CONSEQUENCES AND BIAS | POWER AND RESPONSIBILITY | FOR GOOD OR BAD |

Figure 10.4 Ethical Considerations for AI.

actions. Understanding the intended use of the AI tool is crucial to delivering on ethical outcomes. Here are some questions to consider as you begin the process:

AI Project Considerations:

1. What is the purpose of the AI project, and who are we seeking to help or serve?
2. Who else could be impacted by this tool? Are these stakeholder groups represented on the project team?
3. Is the data quality good?
4. What is the source of the data, and are we permitted to use this data?
5. Where is the bias in the data?
6. How will the data and outcomes be used?
7. Is the code and data auditable?
8. Is there transparency of process and of use of predictive outcomes?
9. Are you controlling for unintended consequences and bias?
10. Who has the power and responsibility in this relationship?
11. Is the AI being used to benefit or to punish people?
12. Does our organization have an AI code of conduct, and is there a governance process in place to ensure that it is being followed?

Data can create erroneous outcomes if the source of the data is unclear, if it doesn't contain diverse voices, or if it includes biased data. As part of the data quality assessment, test for specific groups based on indicators such as race, gender, age, etc. Given your goals, test for use cases that might present problematic outcomes. Transparency of purpose is crucial especially when the data being analyzed falls under data privacy laws. In order to confirm that testing gaps are addressed and vetted, ensure that your testing team includes diverse voices to challenge and raise concerns. Develop a clear AI policy and recommended usage guidelines. Project teams should be provided AI guidelines and codes of conduct to share best practices and to ensure oversight and ethical compliance. Without a clearly defined AI strategy, the process is fraught with problems and can lead to unintended consequences for organizations and the broader stakeholder group.

Amazon has been using AI to track its employees and contractor performance including warehouse workers and drivers. Metrics around performance criteria such as timeliness, package security, and accuracy are evaluated to determine which flex drivers are top performers giving them more routes and deactivating lesser performers. Flex drivers receive machine driven feedback in four categories: Fantastic, Great, Fair, or At Risk. The system is fully automated with machines making decision about drivers' continued employment based on algorithmic results.[13] Drivers complain that the algorithms don't consider real-life issues like traffic or weather and that once terminated from the system there is no recourse to seek remediation. The system appears to be based on the assumption that there will be a never-ending supply of flex drivers. While the nature of the work is "gig," many drivers depend upon this work to survive. Sudden termination puts many already marginalized people at greater risk. One wonders if the voices of drivers were included in this algorithmic model. Decisions on AI tool creation, selection, and usage within the talent ecosystem either support or detract from creating an equitable culture.

Figure 10.5 highlights general ethical principles from the Association for Computing Machinery (ACM) Code of Ethics (Code). The ACM is the world's largest educational and scientific computing society supporting professionals, academics, and researchers. The general ethical principles for computing professionals focus on acting responsibly, reflecting upon the broader impact of decisions and actions, and supporting societal good. In addition to providing guidance, the Code serves as a benchmark or basis for remediation when violations occur. The Code provides further guidance for professional responsibility, and leadership responsibility, and it calls for ethical compliance of every ACM member. It serves as a basis for ethical decision-making for those working in the field of advanced computing either as a scientist or professional.[14] If your organization is looking for a resource on which to model an AI code of ethics, the Code serves as a strong foundational tool.

AI based tools can help to remove bias from the decision-making process through leveraging data and limiting human bias. However, there are limitations to AI capabilities and maturity, and further experience needs to be developed to ensure that these tools function in an unbiased manner. The downside is that certain AI tools penalize segments of the population such as women, BIPOC, and AAPI communities as a result of data limitations and machine learning decision processes. From a data perspective, the data base used to develop AI tools is often not representational of a diverse population. As a result, the data used to create the algorithm and train the AI tool contains biased information. The AI learns from that biased data and incorporates the bias into its decision-making processes. Historically, the data being used to test AI has been predominately male and White. Accordingly, the AI error rates for women, BIPOC, and AAPI are significantly higher. There is the infamous case of Google tagging photos of BIPOC community members as gorillas using its facial recognition algorithms.[16] Without proper vetting and standards, biases can be built into the algorithm because of insufficient representation in the data.

- Contribute to society and to human well-being, acknowledging that all people are stakeholders in computing.
- Avoid harm
- Be honest and trustworthy
- Be fair and take action not to discriminate
- Respect the work required to produce new ideas, inventions, creative works, and computing artifacts.
- Respect privacy
- Honor confidentiality

Figure 10.5   ACM Code of Ethics.[15]

"Gender Shades, a 2018 study of three commercial facial-recognition systems, found they were much more likely to fail to recognize the faces of darker-skinned women than lighter-skinned men."[17] These findings impact all aspects of life such as being stopped at passport control because your reentry photo scan did not match or even being erroneously identified as a criminal. Lack of data representation in algorithms and machine learning results in facial recognition errors impacting the safety of driverless cars. If the vehicle's AI can't identify a darker skinned person, it can impact the safety of pedestrians and bicyclists. Being 95% accurate with this type of technology sounds like a high level of accuracy, but the 5% error rate has a devastating and disproportional impact on those in the 5%. Women of color are more likely to be represented in this 5%.

Conversely, certain groups can be overrepresented in the AI training data. Predictive tools for police departments that predict the probability of crimes in certain areas based on past data such as maps, arrest records, reported crimes, etc. recommend greater police patrolling in predicted hot spot areas. With a greater police presence, the number of arrests rise making this prediction a self-fulfilling prophecy. Other AI tools are based on personal demographics to predict the likelihood of committing a crime and are used by police to thwart individual crimes. This technology is also used by courts to determine the likelihood of an individual to reoffend, and it is used during pretrial and sentencing. As we know, Black men are more than twice as likely to be arrested than White men. With a data set that skews toward Black citizens being deemed more likely to commit a criminal offense, these predictive policing tools produce racist predictions.[18]

In response to the bias in AI and the negative impact that AI tools can have on society, employees are protesting their employer's development and sale of tools such as drones and facial recognition software. As indicated in the examples highlighted in Figure 10.6, employees are pushing back on their own organizations for developing AI-based tools that are being used by the border patrol, military, and law enforcement.

In the case of Amazon's facial recognition, the ACLU performed an experiment with the software in which it incorrectly identified 28 members of Congress as people with arrest records. The implications of identifying someone as having a former conviction results in an escalation and an increase in the potential for use of force.

Salesforce employees protesting a government contract for the sales of technology to US Border Patrol.

Google employees campaigning for greater transparency around building drones for the Pentagon.

Amazon employee wrote an op ed entitled "My Company Shouldn't Sell Facial Recognition Software to Police"

Figure 10.6   Employee Activism against AI.

Even more concerning is that the greatest error rates occurred for members of the Black community.

AI critics view algorithms as a form of "tech washing" with societal bias hidden behind a covering of technology transparency and objectivity. Algorithms often reflect societal biases; it is crucial to actively identify bias and then take steps to debias these algorithms. There are several resource toolkits such as those outlined in Table 10.4. Each of these toolkits has strengths and weaknesses for analyzing machine learning. Microsoft's LIFT tool tests for bias in the data used to train the AI, tests the model using common metrics, and then evaluates the performance outcome using statistical significance.[19] Using these toolkits and others, AI tool and framework developers are better able to assess and address bias across the AI application life cycle.

While we have learned that the data can create bias, so can the models themselves. When learning from past data, algorithms identify trends such as denial of loans based on gender, race, zip codes, and they incorporate those learnings into the machine learning process. IBM's tool Watson OpenScale assists with managing AI through data cleansing, optimization, and planning tools.[20] Using OpenScale, lenders are able to correct their models to minimize generating biased results.

Table 10.4 AI Assessment Toolkits

IBM's AI Fairness 360	https://aif360.mybluemix.net/	Assists in examining, reporting, and mitigating discrimination and bias in machine learning models throughout the AI application life cycle.
Google-What-if-Toolkit	https://pair-code.github.io/what-if-tool/	Supports testing of AI and machine learning performance in hypothetical situations by analyzing the importance of different data features, and visualizing model behavior across multiple models and data sets using a variety AI fairness metrics.
LinkedIn-Fairness Toolkit	https://engineering.linkedin.com/blog/2020/lift-addressing-bias-in-large-scale-ai-applications	The LIFT library supports organizations seeking to analyze the fairness of their own models and data.

The remediation process alters how the AI framework views the biased data by reclassifying the risk status to eliminate the impact on the decision process.[21] Through this process, learned bias is being removed from the algorithm that is used to train the AI tool. Based on the nature of algorithms and machine learning, models improve over time as the data begins to change as a result of less biased decision-making being incorporated into the learning process. If 50 years of data is used to create an algorithm, it will take decades for these issues of bias to organically correct themselves through integrating unbiased data into the AI training function.

In order to attract talent, AI is used to help recruiters sort through applicants and to prioritize candidates based on algorithmic fit. As you may have guessed, these results can be greatly impacted by past data which reinforces higher bias around race and gender. There was evidence that showed that Google search engines showed senior level jobs to men but not to women. In order to address this type of bias, LinkedIn recently revised its Recruiter tool to return a gender mix based on the pool of qualified candidates. While this improved the rankings of women, we know that gender is not binary and that this approach, while improved, is still disadvantaging underrepresented groups.

The European Union (EU) is proposing a law to regulate the use of AI for use in high stakes areas such as critical infrastructure, college admissions, and loan applications. If approved, regulators could fine companies up to 6% of their annual global revenue.[22] The approach is designed to address human and societal risks associated with certain uses of AI. Firms using AI would need to provide details on how their technology works and demonstrate sufficient levels of human oversight. AI including algorithms and machine learning are very much a part of our present and will continue to be part of our future. While leveraging AI tools reduces human bias of individual managers, it also has the potential to increase bias on a more systemic level.

10.6 Ethical Considerations for Artificial Intelligence (AI)

There are NGOs whose mission is to illuminate the social implications and harmful impacts of AI. Table 10.5 lists several of these organizations. Their mission is to provide research in order to equip impacted communities with information and tools to allow their voices to be heard by policy makers, industry leaders, and practitioners to address and eliminate systemic AI bias and its harmful impacts. These NGOs have a

Table 10.5 AI Equity NGOs

Organization	Website
Algorithmic Justice League	https://www.ajl.org
Equal AI	https://www.equalai.org/

number of useful resources to references when developing AI including their Equal AI Checklist to Identify Bias in AI. These types of tools should be referenced by not only developers of AI but also users of the tools to ensure that these best practices have been followed to minimize unintended impacts on underserved communities.

Delivering on AI equity means removing agency and control over how AI systems interact with data from organizations and returning it to the people. As a first step, people need to provide consent that their data be used. They also need to understand how that data will be used and in what situations. Most people are not aware that AI tools are making decisions about them with their personal data in all areas of their lives from schools, job applications, healthcare, and even government. Even a recruitment tool such as video interviewing software can generate bias results. The technology may not fully recognize female voices or faces. Results indicate that it tends to have poor outcomes for people of color or non-native language speakers. Other examples are much more devasting on people's lives, freedoms, and rights. As a society, we need to agree on how our values, rights, and respect for human life will be reflected in AI tools and framework usage. Use in the areas of surveillance, identification for use of lethal force by police, immigration identification, and detainment can all have significant including life-ending consequences. The age of "big brother" is here, and as a society we need to decide how these tools should be used as they impact our rights as citizens. It can't be left to tech companies and their billionaire founders. Reinforcing this issue, in late 2020, 10 members of Congress requested guidance from the EEOC on their authority to investigate bias from AI-based hiring technologies. Recognizing the interconnectivity of societal technology trends and the impacts on organizational practices and policies is a vital step in promoting justice, equity, and inclusion.

Scalable Cooperation at MIT Media Lab (https://www.moralmachine.net/) created the Moral Machine, a platform for gathering human views on moral decision made through machine learning. The current scenario allows participants to act as judges determining the outcome for a variety of scenarios, where a self-driving car has lost its brakes. It is an interesting exercise to identify the moral decisions that need to be considered in machine learning such as the value of a life based upon a variety of factors. In effect, teams are making these kinds of decisions when they decide the acceptable error rate for AI, especially the acceptable impact on human life and the disproportional impact on underserved communities. As part of an organization's J.E.D.I. mission, leaders must consider how these types of ethical decision are embedded into product and service design and the impacts on their stakeholders.

Today, embedded bias is predominately from a White male developer's point of view. While this is not a new phenomenon, to promote J.E.D.I. values we must be more inclusive in our approach to building AI tools and frameworks. For years, engineering has focused on male-based testing. For example, it was 2011 before a female crash dummy was required to be used for safety testing in automobiles. Design bias based on race, ethnicity, class, gender, and sexual orientation remains a significant issue. Unfortunately, we continue to be challenged by equal representation in the tech sector. According to a Paysa report, people accepting jobs in the self-driving car industry were primarily men (69%). Only 6% were women. The remainder didn't disclose their gender. In terms of ethnicity, 43% were White, 37% were Asian, and 22% were undisclosed.[23] Clearly, we have more work to do in order to protect against bias in data, algorithms, and outcomes baked into the AI development process.

The tech industry is full of stories about AI generating bias results because of team and data homogeneity. Examples include Facebook's inability to identify people of color's photos, Amazon's algorithm that excluded women from its candidate pool, and driverless cars that are unable to properly identify pedestrian that are people of color. AI learns from the data and responds to what it is taught. Unless we have a wide representation of voices, faces, experiences included in the development of AI tools and frameworks, the tools' experience and knowledge will only partially represent our population.

In order to change outcomes, we must increase the diversity of those involved in computing science research and those working as computing professions. Table 10.6 includes several organizations that are doing impactful work to ensure that future

Table 10.6 Organizations Supporting Diversity in Tech

Organization	Website	Mission
AI4ALL	https://ai-4-all.org/	Increasing diversity and inclusion in AI education, research, development, and policy.
Girls Who Code	https://girlswhocode.com/	Closing the gender gap in technology.
Code	https://code.org/	Expanding access to computer science in schools and increasing participation by girls and students from other underrepresented groups.
Black Girls Code	https://www.blackgirlscode.com/	Increasing the participation of women of color in the digital space by empowering girls of color in STEM fields and providing Black youth with the skills to enter expanding technology sector.

generations of coders, computer scientists, software engineers, and tech executives represent a diverse cross-section of our communities. Some organizations focus more on bridging the gender divide in technology, and others are reaching out to a cross-section of members of underrepresented groups. These organizations are seeking to improve the diversity of representation and thought in the tech sector as well as to prepare the next generation for good quality jobs that build wealth and a better standard of living.

10.7 Governance and Risk Management

Personal data privacy is a major risk management consideration and in many cases it impacts how people analytics can be used to inform people strategy. It all began with the General Data Protection Regulation (GDPR) launched on 2018 by the EU requiring protection of personally identifiable information (PII). The scope of the GDPR's requirements for employers is significant and includes active and former employees, candidates, and even third parties such as partners and spouses. Organizations are required to have a purpose or reason for collecting and retaining employees' PII data. In addition, employees, candidates, and third parties must be informed that their data is being collected and processed for those disclosed purposes. A schedule is required to be established to review the data for accuracy and relevance, and a process must be in place to purge data that is no longer relevant. Organizations must clarify who internally and externally has access to the data and that the PII data is secure. The GDPR requires that individuals are informed about how their data is being used and allows individuals to have access to their data, request a correction to data, request that their data be deleted and, or not be processed for information or analytical reasons. As part of the security protocols, a data breach response program must be in place. Employees must be informed and trained on the GDPR compliance practices. While the GDPR was the first, California has the California Consumer Privacy Act (CCPA), and Brazil has enacted the LGDP. Over 100 countries have global privacy laws including Australia, Canada, China, Japan, and the U. K. When gathering the PII for reporting on metrics for diversity, equity, and inclusion, it is imperative to know what data is able to be gathered and for which purposes. Data privacy needs to be part of an organization's risk management strategy. Data privacy policies for HCM platforms and people analytics tools should be a consideration during the selection process. Many HCM SaaS solutions have embedded data privacy protocols into their platforms to support data compliance. Best practice includes creating a team that reviews policies, vendor standards, and internal practices in this dynamic regulatory environment to ensure compliance.

In 2020, the GDPR's fines increased 39% rising to the equivalent of $332 million with certain countries such as Italy and Germany being more aggressive about imposing fines. Google received one of the largest fines (€50million; $59 million) in France for its data management practices.[24] According to the United Nations, 128 out of 194 countries have put in place legislation to secure the protection of data and privacy.

As outlined in Figure 10.7, employees can request that employers share any personal information that is gathered on them. Employees can request that updates and corrections be made to the information; they can request that their data be erased, that a copy be given in a digital format, and even that their personal data is not included in any type of processing or data analysis. Employers are required to be transparent with employees on their data gathering policies. They must notify employees regarding the type of data being collected, the purpose of collecting the data, the retention period for the data, and details on how employees can access the data. Under the GDPR, there is personal data and sensitive data. Sensitive data includes personal data revealing racial or ethnic origin, political views, religion, trade union membership, and the processing of genetic data, biometric data, data concerning health, or data concerning a person's sex life or sexual orientation. Processing of sensitive data, which includes many of the data points tracked in DEI metrics and KPI, is prohibited unless certain specific exceptions are met.

One of the challenges in terms of gathering and reporting on diversity, equity, and inclusion data is national laws. Organizations operating within the EU must comply with the GDPR as well as potentially even stricter data privacy requirements of individual member countries.

A recent PWC report, Global Diversity and Inclusion Benchmarking Survey, found that about 55% of organizations gather information on employee demographics, but significantly fewer gather data and stratify it by demographics and compensation, promotion, or performance ratings.[25] Global organizations' DEI programs skew toward talent attraction and retention, and legal compliance with far fewer organizations leveraging DEI initiatives and strategies to enhance performance and business results. These results align with the Society for Human Resource Management (SHRM) research which indicates that the top DEI programs for organizations were:

1. Systematic expanding of the candidate pool to tap new sources of talent.
2. Revising employee policies to expand work and life balance.
3. Develop employee training to enhance cultural respect and tolerances for other differences in the workplace.

Both of these reports reflect that global organizations are at varying levels of J.E.D.I. maturity with most reporting compliance or awareness experiential levels.

| **Right to Rectify** | **Right to Forget** | **Right to Data Portability** | **Right to Object** |
| Request data to be updated or corrected | Request data be erased | Request a copy of data | Object to data being processed |

Figure 10.7   GDPR: Employee Rights.

There are a number of ESG data standards, ranking agencies, and even data tools to facilitate the process of managing an organization's own data and to sharing it transparently with stakeholders. In order to support business leaders seeking data to support data driven decision-making, several new tools have been developed. These tools gather data from internal and external sources to help identify risks and to expand leaders' understanding of what qualifies as risk. These tools are highlighted in Table 10.7.

For example, an organization's HCM policies have not historically received major attention from regulators and investors. As such, many organizations have provided minimal disclosures on people related policies, processes, and procedures. As we have learned, an organization's human capital strategies have an outsized impact on justice, equity and inclusion. The SEC is now requiring disclosure on organizations' human capital practices and strategies. SASB undertook a human capital assessment project to better identify the risks in its industry sector analysis for disclosure criteria. ESG investors are demanding disclosure on organizational J.E.D.I. policies and performance results vs. targets and goals. The social protests in 2020 and 2021 have fully demonstrated the relevance of human capital issues especially around diversity, equity, and inclusion to an organization's risk profile as well as their ability to thrive in a global arena.

Datamaran's software platform leverages an external view and scans regulatory, media, and corporate disclosures to identify and monitor over 400 risk factors impacting today's organizations. While many of these tools initially focused on environmental, climate, and human rights risks, 2020 has brought to the forefront the intersectionality of environmental and social justice. While climate change remains a board level priority, J.E.D.I. related risks and opportunities as well as public health concerns have risen to the top of board agendas. Risk is dynamic and the importance of public health risk in 2020 highlights the reprioritization of materiality, or what is known as the most impactful issues for your organization. In today's volatile and uncertain world, organizations need to assess their risk and their risk identification and vetting practices. Over the past decade, global organizations have been placing an increased emphasis on disclosure of workplace diversity, equity, and inclusion. According to Datamaran analysis based on NLP, S&P Europe 350 places high

Table 10.7 Data-Driven Platform to Assess Risk

Data-Driven Tools	Website	Impact
Datamaran	https://www.datamaran.com	Automated solution to identify and monitor 400+ risk factors.
FigBytes	https://www.figbytes.com/	Connects purpose with data supporting an organization's environmental and social justice.

emphasis on DEI workforce disclosures, and U.S.-based S&P 500 places medium emphasis in their annual financial disclosures. Both the U.S. and the EU-based organizations placed high emphasis on an organization's workplace DEI data disclosures in their annual sustainability reports.[26]

The FigBytes platform focuses internally and brings together data from across an organization to provide information and insights for leadership in order to align strategy and purpose. The platform leverages a balanced scorecard technology to aggregate and share ESG data providing a roadmap for an organization's J.E.D.I. vision. The approach is holistic and includes mission, vision, values, and ethics alignment as well as social and environmental data modules. The end result includes infographics that tell a data-driven ESG story for key stakeholders. Both platforms place a significant priority on the HCM risks and opportunities in an organization. Stakeholder requirements for J.E.D.I. disclosures are rising globally.

10.8 Summary

Driving systemic change requires enhancing our perspective taking to move beyond stereotypes and really understand that people are individuals with their own unique backgrounds, journeys, and futures. Part of the process necessitates moving from managerial decisions based on intuition to decisions based on data and information. In order to effectively make this transition, managers need data to be delivered in a relevant and consistent manner allowing them to incorporate data into their decision-making processes. Technology platforms are available to support data-driven decision-making and when properly implemented and socialized with managers and employees, these tools can provide much needed information to drive organizational change within people, processes, and policies. Alone the tools are not a silver bullet, they are a tool in a toolbox to support an organization's J.E.D.I. strategy. Key to a digital transformation is stakeholder engagement and cross-functional collaboration to drive data sharing, adoption, and ultimately organizational transformation.

While AI-based tools and frameworks are very useful, they must be understood and tested for bias and unintended consequences. When leveraging an analytics solution based on algorithms or machine learning, we must ask questions to ensure that we are not just accepting a blinded solution. Too often, vendors claim proprietary information and are reluctant to share algorithmic variables, which may result in unintended biases. Transparency of process is crucial. Technology application and data usage must be clearly explained to all stakeholders. In addition, as business leaders, we must push major technology companies to be more inclusive in their own hiring practices to ensure that diverse voices are included in the development of AI-based tools. Diversity of thought, experience, and data are all crucial to ensure that we are not developing digital solutions with unintended consequences. While many regulatory agencies have been demanding detailed justification of algorithmic coding and outcomes, the technology sector itself needs to focus on building more diversity of identity, experience, and thought into their product development process. This includes more diversity in employees throughout all levels in technology companies, engagement with diverse customers and communities, and making investments to support diversity in the next generation of tech leaders.

Data privacy is in its nascent stages. In the U.S., we have pockets of regulation, but we do not have a holistic personal data privacy code. For organizations operating globally, many countries have adopted personal data privacy regulations. As leaders seeking to improve our decision-making process through leveraging data, we need to be aware of how data is permitted to be utilized.

Moving to data-based decisions improves an organization's J.E.D.I. outcomes. Arriving at that point of gathering data to provide actionable information is a process that needs to be effectively managed with due diligence to ensure that data quality is sound and that algorithmic outcomes are unbiased.

Questions

1. Where is your organization on its HCM digital transformation journey?
2. What type of AI (algorithms or machine learning) are being used in your organization? How are they being used?
3. Based on the Data-Driven J.E.D.I. Transformation Checklist, how prepared is your organization for moving to data-driven decision-making?
4. How will moving to a data-based decision approach support building a J.E.D.I. culture?
5. How does a pay equity analysis support building a culture that promotes transparency, equity, and inclusion?
6. What recommendations would you make to support socialization of policies and processes to remediate the root causes of pay inequity?
7. What information should be requested of digital tool vendors when considering AI-based tools?
8. If you were leading a technology company developing AI solutions, how might you recommend designing products to promote J.E.D.I.?
9. If you were drafting a Code of AI Ethics for your own organization, what points might you include?
10. How might you address data privacy issues in your organization?

Notes

1 "'Numbers Take Us Only So Far,'" *Harvard Business Review*, November 1, 2017, https://hbr.org/2017/11/numbers-take-us-only-so-far.
2 "Data-Driven Decision Making: A Primer for Beginners," *Northeastern University Graduate Programs* (blog), August 22, 2019, https://www.northeastern.edu/graduate/blog/data-driven-decision-making/.

3 "'Numbers Take Us Only So Far,'" *Harvard Business Review*, November 1, 2017, https:// hbr.org/2017/11/numbers-take-us-only-so-far.

4 "Accountability Drives Action: Diversity, Equity and Inclusion at Johnson & Johnson," Careers, March 10, 2021, https://www.careers.jnj.com/careers/accountability-drives-action-diversity-equity-and-inclusion-at-johnson-johnson.

5 "Accountability Drives Action."

6 1615 L. St NW, Suite 800Washington, and DC 20036USA202-419-4300 | Main202-857-8562 | Fax202-419-4372 | Media Inquiries, "Generation Z Looks a Lot Like Millennials on Key Social and Political Issues," *Pew Research Center's Social & Demographic Trends Project* (blog), January 17, 2019, https://www.pewresearch.org/social-trends/2019/01/17/generation-z-looks-a-lot-like-millennials-on-key-social-and-political-issues/.

7 Sandy Cross and Porter Braswell, "A Data-Driven Approach to Hiring More Diverse Talent," *Harvard Business Review*, December 10, 2019, https://hbr.org/2019/12/why-isnt-your-organization-isnt-hiring-diverse-talent.

8 Cross and Braswell.

9 "Executive Parity Index Calculator - Ascend," accessed April 1, 2021, https://www. ascendleadership.org/page/EPI.

10 "Ascend Foundation Publishes New Research on Silicon Valley Leadership Diversity - Ascend," accessed April 1, 2021, https://www.ascendleadership.org/news/230114/ Ascend-Foundation-publishes-new-research-on-Silicon-Valley-leadership-diversity.htm.

11 "GM Takes Top Spot in Gender Equality Study," accessed April 13, 2021, https://www. freep.com/story/money/cars/general-motors/2018/10/04/gm-study-gender-equality-company/1521497002/.

12 Stephen Miller CEBS, "U.S. Companies Are Working to Fix Pay-Equity Issues," SHRM, May 13, 2019, https://www.shrm.org/resourcesandtools/hr-topics/compensation/pages/ companies-are-working-to-fix-pay-equity-issues.aspx.

13 "Fired by Bot at Amazon: 'It's You Against the Machine,'" *Bloomberg.Com*, June 28, 2021, https://www.bloomberg.com/news/features/2021-06-28/fired-by-bot-amazon-turns-to-machine-managers-and-workers-are-losing-out.

14 "About the ACM Organization," accessed March 30, 2021, https://www.acm.org/about-acm/about-the-acm-organization.

15 "The Code Affirms an Obligation of Computing Professionals to Use Their Skills for the Benefit of Society.," accessed March 30, 2021, https://www.acm.org/code-of-ethics.

16 Alistair Barr, "Google Mistakenly Tags Black People as 'Gorillas,' Showing Limits of Algorithms," *Wall Street Journal*, July 1, 2015, sec. Digits, https://blogs.wsj.com/dig-its/2015/07/01/google-mistakenly-tags-black-people-as-gorillas-showing-limits-of-algorithms/.

17 Michael Totty, "How to Make Artificial Intelligence Less Biased," *Wall Street Journal*, November 3, 2020, sec. Business, https://www.wsj.com/articles/how-to-make-artificial-intelligence-less-biased-11604415654.

18 "Predictive Policing Algorithms Are Racist. They Need to Be Dismantled.," MIT Technology Review, accessed November 4, 2020, https://www.technologyreview. com/2020/07/17/1005396/predictive-policing-algorithms-racist-dismantled-machine-learning-bias-criminal-justice/.

19 "Addressing Bias in Large-Scale AI Applications: The LinkedIn Fairness Toolkit," accessed November 4, 2020, https://engineering.linkedin.com/blog/2020/lift-addressing-bias-in-large-scale-ai-applications.

20 Totty, "How to Make Artificial Intelligence Less Biased."
21 Totty.
22 "Artificial Intelligence, Facial Recognition Face Curbs in New EU Proposal - WSJ," accessed April 21, 2021, https://www.wsj.com/articles/artificial-intelligence-facial-recognition-face-curbs-in-new-eu-proposal-11619000520?st=v2756jsrm9jl9m3&reflink=article_email_share.
23 Marco della Cava, "Who's Hiring for Self-Driving Car Jobs," *USA TODAY*, accessed January 25, 2021, https://www.usatoday.com/story/tech/news/2016/10/17/google-ford-not-only-names-self-driving-car-jobs/92315206/.
24 "European Regulators Have Imposed £245.3 Million in GDPR Fines To Date; 39% More Issued in 2020," CPO Magazine, January 25, 2021, https://www.cpomagazine.com/data-protection/european-regulators-have-imposed-245-3-million-in-gdpr-fines-to-date-39-more-issued-in-2020/.
25 Ip.
26 "TCB-Global-Insights-Report.Pdf," accessed April 23, 2021, https://pages.datamaran.com/hubfs/TCB-Global-Insights-Report.pdf?utm_campaign=GIR%202020&utm_medium=email&_hsmi=102511709&_hsenc=p2ANqtz-8Z9QVi_XvZ4uiVE_5dB4BExpJDA-eAwuCGdcqeZLRWQoO6tCwnak5FvmgsQtXnGMLua4EjloEg6lQfZw_8A_2_Jr-3Ig&utm_content=102511709&utm_source=hs_automation.

Bibliography

"About the ACM Organization." Accessed March 30, 2021. https://www.acm.org/about-acm/about-the-acm-organization.
"Addressing Bias in Large-Scale AI Applications: The LinkedIn Fairness Toolkit." Accessed November 4, 2020. https://engineering.linkedin.com/blog/2020/lift-addressing-bias-in-large-scale-ai-applications.
"Artificial Intelligence, Facial Recognition Face Curbs in New EU Proposal – WSJ." Accessed April 21, 2021. https://www.wsj.com/articles/artificial-intelligence-facial-recognition-face-curbs-in-new-eu-proposal-11619000520?st=v2756jsrm9jl9m3&reflink=article_email_share.
"Ascend Foundation Publishes New Research on Silicon Valley Leadership Diversity – Ascend." Accessed April 1, 2021. https://www.ascendleadership.org/news/230114/Ascend-Foundation-publishes-new-research-on-Silicon-Valley-leadership-diversity.htm.
Barr, Alistair. "Google Mistakenly Tags Black People as 'Gorillas,' Showing Limits of Algorithms." *Wall Street Journal*, July 1, 2015, sec. Digits. https://blogs.wsj.com/digits/2015/07/01/google-mistakenly-tags-black-people-as-gorillas-showing-limits-of-algorithms/.
Careers. "Accountability Drives Action: Diversity, Equity and Inclusion at Johnson & Johnson," March 10, 2021. https://www.careers.jnj.com/careers/accountability-drives-action-diversity-equity-and-inclusion-at-johnson-johnson.
Cava, Marco della. "Who's Hiring for Self-Driving Car Jobs." *USA TODAY*. Accessed January 25, 2021. https://www.usatoday.com/story/tech/news/2016/10/17/google-ford-not-only-names-self-driving-car-jobs/92315206/.
CPO Magazine. "European Regulators Have Imposed £245.3 Million in GDPR Fines To Date; 39% More Issued in 2020," January 25, 2021. https://www.cpomagazine.com/

data-protection/european-regulators-have-imposed-245-3-million-in-gdpr-fines-to-date-39-more-issued-in-2020/.

Cross, Sandy, and Porter Braswell. "A Data-Driven Approach to Hiring More Diverse Talent." *Harvard Business Review*, December 10, 2019. https://hbr.org/2019/12/why-isnt-your-organization-isnt-hiring-diverse-talent.

"Executive Parity Index Calculator – Ascend." Accessed April 1, 2021. https://www.ascendleadership.org/page/EPI.

"Fired by Bot at Amazon: 'It's You Against the Machine.'" *Bloomberg.Com*, June 28, 2021. https://www.bloomberg.com/news/features/2021-06-28/fired-by-bot-amazon-turns-to-machine-managers-and-workers-are-losing-out.

Fountaine, Tim, Brian McCarthy, and Tamim Saleh. "Building the AI-Powered Organization." *Harvard Business Review*, July 1, 2019. https://hbr.org/2019/07/building-the-ai-powered-organization.

"Global-Report.Pdf." Accessed January 13, 2021. https://www.pwc.com/gx/en/services/people-organisation/global-diversity-and-inclusion-survey/global-report.pdf.

"GM Takes Top Spot in Gender Equality Study." Accessed April 13, 2021. https://www.freep.com/story/money/cars/general-motors/2018/10/04/gm-study-gender-equality-company/1521497002/.

Miller, Stephen, and Stephen Miller (CEBS). "U.S. Companies Are Working to Fix Pay-Equity Issues." *SHRM*, May 13, 2019. https://www.shrm.org/resourcesandtools/hr-topics/compensation/pages/companies-are-working-to-fix-pay-equity-issues.aspx.

MIT Technology Review. "Predictive Policing Algorithms Are Racist. They Need to Be Dismantled." Accessed November 4, 2020. https://www.technologyreview.com/2020/07/17/1005396/predictive-policing-algorithms-racist-dismantled-machine-learning-bias-criminal-justice/.

"Numbers Take Us Only So Far." *Harvard Business Review*, November 1, 2017. https://hbr.org/2017/11/numbers-take-us-only-so-far.

Northeastern University Graduate Programs. "Data-Driven Decision Making: A Primer for Beginners," August 22, 2019. https://www.northeastern.edu/graduate/blog/data-driven-decision-making/.

NW, 1615 L. St., Suite 800 Washington, and DC 20036 USA 202-419-4300 | Main 202-857-8562 | Fax 202-419-4372 | Media Inquiries. "Generation Z Looks a Lot Like Millennials on Key Social and Political Issues." *Pew Research Center's Social & Demographic Trends Project* (blog), January 17, 2019. https://www.pewresearch.org/social-trends/2019/01/17/generation-z-looks-a-lot-like-millennials-on-key-social-and-political-issues/.

"TCB-Global-Insights-Report.Pdf." Accessed April 23, 2021. https://pages.datamaran.com/hubfs/TCB-Global-Insights-Report.pdf?utm_campaign=GIR%202020&utm_medium=email&_hsmi=102511709&_hsenc=p2ANqtz-8Z9QVi_XvZ4uiVE_5dB4BExpJDA-eAwuCGdcqeZLRWQoO6tCwnak5FvmgsQtXnGMLua4EjloEg6lQfZw_8A_2_Jr-3Ig&utm_content=102511709&utm_source=hs_automation.

"The Code Affirms an Obligation of Computing Professionals to Use Their Skills for the Benefit of Society." Accessed March 30, 2021. https://www.acm.org/code-of-ethics.

Totty, Michael. "How to Make Artificial Intelligence Less Biased." *Wall Street Journal*, November 3, 2020, sec. Business. https://www.wsj.com/articles/how-to-make-artificial-intelligence-less-biased-11604415654.

Chapter 11

Creating Opportunities for All

Continuing on our J.E.D.I. journey, we focus on best practices and success stories to build new foundational systems to create and support a more equitable and just social and business environment. We have learned that our core societal and business systems require an overhaul to provide equal access and opportunity. These include how we educate our future generation of business leaders, allocate capital and debt, protect our civil rights, and provide access to healthcare. While some might say that these are government problems to address, my recommendation is that we look to partnerships between government, the business community, and community-based NGOs to combine efforts. Leveraging the public-private partnership (PPP) framework creates ecosystems in which we value and appreciate one another's diversity of talents, experiences, and perspectives. Leveraging Appreciative Inquiry as a model to drive change allows for an expanding of the pie not just a reallocation. We have seen that significant positive impact occurs to country's GDP through building a more equitable and inclusive society and economy. If we reimagine what is possible, together, we can create a more just and equitable society for all.

11.1 Public-Private Partnership to Bridge the Gaps

PPPs are collaborations between private parties and governmental or quasi-governmental agencies to address systemic challenges. In order to highlight the significant impact of PPPs, let's take a look back at the pioneering partnership between Dr. Booker T. Washington of the Tuskegee Institute, a Black educator, and Mr. Julius Rosenwald, a White businessperson, who created the Rosenwald schools. In the early

DOI: 10.1201/9781003168072-12

20th century (1912–1937), this partnership between Rosenwald and Washington built 4,978 schools for Black youth primarily in southern states.[1] The collaboration was one of shared vision with Dr. Washington, the educator and thought leader, and Mr. Rosenwald, part-owner of Sears, Roebuck & Co, the underwriter. At the time of this collaboration, most schools in the south for Black students were in very poor physical condition lacking basic materials and funding. Some communities didn't even offer schooling for Black students. The Rosenwald schools were built with the then leading architectural designs including maximizing sunlight, sanitation, and ventilation. These schools had a significant impact on communities and made meaningful strides in closing the education gap between Black and White students offering graduates a better standard of living and higher wages.

The graduates of Rosenwald schools are its greatest legacy including civil rights leaders, Medgar Evers, Maya Angelou, and John Lewis.[2] Medgar Evers was a businessman and civil right activist involved in campaigning to desegregate the University of Mississippi Law School in the 1950s.[3] Dr. Maya Angelou shared her extraordinary talent as a writer serving as a role model for women especially women of color and sharing her message of hope and resilience with the world. John Lewis was a politician and civil rights activist serving in the U.S. House of Representatives. His legacy includes being one of the original 13 Freedom Riders that challenged interstate travel in the southern U.S. states in 1961.[4] His activism in marching with Dr. Martin Luther King in Selma, Alabama, and the televised image of his beating ignited support for the Voting Rights Act in 1965. Unfortunately, the ground gained by this act, striking down the literacy tests required of Black citizens before being allowed to vote, is once again under threat today in places like Georgia with their new voter registration laws. While the House of Representatives passed the John Lewis Voting Rights Act on 2021, which was designed to provide tools to address discriminatory practices enacted by several states that disproportionally suppress voting rights of minorities, the elderly, and youth, it remains bogged down in the Senate. This list of graduates represents just a few that were positively impacted by the Rosenwald schools. This PPP between Rosenwald and Washington serves as an excellent example of what is possible when we reach across divides with a shared purpose and vision of justice and equity.

Today we see PPPs being used to drive transformative change in education, as well. Creating opportunities for underserved youth is vital to reverse and ultimately close the education and wealth gaps and to position the next generation for productive and life-sustaining careers. The following case is a detailed look into IBMs P-TECH program, which is a collaboration with secondary and post-secondary schools, communities, and industry partners to lay the educational foundation and to provide opportunities for today' s underserved youth in the high growth fields of technology, healthcare, and advanced manufacturing. The objective of P-TECH is to educate today's youth and improve their access to the abundant and well-paying jobs of the future as well as to provide a well-trained workforce to meet the needs of 21st century organizations.

IBM DRIVING IMPACT THROUGH P-TECH, A PUBLIC-PRIVATE PARTNERSHIP

OVERVIEW

P-TECH, a PPP, is an innovative education and workforce development model created by IBM in collaboration with school districts, community colleges, and industry partners. This innovative model is designed for students to study high school and college coursework simultaneously while engaging in industry-guided workforce development. P-TECH is helping students achieve their goals for college and careers while delivering skills most in demand by employers in growth industries.

ABOUT

P-TECH is a PPP that leverages the expertise of public school systems, community colleges, industry, and governmental entities to create and support a public education reform model focused on college attainment and career readiness. P-TECH schools support a 9-14 curriculum enabling students to earn both a high school diploma and a 2-year post-secondary degree in a science, technology, engineering, and mathematics (STEM) field. The program including the associate's degree is free to students. Students' education is supplemented by a variety of workplace experiences, such as mentorship, worksite visits and paid internships. After graduation from a P-TECH school, students have both the academic and professional skills needed to succeed. They can either continue their education in a 4-year post-secondary institution or enter into entry-level careers in information technology (IT), healthcare, advanced manufacturing, and other competitive fields. P-TECH is designed to be an inclusive model with no testing or grade requirements for entry into the program. The program serves students from primarily underserved backgrounds.

P-TECH schools foster a community and culture built upon high expectations for students. Rather than seeing graduation from high school as their end goal, students see themselves as college students with a career path starting with their entry into 9th grade. P-TECH schools are in over 28 countries and regions, and growing, including locations in the U.S., Brazil, Canada, New Zealand, Japan, Italy, Canada, Czech Republic, France, Ireland, the UK, and Thailand. The rate of global growth has been exponential as indicated by Figure 11.1. In under 10 years, the program expanded both domestically in the U.S. and around the world as the model was designed for scalability, allowing for rapid replication. The global rate of model adoption and replication demonstrates the effectiveness and impact of the model in driving systemic change related to education and employment for young people.

	2011	2012	2013	2014	2015	2016	2017	2018	2019
	Brooklyn, NY	Brooklyn, NY Chicago, IL	New York Chicago, IL	New York Chicago, IL Connecticut	New York Chicago, IL Connecticut	New York Chicago, IL Connecticut Colorado Maryland Rhode Island Australia	New York Chicago, IL Connecticut Colorado Maryland Rhode Island Australia Morocco	New York Chicago, IL Connecticut Colorado Maryland Rhode Island Texas Louisiana Australia Morocco	New York, Chicago, IL, Connecticut, Colorado, Maryland, Rhode Island, Texas, Louisiana, New Jersey, California Australia, Morocco, Taiwan, Brazil, Colombia, Canada, Ireland, United Kingdom, Korea, Singapore, New Zealand, Philippines

Figure 11.1 P-TECH Global Growth.[6]

In the U.S., P-TECH schools serve urban, rural, and suburban schools. While all of the schools are designed to serve underserved populations, the student demographics vary by region and location. Each of the P-TECH schools' curriculum encompasses a range of STEM fields, including IT, advanced manufacturing, healthcare, and finance. Students that have participated in paid internship programs with IBM have worked in the following business units: Marketing, Communications, Hybrid Cloud, Finance, Global Markets, Global Technology Services, Global Business Services, Global Business Service Center for Applied Insights, Cloud Sales Enablement, and Watson Health. Over 650 business industry partners are part of this program as well. These partners include local, regional, national, and global organizations and they are a vital link in creating workforce experiences for students. Globally, P-TECH schools are serving more than 150,000 students.[5]

MODEL

The P-TECH model is based on six tenets: They

1. Build a PPP between a school district, community college or equivalent, and at least one employer.
2. Create a 6-year integrated program with courses and experiential learning scoped and sequenced to map to both high demand skills and post-secondary education requirements.
3. Open enrollment to all young people. There are no tests or grades required for admission.
4. Ensure students learn workplace skills both in the classroom and with experiential learning, speakers, projects, worksite visits, and paid internships.
5. Offer the program at no cost to the students or their families, including the associated degree.
6. Commit that P-TECH graduates are first in line for entry-level jobs from P-TECH industry partners.

A CONVERSATION WITH GRACE SUH, VP OF EDUCATION, CORPORATE SOCIAL RESPONSIBILITY IBM, P-TECH LEAD[7]

Grace Suh is Vice President, Education, Corporate Social Responsibility at the IBM Corporation. In her position, Grace manages IBM's global education portfolio, including the P-TECH 9-14 School Model, a public education reform initiative spanning more than 240 schools and 28 countries and regions, and SkillsBuild, a newly launched program designed to upskill and reskill adults through online learning, mentorship, and hands-on experiences.

Prior to IBM, Grace worked at the Children's Defense Fund, a national child advocacy organization in Washington, D.C. In addition to the corporate and non-profit sectors, Grace has worked in city government with a focus on juvenile justice issues. Grace serves on a number of education committees and boards, including the Coalition for Career Development, bCahn Fellows Programs and Schools That Can.

Grace has a master's degree in public policy from the John F. Kennedy School of Government at Harvard University and a bachelor's degree from Columbia University.[8]

What Was the Original Vision When You Began P-TECH and How Have the Results Matched with Expectations?

The vision was twofold. We were seeking to address skills gaps in the economy, while also working to address deep inequities in education by giving young people, who have historically and consistently been denied access to quality education and economic opportunity, a supported pathway from school to college and career. We knew that a high school diploma was no longer enough to earn a well-paying job, but at the same time, a 4-year degree was not necessary to garner some of the most exciting career opportunities, including ones in emerging technology areas. Our vision was to break down the artificial silos that exist between high school, community college, and industry, by having these institutions collaborate to ensure that students earned their high school diploma, a cost-free industry-recognized associates degree, along with workplace experiences like mentorships and internships. The vision also was to create a scalable model that could eventually impact hundreds of thousands of young people, rather than just create a single school that would impact 100s. P-TECH was launched in 2011 in Brooklyn.

P-TECH was initially envisioned as a U.S. initiative, but we found that these issues of insufficient "new collar" workers to fill jobs and lack of access and equity for underserved communities are issues that resonate with governments and educators around the world. P-TECH has been replicated in 28 countries and regions with more than 600 global industry partners.

How Has P-TECH Addressed Systemic Challenges That Impede Opportunities for Underserved Populations?

At its core, P-TECH is a partnership between high schools, community colleges, and industry partners, with funding for this new way of high school that spans an extra 2 years – grades 9–14 – generally provided by the state. By combining the expertise of each institution and integrating everything, our goal is to provide underserved youth with a clear and supported pathway from school to career to jobs. In the U.S., we work at the state level to ensure funding and policy changes to enable the model, with long-term sustainability. We also advocated for the reauthorization of the Perkins Act, which provides federal funds to Career and Technical Education (CTE) education, and which states can now use to support P-TECH implementation.

P-TECH is a public high school model so all social services that are available through the public school system continue to be available, such as free and reduced price lunches, and Individualized Education Plan (IEP) accommodations.

Garnering community buy-in is important to ensure that the community supports and enhances the model rather than detracts from it. Our Founding Principal, Rashid Davis, has said that P-TECH helps change the definition of success for many students. Through exposure to mentors and internships students have a new perspective-"What are the kinds of things I can do with my life?"

How Has the Program Experience or Outcome Differed Based Upon the Countries and Partners Involved?

The P-TECH model is based on six design principles allowing the model to be scalable. These design principles provide the blueprint and structure for model replication worldwide. We leverage our IBM Corporate Citizenship Managers, who are part of our Corporate Social Responsibility function, to facilitate meetings with key stakeholders – government officials, education leaders, industry leaders – in countries and regions. Each country has its own complexities such as different education systems, identifying the equivalent of community college, and implementation challenges. Based upon that, we work with our partners to customize the model for local needs, without losing fidelity to the model.

What Lessoned Learned or Best Practices Are You Able to Share to Help Other PPP Projects Improve Diversity, Equity, and Inclusion?

Keeping the user – students – at the center is a best practice for success. Working within a PPP, it is important to understand one another's key strengths. The partnership is most successful when areas of expertise are clearly articulated and respected by partners. Everyone needs to stay in their lanes of expertise. For example, while many people have education backgrounds at IBM, our education partners have delivery responsibility for pedagogy.

Using a clear set of design principles that align with goals keeps the focus on the user and their success. Align mission and metrics to make sure your data gathering, and measurement supports achievement of your goals. A focus on data – and many different data points – is necessary to understand how the work is progressing and if any changes need to be made.

Replication of the model allows for the greatest impact in addressing systemic income and education inequalities. Best practices include making it open source and designing for scalability.

While data is important, sharing of stories really changes hearts and minds. Kudos to Katie Leasor, External Relations Professional, IBM Corporate Social Responsibility for all of the amazing stories she helps us share.

What Impact Has the Program Had on Employees at IBM?

It has had an impact on retention and recruitment of employees. IBM employees are proud of this program and the impact that IBM is having on education inequity and workforce inclusion.

P-TECH is fully integrated into IBM. Ginni Rometty, Executive Chair, IBM, is a crusader for P-TECH, advocating both internally and externally for its widespread replication. Arvind Krishna, CEO, IBM, is also a key voice of the model, sharing its impact and promise with key stakeholders. The model is not just a CSR initiative, it is embedded into IBM. For example, HR provides internships and ultimately positions to recent graduates. We also are reframing the conversation around building a culture of inclusion to welcome and support diversity of identity, experience, and thought.

As another example, employees throughout the company volunteer at P-TECH schools, host worksite visits with students and provide internship opportunities as well. Ultimately, the business units are hiring graduates from the P-TECH program to fill "new collar" jobs.

What Aspect of the Program Makes You Most Joyful?

Our students are so amazing. I really enjoy engaging with them and sharing their stories of success.

Do You Have Anecdotes That You Can Share?

ShuDon Brown has an amazing story. She completed her high school diploma and associate's degree in 2 1/2 years. We are finding that most students who complete P-TECH want to go on to more college. She attended William Peace University in Raleigh, North Carolina, and interned at IBM while there. After graduation, she was hired by IBM, and while working, completed her master's degree and now is working on her PhD.

What Is Next for P-TECH?

Replication, replication, replication. Replicating the P-TECH model with fidelity and quality around the globe. Continuing to build a strong network of P-TECH schools committed to serving students and replicating the model. Building an alumni network to follow alumni and to tell their stories about the journey from education to "new collar" jobs and their continued career paths. Following the alumni's trajectory to better understand P-TECH's impact in addressing systemic barriers. Continuing to build relationships with industry partners so that P-TECH becomes a dedicated source for hiring for "new collar' jobs so that collectively we build more inclusive economies.

HISTORY

To provide a holistic approach to education and workforce development, IBM, the New York City Department of Education, and The City University of New York designed and launched the first P-TECH school in Brooklyn, New York, in September 2011. P-TECH was designed with two primary goals. The first goal was to address the global skills gap by building a workforce with the academic, technical, and professional skills required for "new-collar" jobs. The second goal was to provide underserved youth with a transformative education model that integrated their academic and professional development providing a pathway to career opportunities.

The first class of P-TECH graduated in 2017. The numbers are impressive with 53% of the first cohort graduating with an associate's degree and 74% of the students opting to continue on to a 4-year college. Equally impressive is the 92% attendance rate and the percentage of students reaching college ready preparedness in English Language Arts (74%) and Math (83%).

A CONVERSATION WITH SHUDON BROWN, A GRADUATE OF P-TECH[9]

ShuDon Brown is a graduate of the Pathways in Technology Early College High School Education in Brooklyn. This was the first P-TECH location offering an education that integrates college classes and high school classes. Students have a significant course load and a longer day which includes attending classes at both the high school and college campuses.

ShuDon holds a master's degree from North Carolina Agricultural and Technical State University and a bachelor's degree from William Peace University.

What Key Learnings Have You Taken Away from the P-TECH Program?

That is a loaded question, as I look back on my experience from further out in my career, the answer goes beyond the skills and technical education I received. I really learned about myself – my strengths and weaknesses. With the supportive network at P-TECH, I was able to work on my weaknesses which helped me succeed.

Also, I learned how to communication with students, teachers, and parents especially on technical and complex subjects like coding for which they had no frame of reference. When your parents ask why you are up at midnight working on schoolwork, you need to be able to explain it to them. I have been able to use those communication skills in business to help translate technical speak for non-technical colleagues.

I appreciate the sense of teamwork in the P-TECH community from fellow students and teachers and I learned the value of collaboration in achieving program and personal goals. My fellow students provided guidance and support. My algebra teacher opened her classroom at 7:30 am to help me review material before class because of my hectic schedule. Our principal, Rashid Davis, knew my name and what courses I was taking. He knew all 250 students' names and their areas of study. We felt welcome and valued and we never wanted to leave school. Unlike many experiences of high schoolers, we loved our school!

I also learned how to navigate in a business environment by understanding how businesses operate through courses I took on startups and stock market simulations. I can translate technical requirements into business language because of having been expose to both the business and technical worlds.

How Has the Program Impacted Your Life/Career Trajectory?

Interacting with IBMers gave me a whole new perspective on what is possible. At IBM, people traveled for work and gained exposure to many different cultures. I learned to have a more global perspective and that you can have an impactful career in many places not just NYC. It allowed me to informational interview with people who were doing jobs like software developer or web developer so that I could understand the direction that I was most interested in pursuing. It gave me access and exposure that many people don't receive until well after college.

The workload was intense, but we didn't know that we couldn't do it. We just did it. In retrospect, it seems crazy that we were able to complete both high school and college courses at the same time. I would have robotics then go to track practice and then head off to coding classes. Our days extended at least two hours beyond regular high school hours. I was often doing homework like creating a website at midnight!

The experience changed my perspective about what is possible. My mother is a college graduate, but she had to rely on student debt to attend. I remember celebrating her student debt payment. My father graduated from high school and attended technical school spending his career working for Con Edison. I always planned to attend college and initially wanted to study marine biology, but I always thought student loans were the only way to pay for it. Through the P-TECH experience, I learned about scholarship opportunities. Since I only needed 2 years of college to graduate, it was easier to get funding.

I am now getting my doctorate studying leadership for high school and early college students. I'm planning on writing a case study about how students perceive and develop leadership skills and how models like P-TECH can facilitate the process of building leadership skills in young people.

What Advice Would You Give to Your Younger Self upon Entering the Program?

Stop being scared. Use your voice to advocate for yourself. If you need things to change to support your growth and success, ask for it. If you want to be part of a club, do it. When I came to P-TECH, I was very shy and timid, but I always wore bright colors. I attended a small Jesuit middle school and arrived at P-TECH which had 250 students but was housed in a building with a regular high school bringing the school population to over 900. The size of the school with guards at the door was a whole new experience for me. Through my courses including public speaking and Black theater as well as my student and staff interactions, I began to open up and come into my own personality.

Are There Any Other Reflections That You Would Like to Share?

Going through P-TECH isn't normal, but students don't know that. We have a real sense of pride and accomplishment. Given the opportunity, we rise to the occasion. The P-TECH model proves that through the experience of taking college credit classes that you can handle college.

Impact

P-TECH's impact has been significant in terms of scalability and replication of its model and in improving outcomes for young people. To best assess the impact, it makes sense to take a deeper dive into those programs that have been able to guide students through the entire process. A report prepared by MDRC, a non-profit, non-partisan social and education policy research organization, entitled *Bridging the School to Work Divide: Interim Implementation and Impact Findings from New York City's P-TECH 9-14 Schools* highlights the following key findings for P-TECH NYC-based programs:

- P-TECH students' high school coursework and New York State Regents exams are accelerated. All schools focus on career and technical education (CTE) programs including classes that teach students specific workplace skills aligned with the labor market and "soft skills" such as good work habits and interpersonal skills.
- Student's college coursework typically begins in 10th grade with the pace and progress of courses varying by student. The degree pathways are designed to complement the high school CTE coursework and lead to credentials toward specific careers.
- The specific work-based opportunities available, such as workplace visits, job shadowing, and internships, and levels of participation differed across schools reflecting their region of operation.

- P-TECH students earned more total credits than students in other schools. These additional credits, which are driven by CTE and other non-academic subjects, did not appear to come at the expense of earning academic credits.
- At the end of 2 years of high school, 42% of P-TECH 9-14 students had passed the ELA Regents exam with a score qualifying them for enrollment in City University of New York (CUNY) courses, significantly high when compared with 25% of comparison group students. By the end of 3 years, the gap was smaller but still favored P-TECH 9-14 students.[10]

The P-TECH model is unique as it seeks to integrate workforce development, education, and career rather than segmenting that journey. The model supports students in their journey from education to employment closing many of the holes through which young people fall as they navigate this journey. As the study shows, the P-TECH model demonstrates impressive initial results based on the NYC experience.

Looking at the most mature state-wide P-TECH program provides additional insights. In New York State (NYS), results are impressive. In 2013, New York Governor Cuomo announced NYS P-TECH, a major statewide partnership among the Governor, NYS Education Department, State University of NY, and the Business Council of NYS. The first 16 P-TECH schools were opened in 2014 across a number of industries including advanced manufacturing, IT, health, civil engineering, and agriculture. Figure 11.2 shows the growth of the program and the impact to date. The number of schools has grown to 37 with a presence in all 10 economic development regions in NYS. The number of career and degree pathways has grown to 115 attracting 1,865 incoming 9th graders annually. The number of post-secondary education partners has grown to 30 with over 600 industry partners supporting mentorship, internships, and employment opportunities.

Even more significant, 95% of P-TECH students completed their high school diploma in 4 years compared to the state average of 82.1%. As P-TECH students arrive for post-secondary education, they are better prepared. In 2019, it is estimated that 50% of the of the general student population entering SUNY community college required at least one non-credit remedial course.[12] In comparison, P-TECH students have not needed remedial courses allowing them to move more quickly through degree requirements.

Other programs have less history than the NYS programs but still represent impressive results:

- Students have graduated with both a high school and with an associate's degree on average within 3.5 and 6 years.

Figure 11.2   P-TECH Schools in New York State (2018-2019).[11]

- The first cohort of P-TECH students graduated at four times the on-time U.S. national community college graduation rate and five times the rate for low-income students.
- The program has graduated 246 students with 36 graduates being hired into full-time position upon completion of their associate's degree. Over 70% of graduating students chose to continue with a 4-year degree program.
- IBM has provided 500 paid internship opportunities for students as of January 2020.

Conclusion

The P-TECH story demonstrates the impact of PPPs on systemic barriers. Just like within organizations, silos must be broken down between private and public entities to drive systemic change within our society. Many lessons on collaboration and building for scalability and replication can be taken from this case study as a model for driving impact through a PPP approach. As indicated by the voice of its graduate and further supported by performance metrics, P-TECH has already changed outcomes and created opportunities for students. Thanks to IBM and their partners, many more young people will be served by this innovative education and workforce development model improving their career opportunities and prospects for a bright future.

Programs such as P-TECH have significant impacts in terms of bridging the educational and digital divides advancing pay and wealth accumulation for underrepresented communities. The P-TECH model is scalable and can be translated around the globe driving broad based impact for global youth and changing their future trajectory. Using a collaborative approach, we can find solutions to address education, pay, and ultimately wealth gaps.

11.2 Reallocating Capital

In order to drive the systemic change, the systems that support business capital allocation must be realigned to improve access and to redistribute wealth and power. This includes venture, corporate, and philanthropy investment. Venture capital (VC) funds that are taking up the mantle to improve access to capital include WOCstar Fund, which invests in startups for women of color entrepreneurs. Their entire approach is more holistic than traditional VC firms, which get 80% of their investment return from 20% of their investments. WOCstar uses a "builder capitialist" approach designed to drive success. While they perform the same due diligence in selection of firms to invest as other VC firms, their approach also includes significant feedback and support for the entrpreneur. As a result, more firms, in which they invest, are sucessful. The VC funding dynamic needs to be expanded to create viable investment opportunities as well as viable funding opportunities for BIPOC, AAPI, and women entrepreneurs.

Philanthropy is another area that needs to be restructured to drive more meaningful impact especially in the communities for which these organizations were created to support. As highlighted by Edgar Villanueva, noted author and thought leader, in his book, *Decolonizing Wealth*, the majority of foundation money is retained inperpetuity with only the income from investments being used to support foundation work resulting in only about 5% of foundation money actually supporting its mission. Of this figure, less than 10% goes to BIPOC communities. The problem is multilayered including the foundation's investment model, the undersized impact on BIPOC communities, and the lack of diversity in the board members who make grantmaking decisions. In order to address these disconnects, Villanueva recommends building stronger relationships with the communities that a foundation is created to serve especially BIPOC communities. The approach centers around listening to better understand the community's history, experiences, and requirements. It is about inviting community leaders to the table to better support collaborative development and implementation of meaningful solutions. The philanthropy model needs redesign to incorporate diversity of identity, thought, and experience into its model design and implementation. Significant change requires long-term meaningful financial and resource commitments to recipient community based organizations from the foundation. [13] Too often funding is tied to new initiatives rather than an organization's core competency and operation. Not-for-profits working to support BIPOC communities do not have large endowments; they need long-term financial support for core services to address root causes of racial, social, and environmental injustice.

From a foundation grant-making perspective, we need to consider a more impactful approach that aligns investments with purpose. Resource Generation developed Social Justice Philanthropy Principles to provide recommendations and guidance for young people of privilege and wealth.(https://resourcegeneration.org/social-justice-philanthropy-and-giving/). The following are some tenets of social justice giving for foundations:

1. Focus giving on driving systemic changes to root causes of racial, economic, and environmental injustice.
2. Focus giving to organizations aligned with people most impacted treating them as key decision-makers and respecting their organization's determination for allocating funds.
3. Design your grantmaking process to be clear, simple, and transparent.
4. Consider your other talents to contribute in terms of expertise, knowledge, and skills.
5. Give more than the mandated 5% of assets and invest in non-extractive and regenerative investments.[14]

For example, providing general operating support for BIPOC-led not-for-profits allows them to decide the best allocation of funds for use in programs within their community. While funding is the lifeblood of non-profits, as a foundation you may either have or have access to other resources such as fundraising support, digital

Table 11.1 ESG Impact Screening Criteria

Affordable Housing	Immigrant Rights
Human and Civil Rights	Pay Equity
Community Development	No Funding of Private Prisons
Consumer Protection	Board Diversity
Criminal Justice	Small and Medium Businesses
Education	BIPOC-Owned Businesses
Training and Development	Equal Employment Opportunity
Equitable Food Access	Climate Change
Financial Inclusion	Environmental Justice
Indigenous Rights	Planetary Health

marketing skills, IT capabilities, and finance knowledge that can be invaluable to not for profits, if offered in a collaborative manner.

As endowment investment portfolio decisions are considered, foundation and not-for-profit board members need to consider how their funds are being invested. The investment strategy for the endowment should align with their environmental and social justice missions. Otherwise, foundations are investing in organizations that are exacerbating environmental and social inequities as discussed in the Chevron case in Chapter 1. Table 11.1 includes examples of portfolio screening criteria to consider when developing a socially and environmentally just investment strategy.

In addition, foundation and not-for-profit board members need to look deeply into their own internal practices to promote equity and inclusion including their board composition and representation. As a starting point, the board must define its organization's environmental and social justice mission and vision and how the identity representation of the board aligns with that vision. Foundation board membership is often closely aligned with sponsor organizations with senior members of organizations serving on foundation boards. While S&P 500 companies made strides in increasing their representation of women, Black, and Latino board members in 2020, about 80% of board seats remain occupied by White directors and about 70% remain occupied by men.[15] More diverse board representation is crucial to offer a more diverse perspective and to bring new ideas, networks, and resources to support vision alignment. Boards should establish a governance structure to promote greater transparency for selecting members including defining the roles and responsibilities for board members and the skills and requirements required. They also need to review the board's representation composition to determine if it is reflective of the community in which it operates. To accommodate greater representation, the board size may require expansion and skills and requirements revised to better reflect the communities served.

In terms of foundation investment policies, an analysis of the environmental and social consequences of a foundation's investment allocation needs to be completed. This process should include positive and negative investment screens as well as a review of investment managers for their own representational data. Foundation boards should request an analysis of investment management firms' ownership, portfolio managers, and fund managers. In addition, they need to perform due diligence around their investment managers' screenings and recommendations. Even for cash reserves, impact can be achieved by moving cash to minority-owned financial institutions. Within their sphere of influence, foundation and not-for-profit boards can have significant impact on environmental and social justice issues.

Individual investors can also drive change by considering their own investment guidelines and impacts. Here are some ideas:

1. Move money from Wall Street to invest in communities
2. Redefine return on investment to mean broader social returns

3. Redefine risk to broaden the definition to include a healthy and sustainable planet and communities
4. Consider the investments impact on healing and building solidarity to promote harmonious relationships across class, race, sexual orientation, and gender identity
5. Acknowledge the harm done to the planet and people in the process of wealth accumulation and our complicity in that process[16]

Examples of these actions include making investments with organizations like Seed Commons (https://seedcommons.org/), which is a national network of 25 locally based, non-extractive loan funds giving communities access to sophisticated financial resources. Seed Commons receives investment through a single fund and then allocates funds for local deployment by communities, which lowers risk while driving impact. Their focus is on marginalized communities that have born a disproportional burden from the extractive industry, deindustrialization, and systemic discrimination. Their $7.8 million in funding supports community-based cooperatively owned businesses that create local jobs, build wealth, and reduce inequities.[17]

The Boston Ujima Project (https://www.ujimaboston.com/) is building an ecosystem for change to address challenges being faced by the BIPOC community in Boston such as gentrification, poverty, homelessness, food deserts, unemployment, and lack of access to healthcare. Their approach is to create a multi-stakeholder committee made up of working class BIPOC community members. They are working to create a unique investment vehicle that funds local businesses, real estate, artists, and infrastructure projects that meet their criteria for investing in Boston's BIPOC working class communities. The fund is unique in that each committee member receives a vote on the fund's investment, which is not tied to the amount of money that they have invested. This approach supports building local wealth and jobs as well as supports building community power to address challenges and drive transformative change.[18] These examples of community investment funds highlight the shift that needs to occur in terms of the financial marketplace and how and where funds are being invested.

While this reallocation of investment provides a significant part of the solution, renewal of underserved communities requires a holistic approach. As with any significant project take stock of your current status, gather information, and assess your strengths and weaknesses. Consider your community stakeholders and leverage industry groups, not-for-profits, and local businesses to help support and mentor new businesses, projects, and programs. Create a community space for an incubator to support BIPOC, AAPI, or women entrepreneurs. Leverage partnerships to develop maker spaces to promote innovation and to build an entrepreneurial pipeline. Build technology infrastructure and seek technology-based assistance for community businesses and educational institutions. Leverage the community's NGO stakeholders to provide information, support, and community outreach. Taking a holistic approach recenters power back into the community and reallocates capital in order to drive social and environmental justice.

11.3 Holding Corporations to Their Commitments

Since the murder of George Floyd in May 2020, U.S.-based corporations have pledged tens of billions of dollars to addressing racial inequities. Highlights of these corporate commitmens are included in Table 11.2. The largest commitment, to date, is from JP Morgan/Chase (JPM) at $30 billion.[19] JPM's commitment is targeted toward affordable housing and opening branches in underrepresented neighborhoods.

Several other large banks have made significant pledges including Citigroup and Bank of America with $1 billion pledges coming from each.[20] Bank of America (B of A) pledged to spend $1 billion dollars over 4 years to support communities of color and minority-owned businesses focusing on four areas: Health, Jobs/Training/Reskilling/Upskilling, Support to Small Businesses, and Housing. They have identified the following areas of impact:

Table 11.2 Corporate Racial Equity Commitments

Organization	Amount Pledged	Impact
JP Morgan	$30 billion over 5 years	$8 billion -Mortgages Black and Latinx Household Fund 100,000 Affordable Housing Units Loans -Small BIPOC Businesses Invest in Minority-owned Banks, Credit unions, and Community Development
Bank of America	$1 billion over 4 years	$200 million (M) for Minority Entrpreneurs and Businesses $50M to Minority-owned Depository Institutions $25M Support of Community Outreach and Initiatives $25M in Support of Jobs Initiatiatives
Google	$12 million funding $25 million Ad Grants	Center for Policing Equity ($1M) Equal Justice Initative ($1M)
PayPal	$530 million	20 Not-for-profit Community Partner Grants ($5M) PayPal Empowerment Grant ($10M) Deposited $50M Optus Bank Invested $50M in eight Early-stage Black and LatinX-led VC Funds

(Continued)

Table 11.2 *(Continued)* **Corporate Racial Equity Commitments**

Organization	Amount Pledged	Impact
PepsiCo	$400 million over 5 years	$350M Spent with Black-owned Suppliers $50M Strengthen Black-owned Small Business $25M Scholarship Support $6.5M Community Impact Grants $5M Community Leadership Fellowship program
Amazon	$10 million	Employees Donated $8.5 M. Company Match $17M. Donated to 12 Organizations

Source: Isabel Togoh, "JP Morgan Pledges $30 Billion To Help Remedy Racial Wealth Gap," Forbes, accessed June 3, 2021, https://www.forbes.com/sites/isabel-togoh/2020/10/08/jp-morgan-pledges-30-billion-to-help-remedy-racial-wealth-gap/; "Bank of America Directs $300 Million of Its $1 Billion, Four-Year Commitment to Advance Racial Equality and Economic Opportunity," Bank of America, accessed April 28, 2021, https://newsroom.bankofamerica.com/press-releases/community-development/bank-america-directs-300-million-its-1-billion-four-year; "Standing with the Black Community," Google, June 3, 2020, https://blog.google/inside-google/company-announcements/standing-with-black-community/; Anna Irrera, "PayPal Pledges over $500 Million to Support Minority-Owned U.S. Businesses," *Reuters*, June 11, 2020, https://www.reuters.com/article/us-minneapolis-police-paypal-idUSKBN23I20Q; "PepsiCo's Racial Equality Journey: Black Initiative," PepsiCo, Inc. Official Website, accessed May 6, 2021, http://www.pepsico.com/about/diversity-and-engagement/racial-equality-journey-black-initiative; "Amazon Donates $10 Million to Organizations Supporting Justice and Equity," About Amazon, June 3, 2020, https://www.aboutamazon.com/news/policy-news-views/amazon-donates-10-million-to-organizations-supporting-justice-and-equity.

1. Support virus testing, telemedicine, flu vaccination clinics, and other health services, with a special focus on communities of color.
2. Strengthen relationships with historically Black colleges and universities (HBCUs) and Hispanic-serving institutions in the U.S. for hiring, research programs, and other areas of mutual opportunity.
3. Increase support to minority-owned small businesses, including clients and vendors.
4. Reskilling/upskilling through partnerships with high schools and community colleges.
5. Provide support and investment for affordable housing/neighborhood revitalization, leveraging their nearly $5 billion in Community Development Banking.

6. Increase efforts in recruitment and retention of teammates in low- to moderate-income and disadvantaged communities to build on work the company has already done to serve clients locally.[21]

B of A made its initial investments in September of 2020 investing $300 million. The 4-year commitment is being overseen by Anne Finucane, vice chairman of Bank of America and head of ESG, Capital Deployment and Public Policy. The $25 million in grant funding for jobs initiatives are being used to upskill and reskill Black and Hispanic/Latino individuals in partnership with 11 community colleges and 10 HBCUs and Hispanic-serving institutions. The program involves partnering with major employers to align program targets with hiring needs. The $25 million in community outreach supports philanthropic outreach to underserved and minority communities that were adversely impacted by the global health and humanitarian crisis including personal protection equipment. Direct equity investment of $50 million in Minority Depository Institutions (MDIs)-First Independence Corporation in Detroit, Liberty Financial Services, Inc. in New Orleans, and SCCB Financial Corp in Columbia, SC. The equity investment benefits the communities these MBIs serve through lending, housing, and community revitalization. The largest investment, $200 million, has been allocated to make direct equity investments in Black- and Hispanic/Latino-owned businesses over the next 4 years. The focus of this investment is to build a more robust hiring pipeline for Black and Hispanic/Latino students in order to address the racial wealth gap.[22] Other donations include $13 million to Native American communities impacted by the coronovirus. Recently, B of A raised its commitment to $1.25 billion over 5 years.[23]

Google's funding commitment is less clear as they have not indicated the recipients of the $12 million in funding beyond the initial pledge of $1 million each to Center for Policing Equity and Equal Justice Initative.[24] Since Amazon announced its original pledge of $10 million, employee expressed their desire to contribute and Amazon agreed to match their contibution 100% up to $10,000 per employee. The employees raised $8.5 million dollars, which the company matched, allowing for $17 million in donations to 12 organizations that were selected with input from the Black Employee Network. The groups chosen were: ACLU Foundation, Black Lives Matter, Brennan Center for Justice, Equal Justice Initiative, Lawyers' Committee for Civil Rights Under Law, NAACP, National Bar Association, National Museum of African American History and Culture, National Urban League, Thurgood Marshall College Fund, UNCF (United Negro College Fund), and Year Up.[25]

Walmart, which has 340,000 Black associates in the U.S., in conjunction with the Walmart Foundation has pledged $100 million to create a center on racial equity. With this commitment, the center will support philanthropy in the U.S. in the areas of financial, healthcare, education, and criminal justice system reform to fight exiting barriers.[26] In addition, their CEO, Doug McMillon, has pledged to look at Walmart's own business practices around supplier diversity, especially minority supplier development, to level the playing field and provide economic access to minority owned businesses. From a healthcare perspective, he pledged to provide improved accessibility to their existing health and wellness businesses by increasing Walmart Health Clinics. From an education prespective, he pledged to strengthen their academic support efforts such a Live Better U (https://walmart.guildeduca-tion.com) to provide upskilling, training and education opportunities for employ-ees. From a talent perspective, he has committed to broadening and strengthening recruiting programs with HBCUs. The pledge includes reviewing and evolving hiring rules for returning citizens, community members returning to society after incarceration, to provide better job opportunities.

In order for transformative change to promote opportunities for all to happen, corporate leaders must look deeply at their organizations and rewire their cultures to become one's that value equity and promote belonging. These corporate com-mitments vary from strictly philanthropic donations to investments in communi-ties, BIPOC, AAPI, and women owned business, educational partnerships, and core business realignments. While some organizations have been transparent around their funding of their commitments, others have not. Walmarts commitment is a good example as leadership has considered both internal and external systemic barriers in their strategy. While we are seeing that leaders are making commitments, more work remains to be done to drive systemic change. As organiztions continue on their J.E.D.I. journey, they need to drill deep within their own policies and processes to determine to whom organizational benefits accrue. Even with Walmart's most recent commitment to raising its minimum wage to $15/hour, this rate remains below the $16.54 required for a living wage of $68,808 per year for a family of four.[27] In addi-tion, the living wage level assummes full-time work, which many Walmart associates do not enjoy. Walmart employees' standards of living are impacted by their part-time status resulting in insufficient hours to qualify for healthcare benefits. According to a U.C. Berkley Labor Center report, Walmart pays its workers 12.4% less than retail workers as a whole and 14.5% less than workers in large retail stores. When Walmart enters a county, research indicates that both average and aggregate earnings of retail workers fall. In addition, the share of retail workers with health insurance through their employer also falls. While organization's have moved forward in their J.E.D.I. journey, work remains to be done such as providing well-paying and life-sustaining jobs that promote health and well-being.

Beyond the funding pledges, we are seeing evidence of leaderships' commiments to change business practices, policies, and processes. These commitments include changing business practices such as unlocking Black beauty products in cases at CVS, Walmart, and Walgreens, raising starting wages, and removing or rebranding products that were based on racially charged stereotypes such as the "Aunt Jemima" brand from Quaker Oats.[28] Technology leaders like IBM, Microsoft, and Amazon have committed to stop creating facial recognition software for police usage based on stakeholder concerns of racial profiling and mass surveillance. Many of these commitments focus on realignment with their external systems and stakeholders' requirements. In order to drive organizational systemic change, leaders need to focus on internal policies, processes, and practices to promote equity and inclusion within their talent ecosystems, supply chains, investment and philanthropy policies.

Amazon committed to doubling their representation of Black directors and vice presidents, which they achieved. They have launced inclusion training across the organization and removed racially insentitive language from their technical documentation. They have undertaken an intensive review of their internal policies around hiring, development, and promotions.

AltFinance, a joint venture between three investment firms, Apollo Global Management, Ares Management Corp, and Oaktree Capital Management, was formed to attract more BIPOC talent into the investment industry. The program design includes a mentored fellowship, a scholarshup program, and a virtual curriculum designed by the University of Pennsylvania Wharton School. Students from selected HBCUs, Clark Atlanta, Morehouse College, and Spellman College, will be the initial recipients of the scholarship and fellowship offerings to prepare for careers in private-equity or alternative-credit investing. The virtual program is available to students at any HBCU that elects to participate. By forming a collaborative partnership, these investments have developed a scalable model that builds their BIPOC candidate pipeline and creates better awareness for students of careers in the investment industry.

The mentor fellowship program is being run by Management Leadership for Tomorrow, a not-for-profit focused on diversifying the leadership pipeline for organizations. Students will begin in their sophomore year and they will be paired with mentors from one of the investment firms. The objective is to encourage the students to apply for an internship at any alternative investment firm. Fellows are also eligible for scholarships toward tuition, room, and board at their higher education institution.[29] Coming together to create a joint venture to address systemic barriers within their industry demonstrates the impact that organizations can have through collaboration.

As extensive as all of this sounds, the work is just beginning and creating a culture of equity and belonging for all involves deep systemic work to transform internal systems, policies, and practices. This transformation requires foundational work to establish behaviors and attitudes that support equity and inclusion by creating talent ecosytems for recruitment, hiring, promotion, development that reflect these commitments.

For years, financial institutions have inserted financial covenants into debt instruments that either reward or penalize organizations for reaching or missing financial metrics. The model is now being adopted for ESG targets. BlackRock recently arrranged for a $4.4 billion credit facility from a group of banks, which ties the rate of borrowing to meeting its diversity targets. BlackRock has set goals that include boosting its share of Black and Latino employees to 30% of its workforce by 2024 and to increase the representation of women in senior leadership roles by 3% per year. In its core business, it plans on growing its ESG targeted funds from $200 billion to $1 trillion by 2030.[30] BlackRock's CEO, Larry Fink, made a significant impact by calling on companies to address climate risk as financial risk and to improve shareholder disclosure in his annual 2020 letter. In his 2021 annual letter, he highlights the investment risk of climate change especially in light of the global pandemic. Given the events of 2020, he also highlights the need to address racial equity and sustainability for all stakeholders.[31] BlackRock's culture and internal policies have been under scrutiny after former employees raised concerns about their experience with a lack of inclusion and opportunity in the workplace. In response, BlackRock has established a new group to address workplace complaints and hired a law firm to perform an internal equity audit. While BlackRock is on its own J.E.D.I. journey, as the top asset management firm globally, it serves as a leader for peer organizations to drive systemic social and environmental justice and equity.

Tieing executive compenation to achieving J.E.D.I. goals is a tool to drive impact and increase accountability. Metrics can be both quantative as in the percentage represenation of women and underrepresented groups within your functional areas of responsibility or qualitative as in how have you supported women, AAPI. and BIPOC employee development, growth, and advancement. Starbucks is using an incentive approach by rewarding top executives more shares of stock if the managerial levels of the organization become more respresentative over the next 3 years. Nike announced that it is tieing executive compensation to 5-year goals for improving racial and gender diversity. Over 30% of S&P 500 companies have reported incorporating DEI metrics into their compensation plans.[32] The idea of aligning compensation to desired perfomance outcomes is not new, but the fact that Fortune 500 companies are holding executives accountable on their performance scorecards for J.E.D.I. goals is a significant change. Companies are responding to public demands for action, institutional investor pressure, employee concerns, and customer requirements for organizations to live their J.E.D.I. values.

Despite these initiatives, CEO pay continues to rise, with 2020 executive compensation reaching a record level even in the face of shareholder votes against compensation packages.[33] The time has come to reevaluate the executive compensation models that are being used by boards. While the CEO and executive team lead the stratregy, there are many members of the organization that drive organizational performance. It is time to reallocate the upside benefits of organizational performamce that have been shared disproportionally with senior leaders more equitably across the organization. To drive meaninful change, executive compensation needs to be tied to environmental and social justice metrics not just the metric for total shareholder returns. In order to drive systemic impact, executive, manager, team leader, and individual performance goals also need to be tied to the J.E.D.I. goals.

11.4 Valuing Differences

Creating a culture of belonging to support an organization's J.E.D.I. vision requires moving beyond accepting to valuing differences. The Human Rights Campaign Foundation Corporate Equality Index (CEI) ranks organizations on their LGBTQ+ equality. In 2021, 767 businesses received a score of 100% on the index. These companies come from a wide variety of industries and regions across the U.S. In order to be a highly rated organization by the CEI, these leadership teams created and enacted policies, benefits, and practices to ensure equity for LGBTQ+ workers and their families. The CEI is based on four pillars:

1. Enacting non-discrimination policies across business entities
2. Offering equitable benefits for LGBTQ+ workers and their families
3. Promoting a culture of inclusion (belonging)
4. Engaging in corporate social responsibility[34]

The HRC Foundation evaluates organizations on the inclusion of "sexual orientation" and "gender identity" workforce protections. They also consider inclusive benefits such as employers' provision of health insurance coverage parity for same- and different-sex spouses and partners. Availability of routine, chronic care and transition-related medical coverage for transgender employees and dependents is also evaluated. In terms of supporting an inclusive culture, they evaluate internal education and training practices, as well as other support programs like LGBTQ+ Employee Resource groups and Diversity Councils. Measurement of progress is important; so, the evaluation requires that businesses track and report on LGBTQ+ workforce metrics such as regularly provided education, training, and accountability measures similar to self-identification reporting on diversity and inclusion in the workplace. The organization's outreach or engagement with the LGBTQ+ communities in which they operate such as advertising, public policy engagement, supplier diversity, philanthropy, and sponsorship is also evaluated. Leveraging the CEI criteria as a guideline serves as a tool for leadership in reviewing their own policies, practices, and benefits structures to ensure that they are inclusive to LGBTQ+ workers and their families. The CEI model provides a best practice playbook for organizations that truly seek to create a culture of belonging for the LGBTQ+ community.

The MetroHealth System serves the health needs of communities across Northeast Ohio. Integral to fulfilling its public health mission and vision for health equity, their community engagement is focused on improving health outcomes for everyone, including underserved populations in the Cleveland and surrounding communities. Alan Nevel, SVP, Chief Diversity and Human Resource Officer for MetroHealth Systems in Cleveland shared MetroHealth's DEI transformational journey to promote a culture of inclusion for all stakeholders-patients, staff, and community members. While MetroHealth was already on a DEI journey, the trajectory of the journey changed with the arrival of the COVID-19 pandemic and the growing awareness of racial and social inequity in their community. They doubled down on promoting pay equity for employees and access to healthcare for community members. In support of the LGBTQ+ community, their services through the Pride Network follow the medical guidelines set by the World Professional Association for Transgender Health (WPSTH). The MetroHealth staff are dedicated to serving transgender and non-binary patients in a comfortable, supportive environment that respects gender identity and healthcare treatment.[35] In addition to offering transgender and non-binary health services, they reviewed and revised their internal policies and changed their medical records to reflect gender identity and name preferences for patients to ensure that members of the transgender and non-binary community feel valued and that their health is a top priority.

In 2021, they hosted their 6th year of the Annual MetroHealth Transgender Job Fair. In addition to a variety of employers seeking job candidates including PNC and MetroHealth, the event included several keynote speakers from the transgender community. This event also offered resources and workshops to help with job search, interviewing during COVID-19, career development and job placement. MetroHealth's leadership in the area of LGBTQ+ rights provides an excellent example of what is possible and how organizations can drive the needle in terms of healthcare, income and wealth gaps that plague marginalized communities.

Another way of valuing individuals is to redefine the career path. Moving from a dominant to an equitable culture includes seeking candidates with a nontraditional career path. Incorporating career paths that have breaks for caregiving or other reasons needs to be integrated into an organization's talent pipeline. The applicant tracking systems (ATS) need to be modified so that these resumes are not screened out of the hiring process. Alternative paths and resources need to be provided by organizations to engage non-traditional career path employees. In many ways there isn't a shortage of talent but a lack of innovation by organizations in their talent engagement strategy. Path Forward (https://www.pathforward.org/) is a not-for-profit with a mission to empower people to restart their careers after taking time away from their careers to focus on caregiving. Their approach is to partner with companies to offer "returnships," mid-career internships that support professionals in restarting their careers. The partnership is a win-win as participants get workshops, support networks, and access to organizations and employers gain access to a diverse talent pool. Path Forward has over 80 participating organizations including Walmart, Netflix, Apple, SAP, and Campbells.

Creating a culture that values differences requires viewing the talent acquisition process through an inclusionary rather than an exclusionary lens. Human capital management professionals must think about increasing the size of the pie in this case the talent pool through innovative partnerships, trainings, and program development. If the mechanism for talent engagement remains focused on a narrowly defined pathway that requires specific job titles, employment at certain organizations, or attendance at a handful of colleges or universities, the organization will not be able to reach its goals of creating a more diverse workforce. Without diversity of perspective, the benefits of a J.E.D.I. strategy remain elusive.

11.5 Promoting Transparency

In order to be transparent and to ensure that equity, inclusion, and justice strategies are being implemented in the ways that have been directed by boards and organizational leaders, standards must be developed, measured and verified. While financial audits have been de rigueur for investors, rating agencies, and regulators, we need to think deeply about the information that other stakeholders including customers, employees, and communities need to evaluate organizational J.E.D.I. performance. As we saw in Chapter 1, there are multiple ESG frameworks and rating agencies.

Depending upon an agency's or framework's criteria, weighting, and approach, the same organization often results in a different ranking or rating. In addition, these reports are lengthy, cumbersome, and highly technical making them not very useful to stakeholders. Often, it is difficult for stakeholders to identify organizations that are "green washing" or "woke washing." For example, a firm may have strong performance in a particular area like carbon reduction, but a less-than-stellar record in providing equity and access to underrepresented groups. While industries may have different ESG materiality issues, social issues such as living wages, equal access and opportunity, safety, and inclusive work environments really span all organizations. As ESG compliance and transparency issues rise in stakeholder priorities, it becomes increasingly important to set comparable standards and authentically report on performance on environmental and social justice impact.

11.6 Changing the Conversation

In order to drive meaningful systemic change to promote J.E.D.I., we need to change the conversation around to whom the benefits of organizational success accrue. Organizations thrive because of their people, customers, and communities. For years we have discussed creating shared value, but we have been light on the implementation of actually sharing value to all of the stakeholders. It is time to consider that wealth is created based on access including access to public lands, airways, and communities. Many industries have benefited and even survived because of governmental intervention and bailouts including the financial services sector and auto industry. While taxes have been the primary means of reallocating shared value, we see that numerous loopholes and political maneuvering have pushed down corporate tax rates and the funding of public programs. In order to drive systemic change, a new collaboration between private and public organizations is needed to realistically share both the costs and the benefits.

In order to address the challenges of the 21st century, the Impact Model as depicted in Figure 11.3 has been developed to offer a model to drive collaborative, systemic J.E.D.I. transformation. The model represents a partnership between communities, NGOs, and private companies established to fund and support an incubator for BIPOC, AAPI, and women innovators. Support would come in building out maker spaces, offering professional service, providing office space, and other resources. The initial investment would be funded by commitments made by corporations. The project would also include venture funding for companies with a portion of the gains from successful business launches being contributed back to the venture fund to support future entrepreneurs. To drive systemic change, a new paradigm is required to change the dynamics around who receives governmental support, access to capital and funding, and meaningful opportunities. The implementation of the Impact Model includes incorporating diversity of voices and perspectives from the communities in which organizations live and operate.

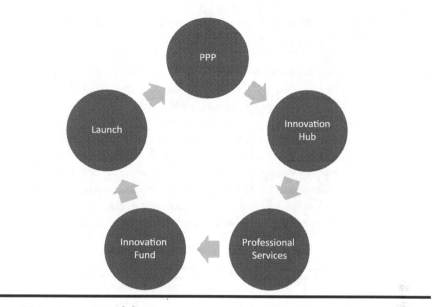

Figure 11.3   Impact Model.

Driving systemic change across our society requires realignment of our foundational pillars around resource distribution, access, and benefit realization. Meaningful change around education, wealth, and healthcare gaps can only be closed by empowering underrepresented groups to have a voice in the changes that are needed and providing resources and tools to drive that change.

11.7 Conclusion

Driving systemic change requires meaningful partnerships where all participants are valued for their expertise and contributions. The P-TECH PPP is an excellent example of organizations from industry, academia, and government coming together to create a scalable model to drive impact for future generations. Moving into the 21st century, we need new tools, technologies, and skilled workers to meet our needs. As we continue to transform as a society, it is crucial that we remember our history both good and bad and that we do not minimize the contributions of BIPOC and AAPI individuals, families, and communities. Redesigning dominate social and organizational cultures is crucial to creating workplaces that promote belonging.

Breaking systemic barriers requires reallocation of capital from institutions, organizations, investors, foundations, and not-for-profits using an approach like the Impact Model. We all must think deeply about the type of world that we wish to inhabit and leave for future generations. The sphere includes both environmental and social impacts as they are intertwined. One cannot have environmental justice without social justice and vice versa.

Guiding an organization on its journey toward its J.E.D.I. North Star vision requires moving forward on the J.E.D.I. maturity continuum further refining strategy and embedding J.E.D.I. values into organizational culture, systems, and daily operations. Creating a culture of belonging to support an organization's J.E.D.I. values is everyone's job from the CEO to the customer service representative. Our attitudes, beliefs, and behaviors impact everyone with whom we come into contact. To drive deep systemic change, requires an assessment of both organizational biases and personal biases to better comprehend how these are incorporated into our organizational policies, processes, and decisions. While technology can help through delivering information to support data-driven decision-making, technology alone will not solve organizational J.E.D.I. challenges. We must adjust our own lenses to see the power and privilege within our society and recognize that part of our work as leaders is to actively support social and organizational equity and inclusion.

Questions

1. As a student, what appeals to you about the P-TECH model?
2. If this educational model had been in existence when you were in high school, would you have chosen this option? Why?
3. As a business leader, what appeals to you about the P-TECH model?
4. What recommendations do you have to bridge the education, pay, and wealth gaps?
5. Corporations have made significant financial commitments to address systemic inequities. Do you think it is enough to drive the transformational change? Why?
6. As a business leader, what would you propose to your own organization to drive impact to justice and equity?
7. As a not-for-profit leader, what investment strategy changes might you make to align your investment strategy with your organization's J.E.D.I. mission?
8. If you were designing standards for J.E.D.I. reporting, what areas of reporting and metrics might you include?
9. How might you use the Impact Model to drive change in your community?
10. What are some of your key takeaways from this book? What is the one action that you are planning to do tomorrow?

Notes

1 "Rosenwald Schools | National Trust for Historic Preservation," accessed April 26, 2021, https://savingplaces.org/places/rosenwald-schools.
2 Andrew Feiler, "The 4,978 Schools That Changed America," *Wall Street Journal*, April 22, 2021, sec. News, https://www.wsj.com/articles/the-4-978-schools-that-changed-america-11619103429.

3 "NAACP | NAACP History: Medgar Evers," NAACP, accessed April 25, 2021, https://www.naacp.org/naacp-history-medgar-evers/.

4 Katharine Q. Seelye, "John Lewis, Towering Figure of Civil Rights Era, Dies at 80," *The New York Times*, July 18, 2020, sec. U.S., https://www.nytimes.com/2020/07/17/us/john-lewis-dead.html.

5 "P-TECH Schools Provide Experience in Growing Fields."

6 "P-TECH Schools Provide Experience in Growing Fields," P-TECH.org, accessed November 23, 2020, https://www.ptech.org/.

7 Grace Suh, A Conversation with Grace Suh, VP of Education, Corporate Social Responsibility IBM, October 14, 2020.

8 "Grace Suh," *Global Business Coalition for Education* (blog), accessed November 24, 2020, https://gbc-education.org/team/grace-suh/.

9 ShuDon Brown, A Conversation with ShuDon Brown, a Graduate of P-TECH, n.d.

10 Inna Kruglaya, "Bridging the School-to-Work Divide," Text, MDRC, May 18, 2020, https://www.mdrc.org/publication/bridging-school-work-divide.

11 Grace Suh, "P-TECH Report January 2020" (IBM, n.d.).

12 Grace Suh.

13 Villanueva.

14 "SOCIAL JUSTICE PHILANTHROPY PRINCIPLES," *Resource Generation* (blog), accessed April 27, 2021, https://resourcegeneration.org/social-justice-philanthropy-and-giving/.

15 Theo Francis and Jennifer Maloney, "WSJ News Exclusive | Big Companies Boost Share of Black and Latino Directors," *Wall Street Journal*, June 16, 2021, sec. Business, https://www.wsj.com/articles/this-years-influx-of-directors-starts-shift-in-boardroom-diversity-11623835801.

16 "Transformative Investment Principles," *Resource Generation* (blog), accessed April 27, 2021, https://resourcegeneration.org/transformative-investment-principles/.

17 "About Seed Commons," *SEED COMMONS* (blog), accessed April 28, 2021, https://seedcommons.org/about-seed-commons/.

18 "Boston Ujima Project," Ujima, accessed October 15, 2020, https://www.ujimaboston.com.

19 Lauren Weber, "Companies Have Promised $35 Billion Toward Racial Equity. Where Is the Money Going?," *Wall Street Journal*, December 21, 2020, sec. Business, https://www.wsj.com/articles/companies-have-promised-billions-toward-racial-equity-where-is-the-money-going-11608570864.

20 Dion Rabouin Witherspoon Andrew, "Fortune 100 Companies Commit $3.3 Billion to Fight Racism and Inequality," Axios, accessed November 21, 2020, https://www.axios.com/fortune-100-companies-donations-racism-inequality-f2a53d37-e587-44f9-ab30-8efc0c088111.html.

21 "Bank of America Announces $1 Billion/4-Year Commitment to Support Economic Opportunity Initiatives," accessed November 21, 2020, https://newsroom.bankofamerica.com/press-releases/bank-america-announces-four-year-1-billion-commitment-supporting-economic.

22 "Bank of America Directs $300 Million of Its $1 Billion, Four-Year Commitment to Advance Racial Equality and Economic Opportunity."

23 "Bank of America Increases Commitment to Advance Racial Equality and Economic Opportunity to $1.25 Billion," Bank of America, accessed April 28, 2021, https://newsroom.bankofamerica.com/content/newsroom/press-releases/2021/03/bank-of-america-increases-commitment-to-advance-racial-equality-.html.

24 "Standing with the Black Community."

25 "Amazon Donates $10 Million to Organizations Supporting Justice and Equity."

26 "Making a Difference in Racial Equity: Walmart CEO Doug McMillon's Full Remarks," Corporate – U.S., accessed November 20, 2020, https://corporate.walmart.com/equity.

27 "Living Wage Calculator," accessed June 24, 2021, https://livingwage.mit.edu/articles/61-new-living-wage-data-for-now-available-on-the-tool.

28 "Living Wage Calculator," accessed June 24, 2021, https://livingwage.mit.edu/articles/61-new-living-wage-data-for-now-available-on-the-tool.

29 Miriam Gottfried, "WSJ News Exclusive | Apollo, Ares and Oaktree Team Up on Initiative to Lure Black Talent," *Wall Street Journal*, June 15, 2021, sec. Markets, https://www.wsj.com/articles/apollo-ares-and-oaktree-team-up-on-initiative-to-lure-black-talent-11623751200.

30 "BlackRock Must Hit ESG Targets or Pay More to Borrow Money – WSJ," accessed May 5, 2021, https://www.wsj.com/articles/blackrock-must-hit-esg-targets-or-pay-more-to-borrow-money-11617769833?st=2labargjcn6wkau&reflink=article_email_share.

31 "Larry Fink CEO Letter," BlackRock, accessed May 5, 2021, https://www.blackrock.com/corporate/investor-relations/larry-fink-ceo-letter.

32 "CEO Pay Increasingly Tied to Diversity Goals – WSJ," accessed June 3, 2021, https://www.wsj.com/articles/ceos-pledged-to-increase-diversity-now-boards-are-holding-them-to-it-11622626380.

33 Theo Francis and Kristin Broughton, "CEO Pay Surged in a Year of Upheaval and Leadership Challenges," *Wall Street Journal*, April 11, 2021, sec. Business, https://www.wsj.com/articles/covid-19-brought-the-economy-to-its-knees-but-ceo-pay-surged-11618142400.

34 "CEI-2021_FINAL.Pdf," accessed February 9, 2021, https://hrc-prod-requests.s3-us-west-2.amazonaws.com/CEI-2021_FINAL.pdf?mtime=20210128123716&focal=none.

35 "Transgender Health Services," accessed May 4, 2021, https://www.metrohealth.org:443/lgbtqi-pride-network/transgender-adult-health-services.

Bibliography

About Amazon. "Amazon Donates $10 Million to Organizations Supporting Justice and Equity," June 3, 2020. https://www.aboutamazon.com/news/policy-news-views/amazon-donates-10-million-to-organizations-supporting-justice-and-equity.

Ajunwa, Ifeoma. "Can We Trust Corporate Commitments to Racial Equity?" *Forbes*. Accessed April 28, 2021. https://www.forbes.com/sites/ifeomaajunwa/02/23/can-we-trust-corporate-commitments-to-racial-equity/.

"Bank of America Announces $1 Billion/4-Year Commitment to Support Economic Opportunity Initiatives." Accessed November 21, 2020. https://newsroom.bankofamerica.com/press-releases/bank-america-announces-four-year-1-billion-commitment-supporting-economic.

Bank of America. "Bank of America Directs $300 Million of Its $1 Billion, Four-Year Commitment to Advance Racial Equality and Economic Opportunity." Accessed April 28, 2021a. https://newsroom.bankofamerica.com/press-releases/community-development/bank-america-directs-300-million-its-1-billion-four-year.

Bank of America. "Bank of America Increases Commitment to Advance Racial Equality and Economic Opportunity to $1.25 Billion." Accessed April 28, 2021b. https://

newsroom.bankofamerica.com/content/newsroom/press-releases/2021/03/bank-of-america-increases-commitment-to-advance-racial-equality-.html.

"BlackRock Must Hit ESG Targets or Pay More to Borrow Money – WSJ." Accessed May 5, 2021. https://www.wsj.com/articles/blackrock-must-hit-esg-targets-or-pay-more-to-borrow-money-11617769833?st=2labargjcn6wkau&reflink=article_email_share.

BlackRock. "Larry Fink CEO Letter." Accessed May 5, 2021. https://www.blackrock.com/corporate/investor-relations/larry-fink-ceo-letter.

"CEI-2021_FINAL.Pdf." Accessed February 9, 2021. https://hrc-prod-requests.s3-us-west-2.amazonaws.com/CEI-2021_FINAL.pdf?mtime=20210128123716&focal=none.

"CEO Pay Increasingly Tied to Diversity Goals – WSJ." Accessed June 3, 2021. https://www.wsj.com/articles/ceos-pledged-to-increase-diversity-now-boards-are-holding-them-to-it-11622626380.

Corporate – US. "Making a Difference in Racial Equity: Walmart CEO Doug McMillon's Full Remarks." Accessed November 20, 2020. https://corporate.walmart.com/equity.

Feiler, Andrew. "The 4,978 Schools That Changed America." *Wall Street Journal*, April 22, 2021, sec. News. https://www.wsj.com/articles/the-4-978-schools-that-changed-america-11619103429.

Francis, Theo and Kristin Broughton. "CEO Pay Surged in a Year of Upheaval and Leadership Challenges." *Wall Street Journal*, April 11, 2021, sec. Business. https://www.wsj.com/articles/covid-19-brought-the-economy-to-its-knees-but-ceo-pay-surged-11618142400.

Francis, Theo and Jennifer Maloney. "WSJ News Exclusive | Big Companies Boost Share of Black and Latino Directors." *Wall Street Journal*, June 16, 2021, sec. Business. https://www.wsj.com/articles/this-years-influx-of-directors-starts-shift-in-boardroom-diversity-11623835801.

Global Business Coalition for Education. "Grace Suh." Accessed November 24, 2020. https://gbc-education.org/team/grace-suh/.

Global Business Coalition for Education. "P-TECH Report January 2020." IBM, n.d.

Google. "Standing with the Black Community," June 3, 2020. https://blog.google/inside-google/company-announcements/standing-with-black-community/.

Gottfried, Miriam. "WSJ News Exclusive | Apollo, Ares and Oaktree Team Up on Initiative to Lure Black Talent." *Wall Street Journal*, June 15, 2021, sec. Markets. https://www.wsj.com/articles/apollo-ares-and-oaktree-team-up-on-initiative-to-lure-black-talent-11623751200.

Grace Suh. A Conversation with Grace Suh, VP of Education, Corporate Social Responsibility IBM, October 14, 2020.

Irrera, Anna. "PayPal Pledges over $500 Million to Support Minority-Owned U.S. Businesses." *Reuters*, June 11, 2020. https://www.reuters.com/article/us-minneapolis-police-paypal-idUSKBN23I20Q.

Kruglaya, Inna. "Bridging the School-to-Work Divide." Text. MDRC, May 18, 2020. https://www.mdrc.org/publication/bridging-school-work-divide.

"Living Wage Calculator." Accessed June 24, 2021. https://livingwage.mit.edu/articles/61-new-living-wage-data-for-now-available-on-the-tool.

NAACP. "NAACP | NAACP History: Medgar Evers." Accessed April 25, 2021. https://www.naacp.org/naacp-history-medgar-evers/.

P-TECH.org. "P-TECH Schools Provide Experience in Growing Fields." Accessed November 23, 2020. https://www.ptech.org/.

PepsiCo, Inc. Official Website. "PepsiCo's Racial Equality Journey: Black Initiative." Accessed May 6, 2021. http://www.pepsico.com/about/diversity-and-engagement/racial-equality-journey-black-initiative.

Rabouin, Dion and Andrew Witherspoon. "Fortune 100 Companies Commit $3.3 Billion to Fight Racism and Inequality." *Axios*. Accessed November 21, 2020. https://www.axios.com/fortune-100-companies-donations-racism-inequality-f2a53d37-e587-44f9-ab30-8efc0c088111.html.

Resource Generation. "Social Justice Philanthropy Principles." Accessed April 27, 2021a. https://resourcegeneration.org/social-justice-philanthropy-and-giving/.

Resource Generation. "Transformative Investment Principles." Accessed April 27, 2021b. https://resourcegeneration.org/transformative-investment-principles/.

"Rosenwald Schools | National Trust for Historic Preservation." Accessed April 26, 2021. https://savingplaces.org/places/rosenwald-schools.

SEED COMMONS. "About Seed Commons." Accessed April 28, 2021. https://seedcommons.org/about-seed-commons/.

Seelye, Katharine Q. "John Lewis, Towering Figure of Civil Rights Era, Dies at 80." *The New York Times*, July 18, 2020, sec. U.S. https://www.nytimes.com/2020/07/17/us/john-lewis-dead.html.

ShuDon Brown. A Conversation with ShuDon Brown, a Graduate of P-TECH, n.d.

Togoh, Isabel. "JP Morgan Pledges $30 Billion To Help Remedy Racial Wealth Gap." *Forbes*. Accessed June 3, 2021. https://www.forbes.com/sites/isabeltogoh/2020/10/08/jp-morgan-pledges-30-billion-to-help-remedy-racial-wealth-gap/.

"Transgender Health Services." Accessed May 4, 2021. https://www.metrohealth.org:443/lgbtqi-pride-network/transgender-adult-health-services.

Ujima. "Boston Ujima Project." Accessed October 15, 2020. https://www.ujimaboston.com.

Villanueva, Edgar. *Decolonizing Wealth: Indigenous Wisdom to Heal Divides and Restore Balance*. 1st edition. Berrett-Koehler Publishers, 2018.

Weber, Lauren. "Companies Have Promised $35 Billion Toward Racial Equity. Where Is the Money Going?" *Wall Street Journal*, December 21, 2020, sec. Business. https://www.wsj.com/articles/companies-have-promised-billions-toward-racial-equity-where-is-the-money-going-11608570864.

Driving J.E.D.I. Toolkit

Cultural Assessment for Environmental and Social Justice Impact

1. What is our organization's mission?
2. Are environmental and social justice organizational pillars included in our mission statement?
3. What are our ESG goals?
   a. How is success defined?
   b. How is progress measured?
4. What is our ESG strategy and is it aligned with our business strategy?
   a. Are we considering the intersectionality of environmental and social factors?
5. How are internal and external stakeholders engaged and informed about our environmental and social justice priorities, actions, and outcomes?
   a. Who is involved in the process?
   b. Who is responsible for external and internal communications?
   c. Is internal and external messaging consistent?
   d. How is stakeholder feedback incorporated into the decision-making process?
   e. How are they communicated?
6. Is the organization involved in private-public partnerships to drive environmental and social impact?
7. How is our organization supporting its ESG strategy?
   a. Is it on the board or C-suite agendas?
   b. Does the CEO speak frequently about our organization's mission to promote a more just and equitable society and organization?
   c. What budget has been designated to support initiatives both internally and externally?
   d. How is the vision of equity and inclusion cascaded to middle management?
   e. What type of organizational systems exists to promote cross-functional collaboration?
   f. Are ESG goals included as part of senior management performance management reviews and tied to compensation?

    g. Who are the champions and leaders of for J.E.D.I. transformation?
       i. What are their roles in the organization?
       ii. How are they involved?
    h. Who is in our supply chain and how is diversity represented in this process?
8. How are we engaging employees on environmental and social justice priorities?
    a. Is environmental and social impact part of everyone's job, or is it the job of one person such as Corporate Social Responsibility Officer or Diversity Equity Inclusion Officer?
    b. Are all employees given J.E.D.I. training?
    c. Is the expense for J.E.D.I. training and programming included in the annual budget allocation process?
    d. What protocols are in place to report harassment or bias?
    e. What tools or resources do we offer?
9. Is our employee diversity representation reflective of our community?
    a. How representative is our talent pipeline across our manager and leadership levels?
    b. What are our recruitment strategies?
    c. What are our retention strategies?
10. How are we tracking J.E.D.I. goals and measuring progress?
    a. How are goals allocated across the organization?
    b. What data are we tracking?
    c. How are we leveraging technology to facilitate data tracking and reporting?
    d. Is executive compensation tied to J.E.D.I. goals?
    e. How is this information being incorporated into the decision-making process?
11. What activities or programs are our employees involved with to support environmental stewardship or community investment?
    a. How aligned are these volunteer programs with your community's interests or requirements?
    b. Are these activities being performed in the name of the corporation?
    c. What types of resources does the corporation provide for volunteer activities and programs?
    d. How are initiatives promoted internally and externally?

Employee J.E.D.I. Survey Questions

1. What does diversity mean to you?
2. What does inclusion mean to you?

3. What does equity mean to you?
4. What does a culture of belonging mean to you?
5. How well do you feel our organization does diversity, equity, and inclusion?
6. How do you feel when you come to work?
7. Do you feel you can bring your full self to work?
8. Have you ever felt marginalized or discriminated against in our workplace?
9. What could we do to improve our culture of belonging?
10. What challenges do you face in bringing your full self to work?
11. What practices and processes help you feel valued and welcome?
12. What practices or processes act as barriers to your work experience?
13. What practices promote distributive, procedural, interpersonal, and informational justice?
14. What practices deter distributive, procedural, interpersonal, and informational justice?

Organizational Justice, Equity, Diversity, and Inclusion (J.E.D.I.) Framework

1. How is our organizational culture described by the following stakeholders?
   a. Board/C-suite
   b. Managers
   c. Employees
   d. Suppliers
   e. Community
   f. Other Stakeholders
2. How are J.E.D.I. values reflected in our organizational pillars?
   a. Vision
   b. Goals
   c. Priorities
   d. Strategy
3. How are J.E.D.I. principals reflected in our culture and operations?
   a. Values
   b. Norms
   c. Shared Beliefs
   d. Role Models
   e. Resource Allocation
   f. Behaviors and Actions
   g. Artifacts
4. How is DEI reflected in our organization's performance goals?
   a. Internal
      i. C-suite Scorecard
      ii. Senior Manager Goals

        iii. Middle Manager Goals
        iv. Team Goals
        v. Individual Goals
    b. External
        i. Supplier Goals
        ii. Community Goals

5. What is the diversity representation of our …?
   a. Board of Directors
   b. C-suite
   c. Senior Management
   d. Middle Management
   e. Employees

6. How effective are our internal policies, processes and systems in promoting our J.E.D.I. vision?
   a. How do they promote an inclusive culture?
   b. How do they act as barriers to an inclusive culture?
   c. Where are we doing well?
   d. Are we considering both internal and external impacts?
   e. How do we compare to our industry peers?
   f. Are our leaders serving as role models in policy adoption and execution externally?
   g. Where do we need help?

7. How are our people management systems impacting the J.E.D.I. goals?
   a. What are our recruitment and talent acquisition diversity metrics?
   b. What development opportunities are being offered to support awareness and understanding of the culture, history, and experience of underrepresented communities?
   c. How are we managing our career development?
   d. What are the diversity metrics for our leadership program?
   e. What are the diversity metrics for our high potential employees?
   f. How are we recommending and delivering talent development?
   g. What tools are we offering to support employees needs for work life balance?
   h. What are our community based talent interactions?
   i. How reflective of our community is our workforce representation?

8. What are our talent recruitment strategies?
   a. How do we recruit talent?
   b. Where do we recruit talent?
   c. Are we recruiting from diverse sources?
   d. What is the diversity of our talent recruitment pipeline?
   e. What language(s) do we use in job postings?
   f. How are we addressing unconscious bias in the hiring process?

9. What are our talent retention strategies?
   a. How reflective of our community is our talent diversity representation?
   b. How are new opportunities shared?
   c. How is talent developed?
   d. How do we define meritocracy?
   e. How do we demonstrate that we value employees?
   f. What are our turnover rates? By category?
   g. How do we compare to our peers?
   h. What do our employee engagement(EE) surveys reflect?
   i. How are promotions and raises determined?
   j. Who is eligible for leadership development?
   k. Are we auditing talent policies and processes for conversion and retention leakages?
10. How do we develop leaders?
    a. What core competencies do we identify and prioritize?
    b. Who sponsors employees for selection in leadership development programs?
    c. How transparent is this process?
    d. How diverse is our leadership pipeline?
    e. What curriculum is included in leadership development to support J.E.D.I. capacity building in future leaders?
11. How do we engage with middle managers on topics related to J.E.D.I. initiatives and priorities?
    a. What training and development is given to middle managers?
    b. How are outcomes measured?
    c. What is the impact on middle managers performance scorecard?
    d. What expectations do we have of managers?
12. How are teams designed?
    a. Do teams reflect diversity of identity, experience, thought?
    b. Do we promote psychological safety?
    c. Do we promote inclusive norms?
    d. Do we avoid tokenism?
13. What tools are available to build capacity and support J.E.D.I. goals?
    a. Training
    b. Development
    c. Mentoring, Reverse Mentoring, Shadowing
    d. Allyship
    e. Sponsorship
    f. Storytelling
    g. Employee Resource Groups-ERGs
    h. Town Halls
    i. Flexible Work Policies
    j. Metrics and Reporting

14. What technologies allow for scaling of solutions across the organization?
    a. Process improvement
    b. Workflow automation
    c. Data-based decision-making
    d. Artificial Intelligence tools
    e. Reporting
    f. Communication
15. What are our J.E.D.I. standards for procurement and suppliers?
    a. Percentage spent with BIPOC owned businesses?
    b. Percentage spent with AAPI owned businesses?
    c. Percentage spent women-owned businesses?
    d. Percentage spent with LGBTQ+ owned businesses?
    e. Are we including professional service firms?
    f. Do we have a supply chain J.E.D.I. questionnaire?
    g. Do we request remediation plans from suppliers?
    h. Do we have an outreach program to support underrepresented businesses?
    i. Is a supplier scorecard used?
    j. Do we maintain a supplier ranking matrix based on scorecard performance?
16. How are our J.E.D.I. commitments reflected in community outreach?
    a. How do we define our community?
    b. What are the demographics of the communities in which we operate?
    c. How do we engage our community? (CSR outreach)
    d. How do our philanthropic beneficiaries align with community demographics?
    e. What programs and outreach are we engaged with in the communities?
    f. Which community members are included on advisory boards?
    g. What employee volunteer programs are we supporting as an organization?
    h. Where are our employees choosing to spend their volunteer time?
    i. How well does our community feel our CSR initiatives support a culture of belonging and inclusion?
17. How do we hear the voices of our employees on J.E.D.I. issues?
    a. How often do we conduct employee engagement surveys?
    b. Are survey results shared? If so, how?
    c. What is done with the information?
    d. How is this information translated into action?
    e. What is the timeframe for actions or remediations?
18. How do customers perceive our organization's J.E.D.I. strategy?
    a. How is our J.E.D.I. strategy reflected in our branding and image?
    b. How are we receiving feedback from customers?

  c. What are our marketplace J.E.D.I. commitments?
  d. Is there alignment between external messaging and internal actions?
19. How do we engage with industry associations and peer organizations?
  a. Who attends these events from our organization?
  b. Who leads the J.E.D.I. agenda in these groups?
  c. What roles do our out leaders play in these organizations?
  d. How active is our CEO in championing J.E.D.I. issues within this ecosystem.

Communication Strategy

1. What is our goal?
2. What is the message(s) that we want to deliver?
3. What outcome are we seeking?
4. Who can help deliver the message?
5. What is our budget?
6. What is our action plan and timeline?
7. Which communication channels will be most effective?
8. How are we going to measure impact?
9. How will we gather feedback from our audience?
10. How will we inform senior management about stakeholder feedback?
11. How will we keep stakeholders informed about the impact of their feedback?

Implicit Association Test Reflection Questions

1. What is your initial reaction to the test results?
2. Are the results aligned with your self-perception? Are they misaligned?
3. Does this alignment create acceptance or resistance to the results?
4. Are you able to identify any experiences or interactions that may inform these results?
5. How might these unconscious biases impact your interactions in your personal or professional life?
6. How might these biases impact your role as a leader?
7. How might these biases impact designing organizational systems around hiring, promotion, compensation and opportunities?
8. How might these biases impact team member relationships and dynamics?
9. How might these biases impact vendor or contractor selection?
10. How might these biases impact who is selected as a high potential employee of future leader?

Cultural Tools

1. What's Your Cultural Profile (https://hbr.org/2014/08/whats-your-cultural-profile)
   a. What surprised you about your results?
   b. Try taking an assessment for a different country. How culturally aligned are your practices with the business culture of that country?
   c. What are your key learnings from this exercise?
2. "Killing Me Softly" by Fobazi M. Ettarh, (http://fobettarh.github.io/Killing-Me-Softly/)
   a. How did this exercise make your feel?
   b. What perspective have you gained from this exercise?
   c. What might you do differently in your personal and professional interactions?
   d. What changes might you suggest in your organization to create a culture of belonging?

Data Driven J.E.D.I. Transformation Checklist

1. Do we have senior leadership support? Who from senior leadership is our champion?
2. Who needs to be on the team?
3. What information are we seeking, and data are we trying to gather?
4. Who will be using this data and how will they be using it?
5. Where is data located? Is it in a single system or multiple systems?
6. How can we access the data?
7. Do we need technical expertise on an ongoing basis to leverage this technology?
8. Who needs to authorize data access?
9. Is use of the data protected by regulation such as GDPR, CPRA, other? If so, what compliance action are required?
10. What tools are available to support the process of gathering data and then reporting and sharing information? Do we need new tool?
11. What information and metrics will be reported?
12. Will we offer periodic reporting, dashboards, or system driven reports?
13. How will the new tool or dashboard be socialized with leadership and managers to promote data driven decision?
14. Will leadership need training and support to incorporate data driven decision making?
15. How will the culture change toward data driven decisions be socialized with employees?
16. How will managers be held accountable for decisions that impact DEI metrics and KPI?

17. What behaviors, policies, procedures need to be changed to drive impact?

AI Project Considerations

1. What is the purpose of the AI project and who are we seeking to help or serve?
2. Who else could be impacted by this tool? Are these stakeholder groups represented on the project team?
3. Is the data quality good?
4. What is the source of the data and are we permitted to use this data?
5. Where is the bias in the data?
6. How will the data and outcomes be used?
7. Is the code and data auditable?
8. Is there transparency of process and of use of outcomes?
9. Are you controlling for unintended consequences and bias?
10. Who has the power and responsibility in this relationship?
11. Is the AI being used to benefit or to punish people?
12. Does our organization have an AI code of conduct and is there a governance process in place to ensure it is followed?

Index

Page numbers in **bold** indicate tables, page numbers in *italic* indicate figures.